Jung and Philosophy

Although the works of C.G. Jung have received worldwide attention, there has been surprisingly little engagement by philosophers. In this volume, internationally recognized philosophers, Jungian analysts, and scholars attempt to fill this void in the literature. Although Jung did not have a formalized, systematic philosophy, the philosophical implications of his thought are explored in relation to his key theoretical postulates on archetypes, the collective unconscious, the mind-body problem, phenomenology, epistemology, psychology of religion, alchemy, myth, ethics, aesthetics, and the question of transcendence. Through analyzing Jung philosophically, new vistas emerge for enhanced explication, theoretical refinement, revision, and redirecting shifts in emphasis that lend more proper cohesion to Jung's philosophy.

For the first time we may observe philosophers attempting to unpack the philosophical consequences of Jung's thought applied to many traditional topics covered in the humanities and the social sciences. Given that Jung has not been historically taken up by philosophers, critiqued, nor applied to contemporary theories of mind, culture, and human nature, this is the first book of its kind. It is argued that a new generation of research in analytical psychology can benefit from philosophical scrutiny and theoretical fortification.

Jung and Philosophy will be of interest to psychoanalysts, philosophers, cultural theorists, religious scholars, and the disciplines of depth psychology and post-Jungian studies.

Jon Mills, PsyD, PhD, ABPP is a philosopher, psychoanalyst, and clinical psychologist. He is Professor of Psychology and Psychoanalysis at Adler Graduate Professional School, Toronto and is the author of numerous works in psychoanalysis, philosophy, and cultural studies. He runs a mental health corporation in Ontario, Canada.

Philosophy and Psychoanalysis Book Series
JON MILLS

Series Editor

Philosophy & Psychoanalysis is dedicated to current developments and cutting-edge research in the philosophical sciences, phenomenology, hermeneutics, existentialism, logic, semiotics, cultural studies, social criticism, and the humanities that engage and enrich psychoanalytic thought through philosophical rigor. With the philosophical turn in psychoanalysis comes a new era of theoretical research that revisits past paradigms while invigorating new approaches to theoretical, historical, contemporary, and applied psychoanalysis. No subject or discipline is immune from psychoanalytic reflection within a philosophical context including psychology, sociology, anthropology, politics, the arts, religion, science, culture, physics, and the nature of morality. Philosophical approaches to psychoanalysis may stimulate new areas of knowledge that have conceptual and applied value beyond the consulting room reflective of greater society at large. In the spirit of pluralism, *Philosophy & Psychoanalysis* is open to any theoretical school in philosophy and psychoanalysis that offers novel, scholarly, and important insights in the way we come to understand our world.

Titles in this series:

Progress in Psychoanalysis: Envisioning the Future of the Profession
Edited by Steven D. Axelrod, Ronald C. Naso and Larry M. Rosenberg

Lacan on Psychosis: From Theory to Praxis *Edited by Jon Mills and David L. Downing*

Ethics and Attachment: How We Make Moral Judgments *Aner Govrin*

Jung and Philosophy *Edited by Jon Mills*

Jung and Philosophy

Edited by Jon Mills

Routledge
Taylor & Francis Group

LONDON AND NEW YORK

First published 2019
by Routledge
2 Park Square, Milton Park, Abingdon, Oxon OX14 4RN

and by Routledge
52 Vanderbilt Avenue, New York, NY 10017

Routledge is an imprint of the Taylor & Francis Group, an informa business

British Library Cataloguing-in-Publication Data
A catalogue record for this book is available from the British Library

Library of Congress Cataloging-in-Publication Data
Names: Mills, Jon, 1964– editor.
Title: Jung and philosophy / edited by Jon Mills.
Description: 1 Edition. | New York : Routledge, 2019. |
Series: Philosophy and psychoanalysis |
Includes bibliographical references and index.
Identifiers: LCCN 2018060241 (print) | LCCN 2019001901 (ebook) |
ISBN 9780429261763 (Master) | ISBN 9780429523885 (Adobe) |
ISBN 9780429552052 (Mobipocket) | ISBN 9780429537356 (ePub) |
ISBN 9780367204839 (hardback : alk. paper) |
ISBN 9780367204846 (pbk. : alk. paper)
Subjects: LCSH: Psychoanalysis. | Jungian psychology. |
Psychology–Philosophy.
Classification: LCC BF173 (ebook) |
LCC BF173 .J626 2019 (print) | DDC 150.19/54–dc23
LC record available at https://lccn.loc.gov/2018060241

ISBN: 978-0-367-20483-9 (hbk)
ISBN: 978-0-367-20484-6 (pbk)
ISBN: 978-0-429-26176-3 (ebk)

Typeset in Times New Roman
by Newgen Publishing UK

Printed and bound by CPI Group (UK) Ltd, Croydon, CR0 4YY

Contents

About the Contributors

Garth Amundson, PsyD is a clinical psychologist, now semi-retired in Yellow Medicine County, Minnesota. For twenty-five years he practiced privately in Chicago, Illinois. He has published in the areas of the sociocultural background of developments in American psychoanalytic theory, and the outpatient treatment of psychosis from a Jungian perspective. Dr. Amundson is an active student of modernist American poetry, particularly the works of Wallace Stevens, and Buddhist philosophy.

Marco Heleno Barreto, PhD is a Jungian psychotherapist working in private practice. He teaches philosophy at FAJE – Faculdade Jesuíta de Filosofia e Teologia, in Belo Horizonte, Brazil. He is the author of *Símbolo e Sabedoria Prática. C.G. Jung e o Mal-estar da Modernidade* (2008), *Imaginação Simbólica. Reflexões Introdutórias* (2008), *Pensar Jung* (2012), *Homo Imaginans. A imaginação criadora na estética de Gaston Bachelard* (2016) and *Estudos (Pós)Junguianos* (forthcoming). He also has contributed articles to *Spring Journal*, *International Journal of Jungian Studies*, *Journal of Analytical Psychology*, and *Jung Journal*. He presently serves on the Executive Committee of the International Society for Psychology as the Discipline of Interiority (ISPDI).

Robin McCoy Brooks, MA, TEP has been a psychoanalyst in private practice in Seattle Washington for over thirty years. She is a founding member of the New School for Analytical Psychology, active analyst member of the Inter-Regional Society of Jungian Analysts, and the International Association for Analytical Psychology. She is a nationally certified Trainer, Educator and Practitioner of Group

Psychotherapy, Psychodrama, and Sociometry. Her published works incorporate philosophical, psychoanalytical, and scientific perspectives into the enigma of being human.

Erik D. Goodwyn, MD is Director of Psychotherapy Training and Assistant Professor of Psychiatry at the University of Louisville where he teaches residents and medical students dream interpretation methods along with psychodynamic theory and general subjects in psychiatry. He is the author of several articles and books including, *The Neurobiology of the Gods* (Routledge, 2012), *A Psychological Reading of the Poem Beowulf: Understanding Everything as Story* (Mellen, 2014), *Magical Consciousness* (Routledge, 2015), *Healing Symbols in Psychotherapy: A Ritual Approach* (Routledge, 2016), and *The Invisible Storyteller* (Routledge, 2018).

Ladson Hinton, MD trained as a psychiatrist at Stanford University Medical Center, and completed his analytic training at the C.G. Jung Institute of San Francisco. He is a member of the Society of Jungian Analysts of Northern California, the Institute for Contemporary Psychoanalysis in Los Angeles, and a founding member of the New School for Analytical Psychology in Seattle. He serves on the editorial board of the *Journal of Analytical Psychology* and practices, consults, and teaches in Seattle. In 2009, he received an Award for Distinguished Contributions to Psychoanalytic Education from the International Forum for Psychoanalytic Education, and was nominated for a Gradiva Award in 2016 for his article, "Temporality and the Torments of Time." He is the co-editor of *Temporality and Shame: Psychoanalytic and Philosophical Perspectives* (Routledge, 2017), winner of the 2018 American Board and Academy of Psychoanalysis Book Prize for best edited book.

George B. Hogenson, PhD is a senior training analyst at the C.G. Jung Institute of Chicago. He holds a PhD in philosophy from Yale University and an MA in clinical social work from the University of Chicago. He is on the editorial board of the *Journal of Analytical Psychology* and is currently Vice President of the International Association for Analytical Psychology. He has a private practice in Chicago, Illinois.

Raya A. Jones, PhD is a Reader in the School of Social Sciences, Cardiff University, UK. She is the author of numerous articles and books including *Personhood and Social Robotics* (Routledge, 2016), *Jung, Psychology, Postmodernity* (Routledge, 2007), and *The Child-School Interface* (Cassell, 1995); editor of *Body, Mind and Healing after Jung* (Routledge, 2010) and *Jung and the Question of Science* (Routledge, 2014); and co-editor of *Jungian and Dialogical Perspectives* (Palgrave Macmillan, 2011), *Cultures and Identities in Transition* (Routledge 2010), and *Education and Imagination* (Routledge, 2008).

Stanton Marlan, PhD, ABPP, FABP, LP, is a Jungian analyst and clinical psychologist in private practice in Pittsburgh, Pennsylvania, and an adjunct Clinical Professor of Psychology at Duquesne University from where he graduated with two PhDs (Clinical Psychology and Philosophy). He is a training and supervising analyst with the Inter-Regional Society of Jungian Analysts, and President of the Pittsburgh Society of Jungian Analysts. He is board certified in both clinical psychology and psychoanalysis from the American Board of Professional Psychology (ABPP) and board certified in adult psychoanalysis and a Fellow of the American Board of Psychoanalysis (FABP). He is a director on The American Board and Academy of Psychoanalysis (ABAPsa) and its past President. Dr. Marlan has published numerous articles on Jungian psychology and is the editor of four books including *Archetypal Psychologies: Reflections in Honor of James Hillman*. He has lectured widely internationally, was a Fay lecturer at Texas A&M and the author of *The Black Sun: The Alchemy and Art of Darkness*. He has taught at the C.G. Jung Institut–Zürich and other Jungian institutes and universities. He is currently working on a new book entitled *The Philosophers' Stone: The Alchemy and Art of Illumination*.

Christian McMillan, PhD is a researcher on a two-year research project titled "'One World': Logical and Ethical Implications of Holism" funded by the Arts and Humanities Research Council, UK in the Department of Psychosocial and Psychoanalytic Studies at the University of Essex.

Jon Mills, PsyD, PhD, ABPP is a philosopher, psychoanalyst, and clinical psychologist. He is Professor of Psychology & Psychoanalysis at Adler Graduate Professional School in Toronto and runs a mental health corporation in Ontario, Canada. Recipient of numerous awards for his scholarship, he is the author and/or editor of twenty books in psychoanalysis, philosophy, psychology, and cultural studies including *Inventing God* (Routledge, 2017), *Underworlds* (Routledge, 2014), *Conundrums: A Critique of Contemporary Psychoanalysis* (Routledge, 2012), *Origins: On the Genesis of Psychic Reality* (McGill-Queens University Press, 2010), *Treating Attachment Pathology* (Rowman & Littlefield, 2005), *The Unconscious Abyss: Hegel's Anticipation of Psychoanalysis* (State University of New York Press, 2002), and *The Ontology of Prejudice* (Rodopi, 1997).

Robert A. Segal, PhD is Sixth Century Chair in Religious Studies, University of Aberdeen. Previously, he was professor at Lancaster University, England. Before he came to Lancaster in 1994, he taught religious studies at several universities in his native United States. He writes and teaches on theories of myth and theories of religion as well as on Gnosticism. He was introduced to Jung by a philosopher of religion at Princeton University, where he studied for his PhD in religious studies. Among the books he has written or edited are *The Poimandres as Myth* (Mouton de Gruyter, 1986); *Joseph Campbell* (1987, rev. ed. 1990), *In Quest of the Hero* (Princeton University Press, 1990), *Explaining and Interpreting Religion* (Peter Lang, 1992), *The Gnostic Jung* (Princeton University Press and Routledge, 1992), *The Myth and Ritual Theory* (Blackwell, 1998), *Jung on Mythology* (Princeton University Press, 1998), *Theorizing about Myth* (University of Massachusetts Press, 1999), *Hero Myths* (Blackwell, 2000), *Myth: A Very Short Introduction* (Oxford University Press, 2004, rev. ed. 2015), *Blackwell Companion to the Study of Religion* (Blackwell, 2006), *30 Second Mythology* (Ivy Press, 2012), *Hero's Quest* (Salem Press, 2013), and *Vocabulary for the Study of Religion*, 3 Vols. (Brill, 2015).

Cecile T. Tougas, PhD taught philosophy at the University of Massachusetts-Lowell, the University of Southern Maine, and currently teaches Latin at the North Carolina School of Science and Mathematics, Durham. She has published articles on analytical psychology and phenomenology including the book, *The Phenomena of Awareness: Husserl, Cantor, Jung* (Routledge, 2013).

John R. White, PhD, Jungian Diplomate, is a practicing Jungian psychoanalyst and licensed mental health counselor. His original training was in philosophy. He completed his doctorate in philosophy at the International Academy of Philosophy, and subsequently taught philosophy at three different institutions over the span of twenty years. His publications are mainly in Continental philosophy, ethics, environmental philosophy, and the philosophy of psychoanalysis. He is currently a Scholar-in-residence at the Simon Silverman Phenomenology Center, Duquesne University, Pittsburgh PA. He obtained his Masters in mental health counseling and his diploma as a Jungian psychoanalyst from the Inter-Regional Society of Jungian Analysts. He is a member of the Pittsburgh Society of Jungian Analysts and of the Board of Directors of the Pittsburgh Psychoanalytic Center. He is the author of *Adaptation and Clinical Practice: Robert Langs' Adaptive Psychotherapy in the Light of Analytical Psychology*.

Introduction

Philosophizing Jung

Jon Mills

Unlike Freud, Jung has received little attention from philosophers. This may be in part due to the fact that while Freud was intent on systematizing his theories, Jung was not. This cool receptivity by philosophers may also be due to the fact that Jung often disparaged philosophy in his writing while exalting religion, despite the fact that much of his corpus involves direct engagement with ancient, Gnostic, medieval, modern, Continental, and Eastern philosophical texts. This salient contradiction underlies a fundamental tension in Jung's thinking about the value of philosophizing analytical psychology.

At times Jung goes to extreme lengths to deny his philosophical penchants, unconvincingly I might add. Shamdasani (2003) tells us that in 1951 Jung wrote to his translator Richard Hull clamoring: "Don't forget; I am definitely no philosopher and my concepts are accordingly empirical and not speculative" (p. 167, fn 12). Elsewhere he states: "I approach psychological matters from a scientific and not from a philosophical standpoint" (Jung, 1938/1940, p. 6; 11, § 2). And in an interview near the end of his life, he proclaims: "I have no system, no doctrine, nothing of that kind. I am an empiricist, with no metaphysical views at all" (Jung, 1977, p. 419). Why would Jung say such things? Presumably to shelter his views from skepticism by evoking science, thereby safeguarding his psychological theories would be deemed respectable "hypotheses." But in reality Jung himself was a very ambivalent thinker, vacillating between the world of evidence and ideas, speculation and experience, imagination and reality, truth and myth—all vying for legitimacy under the rubric of knowledge. His ambivalence suffuses his writings throughout his career; perhaps in part owing to never feeling truly satisfied by privileging science as the master discourse. But despite his late turn to alchemy in search of the *lapis philosophorum*, his writings retained an unbelievable reservation, if not an absence of reflection, on the compatibility between philosophy and science, almost bordering on a crass denial, and hence deceiving his readers into thinking he is talking about facts, only then to return them to the status of hypotheses, thus back-paddling further and further into a false binary, the so-called dichotomization of science and philosophy.

Denial or Posturing?

Why would Jung go to such exaggerated efforts to polarize the value of science over philosophy when much of the subject matter Jung was most passionately interested in and engaged with throughout his life would fall within the domain of the humanities outside of the confines and methodology of natural science? In *Mysterium Coniunctionis* (1954), his final great last work on alchemy, he attempts to introduce an obfuscating cleavage between psychology and philosophy most forcefully when he says: "any attempt at scientific explanation gets into the grotesque situation of being accused in its turn of offering a metaphysical explanation" (p. 547). Here this equally applies to Jung's philosophy of the archetypes and the collective unconscious, for he is intimately aware that he is tarrying in metaphysical country when postulating these concepts.

Elsewhere Jung shows more affinity for philosophy, hence revealing more indecision, if not prevarication, in his identifications, yet he ultimately equates philosophy with religion:

> I can hardly draw a veil over the fact that we psychotherapists ought really to be philosophers or philosophic doctors—or rather that we are already so, though we are unwilling to admit it because of the glaring contrast between our work and what passes for philosophy in the universities. We could also call it religion *in statu nascendi*, for in the vast confusion that reigns at the roots of life there is no line of division between philosophy and religion.
>
> (Jung, 1943, p. 79; *CW*, 16, § 181)

Yet still Jung sees that every science hinges on human subjectivity, that the object of science is contingent on the subjectivity of the scientist, and that what is deemed empirical is equally determined by psychological factors as well as methodological considerations. And when the psyche is the subject matter of science, it cannot step outside of itself as a self-observing, purely objective reflective cogito that it must become—for there is no unadulterated scientific apparatus, no pristine epistemology, no God's eye view of the universe. This false dichotomy problematizes the methodology of science with phenomenology, which it must reconcile, for both approaches to observation and experience are procedurally intertwined. In fact, Jung even radicalizes the phenomenology of psychic experience as the ontic ground of "everything":

> The psyche is an extremely complex factor, so fundamental to all premises that no judgment can be regarded as 'purely empirical' but must first indicate the premises by which it judges. Modern psychology can no longer disguise the fact that the object of its investigation is its own essence, so that in certain respects there can be no 'principles' or valid judgments at all, but only *phenomenology*—in other words, *sheer experience*. On this level of knowledge, psychology has to abdicate as a science, though only on this very high level. Below that, judgments and hence science are still possible, provided that the premises are always stated … The premise underlying my judgments is the *reality* [*Wirklichkeit*] *of everything psychic*, a concept based on the appreciation of the fact that the psyche can also be pure experience.
>
> (Jung, 1935, pp. 774–775; *CW*, 18, §§ 1738, 1740)

Roger Brooke (2015) has been most instrumental in showing that Jung was a phenomenologist of the mind and his writings should be understood within this framework despite the fact that Jung was quite "inconsistent," "unsophisticated," and "poorly disciplined" in this regard (p. xvi). Although Jung interjected his own unique phenomenological style to his theorizing, he often did so at the expense of distancing himself from the discipline of philosophy, when in fact he was most notably critical of speculative metaphysics and tended to lump all philosophy into the same basket with a flare of negation. Throughout his *Collected Works* Jung stubbornly emphasized that he was no philosopher, and that he was not theorizing or engaging in speculative arguments or doctrines about the ideas (concepts) he developed throughout his corpus regarding psychical life (see Jung, 1976, *Letters Vol. II*, pp., zl-zlii). He repeatedly claimed that he did not engage in philosophical or positivist approaches to make his arguments, except for that *when he did*, heralding a kind of hybrid-empiricism that he alone created, it was couched in phenomenological language: "Not being a philosopher, but an empiricist, I am inclined in all difficult questions to let experience decide. Where it is impossible to find any tangible basis in experience, I prefer to leave the question unanswered" (Jung, 1926, § 604). Here Jung rebukes ultimate questions of reality, hence first principles, in favor of the phenomenology of lived experience while claiming simultaneously "the reality of everything psychic." Let's get our ontological premises straight.

Jung as Philosopher

Rather than remain hung up on professional roles and titles, or class distinctions based on occupations, I believe it is important for Jungians and post-Jungians to embrace the philosophical implications of Jung's thought, which has the potential to be extended into a more formalized, systematic philosophy (see Mills, 2014). While this endeavor is beyond the scope of this immediate project, it becomes incumbent on me to demonstrate more persuasively why Jung's philosophical corpus should be identified as encompassing metaphysical, as well as psychological and phenomenological parameters. If all the experiences we have are conditioned on and come from a collective psyche as the primordial base dispersed as ontic forms superimposed on all the various layers that comprise human psychic reality, and that we ultimately only know and experience them as our inner world, then if this is not a grand philosophy, I don't know what else it would be. The mere fact that Jung (1961, pp. 158–159) can introduce a theory of the collective unconscious *derived from his own dream*, as reported in *Memories, Dreams, Reflections*, shows the creative advance of imagination that seeks to wed higher (universal) unitive forces with the content of dreamt psychic material believed to emanate from a real external correspondent reality he called the archetypal. This is metaphysics at its finest! It is time for Jungians to welcome the philosophical positions inherent in Jung's writings in order to engage or revise them, as well as enter the fray of empirical (academic) psychology if depth psychology is to survive as a vibrant intellectual discipline.

Also when Jung (1952) employs these defensive side-stepping strategies in his caveats of disavowing any intent to offer a "system nor a general theory" (*CW*, 18, p. 666), this does not mean his collected body of works on various topics do not constitute a treatise on human nature, which I argue they do. Jung's caveats belie a transparent intention, that is, they are designed to insulate him from external criticism and are interjected selectively where he sees fit.

When Jung (1937) states that he wants to "eschew any metaphysical or philosophical considerations" (*CW*, 11, p. 16) from his "empirical" take on the phenomenological manifestations of human psychology, what does he mean by this? Granted that he wants to set his investigations within the context of a particular domain of study or inquiry (here, from this last longer quote, it is religion), but he cannot "eschew" metaphysics, especially when religion is ultimately concerned (historically) with the question of God, itself a metaphysical posit. Psychology *is* ontology: our psyches define and shape lived reality, and hence animates being itself with a certain psychic presence. This is very much an idealist position, namely, that the structures of subjectivity necessarily condition our experience of the world, and in this way construct reality (cf. Mills, 2010, pp. 208–212). I don't think Jung (1957) would disagree with this statement given he says that "metaphysical assertions ... *are statements of the psyche*" (p. xxxvii).

I realize that orthodox Jungians will likely bemoan any analysis of Jung's pivotal concepts that define the historical landscape of his theoretical legacy, but I believe critique and progressive development will only add to philosophical enrichment. After all, we are drawn to Jung's theories for a reason. Why not improve them? It is for this reason that I have asked many internationally recognized scholars to address the philosophical implications of Jung's far-ranging ideas, from traditional metaphysics, philosophy of mind, epistemology, philosophical psychology, phenomenology, psychology of religion, myth, physics, alchemy, ethics, aesthetics, and the question of science. Here, for the first time in a comprehensive manner collected throughout these chapters, we may observe philosophers attempting to unpack the philosophical consequences of Jung's thought as they are applied to many traditional topics covered in the humanities and the social sciences.

Given that Jung has not been historically taken up by philosophers, critiqued, and applied to contemporary theories of mind, culture, and human nature, this is the first book of its kind. I hope this encourages a new generation of research in analytical psychology that can benefit from philosophical scrutiny and theoretical fortification.

In the first chapter, I challenge the most basic tenet of Jung's analytical psychology, namely, the existence of the collective unconscious. Despite the fact that there are purported to be universal processes and ontological features of mind throughout all psychoanalytical schools of thought, Jung's is unique in the history of psychoanalytic ideas for positing a supraordinate, autonomous transpersonal psyche that remains the source, ground, and wellspring from which all unconscious and conscious manifestations derive. This bold claim is analyzed through a close inspection of Jung's texts that questions the philosophical justification for postulating a supernatural macroanthropos or reified collective mind. Pointing out the problems of agency and fallacies of hypostatization, it is not necessary to evoke a transpersonal cosmogony to explain how universality suffuses individual subjectivity within social collectives. Here we may conclude that the collective unconscious construct is a signifier for the common psychological dynamics and characteristics of shared humanity. In this sense, the myth of the collective unconscious is better understood as a metaphor for a higher abstraction or ideal principle ordained with numinous value.

In Chapter 2, George Hogenson tackles the archetype debate that was revived in 2001 at a conference held at Cambridge University. The debate focused on the role evolutionary biology played in Jung's thinking, and the degree to which evolutionary psychology could inform Jungian theory. Following the debate a series of papers appeared, with differing interpretations of Jung's theory, but largely proposing an interpretation based on emergence rather than stable patterns. This chapter argues that much of the confusion that arose at this time resulted from a failure to fully investigate the background to Jung's theory, particularly in relation to the French somnambulistic tradition found in the psychologists Pierre Janet and Theodore Flournoy, and the philosopher, Henri Bergson. Additionally, Jung's debate with Freud over the nature of libido and the phenomena associated with Dementia Praecox played a role in the development of the theory of archetypes. With this background in hand it is possible to identify contemporary trends in theorizing that are closer to Jung's original concerns.

Erik Goodwyn examines Jung's views on psyche and soma in Chapter 3. Any psychology begins with (often unstated) assumptions about its subject matter: to discuss the characteristics of the mind, conscious experience, the unconscious, etc., we must already have some idea of what the categories of "mind" and "matter" are to begin with. This of course invites the age-old issue of what comprises or characterizes each, and this is known as the Mind–Body Problem (MBP). For some psychological theories this fact does not cause many problems, but for Jungian theory it poses certain challenges because of the way Jung himself—particularly later in life—presented the concepts of the archetype as metaphysical entities. Unfortunately, Jung shied away from metaphysics, however, leaving us with some long-standing conceptual problems that this chapter attempts to sort through. Here, several metaphysical approaches to the MBP are examined to see which best suits Jungian psychology.

In Chapter 4, Marco Heleno Barreto examines Jung's epistemology. From an epistemological standpoint, Barreto argues that Jung is a skeptical thinker, although his skepticism has not been duly characterized and stressed. The skeptic dimension of his self-proclaimed empiricism is demonstrated under the forms of metaphysical skepticism and epistemic skepticism, the latter leading to a conception of science in terms of a skeptical statistical probabilism. The empiricist-skeptic outlook of Jung's typological and phenomenological standpoints is also highlighted. Jung's adoption of the fundamental premise of the reality of the psyche (*Wirklichkeit der Seele*), which brings in ontological presuppositions, leads to a final characterization of his epistemological standpoint as being that of a mitigated epistemic skepticism. On the other hand, Jung's opposition to skepticism is examined, disclosing a tension between his epistemological standpoint and psychotherapeutic goals in analytical psychology. The outcome of this unresolved tension is a *sacrificium intellectus* for the sake of "immediate experience," which establishes the problematic (and often denied) place of belief in Jung's thought, both on its theoretical aspect and on its psychotherapeutic conception. Finally, it is shown how skepticism and belief meet in Jung's notion of symbol and symbolic experience.

In Chapter 5, Robin McCoy Brooks critiques aspects of C.G. Jung's epistemological basis for psychic reality that contributes to a view of the self that is ungrounded in biological life and the material world because of his para-psychological biases. Thus, Jung's attempt to establish the prominence of the objective psyche as a foundation to the other sciences of his era had the unfortunate effect of disregarding the material realities inherent in self-formation. The author investigates the historical contexts to which Jung was inured as a means of determining what of his corpus regarding a dis-embodied self remains relevant today amidst our present scientific revolution and analytical psychology's contemporary identity crises. The critique into Jung's prevailing psychical biases focuses on the historical tensions that contributed to Jung's ambiguous relationship to natural (*Naturwissenschaften*) and human (*Geisteswissenschaften*) sciences throughout his lifetime that led him to rely on new-Kantian philosophical ideas (a foundational ontology) and turn away from contemporary developments advanced by philosophical phenomenology and Freud's biological model of personhood. Brooks contends that analytical psychology today has been dealt a fatal theoretical blow if we do not radically reconsider the indivisibility of material and more than material realities as viable influences in self-formation.

In the next chapter, Cecile Tougas explores Jung's phenomenological method. Phenomenology is a practice of paying attention to *phenomena*—"appearances" in the root sense of the word, "whatever is given for awareness" in the current general sense. Jung's detailed study of "psychological types" as typical acts of perception, ways of making judgments, and attitudes towards the givens, qualifies him early on as a rigorous student of activities of awareness in its many forms. His philosophical insights about awareness were manifold yet in several ways coincide with some insights of Indian philosophy, Aristotle, Husserl, Kate Soper, Kant, Schopenhauer, Socrates, Sylvia Brinton Perera, Marie-Louise von Franz, and Jacqueline M. Schectman. Finding insight in Jung and others involves experiencing the insight for oneself firsthand; and so, following phenomenological practices, Tougas attends to personally lived experience and describes it with the aim of putting such meaning before others as evident in various ways.

Jung's (1958) *Answer to Job* is his contribution to the further unfolding of a new, culturally-relevant system of symbols of the divine, a highly personal, even prophetic response to what he calls the spiritual crisis of modernity. In Chapter 7, Garth Amundson examines how throughout his life Jung sought to remedy this cultural malady by reintroducing ancient mythic perspectives on the human condition into the Western worldview, in ways that honor the demand of modern persons for symbols of the divine that withstand critical scrutiny; that is, that *make sense* by conforming to the phenomenology of collective modern consciousness. Jung pursued this agenda while also giving pride of place to another dimension of our sensibilities, that is, the fact that the satisfaction of a sensible viewpoint is rooted in its synergy with our aesthetic faculties, which are emotional and instinctive. These are our "irrational" or "supra-rational" desires for concretely felt— that is, sensate—experiences of reality that may yield an unbidden, vitalizing awareness of the transcendent. In all this Jung is cautious, insisting that the existence of a metaphysical object is not provable objectively. Rather, he seeks to forward a perspective on spirituality that embraces rather than ignores the vicissitudes of our habitation of an increasingly secular world.

In *Answer to Job*, Jung uses the Biblical character Job's harsh yet reasoned critique of Yahweh's character to argue that modern Western religious faithful must critically reevaluate the qualities of the God imago that has been handed down to them by history, or risk falling into irrelevance. Specifically, Jung insists that we have yet to integrate the archetypal "dark," daemonic aspect of the God imago into collective consciousness, such that this emerges, unmodified by awareness, into modernity as the pervasive blight of personal psychic anomie and dangerous mass movements. Elaborating upon Jung's perception of our spiritual rootlessness, Amundson extrapolates on the work of religious philosopher Rudolf Otto, which Jung liberally applied to outline his position in *Answer to Job*, as well as variations of phenomenological, pragmatic, social psychological, and eco-feminist views to argue for the centrality of our need for a redemptive relation to the Absolute that resonates with modern Western sensibilities.

Building upon this tradition, in the next chapter John White shows how Rudolf Otto's notion of the numinous plays a central role in Carl Jung's analytical psychology. However, both Jung's and Otto's treatment of the numinous tend to treat religious experience as something purely immanent to the psyche, i.e. as lacking what phenomenology terms "intentionality" or meaningful transcendence to something beyond the experience. In Otto's case, the development of the numinous is in part in contrast to traditional natural theology, which Otto rejects wholesale as too rationalist, an attitude Jung shares. In this chapter, White questions the binary Otto and Jung implicitly pose between (1) a purely transcendent and rationalist conception of God, and (2) a treatment of God in terms of numinous experience purely immanent to the psyche. Prior to the rationalist tradition, traditional natural theology opted for neither immanence nor transcendence but rather assumed the experience of the divine occurs in the tension between immanence and transcendence. Once this point is clarified, it is seen that the binary of immanence and transcendence need not be assumed in psychology of religion and further that Jung can be read as making potentially important contributions to a psychology of religion more attuned to traditional natural theology and to the tension between immanence and transcendence.

Chapter 9 by Robert Segal begins by distinguishing nineteenth-century approaches to myth from twentieth-century ones. Freud and Jung are far more akin than distinct. They share the twentieth-century view that myth is other than the primitive counterpart to modern science. But going beyond fellow twentieth-century theorists, they reject both the nineteenth-century subject matter and the nineteenth-century function of myth. Not only is myth not about the physical world, but it is not an explanation of anything. Jung's theory turns out to be pitted at least as much against nineteenth-century theorists like Tylor and, especially, Frazer as against Freud. Segal takes Jung's interpretation of the myth of the puer archetype, and in turn of Adonis as a case of a puer personality, to exemplify his distinctive approach to myth.

In Chapter 10, Stanton Marlan affirms the importance of philosophizing in the forging of Jung's psychology of the unconscious as developed in his study of alchemy. Following alchemical and religious philosophers, Jung saw both mind and spirit as essential aspects of alchemical studies. In this way, he goes beyond philosophical materialism as a basis for viewing alchemy simply as a proto-science of chemistry. For Jung, alchemy was also a psychological, symbolic, and spiritual discipline. However, in terms of the latter, he was aware of the limits of an "ontology of spirit," which rejected what it considered to be the vulgar filth of natural and worldly *materia*—but which Jung held to be an indispensable dimension of alchemical recipes and practice. What's the matter with alchemical recipes is that the "matter" was literalized and ejected, split off from our understanding of alchemy. The nature of this "matter" remains an important question. For Jung, the philosophical divide between pure and impure, spirit and matter, subject and object, self and world, the godly and the demonic, was too simplistic for the complexity needed to establish an adequate ground for a psychology of the unconscious. In an attempt to go beyond such binaries, Jung reclaimed what was rejected and emphasized a dialectic of wholeness and an archetypal view of psychic reality rooted in notions of imagination and the self as a way of surpassing fixed traditional ontologies of materialism and idealism. Jung's dynamic vision is illustrated by active imagination, a transformative process which reveals a phenomenological subtle body and a view of the soul that resists reduction into known categories of understanding. The need for further philosophical clarification is important, but it must account for the rejected filth that muddies our intellectual clarity. It must help us to understand how rejected "vulgar monsters," such as the ouroboros, can play an important role in scientific discovery, such as the benzene ring and in the healing of analytic patients.

In Chapter 11, Ladson Hinton explores the parameters of time in Jung's ethics. The lens of temporality yields many insights into the ethical perspective of C.G. Jung. In order to provide a context for discussion, Hinton first elaborates some broader perspectives on temporality, providing a brief genealogy illustrating the intimate connection between the emergence of temporality and the emergence of human culture. As philosophical thought evolves, Aristotle states that we cannot fully know the past or predict the future, arguing for the perspective of *phronesis*, or practical wisdom: an ethical knowledge that only emerges in time. He contrasts his ideas with the Platonic perspective of *epistêmê*, or 'timeless' truth. Influenced by the latter tradition, Jung often privileges 'timeless' archetypes, unfavorably contrasting that perspective with the 'personal unconscious,' the experience of everyday temporality. Although he consistently affirms the moral obligation of consciousness, his theories often seem to undermine his intent, and leave one with the impression that the 'archetype' is responsible for human actions.

Hinton specifically elaborates these tendencies in Jung's thinking, first focusing on his early poem, *Septem Sermones Ad Mortuos* (The Seven Sermons to the Dead). That work clearly privileges a 'timeless' dimension. Examples from his other writings further illustrate a devaluation of lived time, the personal unconscious, in favor of a 'timeless' archetypal perspective. This detracts from our everyday experience of ethical responsibility. Sophocles' *Oedipus Rex* dramatically highlights the connection of time, memory, and ethical knowledge. Later in his life, Jung's deep interest in alchemy seems to represent a step toward a more process-oriented perspective, with an emphasis on the importance of the *prima materia*, the 'stuff' of life that is often rejected and thrown away. This implies a degree of shift in his ethical perspective, toward valuing the everyday process of temporal experience. Here there is less sense of division between the archetypal and the everyday. Some late statements from his *Letters* amplify that viewpoint.

In the next chapter, Christian McMillan examines Jung's views on literature and aesthetics. Jung appears to have had a troubled relationship with the philosophical discipline associated with aesthetics. A discipline whose origins are often credited to the German philosopher Alexander Gottlieb Baumgarten (1714–1762), aesthetics is commonly concerned with the nature and appreciation of art, beauty, and taste. This preoccupation with 'beauty' is responsible for some of Jung's resistances to aesthetics and what he regards as the lack of ethical and moral obligation that aesthetic engagements convey. In this chapter McMillan critically reflects on Jung's encounter with Joyce's (1882–1941) *Ulysses* upon which he wrote a monologue (1932). Jung's encounter is used as a vehicle to examine some of his assumptions regarding the nature of moral and ethical obligations in relation to aesthetics. Given the German origins of aesthetics as a discipline and its important influence on post-Kantianism, McMillan draws upon two detailed studies of Jung's engagement with aesthetics in order to illuminate the vistas that Kant and post-Kantian's opened up concerning the 'depth' of the synthetic genesis of experience as well as the transformative ethical potential of aesthetic encounters. With respect to Jung's aesthetic 'encounter' with *Ulysses* and its philosophical dynamics, McMillan refers throughout to the work of Deleuze (1925–1995) who was not only influenced by Jung, but who wrote extensively on Kant/post-Kantianism, 'modern art,' sensation, and ethics, thus bringing together the two themes of this chapter; the modalities of synthesis engendered by an aesthetic encounter and the extent to which this sits uncomfortably (not incompatibly) with analytical psychology.

In the final chapter, Raya Jones examines Jung's views on science and technology. Jung's ambivalent attitude to science and technology should be considered in view of his agenda for analytical psychology pitched against the backdrop of how science was generally understood in the early twentieth century, the history of psychology as a science, and the traditional view of technology as the practical application of science. This chapter first highlights Jung's timely defense of science in lectures presented to educators in the 1920s, noting how significant omissions and alterations in a 1946 revision of the lectures correspond to changes in the backdrop against which Jung was pitching analytical psychology. Next, Jung's untimely method of investigation is identified, noting that Jung was perceived by his contemporaries as betraying the dream of a scientific psychology. Jung's own exposition of the dilemma of modern psychology is reviewed in relation to the history of modern psychology. Turning to Jung's contemplation of technology, this chapter takes a close look at his letter to the editors of *Zürcher Student* in which he speculates about the effect of technology on the psyche. Finally, it is proposed to reposition analytical psychology as a technology of the self.

Taken together as a whole, this edited volume is the first endeavor to evaluate Jung among the philosophers and examine how his psychological theories have philosophical merit despite their purported shortcomings. With this in mind, philosophizing Jung's theories may lead to future research that refines his theoretical contributions and inaugurates new directions in post-Jungian studies.

References

Brooke, R. (2015). *Jung and Phenomenology*. Classic Edition. London: Routledge.

Jung, C.G. (1977). *C.G. Jung Speaking: Encounters and Interviews*. Eds. W. McGuire and R.F.C. Hull. Princeton, NJ: Princeton University Press.

———(1976). *Letters Vol. II 1951–1961*. Eds. G. Adler and A. Jaffé. Princeton: Princeton University Press.

———— (1961). *Memories, Dreams, Reflections*. New York: Vintage.

———— (1957). Psychological Commentary. *The Tibetan Book of the Dead, 3rd Ed.* Ed. W.Y. Evans-Wentz; Trans. R.F.C. Hull. Oxford: Oxford University Press, pp. xxxv-lii.

———— (1954/1963). *Mysterium Coniunctionis. CW*, 14.

———— (1952). *A Reply to Martin Buber. CW*, 18, pp. 663–670.

———— (1943). *Psychotherapy and a Philosophy of Life. CW*, 16.

———— (1938/1940). *Psychology and Religion. CW*, 11.

———— (1937). *Psychology and Religion. CW*, 11, pp. 3–200.

———— (1935). *Foreword to von Koenig-Fachsenfeld: "Wandlungen des Traumproblems von der Romantik bis zur Gegenwart". CW*, 18.

———— (1926). *Spirit and Life. CW*, 8.

Mills, J. (2014). Jung as Philosopher: Archetypes, the Psychoid Factor, and the Question of the Supernatural. *International Journal of Jungian Studies*, 6 (3), 227–242.

———— (2010). *Origins: On the Genesis of Psychic Reality*. Montreal: McGill-Queens University Press.

Shamdasani, S. (2003). *Jung and the Making of Modern Psychology.* Cambridge: Cambridge University Press.

Chapter 1

The Collective Unconscious

Jon Mills

What do Jung's theories mean to Jungians? In *The Wisdom of the Dream* (Segaller, 1989), Robert Johnson says the following: "The collective unconscious is that set of building blocks in which human reality is made. It is as if there is this great reservoir outside time and space—patterned energy. Mankind struggles to give it definition, like this from which everything is drawn or everything is made." This statement, I suggest, personifies what Jung means to the world and what Jung represents to Jungians. For Jung, all of psychic reality is conditioned on the bedrock of a collective unconscious mind that precedes each of us. We know the marbled instantiations of this generative "objective psyche" through the archetypes, which are symbolic forms that make their way into lived, personal (conscious) reality radiating from a timeless unconscious ground originating from a universal principle, yet awakened within the archaic life of mankind and passed along the aeons through encoded genetic transmutations and the transgenerational transmission of culture. Here Jung commands a very distinct philosophy in the history of ideas, one based on *transpersonal supervenience* from a collective unconscious agency, which I argue is a form of *cosmic emanationism* (Mills, 2014, p.16). If all psychic reality derives from or flows out of an original wellspring we call the archetypical collective, then we must ponder the metaphysical and mystical implications of this radical idea.

In this chapter I wish to examine a central notion of analytical psychology, if not the fulcrum on which Jung's philosophy of mind and human culture rests. Here I will take up a very specific question with a narrow scope of analysis; namely, Is there a Collective Unconscious? And if so, What is it, exactly? Jung himself actually gives a very scant account of the collective unconscious throughout his *Collected Works*, instead focusing almost entirely on the archetypes, the presupposed contents of a collective psyche. Rather than focus on content, I wish to sustain the question of original ground, the metaphysical womb of all becoming. Indeed, although the archetype is purported to be its own original form (*arché*—origin, type—form), the collective unconscious is the original *source* of these innumerable self-instantiating forms, the foundation, wellspring, or encompassing principle in which archetypes originate— the ultimate cause and basis of appearances as such. Although this inquiry may amount to heresy within certain orthodox circles, in order to lend coherence and credibility to this theoretical postulate, it is incumbent upon us to offer a philosophical defense of this most important and radical concept that grounds the entire edifice of Jungian thought.

As a universal and necessary a priori condition for psychic life to exist and emerge, the collective unconscious becomes the most ontologically dependent force and locus of all human activity, perhaps even presupposing a transpersonal matrix that yields cosmic, if not supernatural, significance. But before we draw any conclusions, it becomes important for us to unpack Jung's concept of the collective unconscious and see if the philosophical implications of his theory bears plausibility and merit, if not pragmatic utility.

In the Jungian literature, there has been a great deal of critique on the notion of archetypes. In fact, this concept may very well be the most controversial aspect of Jung's analytical psychology. But whatever analysis we derive at, we must not forget that archetypes are conditioned on something far more ontologically basic, that is, indispensably primordial.

Because archetypes are essentially the contents of the collective psyche that are said to be emitted into individual minds—itself a presumptive assertion that requires justification, this further challenges Kant's formalism where only a priori categories for understanding and forms of sensibility exist, which are the formal mental structures that allow us to apprehend objects of experience; whereas Jung imports content (the archetypes) at the very beginning that constitutes the pre-subjective agent—that is, the ontological preconditions that make subjectivity possible, thus present at birth without the aid of sense perception, space, and time. This becomes problematic unless one is willing to grant that the contents of past ancestral experience become incorporated, organized, preserved, and recapitulated by humankind, is transmitted phylogenetically, and reemerges in subsequent transgenerational instantiations in future historical timelines of the human race. Here we must differentiate between an *original source* versus the forms, contents, and aims of manifestation. Recall that transitioning from the non-manifest to the manifest is realized and accomplished through the archetypes. Is the collective unconscious the true *arché*, the true beginning, or should this be more properly ascribed to the archetypes themselves, presuming they exist, which further needs an argument?

Perhaps the collective unconscious is merely a symbol, a metaphor for the Center, or does it have a distinct ontology—the "really real," the zone of an absolute reality? If we push this issue further, boundaries quickly become blurred to the point that the collective unconscious could be synonymous with the concept of God, the actor and act of creation taking place in and at the center of the cosmos. If we adopt this point of view, viz., of deifying the collective unconscious as a supernatural macroanthropos, it would be disastrous for Jungian studies, as the theoretical foundation of analytical psychology would succumb to inventing unverifiable fictions that satisfy the wishful fantasies of imagination at the expense of reason, logic, and science.

Jung on the Collective Unconscious

Jung's first use of the term appears in *Symbols of Transformation* (1912, *CW*, 5, p. 177n), what he initially referred to as a "supra-individual universality" (p. 177), "the archaic heritage of humanity" (p. 178), the birth of "spirit" (p. 413). Here Jung makes a bold claim: spirit (*Geist*) comes from a collective unconscious and appears as archetypes, both as "primordial images" and "primary forms" (p. 413). In his Foreword to the 4th Swiss Edition, Jung concludes that "The psyche is not of today; its ancestry goes back many millions of years ... from the perennial rhizome ... the root matter" of the unconscious, "the mother of all things" (p. xxiv). In other words, mind and its contents come from a pre-ontological substrate that conditions the coming into being of all psychological events up to our current times.

Jung makes many statements in his writings that enlist a nativist view of the psyche derived from innate substructures that favor evolutionary explanations (Jung, 1961, p. 348), but he also conflates the contents of mind (archetypes) with the collective unconscious itself. He specifically says that "The collective unconscious does not develop individually but is inherited" (*CW*, 9i, p. 43). How is a collective unconscious belonging to archaic humanity inherited? How can an unconscious collective mind be congenital? This would seem to suggest that we actually inherit some other supraordinate mind that is operative in us and dominates us from the start as some foreign process superimposed on our consciousness. In other words, we inherit another Mind or many people's minds that are lumped into a categorical abstraction called the world soul (*anima mundi*). How is this possible? Of course we inherit inborn structures, but to claim that "images" or supraordination is inborn is another matter.

How is the so-called collective unconscious "identical in all individuals" but does not develop individually? How could a suprapersonal configuration—a complex organization—be inborn? One way of interpreting these claims is to collapse the concept of a collective unconscious into a general abstract category subsumed within evolutionary biology, as Jung does when he first identifies the instincts (*Triebe*) with innate images and patterns of behavior derived from unconscious processes. Here the collective unconscious becomes merely a placeholder for something common in all people, our base embodiment that gives rise to conscious experience. So far there is no new thesis being advanced from that of classical psychoanalytic theory.

But Jung soon throws down the gauntlet. In his insistence that there are "universally present formal elements" in the psyche, he quickly jumps to posit the content of the archetypes and asks: "are there or are there not unconscious universal forms of this kind? If they exist, then there is a region of the psyche which one can call the collective unconscious" (*CW*, 9i, p. 44). But why this inferential leap? Why are universal forms equated with archetypal content? How is formalism the same as particularities? Is there a difference between unconscious structure, form, and content (as process, as the preconditions for cognition to transpire)? These differential classifications of explanation make a difference in how we come to conceptualize the notion of a collective unconscious. Jung's hasty generalization is furthermore met with a disclaimer followed by an assertion that "the collective unconscious is neither a speculative nor a philosophical but an empirical matter" (*Ibid.*). What is "empirical" is the mere fact of our biological embodiment that is innately equipped with evolutionary pressures, drives, desires, affects, and a priori cognitive structures that allow all human beings to experience the world and their psychological realities, while positing a transcendental collective or objective (objectified) psyche is a "speculative" "philosophical" construct that must be justified with logical arguments and empirically demonstrated. So far Jung has failed to argue—let alone demonstrate—that just because there are universal structures of mind common to all people that they derive from a collective source or cosmic web of all becoming. Here becomes the first problem in grounding a theoretically justified transpersonal ontology, especially when it is inflated to the realm of cosmogony.

When Jung blurs his definition of the collective unconscious and makes it synonymous with the archetypes, he problematizes his project even further. He declares that the collective unconscious consists of instincts and their "correlates, the archetypes," which everyone possesses, but they also possess "a stock of archetypal images" (*CW*, 8 ¶ 281, p. 138). This would mean that "images" are stored in a collective psyche and transmitted over the ages through the evolutionary mechanisms that have created or given shape to the emergence of modern day *homo sapiens*. Reductive implications aside, at the very least Jung believes (stipulated under the guise of a hypothesis) that images are experienced by humankind and evolutionarily stored in the brain, which are transgenerationally transmitted genetically and culturally, and that they have fixed universal meaning in their symbolism. This is a very deterministic model of evolutionary emergence where image and symbolic meaning appear to be prearranged, programmed, or encoded. There also appears to be no real distinction between the content of the collective unconscious and an agency that produces such content. Why presume a stockpile of images exuding from an archaic mind that is purported to be present at birth and spews forth in the psyche when the same phenomena can be explained from innate cognitive processes that we are evolutionarily engineered to have in order to experience and adapt to our world in which we are thrown?

On the Question of Agency

Jung explicitly states early on that "The instincts and the archetypes together form the 'collective unconscious'" (*CW*, 8, pp. 133–134). Here he makes desire, as part of our drives, along with the formative role of imagoes, the substance of what comprises the collective unconscious. This means that our pulsions, which are part of our embodiment, as well as inborn images, form the organization and content of the collective unconscious. But what about agency? How are the drives and imagoes released or discharged into the psyche? How are the personal or subjective aspects of mind agentically constituted, let alone come from a collective provenance or supraordinance? Here Jung fails to answer to these basic theoretical elements.

To set out my first set of criticisms, we must establish that Jung does indeed at times conflate the collective unconscious *and* archetypes with agency, while at other times, even in some of his later writings, he is more careful in his theoretical propositions. Let us first look at some of his statements of reification. When discussing mythology, Jung explicitly says that "the whole of mythology could be taken as a sort of projection of the collective unconscious;" and when referring to the astrological influence of the stars, he asserts that "these influences are nothing but unconscious, introspective perceptions of the activity of the collective unconscious" (*CW*, 8 ¶ 325, p. 152). Rather than situating these determinative perceptions and judgments within the subjective mind of an individual, here he objectifies them as a concrete thing performing cognitive acts. He commits the fallacy of treating an abstraction as though it is a real entity or thing. This type of theoretical concretization as hypostasis is philosophically problematic, if not simply untenable.

When Jung refers to the collective unconscious as "regulators and stimulators" or "dominants" (*CW*, 8 ¶ 403, p. 204), the notion of agency is further attributed to the collective unconscious as an organizer of mental processes; although he refers to this psychic constellation as "impersonal," hence lacking selfhood, here presumably referring to its functions rather than an agent in its own right. But this is by no means clear and is open to interpretation, especially given that he refers to the archetypes as "entities" (*CW*, 8, p. 231) and "spontaneous agencies" (*CW*, 8, p. 216) elsewhere. Given Jung's preoccupation with the archetypes, the collective unconscious appears at times to be presupposed without offering a philosophical argument or theoretical justification for why it is necessary to even posit such an entity in the first place. In his early work, *Symbols of Transformation*, when focusing on the content of the "stock of primordial images" as "inborn forms peculiar to the instincts," hence collapsing imago within drive (rather than an agentic function that generates images and experiences internal impulses), he refers to "this 'potential' psyche the collective unconscious" (*CW*, 5, p. 408). Here the collective is only a potentiality. But "in this world of the collective unconscious spirit appears as an archetype" (*CW*, 5, p. 413). How do we go from potentiality to actuality, from the possible to the real? Jung is quick to suggest that spirit (*Geist*) emerges from a collective psyche and appears as content (archetypes). Collective or experiential universal images do not have to come from a collective mind. Why such a persistent (if not perfunctory) inferential leap? The psyche is obviously designed a priori to encounter, apprehend, and perceive images of experience, so why suggest they come from a suprastructural, transpersonal mind? There is no logical defense in making this claim other than being an intellectual intuition, which is paraded under the scientific language of a "hypothesis." But here Jung's hypothesis that there is a collective mind is rather suspect. Why is it needed to explain the phenomena of consciousness that are conditioned on unconscious processes that can be generalized to all human beings without the added theoretical onus of importing and justifying a suprapsyche that pulls all the strings behind the anthropic curtain? This would imply that the collective unconscious is a macroanthropos (Mills, 2013), a rather antiquated way of looking at the psychological diversity of socialization and cultural diffusion that springs from a so-called cosmic godhead. Let us return to Jung's ambivalence in how he came to struggle with and advance his theory.

A Return to Basics

Jung was obsessed with the "activity of the psyche" (*CW*, 8, p. 233), but was quick to attribute it to a supreme cause. Here he cannot escape the influence of his theological inculcations and Christian upbringing. But let us examine more soberly his rational side. Although he flip-flops in his thoughts and writings in a rather haphazard manner, he is obviously struggling with what he wants to convey to his audience based on his mood or psychological temperament at the time, something akin to his theory of typology—as each psychological configuration(s) offers its own insights. In a rather inconsistent fashion, we witness how

Jung is inclined to contradict himself by offering contrary and incongruous ruminations. Let us examine some of his more sensible and insightful ideas.

In one of his early writings on aesthetics, Jung states that "the collective unconscious is not to be thought of as a self-subsistent entity; it is no more than a potentiality handed down to us from primordial times in the specific form of mnemonic images or inherited in the anatomical structure of the brain. There are no inborn ideas, but there are inborn possibilities of ideas" (*CW*, 15, pp. 80–81). This is a most sensible assertion despite his later pronouncements to the contrary. Here he is affirming that the collective psyche is not a being in itself, but rather is merely a receptacle of experientially inherited images from the early times of man that have been incorporated within our evolutionarily informed cognitive structures, which give rise to potential ideas encountered in our experience of the world. This is theoretically compatible with nativist views from Kant to evolutionary psychology. Jung is merely reinforcing the point that what is collective is universal to all humans regardless of time, geography, and context, what we typically think of today as our common human nature. But despite the fact that he does concede that the collective unconscious should not be conceived as a "self-subsistent entity," he does nonetheless insist on a basic division between the personal and collective unconscious, when this categorical separation is far from clear or is justified. If every subject has one's own subjective experience of the world but is conditioned on objective universal features of the mind that belong to the human species, then what is subjective or personal is also simultaneously informed by the very psychic structures that permit subjectivity to emerge in the first place. So far in our investigation, I see no need to create a binary between the personal and the universal when both are operative within the minds of all people at any given time. Here the real distinction is between the experiential idiosyncrasies of a unique individual or subject that are peculiar to that specific person as a distinct personality versus what is a common organic and structural a priori substrate that belongs to and unconsciously conditions the human race on a universal level.

So far, the "collective" is merely a signifier for "universal," namely, that which is common to us all. If the collective is then reified (or deified) to the status of a suprastructure, let alone a supraordinant entity, then we have some serious philosophical conundrums to contend with; similar to justifying the question of God or positing a supreme being that conditions all the activities of the psyche. Can we appeal to universal psychic structures without importing a collective mind that supports emanationism or onto-theology? Kant, as well as Hegel and Freud, had little problem in doing so because each affirmed an objective aspect to mind that serves as the preconditions for subjective experience and epistemology. For Kant (1781) it was the intuitive forms of sensibility and the categories for understanding mediated through the transcendental unity of apperception, while Freud (1923, 1932–33, 1940) introduced a more proper discourse on the unconscious processes that bring these faculties about. Even when Hegel (1807) argued for an objective mind or spirit (*Geist*), despite stipulations and scholarly disputes, this was ultimately grounded in dialectical logic rather than a presupposed, transpersonal grand agent or cosmogony that conditions all psychic acts, such as Jung's concept of the collective unconscious. So where do we go from here? Let us return to his treatment of universal human experiences.

Jung first focuses on images, which he rightfully insists gives form "to countless typical experiences of our ancestors ... the psychic residua of innumerable experiences of the same type" (*CW*, 15, p. 81). He then immediately says these primordial images are the "products of creative fantasy" mediated ("translated") through language. But these mediatory concepts signify "the unconscious processes that lie at the roots of the primordial images" (*Ibid.*). What Jung thinks lies at the "roots"—the rhizome—is the collective unconscious, which is presumed to *generate* such images that are laid down within an ancestral psyche. Here a certain hypostatization is suggested, and the archetypes are quickly evoked. Are we justified in positing an ancestral psyche in the first place, what Jung calls the "objective" psyche, or are we merely referring to archaic mind that belonged to humans in the past, not as one source point or supernatural procreative entity, but rather as an abstract idea used to denote a common universal feature attributed to all people, which now evolutionarily and culturally informs the current mental processes of collectives? If we stay attuned to the creative power of imagination to form meaning through semiotic and symbolic mediation, then we may argue that a hypostasized collective psyche is hardly theoretically necessary, for fantasy is the basis of (and is the basic language of) all of humanity.

Jung places a great deal of importance on the emotional intensity of experience and at times makes hasty inferences and generalizations to import some greater Über source as the foundation or cause of affective intensity, when this can simply be fated to the universal processes of psychic organization and developmental emergence common to all humans. Just because we are seized by emotions does not mean they come from an ultimate collective receptacle or wellspring that causes phylogenetic resonances. Jung claims: "At such moments we are no longer individuals, but the race; the voice of all mankind resounds in us" (*CW*, 15, p. 82). Although Jung attributes this to the "hidden forces of instinct," he also believes these reflect "the spirits of [our] ancestors." Rather than claim that the intensity of affect is both the evolutionary residue of history within developmental maturation and cultural diffusion coming from a particular place and epoch in time, he suggests a reification of an original prototype to "the realm of the ever-enduring" that is reactivated in the personal encounter. While equating the overwhelming power and sense of affective release to archetypal experience rather than just psychic experience, he makes a philosophic leap of faith to generalize such emotional intensity to the universal—but not just any universal: rather he makes it a Collective Psyche. Not only is this similar to Hegel's Objective Spirit, it is objectified as a transpersonal mind. Rather than emotional intensity being duplicated in collectives due to a confluence and inseparable interpenetration of biology and culture, it becomes The Collective—the encompassing matrix of everything, the Neoplatonic One.

In many places in his writings, Jung equates the collective unconscious with a corresponding world soul (*anima mundi*) portrayed as an Anthropos (*CW*, 12, pp. 189, 233) enveloped within a wider unified, metaphysical cosmos, namely, the *unus mundus* (see *CW*, 14, pp. 462–465), presumably yoked together by God (see *CW*, 9, ii, pp. 194–195). We may further conclude that the collective unconscious posit serves as its own godhead and is either a symbol or surrogate for original divine creation and causal point of origin. May I suggest that this leap is not philosophically necessary to ground a theory of the archetypes that stand in relation to archaic ontology. One does not need to evoke a transpersonal cosmogony to explain how universality suffuses the individual within masses. It becomes a matter of teasing out how universality operates within plurality, difference, individuality, and expressions of collectives rather than attributing it to one supraordinate psychic source that conditions all psychological productions within individuals and societies worldwide.

Confounding Source with Form and Content

Jung frequently equates archetypes with the collective unconscious when they are, strictly speaking, two fundamental categories. One is *ab origine*, based on primal ontic ground, while the other is *derivative* from such original source. This confusion is exemplified when Jung asserts that we inherit a "stock of primordial images which everybody brings with him as his human birthright, the sum total of inborn forms peculiar to the instincts. I have called this 'potential' psyche the collective unconscious" (*CW*, 5 ¶ 631, p. 408). Here Jung equates *images* with inborn *forms* that belong to the *drives*, which he then hesitantly attributes to a "potential" collective psyche. Originally written in 1912, Jung is navigating himself away from Freud but has not yet taken the plunge to make the collective unconscious the heir to the drives. Here we may see how he wants to make inborn forms (archetypes) imaginal (imagoes), which are laid down within the biological substrates of the human mind, and hence are instinctual involuntary contents and natural events. Jung goes on to emphasize the equiprimordiality of the image inherent in myth within a collective birthplace as transcending any personal subjectivity of individual agents, and hence arises from the ontological fabric of a collective fountainhead.

> The image is called *primordial* when it possesses an *archaic* character. I speak of its archaic character when the image is in striking accord with familiar mythological motifs. It then expresses material primarily derived from the *collective unconscious*, and indicates at the same time that the factors influencing the conscious situation of the moment are *collective* rather than personal.
>
> (*CW*, 6 ¶ 746, p. 443)

Here Jung is emphasizing all people rather than just one person, or the subjective personality of an individual, but he is situating his argument in such a manner that it may be considered a false binary. All personal subjectivities participate within collective organizations that are universal even though they may be enacted in a peculiar way from a specific person not reflective of other personalities; but this does not justify an ontological distinction between the individual and the collective. Collectivity is simply shorthand for the universal dimensions of human nature. The collective does not trump or supersede the personal, nor does the individual override the collective: both are equiprimordial and dialectically conjoined even if they are unfolding complementary, parallel processes.

In his evolving thought, Jung continues to privilege the collective over the individual in such a manner that he elevates it from mere commonly shared attributes of humanity to that of a supraordinate construct that developmentally conditions all particularities of consciousness and culture. This is when he begins to move away from generic references to the collective unconscious through a displacement and preoccupation with the archaic content of archetypes as imaginal forms that populate the psyche. "The primordial image, elsewhere also termed *archetype*, is always collective, i.e., it is at least common to entire peoples or epochs. In all probability the most important mythological motifs are common to all times and races" (*CW*, 6 ¶ 747, p. 443). Despite his hasty generalization, source, form, and content are ontologically inseparable, although there is a cleavage forged between the generative wellspring and the manifest product. The collective unconscious presumably produces archetypes, yet the archetypes are phenomenal appearances, while the so-called objective psyche remains obscured, inaccessible to direct experience or observation: it therefore remains a hypothesis, an informed inference, an educated guess.

For Jung, primordial images are innate and inherited, given over a priori, not through conscious experience that are then mnemonically laid down in the unconscious, but rather instead they belong "to certain inner determinants of psychic life" (*CW*, 6 ¶ 748, p. 444). The image becomes "a condensation of the living process" that dislodges psychic energies upon encountering perceptual stimuli in one's environment, which lends meaning and order to consciousness and motivates paths of action connected to such meaning (*CW*, 6 ¶ 749, p. 445). For Jung, the archetype is a spontaneous "self-activating organism" that releases its vital energies in the psyche as procreative powers (*CW*, 6 ¶ 754, p. 447). Jung continues to elaborate:

The primordial image is an inherited organization of psychic energy, an ingrained system, which not only gives expression to the energic process but facilitates its operation. It shows how the energic process has run its unvarying course from time immemorial, while simultaneously allowing a perpetual repetition of it by means of an apprehension or psychic grasp of situations so that life can continue into the future.

(*CW*, 6 ¶ 754, p. 447)

Whether one reads this passage through the lens of evolutionary psychology[1] or as an innate animating process belonging to psyche (ψυχή), soul (*Seele*), or spirit (*Geist*), what is clear is that the archetype has moved from being a mere content or product of the collective unconscious to being a self-activating system or organizing principle in its own right, in other words, an autonomous entity teaming with psychic energies. In Jung's shift from the collective unconscious to the nature and function of the archetype, he is, albeit unintended by him, paving a theoretical scaffolding that draws into question the nature of origins. If an archetype is self-activating, autonomous, systemically self-contained, and self-generative, then the collective unconscious becomes an unnecessary category: theoretically it is superfluous. In other words, if the archetype becomes the prototype for the collective mind of the human species and is autonchronous, the collective unconscious becomes a redundant concept.

Early in his conceptualization of the collective unconscious, Jung was more faithful to the scientific naturalism of his day, as was Freud, espousing evolutionary paradigms that gave credibility to the rise of modern psychology. In *Psychological Types*, an early work of renowned importance, Jung is already preoccupied with the "wrappings of collectivity" (*CW*, 6 ¶ 12, p. 10). By the time he wrote *Alchemical Studies* in his late period, he equates the collective unconscious to the cognitive neurological processes operative in all human beings irrespective of race, time, location, and cultural relativity.

The collective unconscious is simply the psychic expression of the identity of brain structure irrespective of all racial differences. This explains the analogy, sometimes even identity, between the various myth motifs and symbols, and the possibility of human

communication in general. The various lines of psychic development start from one common stock whose roots reach back into
the most distant past. This also accounts for the psychological
parallelisms with animals.

(*CW*, 13 ¶ 11)

Here he stays faithful to the scientific party-line, reducing collective
psychological functions to universal "brain structure," which by and
large is no different than neuroscience today, with the exception that
Jung wanted to include every aspect of the human race, whereby
during his time eugenics was on the rise in popularism. In identifying
with collective humanity, in groping for a way to express the sentiment
of a union of all people, Jung was likely struggling with a universal
psychological theory that the philosophers, mystics, Gnostics, and
medievalists alike were wrestling with in their own ways long before
him. But Jung later parted company with a purely evolutionary account
of psychology, for it could not fill the bill. What was missing from
these reductive ontologies was the *mysterium* of the transcendent, the
religious, the soliloquy of affective life, the resonance of pre-linguistic
experience, and that which is occluded from linguistic mediation, such
as intuitive internal reverberations or self-states, aesthetic and moral
intuitions, and the pursuit of the numinous and sublimity.

Jung's Later Metaphysical Commitments

Jung's conceptualization of the collective psyche differs from Freud's
in the sense that he presumed a whole hoard of content in the form of
primordial images and cultural-mythological motifs to exist at birth,
and more specifically, that they predate and preexist within a transpersonal potential realm or psychic spacing prior to the birth of any one
individual. Such content (i.e., the archetypes) is the alchemical *prima
materia* of the psyche, an outpouring of the unconscious that when
taken up by consciousness can be reactivated and reorganized within
a newly assimilated order of meaning (*CW*, 5, p. 408). This "potential" psyche is often objectified or reified by Jung as an entity or being
in-itself; this is when Jung gets into philosophical trouble because he
does not take the care to rigorously delineate his theoretical propositions. On the one hand, Jung succeeds, like Freud, in offering a

metapsychology articulating the universal unconscious characteristics of the human mind. Empirical apologists are content in subsuming the collective unconscious within this universal rubric whereby unconscious contents become reliably emergent despite wide variations in context and social environments. But, on the other hand, for Jung, the animation of the collective unconscious becomes much more than just the unconscious infrastructure we all possess as human beings; it is *supernatural.*

In many of his writings he makes the collective a world soul, deified entity, or transpersonal subject that conditions all unconscious productions. Here is where he elevates the collective unconscious in ontological priority and makes it a first principle, the ultimate origin and prototype of Mind. This theoretical move from mere formal universality to cosmogony, from evolutionary psychology to hierophany, constitutes the Neoplatonic enlistment of a godhead or macroanthropos that supervenes on humanity; hence it disperses its essence and properties within the psyches of all people over eons since time *in memoriam* through some ill-defined emanationist process. Here the collective unconscious becomes a transcendent first reality where everything else is derived. This all-encompassing, supraordinate metaphysical order or cosmic force presupposes a unitary divinity principle or archaic ground upon which all else materializes and appears. The collective unconscious becomes the root of all things that emerge or flow from an ontic fountain as absolute ground that gives rise to the phenomenal psychic universe belonging to humankind, but it could very well be a form of panpsychism that interpenetrates everything in the cosmos. This would make the personal unconscious a hypostasis from a grand metaphysical originator. If all the a priori contents of mind are natively implanted and conditioned by a higher spiritual principle that begets the *anima mundi*, then the collective unconscious would constitute an Over-Soul.

Given the aporetic nature of the collective unconscious construct, we may wish to ask, Why do we need a reified collective psyche to perform these mental functions and why not simply a generic unconscious that is common to us all? If the unconscious is merely universal *and* subjective, there is no need to posit a transpersonal agency or macroanthropos pulling the strings behind the curtain of the psyche. To appropriate Jung's language, the "personal" unconscious explains it all, while the objectified collective unconscious *qua* supraordinate entity is merely a *myth* in-itself. You can have unconscious subject-ivity (viz., an unconscious ego at the center of agency that is uni-versal in all people) that performs these activities of mind, which gives rise to higher forms of consciousness without the need to appeal to a supraordination directing these psychological processes. Jung's reliance on a macroagent that is the source point for generating archetypes also introduces the debacle of an infinite regress where we would need to account for how a collective unconscious agency and the contents of mind got there in the first place. Without attention paid to such complications, Jung embarks on a theoretical leap of faith and introduces all kinds of philosophic problematics, such as the question of origins, the question of agency, of ground, of how the personal unconscious is colored or conditioned by another entity, of freedom and determinism, and so forth. Viewed from this perspective, the collective unconscious seems like a magical construct that eman-ates and descends from an imaginative sky and induces content as some form of *supravenience* over the psyche. From this vantage point, I argue, the collective unconscious postulate is not necessary. Psychic life can be partially explained from the standpoint of universal uncon-scious processes that condition the unique subjectivities of each agent. Such a universal unconscious is not an entity, but rather is the given hardware of the psyche, a necessary albeit not a sufficient condition for mental life. On the one hand, the unconscious is transsubjective, transhistorical, and universal, hence comprised of a priori structures, features, and organizations that allow for subjective psychic life to arise; while on the other hand, it is merely a formal, non-personal organizing principle, the ontic foundation that gives rise to conscious-ness and individual personality. So when I refer to the *universal uncon-scious*, I am merely highlighting the ubiquity of unconscious structure that underlies mental processes and conditions the manifestation or appearance of all psychological phenomena.

If the logical operations of mind observe a path where conscious-ness must arise from a prior ontic ground, then following the prin-ciple of sufficient reason, every mental object must stand in relation to its prior occurrence, hence its origins or archaic ground. There must be some preordering or internal regulatory organization to the psyche (i.e., following teleonomic and telic processes) that allows us to experience the world of consciousness. Consciousness arises from unconscious configurations even if they are crude and biologically informed. I would first describe these basic organizations as constellating through unconscious schemata that take self-apperceptive forms of desire and drive, sentience and affect, only then to breach into consciousness as percept and image, imagination and fantasy, and eventually thought proper, even though we may say that any form of mentation is implicit mediatory thought (Mills, 2010). Reason or logic is the culmination of thought and must derive from its earlier constituencies. In fact, imagination is the mediatory faculty between intuition and thought in many of the great Modern and German Idealist traditions, which leads Hegel (1817) to conclude that "phantasy is reason" (§ 457). You really cannot think without imagination. Logic is imaginative as well as ordered. Mathematics is the invention of the imaginative mind, even if it is the sublation of reason. As the source of imagination, the unconscious is the house of Being.

When Jung sinks into his Neoplatonic identifications, the collective unconscious posit is elevated to the supraordinate sphere of the godhead, the *Anima Mundi* within the *Unus Mundus*. It is unfortunate that he never worked through these theoretical complexifications in his system. Rather than eschewing metaphysics in his writings, he should have embraced it more fully. Here his theory suffers because he is not able to account for these details. Claiming that metaphysics is mere speculation and antithetical to science, he falls into the professional (and political) dualism of his day: empiricism is the only so-called credible road to truth, while philosophy and theology (despite his constant engagement with both disciplines) take a back seat to revealing true reality and knowledge. Yet this is merely a party line, an appearance to win him professional credibility. He would not have wasted his time studying these traditions in the humanities if he did not have a personal investment in the outcome. Jung delved into all matters contrary to extraspective science, not merely philosophy, but Gnosticism, theosophy, medieval alchemy, the occult, orientalism, and everything that hinted at the supernatural. Attempting to distance himself from theology despite his strong personal inclinations and identifications, he made psychology the new godhead. And with good reason. All human experience is psychologically mediated. This is an uncontested empirical fact. But it does not mean that human psychology is animated from a godhead (Mills, 2017). In his more monistic attempts at theoretical posturing, Jung makes the following claim:

> While the concept of the *unus mundus* is a metaphysical speculation, the unconscious can be indirectly experienced via its manifestations. Though in itself an hypothesis, it has at least as great a probability as the hypothesis of the atom. It is clear from the empirical material at our disposal today that the contents of the unconscious, unlike conscious contents, are mutually contaminated to such a degree that they cannot be distinguished from one another and can therefore easily take one another's place, as can be seen most clearly in dreams. The indistinguishableness of its contents gives one the impression that everything is connected with everything else and therefore, despite their multifarious modes of manifestation, that they are at bottom a unity.
>
> (*CW*, 14 ¶ 660, pp. 462–463)

Here we can discern the mystical elements of Jung's thought as he moves from phenomenological manifestation to underlying ontological unity. He starts with the Plotinic One, only then to modify and differentiate its essence into particularities, which eventually return to the cycle of being as the recapitulation of its divided unity brought together again as an eternal recurrence. But given that the contemporary field of physics speculates that the universe is interconnected in all its multifarious details, Jung would be among good company. From the *Upanishads* to CERN, the European Organization for Nuclear Research, metaphysics is hardly an antiquated topic.

In Jung's more informal correspondences in his *Letters*, he takes up the notion of oneness in more mystical ways, but with imported metaphysical implications nonetheless. When referring to the collective unconscious, Jung tells us:

> This particular psyche behaves as if it were *one* and not as if it were split up into many individuals. It is *non-personal*. (I call it the "objective psyche.") It is the same everywhere and at all times. (If it were not so, comparative psychology would be impossible.) As it is not limited to the person, it is also not limited to the body. It

manifests itself therefore not only in human beings but also at the same time in animals and even in physical circumstances.

(*Answers to Rhine's Questions*, 1945, p. 395)

Notice the reification of the psyche as one enlarged cosmic mind, the tendency to collapse difference and individuality within an overarching medium—the "substance" from Aristotle to Spinoza, the undifferentiated beginning of sameness throughout world history, and the suggestion that such supraordination supervenes on yet transcends the body, hence it is immaterial.

In his letter to Pastor Max Frischknecht, Jung (1946) writes:

> The collective unconscious, on the contrary, is made up of contents which are formed personally only to a minor degree and in essentials not at all, are not individual acquisitions, are essentially the same everywhere, and do not vary from man to man. This unconscious is like the air, which is the same everywhere, is breathed by everybody, and yet belongs to no one. Its contents (called archetypes) are the prior conditions or patterns of psychic formation in general. They have an *esse in potentia et in actu* but not *in re*, for as *res* they are no longer what they were but have become psychic contents. They are in themselves non-perceptible, irrepresentable (since they precede all representation), everywhere and "eternally" the same. Hence there is only one collective unconscious, which is everywhere identical with itself, from which everything psychic takes shape before it is personalized, modified, assimilated, etc. by external influences.
>
> (*Letters, Vol. 1*, p. 408)

Here Jung acknowledges a minor modification to his theory, namely, that personal elements of experience may *slightly* alter the collective psyche of humanity and its confluence on the individual, but he holds steadfast to his theory of universality as being "the same everywhere" without variation in the life of "man." These contents—the archetypes—are said to "precede all representations" when as logical argument they *re-present* original images that are stored in a so-called collective psychic receptacle. Here Jung problematizes the question of primordiality and the transmission of the archaic. But he then moves from the actual (contents) to the potential (imperceptible and ineffable) domain of a shrouded reality we can never know in-itself, the *mysterium* where everything is "identical" and "'eternally' the same." Here we may conclude that Jung is groping for a way to explain the problem of the one and the many, differentiation from unity, the particular from the universal.

At the height of his convolution, Jung wades out into even deeper waters of speculation when describing the archetypal, giving it a magical ambiance in its own right.

> The primordial images which, in their totality, constitute a psychic mirror-world. It is a mirror with the peculiar faculty of reflecting the existing contents of consciousness not in their known and customary form but, as it were, *sub specie aeternitatis,* somewhat as a million-year-old consciousness might see them. Such a consciousness would see the becoming and passing away of things simultaneously with their momentary existence in the present, and not only that, it would also see what was before their becoming and will be after their passing hence.
>
> (*CW*, 6 ¶ 649, p. 395)

Let us begin with the claim that the image constitutes a mirror reflection of a "million-year-old consciousness," as if representations are laid down mnemonically as they would have originally occurred and transpired in the minds of primitive ancestors over a million years ago, as if this would be remotely possible. This notion by definition harnesses a hard psychic determinism of pure replication of original content, when at most we can say is that representations undergo mediation, translation, transmogrification, and a displacement of subjective experience into any reiteration, recurrence, and interpretation of the past. There is no pristine undiluted reproduction of archetypes, for everything in the psyche is mediated and subject to translation and reinterpretation of so-called inscribed archaic events through the lingering resonance of after-effects (*Nachträglichkeit* or *après-coup*), or perhaps more appropriately, aftershocks. Here the universal "collective representations" thesis is deemed suspect at best. When Jung continues with his hypostasized language of making the image a psychological "faculty" that has its own "consciousness" that is regenerated as pure and unadulterated replication of its original instance in antiquity, he has reified archaic mind and has superimposed it as a fixed artifact on the contemporary psyche without considering how evolutionary and cultural forces would have mutated and shaped our contemporary understanding of cognition today. When Jung further evokes the fantasy of a supraordinate, omnipotent consciousness that can observe the coming into being and passing away of everything that has ever transpired in the collective experience of humankind, he has succumbed to a mystical metaphysical theory of consciousness that lacks argumentation, theoretical justification, or empirical support. By today's standards, at face value, Jung's theory is antiquated and unsubstantiated from the domain of logic and modern scientific principles.

The notion that the archetype is a "mirror-world" of a previous world experienced in the minds of archaic men and women suggests that our psychic representations are the holographic duplication or reiteration of the experience of another person or agent in the past, rather than our own unique phenomenal engagement with the world. Equating my current experience with an amorphous, ancestral supraordination or entity that determines how I perceive and encounter the world is illogical, if not delusional. How could a cosmic mind be distributing its essence into my mind as dispositional content and thought? How could that possibly work, let alone be remotely probable? At most, this may be psychologically explained, I suggest, as a merger fantasy with an omnipotent object such as a godhead, or as a repetition of the myth of eternal recurrence—of the cycle of timeless, infinite pervasiveness through modified form only to reconnect with its original lost source and unity motivated by the longing for return, rebirth, and regeneration. Here we may conclude that the collective unconscious construct is nothing more than a signified abstraction based on identification with the universal unconscious structures and features of shared humanity.

Concluding Reflections

By making the collective unconscious a hypostatization, Jung commits the fallacy of misplaced concreteness, viz., he makes the *qua* idea or abstraction a concrete entity or reality in its own right. Such concretism or thing-making by lending real identity and existence to a concept elevated to the incorporeal heavens yet occluded from direct observation or epistemology is mythology at its finest. In this sense, the myth of the collective unconscious is better understood as a metaphor for rhetorical effect, or when symbolized, an imagined representation of a higher abstraction or ideal principle ordained with value. Here we may compare the collective with the idea of infinity, eternity, timelessness, the *apeiron* of the Greeks, the numen of the Romans, or the Platonic *chora*—the womb, matrix, or interval of all becoming. As a theoretical placeholder—a spacing that transfers form and begets ideality, the collective unconscious construct becomes a conduit or medium for representing surplus value, much like the metaphor of the World Soul or Universal Spirit, which represents the values of shared humanity as personifications.

The hypothesis of the collective unconscious is only tenable through naturalized psychology conceived as a construct that signifies the universality and deep psychic contours of the unconscious mind, whether considered from nativist evolutionary perspectives or as a priori faculties belonging to the functional structures and processes informing the emergence of psychic life. As such, the collective unconscious is not a noun, is not a thing, rather it is a signifier for collective *unconsciousnesses* of the masses—the unconscious minds of subjects—of people—who comprise collectives within society and across cultures historically subsumed within certain epochs throughout the rise and development of human civilization.

It does not make sense that a collective unconscious would be a reified entity without importing onto-theology, emanationism, or supervenience from a divine artificer or cosmic source as the "matrix of everything," and hence pejoratively devalue the concept by making it a supernatural force pulling the levers behind the machinery of the universe. This is really tantamount to the belief in magical thinking whereby the myth of the collective unconscious devolves into its own recalcitrant dogma or sacred religiosity. So where does this leave us? What can we reasonably conclude about a universal collective?

In order for there to be *représentations collectives*, there must be a process of memorialization that is inscribed on the psyche and left like a mark or trace, which is transmitted as a semiotic on a collective scale. Without memory or replicators, if using the language of evolutionary biology, then cultural motifs would not be universal. But we see recurrent forms or patterns in all civilizations—from the primitive to the refined. Now it makes no sense, as suggested earlier, that this collective unconscious is a Cosmic Mind or Universal Psyche in-itself, as this would make the collective or cultural unconscious a macroanthropos tantamount to a godhead or supraordinate transpersonal agent or being. Rather, collective representations must be encoded and retained as concrete universals within the material structures of objective society (e.g., in educational institutions, museums, libraries, archeological sites, public facilities, etc.) only to be reiterated as images and symbolic patterns instantiated in a particular social context and cultural milieu. This is why we have variations of content within replications of forms and patterns that are similar across cultures, societies, time, and historical eons.

If the collective unconscious is the *fount*, how are re-presentations (*Vorstellung*) preserved and memorialized on some cosmic psychic scale and then imparted to each person upon birth? Would it not be sufficient to merely conceive of such a process as a naturalized occurrence explainable through reason, logic, and science, either from the standpoint of metaphysics, cultural transmission, cognitive science, or evolutionary theory despite wide variations in scope and speculation? Recall that I am not talking about the archetypes per se, but rather a more fundamental source or abyss *in illo tempore* from where everything is said to come, arise, and is ontologically dependent upon for any possibility for manifestation to occur. The collective unconscious construct as semiosis may be viewed as a heuristic to explain the process in which replication and presence, that is, *re-presented* form and content, are laid down *ab origine*, memorialized, and activated over the historical development of the human race in transmogrified ways as collective repetition. What are in fact archaic are not merely the archetypes as *pre-representations* that arise within consciousness, but the primordial unconscious organizations or psychic structures within the organism that make memorialization, reactivation, semiotic transmission, and symbolic reduplication possible. Here we may say that the collective unconscious becomes a semiosis that confers *meaning*; moreover, the notion of an overarching encompassing collective signifies an existential meaning of supraordinate importance, namely, ideal value.

Although a collective unconscious is universal, it is merely a theoretical description and *explanandum* of phenomena referring to universal psychological processes inherent in the human species that saturates the cultural ethos of collectives, but it is not an *explanans*. In fact, Jung's predication that the collective psyche is an explication for the phenomena in question is to presuppose the existence of the very thing that needs an explanation; hence he is begging the question. When he reverts to archetypes as the products of a collective unconscious, he makes them synonymous with the collective and hence their ontic manifestation is causally conditioned on the original presupposition of a collective Mind. And when Jung theoretically justifies collective phenomena oozing from an originating collective ground, this collapses into tautology. Here we may say that the collective unconscious is tantamount to a myth as *explanans* for it provides a story—of origins, of functions, of structures inherent to human mental processes. In fact, the generalization and reification, if not deification, of the collective unconscious has generated its own myth among many Jungians where a collective psyche is thought to maintain its own ontological independence, which thereby grounds, conditions, and is the foundation of all productions of consciousness, supervenes on our subjective minds through supernatural means such as emanationism, and is of divine provenance, namely, the presence or derivative of the mind of God.

Note

1   Cf. "The human psyche possesses a common substratum transcending all differences in culture and consciousness. I have called this substratum the collective unconscious. This unconscious psyche, common to all mankind, does not consist merely of contents capable of becoming conscious, but of latent predispositions towards identical reactions" (*CW*, 13 ¶ 11).

References

Freud, S. (1923). *The Ego and the Id. Standard Edition*, 19. London: Hogarth Press.

——— (1932–1933). *New Introductory Lectures on Psycho-Analysis. Standard Edition*, 22. London: Hogarth Press.

——— (1940 [1938]). *An Outline of Psycho-Analysis. Standard Edition*, 23, pp. 144–207. London: Hogarth Press.

Hegel, G.W.F. (1807[1977]). *Phenomenology of Spirit*. Trans. A.V. Miller. Oxford: Oxford University Press.

────── (1817/1830[1978]). *Philosophy of Spirit*. In *Hegel's Philosophy of Subjective Spirit*. Vol. 3: *Phenomenology and Psychology*. Trans. and Ed. M.J. Petry. Dordrecht, Holland: D. Reidel Publishing Company.

Jung, C.G. (1953–1977). *Collected Works of C.G. Jung*, Bollingen Series, 20 vols. Eds. H. Read, M. Fordham, & G. Adler; Trans. R.F.C. Hull. London: Routledge & Kegan Paul; Princeton: Princeton University Press. (hereafter referred to *CW* by vol. no.)

────── (1912). *Symbols of Transformation. CW*, 5.

────── (1919). *Instinct and the Unconscious. CW*, 8, pp. 129–138.

────── (1921). *Psychological Types. CW*, 6.

────── (1931). *On the Relation of Analytical Psychology to Poetry. CW*, 5, pp. 65–83.

────── (1936). *The Concept of the Collective Unconscious. CW*, 9, i: pp. 42–53.

────── (1947). *On the Nature of the Psyche. CW*, 8, pp. 159–234.

────── (1951/1973–1975). *C.G. Jung Letters, Vol.1*. Selected and edited by G. Adler in collaboration with Aniela Jaffé. Translations from the German by R.F.C. Hull. Volume 1 1906–1950. London: Routledge and Kegan Paul.

────── (1931). *The Structure of the Psyche. CW*, 8, pp. 139–158.

────── (1944/1952). *Psychology and Alchemy. CW*, 12.

────── (1955). *Mysterium Coniunctionis. CW*, 14.

────── (1959). *Aion. CW*, 9, ii.

────── (1961). *Memories, Dreams, Reflections*. New York: Vintage.

────── (1967). *Alchemical Studies. CW*, 13.

Kant, I. (1781[1965]). *Critique of Pure Reason*. Trans. N.K. Smith. New York: St. Martin's Press.

Mills, J. (2010). *Origins: On the Genesis of Psychic Reality*. Montreal: McGill-Queens University Press.

────── (2013). Jung's Metaphysics. *International Journal of Jungian Studies*, 5 (1), 19–43.

────── (2014). *Underworlds: Philosophies of the Unconscious from Psychoanalysis to Metaphysics*. London: Routledge.

────── (2017). *Inventing God: Psychology of Belief and the Rise of Secular Spirituality*. London: Routledge.

Segaller, S. (Director) (1989). *The Wisdom of the Dream: Carl Gustav Jung* [TV Mini-Series]. Segaller Films.

Chapter 2

The Archetype Debate

George B. Hogenson

A discussion of Jung's theory of archetypes necessarily begins with a critical distinction between the archetype-as-such (*archetypes-an-sich*) or in-itself and the archetypal image or representations (*Die archetypischen Vorsellungen*)—the phenomenal instantiation of the archetype-as-such. Virtually the entire discussion of archetypes involves the question of how to conceptualize the archetype-as-such, with very little attention paid to the archetypal image. This may be a questionable strategy because the relationship between the two elements is central to Jung's overall analysis, but the distinction is nevertheless important to keep in mind. In his 1931 essay, "On the Nature of the Psyche," Jung clearly lays out the distinction:

> The archetypal representations (images and ideas) mediated to us by the unconscious should not be confused with the archetypes as such. They are very varied structures which all point back to one essentially "irrepresentable" basic form. The latter is characterized by certain formal elements and by certain fundamental meanings, although these can be grasped only approximately.
>
> (Jung, 1970c, para. 417)

Earlier in the same essay, Jung gives the following description of an image:

> Instinct and the archaic mode meet in the biological conception of the "pattern of behaviour." There are, in fact, no amorphous instincts, as every instinct bears in itself the pattern [Gestalt] of its situation. Always it fulfils an image [*Bild*], and the image has

fixed qualities. The instinct of the leaf-cutting ant fulfils the image [*Bilde*] of ant, tree, leaf, cutting, transport, and the little ant-garden of fungi [Lloyd Morgan: *Habit and Instinct*]. If any one of these conditions is lacking, the instinct does not function, because it cannot exist without its total pattern [*Gestalt*], without its image [*Bild*]. Such an image [*Bild*] is an a priori type.

(Jung, 1970c, para. 398)

We will encounter Conway Lloyd Morgan, Jung's source for this example, again shortly, but first several aspects of this paragraph need to be noted. Jung's comments certainly add to the sense that he is pursuing an evolutionary biological model of the psyche, as is argued by Anthony Stevens, amongst others. The discussion of the leaf-cutting ant, is one of many examples Jung draws on to illustrate his notion of the image—indeed, the archetypal image. I have interpolated the German to highlight the relation between the image, *Bild*, and the pattern, *Gestalt*. If we think in terms of an archetypal image Jung is suggesting that we need to think of a complete situational gestalt, rather than an isolated or discrete artifact or representation. I will return to this point as it informs how we think about archetypes, but first some groundwork needs to be done to understand the context within which Jung worked when first proposing the theory of archetypes.

Beginnings

A serious impediment to coming to terms with Jung's theory of archetypes, as well as forming an assessment of its viability as an explanation for psychological phenomena, is Jung's ambiguity in defining exactly what he means by the term archetype. Jean Knox identifies four basic models in Jung's writings (Knox, 2003, p. 30ff.):

1) Biological entities in the form of information, which is hard-wired in the genes providing a set of instructions to the mind as well as to the body.
2) Organizing mental frameworks of an abstract nature, a set of rules or instructions but with no symbolic or representational content, so that they are never directly experienced.

3) Core meanings which do contain representational content and which therefore provide a central symbolic significance to our experience.
4) Metaphysical entities which are eternal and are therefore independent of the body.

As we will see, however, the ambiguity may be less pronounced once one comes to terms with more of the background for Jung's theorizing, particularly in the early stages of his thinking about archetypes.

The term, "archetype" first appears in Jung's 1919 paper, "Instinct and the Unconscious," delivered at a joint meeting of the Aristotelian Society, the Mind Association, and the British Psychological Society, at Bedford College, London University (Jung, 1969). To grasp the paper's significance, and to understand the degree to which it can be misconstrued without a better understanding of the background to its formulation, it is necessary to review Jung's course of theoretical development up to that point. In 1900, Jung, newly graduated in psychiatry from the University of Basel, joined the staff of the Burghölzli Hospital in Zurich as assistant to its director, Eugen Bleuler. Bleuler's approach to treatment, which he imposed on his subordinates, required extended intensive engagement with the patients and detailed attention to symptomatology. He also mandated attention to new developments in psychology and psychiatry, which was how Jung and the Burghölzli group first came into contact with the work of Freud, when *The Interpretation of Dreams* was published. Jung's first order of business upon arrival, however, was the completion of his dissertation, "On the Psychology and Pathology of so-called Occult Phenomena" (Jung, 1970a).

The dissertation involved a study of a young female medium—in fact Jung's first cousin, Helene Preiswerk (Ellenberger, 1983)—who produced a variety of personalities including both recently deceased relatives as well as more mysterious figures while in trance states. Jung's discussion of the case ranges widely over the psychiatric literature of the time but pays particular attention to the phenomena associated with somnambulism. He cites Freud in passing, but it is clear that his primary inspirations at this point are William James and the French psychologists Pierre Janet and Theodore Flournoy. Flournoy's 1900, *From India to the Planet Mars*, gave an account of a similar somnambulist, "Hélène Smith," whose trance fantasies involved her previous lives in India and on Mars. Flournoy was a close friend of Janet, James, and Henri Bergson, as well as the American child psychologist and evolutionary theorist, James Mark Baldwin. Baldwin had been forced out of his position at Johns Hopkins due to a sexual scandal but was received in France by Janet and Flournoy. Through them he came into contact with Bergson (Scarfe, 2009). Jaan Valsiner has gone farther and argues that Baldwin was an important influence on Bergson's *Creative Evolution* (Bergson, 1998). Valsiner writes, "Undoubtedly there is a clear intellectual closeness between Bergson's ideas and James Mark Baldwin's "postulates of genetic science" (e.g., Baldwin, 1906, pp. 21–24). Indeed, Bergson relied on Baldwin's developmental ideas directly (e.g., Bergson, 1911a, p. 32)" (Valsiner, 1998, pp. 180–181).

Following the completion of his dissertation, Jung spent the winter term of 1902–1903 in Paris where he attended Janet's lectures. The core of Janet's psychology was his study of dissociative states and Jung's frequent references to Janet in his early research into complexes by way of the word association test shows the continuing influence of the French psychologist (Jung, 1970b). Appreciative comments regarding Bergson also appear throughout Jung's works. Any consideration of Jung's theories, therefore, must take into account this early French influence, (Gunter, 1982; Haule, 1983; Haule, 1984) and the significance within that tradition of the somnambulistic unconscious (Kerslake, 2006; Kerslake, 2007a; Kerslake, 2007b; Pilard, 2015).

To understand the somnambulistic model of the unconscious it is necessary to begin with the observations by the French naturalist Georges Cuvier (1769–1832), and the entomologist, Jean-Henri Fabre (1823–1915) (Kerslake, 2006, p. 1). Fabre, in particular, interests us due to his observations of the behavior of the Ammophila Hirsuta wasp, which Bergson cites in *Creative Evolution* (1907). The Ammophila Hirsuta is a solitary ground-nesting wasp that attacks the cutter worm—a caterpillar—and stings the caterpillar in its nerve ganglions and squeezes its head, thereby paralyzing—but not killing—it. The wasp then drags the caterpillar to its nest and lays its egg on the caterpillar, providing living food for its larva once it hatches. The behavior of the wasp and a number of other strange animal behaviors were of great interest at the end of the nineteenth and early twentieth centuries. Within the context of the somnambulist model of instinct these behaviors took on more significance, given that the behaviors were manifestly not learned, as the insects, in particular, were solitary, or as in the case of the Yucca moth, which would become a touchstone for Jung, their particular behavior was limited to one night in their otherwise very short life cycle.

Bergson's explanation for the behavior of the wasp was based on what Kerslake refers to as a kind of "divinatory sympathy" (Kerslake, 2007c, p. 54) between the wasp and the caterpillar. Bergson's formulation in *Creative Evolution* is important for understanding the process:

> But the whole difficulty comes from our desire to express the knowledge of the Hymenoptera in terms of intelligence. It is this that compels us to compare the Ammophila with the entomologist, who knows the caterpillar as he knows everything else—from the outside, and without having on his part a special or vital interest. The Ammophila, we imagine, must learn, one by one, like the entomologist, the positions of the nerve-centres of the caterpillar— must acquire at least the practical knowledge of these positions by trying the effects of its sting. But there is no need for such a view if we suppose a sympathy (in the etymological sense of the word) between the Ammophila and its victim, which teaches it from within, so to say, concerning the vulnerability of the caterpillar. This feeling of vulnerability might owe nothing to outward perception, but result from the mere presence together of the Ammophila and the caterpillar, considered no longer as two organisms, but as two activities. It would express, in a concrete form, the relation of the one to the other. Certainly, a scientific theory cannot appeal to considerations of this kind. It must not put action before organization, sympathy before perception and knowledge. But, once more, either philosophy has nothing to see here, or its rôle begins where that of science ends.
>
> (Bergson, 1998, pp. 173–174)

Implicit in this discussion is the sense that underlying the duality of wasp and caterpillar is a deeper unity, almost a single organism that manifests itself in two forms. This was, in fact, a position that Bergson had taken in *Matter and Memory* of 1896 where he writes:

Matter, in our view, is an aggregate of "images." And by "image" we mean a certain existence which is more than that which the idealist calls a representation, but less than that which the realist call a thing—an existence placed halfway between the "thing" and the "representation."

(Bergson, 1990, p. 9)

We will return to this issue when at the conclusion of this chapter.

Psychosis, Myth, and the Schreber Case

In his 1911 study of schizophrenia (Bleuler, 1911), Eugen Bleuler, director of the Burghölzli psychiatric hospital and arguably the foremost psychiatrist in Europe, provided a series of verbatim records of the delusional fantasies of schizophrenics, which he characterized as containing a "plethora of mythic and symbolic material" (Escamilla, 2016, p. 137). "For Bleuler," Escamilla continues, "symbols and myths were representative of how unconscious complexes manifested themselves, and symbols appeared in modes of thinking that approached that seen in dreams and other states where there was an *abaissement du niveau mental*" (*Ibid.*). Bleuler did not delve more deeply into the nature of the myth-like patterns of psychotic discourse, but his assistant, C.G. Jung, took up the issue in detail in his major early study, *Wandlungen und Symbole der Libido: Beiträge zur Entwicklungsgeschichte des Denkens* (Jung, 1912), translated in 1916 as *The Psychology of the Unconscious* (Jung, 2001) and later revised as *Symbols of Transformation*, Volume 5 of the *Collected Works* (Jung, 1967). The publication of the second section of this book is often credited with being the final blow to Jung's relationship with Freud, and it is certainly the case that the view of libido, and the functioning of symbolic patterns in the transformation of libido, was a significant deviation from Freud's position.

The debate regarding libido had begun with their earliest exchanges of letters, and eventually turning into a major dispute, regarding the interpretation of psychotic states. The outlines of this argument need to be understood because the debate informs the questions Jung tried to resolve by way of his theory of the collective unconscious, and its contents, the archetypes. In broad terms the debate begins with Freud's notion of the regression or libido toward unconscious contents. Leaving aside, for the moment, the frequently ignored but essential element in Freud's model, primal repression (*Urverdrängung*), the contents of the unconscious in Freud's model are comprised of repressions of previously conscious contents. In other words, a wish or drive object has to have first been present in consciousness and then repressed and "stored" in the unconscious. Regression, in Freud's model, is, therefore, regression toward these repressed contents, and, as he repeatedly argues in his correspondence with Jung, the objective of the regression is the restoration of infantile autoerotic gratification. As early as 1907, however, Jung is questioning Freud's insistence that regression is always autoerotic, particularly in cases of dementia praecox—schizophrenia. He writes:

> But why the regression to the autoerotic stage? Autoerotism is certainly something infantile, and yet infantilism is utterly different from D. pr. I have even seen that in the galvanometric investigations the splitting off of affects in Dem. praec. goes so far that strong physical stimuli do not exert the slightest influence, whereas psychological stimuli still provoke affects. Thus, even with complete analysis and transference no revolutionizing of the personality occurs as it does in hysteria.
>
> (Freud & Jung, 1974, p. 31:19J)

Jung's argument, even at this early stage, was that Freud relied too heavily on the observation of behavior that appears similar to sexual satisfaction, for example in the nursing infant. Lothane, drawing on Vandermeersh (Vandermeersch, 1991) summarizes the dispute, writing:

> Freud's libido theory envisaged a process of coalescing of sexually-toned infantile component drives into adult forms of sexual aim and love object choice and was the basis of a theory of pathogenesis of neuroses and psychoses according to which symptoms represented a return to fixation points created in the course of libidinal development. By contrast, Jung argued for a genetic, or evolutionary, conception of a holistic, vital drive, or primordial libido, concerned with self-preservation only, which only at a later stage became differentiated into sexuality. Jung's theory of pathogenesis stressed the role of a real, actual conflict in the patient's adult life as a result of which "libido became introverted and regressively

formed the fantasies which Freud has mistakenly considered to be the origin of neurosis." Jung proposed this theory for psychoses in general and for Schreber in particular. For Freud, the two theories were on an irreconcilable collision course.

(Lothane, 1997, p. 110)

In 1910 Jung gave Freud a copy of Daniel Paul Schreber's *Memoirs of My Nervous Illness* (Schreber, 1955). Jung had already referred to Schreber in his 1907 monograph on dementia praecox (Jung, 1960a) but he had not taken up Schreber's case in detail. Freud, on the other hand, would turn the Schreber case into a major theoretical study of paranoia (Freud, 1958). By this time, however, the issue of libido had become far more acute. Jung was arguing that Freud's account of libidinal withdrawal, as spelled out in the *Three Essays on a Theory of Sexuality*, was insufficient for a description of dementia praecox. In the Schreber case itself, Freud had acknowledged that his position on withdrawal from a specific object, as was the case in the formation of a neurosis, was problematic, when faced with the global withdrawal of the dementia praecox patient. Writing to Freud in December of 1911 Jung pressed this point home:

As for the libido problem, I must confess that your remark in the Schreber analysis,[1] has set up booming reverberations. This remark, or rather the doubt expressed therein, has resuscitated all the difficulties that have beset me throughout the years in my attempt to apply the libido theory to Dem. praec. The loss of the reality function in D. pr. cannot be reduced to repression of libido (defined as sexual hunger). Not by me, at any rate. Your doubt shows me that in your eyes as well the problem cannot be solved in this way. I have now put together all the thoughts on the libido concept that have come to me over the years, and devoted a chapter to them in my second part. I have got down to a fundamental discussion of the problem and arrived at a solution which I am afraid I cannot discuss in *extenso* here. The essential point is that I try to replace the descriptive concept of libido by a *genetic* one. Such a concept covers not only the recent-sexual libido but all those forms of it which have long since split off into organized activities.

(Freud & Jung, 1974, p. 471:287J)

Jung is arguing that the global loss of reality seen in psychotic states, as distinct from neuroses, could not be a matter of withdrawal of a purely sexualized libido from a particular object. More importantly, for the question of archetypes was the nature of the unconscious domain to which psychotic regression moved. Beginning with the observations Bleuler made in his study of schizophrenia regarding the mythic qualities of psychotic discourse, which the entire staff of the Burghölzli was engaged in supporting, and Jung's investigations in *Wandlungen*, Jung was coming to the conclusion that an unconscious domain had to exist that was not simply the repository of previously conscious repression. This domain appeared to give rise to systems of ideation that had precisely those qualities associated with myths, and those qualities, taken over the population of patients he and the rest of the Burghölzli psychiatrists were treating had commonalities that could not be reduced to individual complexes, as was the case with neurotics.

Jung would argue this point in more detail in 1914, a year after their final break and just as he was beginning his investigations leading to the *Red Book*, that Freud's 1911 analysis of the case of Daniel Paul Schreber (Freud, 1958) had only gone half way in his interpretation:

> When we apply these insights to the psychology of that class of mental patient to which Schreber belongs, we must, from the "objective-scientific" standpoint, reduce the fantasy-structure to its simple, fundamental elements. This is what Freud has done. But that is only one half of the work. The other half is the constructive understanding of Schreber's system. The question is: What is the goal the patient tried to reach through the creation of his system?
>
> (Jung, 1960b, para. 408)

As we will see below, Jung's notion that a full understanding of Schreber's case entails an understanding of the goal toward which his symptoms are striving—Jung's teleological understanding of psychic states—was of long standing. "If we look at the delusional system without prejudice," Jung goes on:

> and ask ourselves what it is aiming at, we see, first, that it is in fact aiming at something, and second, that the patient devotes all his will-power to the completion of his system. There are patients who elaborate their delusions with scientific thoroughness, often

dragging in an immense amount of comparative material by way of proof. Schreber belongs to this class.

(Jung, 1960b, para. 410)

The distinction Jung is drawing here between his system and Freud's is central to our understanding of archetypes, and to the nature of the debate that currently surrounds them. Reiner Schümann, in a context unrelated to the Jung/Freud debate, gives us a clue to what is at stake:

The complementary notion to *archē* is *telos*; that to 'principle' is something entirely different, namely the sequent, the consequence, the derivative, the "issue.'" As the concept of origin changes its linguistic milieu, it also changes its strategy. Origination still means inception and domination; no longer, however, of a becoming, but of a hierarchical order.

(Schürmann, 1987, p. 107)

Jung's view of Freud's interpretative strategy, we could say, was that it was based on a principle or *principe*—the singular nature of libido and reduction of symptoms to sexuality—could not account for the teleological imperative Jung saw in the systems devised by psychotics. These systems, as Bleuler had noted in his study of schizophrenia, displayed the characteristics of mythologies, and Jung's subsequent studies of myth and psychotic discourse led first to his experiments with a deep *abaissement du niveau mental* in *The Red Book*, and subsequently in his theory of archetypes. To what degree Jung chose the term "archetype" to capture the element of telos is uncertain—he traces out the history of the term is several places—but Schümann's gloss remains instructive and the teleological element in Jung's system continues to inform aspects of the issues surrounding archetypes in the contemporary world of Jungian theory. To flesh this argument out, however, it is necessary to examine other influences on Jung's thinking.

Instinct and the Unconscious

Before directly addressing "Instinct and the Unconscious" we need to return to the discussion of somnambulism and Jung's penchant for examples drawn from the behavior of insects.

Gunter estimates that Jung probably first read Bergson's *Creative Evolution* in 1912 (Gunter, 1982, p. 642) and used Bergson's work to further extend his dispute with Freud over the nature of psychic energy or libido. Kerslake views this reading of Bergson, and his theory of instinct as central to Jung's first comments on archetypes, writing, "Indeed, Jung's first use of the concept of the archetype emerges out of an interpretation of this Bergsonian theory" (Kerslake, 2006, p. 2). Similarly, as Nathalie Pilard points out in her indispensable *Jung and Intuition*, "The centrality of the *Anschauung* in Jung's psychology historically started with the first appearance of the term 'Archetype' in 1919. Jung did not write of the (German) *Archetypen*, but of the *Archetypen des Anschauunger*, 'the archetypes of intuition' (Pilard, 2015, p. xv).

In "Instinct and the Unconscious" Jung turns to another naturalist, the botanist Anton Joseph Kerner, whose *Natural History of Plants*, published in two volumes in 1890 and 1891, gives an account of the reproductive behavior of the yucca moth. The yucca moth is an obligate pollinator of the yucca plant, meaning that only the yucca moth can pollinate the plant. The plant opens for only one night, and the moth must at that point deposit its eggs in the plant and then form a small ball of pollen, which they also place in the plant to fertilize the plant's seeds. The larva of the moth then feeds on the seeds until they emerge as moths. This is now viewed as an example of prolonged co-evolution, although precisely how the co-evolutionary process began and progressed is still not understood. Like the mutualism of the Ammophila wasp, however, it provides an example of the kind of complex behavior that implies an intricacy of relationship that is not purely linear or causal. For Jung, the behavior of the moth is related to intuition:

> Such cases are difficult to explain on the hypothesis of learning and practice. Hence other ways of explanation, deriving from Bergson's philosophy, have recently been put forward, laying stress on the factor of intuition. Intuition is an unconscious process in that its result is the irruption into consciousness of an unconscious content, a sudden idea or "hunch." It resembles a process of perception, but unlike the conscious activity of the senses and

introspection the perception is unconscious. That is why we speak of intuition as an "instinctive" act of comprehension.

(Jung, 1969, para. 269)

In the next paragraph, Jung introduces both the collective unconscious and the archetypes. After first acknowledging Freud's unconscious, but labeling it the "personal unconscious," Jung writes:

But, over and above that, we also find in the unconscious qualities that are not individually acquired but are inherited, e.g., instincts as impulses to carry out actions from necessity, without conscious motivation. In this "deeper" stratum we also find the a priori, inborn forms of "intuition," namely the archetypes of perception and apprehension, which are the necessary a priori determinants of all psychic processes.

(Jung, 1969, para. 270)

Jung also cites the English comparative psychologist, Conway Lloyd Morgan in "Instinct and the Unconscious." In his book, *Habit and Instinct* (Lloyd Morgan, 1973), published in 1896, Lloyd Morgan cites Kerner's example of the yucca moth, as well as providing Jung with the example of the leaf-cutting ant. Lloyd Morgan was interested, in the development of a relationship between instinct and habit, wherein an instinctual action "on the occasion of the first performance is automatic, and cannot be regarded as under the guidance of consciousness; but that the carrying out of the activity furnishes data to consciousness in the light of which subsequent performances of a like activity may be perfected, or modified, or checked" (Lloyd Morgan, 1973, p. 136). This and other passages in Lloyd Morgan's early work are among the first steps in the development of his theory of emergent evolution, which, in conjunction with the theorizing of James Mark Baldwin, will come to be known as the Baldwin effect[2] (Baldwin, 2015).

Framing the Debate

This background material is necessary to frame the contemporary debate over the question of archetypes. To review, Jung comes to the relationship with Freud from a background heavily influenced by the French somnambulists, as Haule pointed out as early as 1983. He was also influenced by his work with Bleuler, which identified a form of discourse in psychotic patients that resembled mythical structures and emphasized the total loss of one reality and the construction of a new one. His deep immersion in the world of dementia praecox increasingly informed his debate with Freud, culminating in the dispute over the case of Schreber. As Deleuze pointed out in his early essay, "From Sacher-Masoch to Masochism:"

> *On Freud and Jung.* All these points refer us back generally to the differences between Freud and Jung. To understand these essential differences properly, one has to take into account that the two authors did not work on or privilege the same clinical material. The primary Freudian concepts (for example, repression) are marked by the domain of hysteria. They always will be, even though Freud's genius was to sense the necessity of reformulating them in terms of other cases which deepen their meaning (such as obsession and anxiety). It is, moreover, the case that Freudian methodologies are appropriate mainly for young neurotics whose disorders are related to personal reminiscences and whose problems are about reconciling themselves with the real (loving, making oneself lovable, adapting, etc.), without regard for the role of any interior conflicts. But there are neuroses of quite another type which are nearer to psychosis. There are adult neurotics who are burdened by "Images" which transcend every experience; their problem is to be reconciled with themselves, that is, to reintegrate in their personality those very parts which they neglected to develop, and which are as if alienated in Images, where they lead a dangerously autonomous life. Freud's analytic method is no use for relating to these primordial Images. They are irreducible and they can be approached only by a synthetic method which searches beyond the experience of the subject for the truth of the neurosis, and looks to this truth for possibilities by means of which the subject might personally assimilate for himself the content of these images. Jung can therefore reproach Freud for having left in the dark both the real dangers present in a neurosis and the treasures it can contain.
>   (Deleuze, 2004, p. 133 note 25)

The contemporary debate regarding the theory of archetypes, however, begins at the congress of the International Association for Analytical Psychology, held at Cambridge University in 2001 between Anthony Stevens and myself (Hogenson & Stevens, 2003). In 1983 the Jungian analyst, Stevens published the most detailed argument for a reading of Jung's theory as a precursor of sociobiology—later evolutionary psychology—which viewed the archetypes-as-such as biologically inherited functions (Stevens, 1983; Stevens, 2015). Stevens was also concerned to debunk the notion that Jung was a Lamarckian as was unquestionably the case with Freud (Sulloway, 1992). *Archetype: A Natural History of the Mind* was a major contribution to theorizing about Jung and archetypes, and reflected a solid grasp of the sociobiological model promoted at the time by E.O. Wilson and others. Much of Stevens' argument rested on Jung's frequent seeming reference to his own biological, indeed apparently Darwinian, commitments scattered throughout his texts, such as his comments on the leaf-cutting ant, and it appeared to many that Stevens had developed a truly compelling interpretation of Jung's theory. Bergson, and the French tradition, however, is not mentioned in his book.

The difficulty with Stevens' position was that sociobiology as developed by Wilson, and its successor discipline, evolutionary psychology, were, from the beginning, subject to a variety of criticisms, some seemingly more political than scientific (Kamin, Lewontin, & Rose, 1984), but also reflecting scientifically detailed and philosophically well-grounded critiques (Kitcher, 1985; Shapiro & Epstein, 1998; Panksepp & Panksepp, 2000; Saunders, 2003; Foley, 1995). Added to this problem, myself and others argued, was the fast pace of change in the sciences, and the inherent challenges posed by interdisciplinary research programs—a problem that also goes back at least to Freud and Jung (Kitcher, 1995). The criticism of the strongly evolutionary model by Knox, myself, Merchant, and Roesler (Knox, Merchant, & Hogenson, 2010; Roesler, 2012) went further following the appearance of papers by the psychiatrist Erik Goodwyn (Goodwyn, 2010) and an exchange between me and the Jungian analyst, Alan Maloney (Maloney & Hogenson, 2003a; Maloney & Hogenson, 2003b). Their argument in these exchanges was that the demands being placed on phylogenetic transmission as an account for archetypes could not be sustained given the current state of our understanding of the genome, and the processes involved in evolution, which were rapidly under-going change directed at more developmental theories.

All of these problems were already beginning to play a role in the interpretation of Jung's theories by the early 1990s with the appearance of research by the Jungian analyst, John van Eenwyk, arguing for an interpretation of archetypes as manifestations of strange attractors, a term drawn from what was at the time referred to as chaos theory, and would subsequently be called complex dynamic systems theory (Eenwyk, 1991; Eenwyk, 1997). In 1996 the Jungian analyst, David Tresan published a paper in the *Journal of Analytical Psychology* entitled "Jungian Metapsychology and Neurobiological Theory" that argued for a more sophisticated integration of Jungian theory with neuroscience and drew explicitly on the philosopher Jaegwon Kim's discussion of emergence as supervenience as a way of thinking about Jung's description of psychological phenomena, including the archetypes (Tresan, 1996). Emergence had already been identified as an issue in Jung's overall theorizing by Marilyn Nagy in her book *Philosophical Issues in the Psychology of C. G. Jung* (Nagy, 1991), but Tresan's paper is arguably the critical inflection point in the emergence of emergence as an aspect of Jungian theorizing, in part due to a timely crossover with my engagement with Jung's theorizing.

My early work on Jung dealt largely with the early history of psychoanalysis and analytical psychology (Hogenson, 1983; Hogenson, 1994), but in the late 1980s I became directly engaged with the Santa Fe Institute and the developing research on complex adaptive systems— the chaos theory of van Eenwyk's paper—as well as the study of emergence in biological systems as discussed by Tresan. In 1999, drawing on these and related research programs, most notably the work of the neuroscientist and anthropologist Terrence Deacon on human symbolic abilities (Deacon, 1997) and the theoretical roboticist, Horst Hendriks-Jansen (Hendriks-Jansen, 1996), I presented a paper at the North American conference of Jungian analysts titled "The Baldwin Effect: A Neglected Influence on C. G. Jung's Biological Thinking." This paper drew heavily on research at the Santa Fe Institute that was returning to the work of James Mark Baldwin and, although not as directly acknowledged, Conway Lloyd Morgan, to the mainstream of thinking about evolution and the emergence of new biological phenomena. My position could be called a strong emergent position in that at this point I essentially rejected the notion of an underlying pattern for archetypal phenomena, writing that "the archetypes do not exist in some particular place, be it the genome or some transcendent realm of Platonic ideas. Rather, the archetypes are the emergent properties of the dynamic developmental system of brain, environment, and narrative" (Hogenson, 2001, p. 607). In the debate with Stevens, I drew heavily on these models of emergence, but also research based on artificial simulation of living systems to demonstrate my argument that the complex animal behavior Jung found so compelling could be explained by very simple rules and did not require the complex algorithmic structures proposed by evolutionary psychology and Stevens' model of archetypes (Hogenson, 2002).

In a notable publishing confluence, 2001 also saw the appearance of papers addressing the question of archetypes and taking up the theme of emergence by the theoretical biologist, Peter Saunders and the Jungian analyst, Patricia Skar as well as the Jungian analyst Maxson McDowell (McDowell, 2001; Saunders & Skar, 2001). Saunders and Skar argued that archetypes could be conceptualized as emergent patterns that developed out of progressively denser aggregations of complexes, Jung's more elementary and more readily accessible psychological structures, while McDowell, who had set the stage in an earlier paper (McDowell, 2000), took a more mathematical approach, based on complex systems theory to outline a way of mathematically identifying archetypal images. The British analyst, Jean Knox also initiated her investigation of archetypes in 2001 with an appeal to developments in cognitive science, particularly the work of Annette Karmiloff-Smith (Karmiloff-Smith, 1996) and the cognitive linguist, George Lakoff (Knox, 2001). Once again, the theme was emergence, but in this instance the form emergence took was more developmental in focus and provided a cognitive foundation for an understanding of the archetype-in-itself, which Knox associated with the image schemas of Lakoff. Knox followed this 2001 article with her important and influential book, *Archetype, Attachment, Analysis: Jungian Psychology and the Emergent Mind* (Knox, 2003). Also following a more developmental model of emergent phenomena, the Australian analyst and academic, John Merchant, proposed an interpretation of shamanism as an emergent property of certain developmental patterns (Merchant, 2006). I published several additional papers on dynamic systems theory, emergence, and archetypes including an overview of the state of thinking about archetypes in 2004 (Hogenson, 2004a).

Although it was not evident to observers at the time, in retrospect it is safe to say that by 2004 the discussion of archetypes among the more theoretically minded Jungian analysts and associated scholars was in a state of confusion. Stevens revised his book to address the positions taken by Hogenson and Knox, arguing that they were confusing archetypal images with the archetype-as-such, but without taking into consideration the extensive source materials on which they built their arguments. Emergence, as a general organizing principle for archetypal theory was widely held in the community; differing views on what emergence meant to each researcher, however, had not been worked out. It was also the case that among the various positions on offer in the discussion, only my 2001 Baldwin Effect paper came close to incorporating the implications of the Bergsonian view of the somnambulistic unconscious by way of explicitly addressing the influence of Baldwin and Lloyd Morgan on Jung. This aspect of Jung's thinking was also captured in my debate with Stevens and my emphasis on simple rules giving rise to complex behavior. This became more evident with the ongoing research into Jung's somnambulistic assumptions by Kerslake and others cited above and with the publication of more of Jung's writings and seminars.

Roughly twenty years after writing "Instinct and the Unconscious," in Jung's seminar on *Dream Interpretation: Ancient and Modern* conducted between 1936 and 1941, Carol Baumann presented a paper based on Eugène Marais' book, *The Soul of the White Ant*, published in Africaans in 1925 and translated into English in 1937 (Jung, 2014, p. 94). Marais was a South African naturalist and ethologist, and the "white ant" referred to the termites that were common in the African bush. Baumann's paper no longer exists, but Jung's comments engage the question of termite behavior by way of an implicit reference to Bergson:

> We would be mistaken to assume, however, that collective images, because they are independent of environmental influences, remain enclosed in the soul to no effect... ... These are processes that can only be explained by *sympathy* (Greek *sympathein*: to suffer together). There a transmission without words and visible signs

takes place; the contents go directly from one unconscious to the other.

Such a living out of "sympathy" is extremely pronounced in termites. One could integrate the multiplicity of individual termites and imagine them as a single being.

(Jung, 2014, p. 97)

The behavior of termites, as well as other social insects, is now examined under the theory of swarm behavior (Bonabeau, Theraulaz, & Dorigo, 1999; Malone & Bernstein, 2015), which relies on the aggregation of simple interactions among organisms to create what appear to be complex behaviors. The same processes account for the intricate patterns of flocking birds and schools of fish. Beyond these patterns, however, swarming behavior is increasingly seen in human social interactions that involve large collectivities such as the internet (Kundu & Ji, 2012). The behavior of swarming systems is, however, once again a form of emergence, but now based on a deeper collective dynamic. The issue of deep structures has since informed several contributions to the theorizing regarding archetypes and, increasingly, the entire structure of the psyche.

In 2002, Joseph Cambray for the first time broached the question of emergence and archetypes in a psychoanalytic journal with his paper "Synchronicity and Emergence" (Cambray, 2002). This was followed by a more clinical paper, "Towards the Feeling of Emergence" in 2006 (Cambray, 2006), but Cambray took a decisive step with his Fay lectures at the Texas A & M University, published in 2009 (Cambray, 2009). In these lectures Cambray moved the discussion of synchronicity into a central position linking synchronistic phenomena, which are closely related to archetypes in Jung's later works, to developing theories of psyche and matter taking place in quantum mechanics, particularly at the Institute for Frontier Areas of Psychology and Mental Health at Freiburg University under the direction of the physicist, Harald Atmanspacher.

Atmanspacher and his colleagues at Freiburg were engaged in the study of extraordinary experiences such as out of body events, near-death experiences, and other forms of altered perception. The theoretical focus of this work is based on a dual aspect metaphysics that views physical and psychological phenomena as epistemic points of view on an underlying non-dual substrate. Atmanspacher's research into this field and its implications for analytical psychology is extensive (Atmanspacher, 1994; Atmanspacher & Primas, 1996; Atmanspacher, 1997; Atmanspacher & Wiedenmann, 1999; Atmanspacher, 1998). In 2013 in collaboration with his Freiburg colleague, Wolfgang Fach, he published an overview of the dual aspect model in the *Journal of Analytical Psychology* with a commentary by David Tresan (Atmanspacher & Fach, 2013; Tresan, 2013). During this same period I shifted my attention to the underlying structural characteristics of symbolic patterns culminating in an argument for the importance of fractal geometry for understanding the significance of Jung's attention to mandala symbols as fundamental symbolic representations of individuation (Hogenson, 2004b; Hogenson, 2005; Hogenson, 2007; Hogenson, 2009a; Hogenson, 2009b; Hogenson, 2014; Hogenson, forthcoming), working from research into the mathematics of symbols systems first developed by the Harvard linguist, George Kingsly Zipf (Zipf, 1949) but more recently developed by research at the Santa Fe Institute and elsewhere (Ferrer i Cancho & Solé, 2003; Ferrer i Cancho, Solé, & Köhler, 2004; Vogt, 2004; Vogt, 2005; Vogt, 2012). Cambray has similarly extended his investigations into universal structures, also including the fractal patterns of Jung's illustrations in the *Red Book*, the symbolic importance of cosmological structures and the metaphysics of Wha Yen, or Kegon Buddhism (Cambray, 2014; Cambray, 2016; Cambray, 2017).

Conclusion

In 2014 the Jungian analyst, Warren Colman, delivered a lecture at the International School for Analytical Psychology in Zurich entitled "Act and Image: The Emergence of Symbolic Imagination" (Colman, 2016). Based on a wide-ranging review of anthropological literature, Colman concluded that the dynamics of symbols and his reading of the discussion of the emergence of the emergence theory of archetypes, he writes:

> Over the past fifteen years or so, archetype theory has been reconfigured in terms of emergence theories, notably by Jean Knox and George Hogenson. In view of this, I argue that the notion of archetype has become redundant since emergent forms cannot

properly be described with a term that, by definition, refers to pre-existent forms.

(Colman, 2016, p. 4)

What are we to make of this claim by a leading Jungian analyst? Is it the case that in the end the effort to work out a theory of archetypes results in the elimination of the object of theorizing? To respond to this question, at least provisionally, we need to examine the basic notion of what archetype means. We have already seen Reiner Schürman's comment that Archē carries with it the complementary sense of telos. In this he is following Heidegger who writes:

The Greeks usually hear two things in this word: on the one hand, *archē* means that from which something takes its egress and inception; on the other it means that which, as such egress and inception, at the same time reaches beyond whatever emerges from it, thereby dominating it. *Archē* means both inception and domination inseparably.

(Heidegger, 1976)

Tupos is frequently taken to mean an impression, as in striking a coin, thus, archetype is understood as assumed to mean some form of imposed foundational structure. *Tupos*, however, also has the meaning of a fundamental exemplar or definition, as in the Christian cross being the type of all subsequent iconography—everything refers back to the type, but the type is not an impression or definitive form (Marion, 2003). How does this relate to emergence? First of all, emergence as discussed in philosophy—for example, Kim's supervenience—or in the literature of complex dynamic systems is not simply a process of things appearing, as in a blade of grass emerging from the soil. Emergence, as discussed in the sources referenced in this chapter is a rather more complex, and in fact rather more constrained process than Colman appears to realize. This is the argument of the work that has been done on archetypes after the initial formulation of the concept in the late 1990s and early 2000s. We come at last to the current work of Atmanspacher, Cambray, and myself, that in varying ways examine deep structural patterns that still, as I argue in 2001, do not inhere in any place but nevertheless appear to give shape to phenomena as wide-ranging as symbol systems, synchronicity and the distribution of matter in the universe. The early somnambulists, whose influence on

Jung is only now beginning to be fully understood, set his theorizing on a course that eventually brought him to his work with Wolfgang Pauli and the formulation of the Pauli/Jung conjecture, the presence of a unified substrate or *Unus Mundus* to the psychological and physical that is the foundation of the dual aspect monism proposed by Atmanspacher (Atmanspacher & Fuchs, 2014).

The investigation of Jung's theory of archetypes is not closed, but remains a compelling area of investigation in analytical psychology, with implications far beyond the individual consulting room. A great deal of material needs to be added to what is presented in this chapter, but that will necessarily await another opportunity.

Notes

1   Jung refers to the following comment in Freud's study of Schreber: "(3) A third consideration which arises from the views that have been developed in these pages is as follows. Are we to suppose that a general detachment of the libido from the external world would be an effective enough agent to account for the 'end of the world'? Or would not the ego-cathexes, which still remained in existence, have been sufficient to maintain rapport with the external world? To meet this difficulty we should either have to assume that what we call libidinal cathexis (that is, interest emanating from erotic sources) coincides with interest in general, or we should have to consider the possibility that a very widespread disturbance in the distribution of libido may bring about a corresponding disturbance in the ego-cathexes. But these are problems which we are still quite helpless and incompetent to solve" (Freud, 1958, p. 73).

2   The Baldwin effect, or as Baldwin referred to the concept, organic selection, is a variant on Darwin's natural selection which argues that actions undertaken by an organism can alter the environment in which selection is taking place in ways that provide a gradient toward some new genetic adaptation. A classic example is the development of lactose tolerance in adults inhabiting northern regions with little sunlight. Migration into these areas would only be possible if vitamin D could be acquired by means other than sunlight, but the major alternative source of vitamin D is milk, for which most adult mammals lose their tolerance. Through processes of fermentation or other transformations of milk, however, some portions of the population are able to maintain tolerance, and eventually establish a complete population with widespread adult lactose tolerance, thereby making it possible to thrive in areas with little sunlight.

References

Atmanspacher, H. (1994). Complexity, Meaning and the Cartesian Cut. *Journal of Consciousness Studies*, 1 (2), 168–181.

Atmanspacher, H. (1997). Cartesian Cut, Heisenberg Cut, and the Concept of Complexity. *World Futures: Journal of General Evolution*, 49 (3–4), 333–355.

Atmanspacher, H. (1998). Commentary on Chris Nunn's 'Archetypes and Memes. *Journal of Consciousness Studies*, 5 (3), 355–361.

Atmanspacher, H., & Fach, W. (2013). A Structural-Phenomenological Typology of Mindmatter Correlations. *Journal of Analytical Psychology*, 56 (4), 274–280.

Atmanspacher, H., & Primas, H. (1996). The Hidden Side of Wolfgang Pauli: An Eminent Physicist's Extraordinary Encounter with Depth Psychology. *Journal of Consciousness Studies*, 3 (2), 112–126.

Atmanspacher, H., & Wiedenmann, G. (1999). Some Basic Problems with Complex Systems. *Theory and Applications* (pp. 1059–1066). Amsterdam: Elsevier.

Atmanspacher, H., & Fuchs, C.A. (2014). *The Pauli-Jung Conjecture and its Impact Today*. Exeter: Imprint Academic.

Baldwin, J.M. (2015). *Darwin and the Humanities*. New York: Irving Lewis Press.

Bergson, H. (1990). *Matter and Memory*. New York: Zone Books.

Bergson, H. (1998). *Creative Evolution* (A. Mitchell, Trans.). London: Dover Publications.

Bleuler, E. (1911). *Dementia praecox: oder Gruppe der Schizophrenien*. Leibzig: F. Deutiche.

Bonabeau, E., Theraulaz, G., & Dorigo, M. (1999). *Swarm Intelligence: From Natural to Artificial Systems*. Oxford: Oxford University Press.

Cambray, J. (2002). Synchronicity and Emergence. *American Imago*, 59, 409–434.

Cambray, J. (2006). Towards the Feeling of Emergence. *Journal of Analytical Psychology*, 51, 1–20.

Cambray, J. (2009). *Synchronicity: Nature and Psyche in an Interconnected Universe*. College Station, TX: Texas A&M University Press.

Cambray, J. (2014). *The Red Book*: Entrances and Exits. In T. Kirsch & G. Hogenson (Eds.), *The Red Book: Reflections on Jung's* Liber Novus (pp. 36–53). London: Routledge.

Cambray, J. (2016). Darkness in the Contemporary Scientific Imagination and its Implications. *International Journal of Transpersonal Studies*, 35 (2), 75–87.

Cambray, J. (2017). The Emergence of the Ecological Mind in Hua-Yen/Kegon Buddhism and Jungian Psychology. *Journal of Analytical Psychology*, 62 (1), 20–31.

Colman, W. (2016). *Act and Image: The Emergence of Symbolic Imagination*. New Orleans: Spring Journal.

Deacon, T. (1997). *The Symbolic Species: The Co-evolution of Language and the Brain*. New York: W. W. Norton & Company.

Deleuze, G. (2004). From Sacher-Masoch to Masochism. *Angelaki: Journal of Theoretical Humanities*, 9 (1), 125–133.

Eenwyk, J.V. (1991). Archetypes: The Strange Attractors of the Psyche. *Journal of Analytical Psychology*, 36, 1–25.

Eenwyk, J.V. (1997). *Archetypes & Strange Attractors: The Chaotic World of Symbols (Studies in Jungian Psychology by Jungian Analysts)*. Toronto: Inner City Books.

Ellenberger, H.F. (1983). C. G. Jung and the Story of Helene Preiswerk: A Critical Study with New Documents. In M. Micale & F. Dubor (Eds.), *Beyond the Unconscious: Essays of Henri F. Ellenberger in the History of Psychiatry*. Princeton: Princeton University Press.

Escamilla, M. (2016). *Bleuler, Jung, and the Creation of the Schizophrenias*. Einsiedeln: Daimon Verlag.

Ferrer i Cancho, R., & Solé, R.V. (2003). Least Effort and the Origins of Scaling in Human Language. *Proceedings of the National Academy of Sciences*, 100 (3), 788–791.

Ferrer i Cancho, R., Solé, R.V., & Köhler, R. (2004). Patterns in Syntactic Dependency Networks. *Phys Rev E Stat Nonlin Soft Matter Phys*, 69 (5 Pt 1), 051915.

Foley, R. (1995). The Adaptive Legacy of Human Evolution: A Search for the Environment of Evolutionary Adaptedness. *Evolutionary Anthropology: Issues*, 4 (6), 194–203.

Freud, S. (1958). Psycho-Analytical Notes on an Autobiographical Account of a Case of Paranoia (dementia paranoides)(1911) (J. Strachey, Trans.). In *The Standard Edition of the Complete Psychological Works of Sigmund Freud, Volume XIII: The Case of Schreber, Papers on Technique and Other Works* (pp. 1–82). London: Hogarth.

Freud, S., & Jung, C.G. (1974). *The Freud/Jung Letters: The Correspondence between Sigmund Freud and C. G. Jung (Bollingen Series, No. 94)*. Princeton: Princeton University Press.

Goodwyn, E. (2010). Approaching Archetypes: Reconsidering Innateness. *Journal of Analytical Psychology*, 55, 502–521.

Gunter, P.A.Y. (1982). Bergson and Jung. *Journal of the History of Ideas*, 43 (4), 635–652.

Haule, J.R. (1983). Archetype and Integration: Exploring the Janetian Roots of Analytical Psychology. *Journal of Analytical Psychology*, 28, 253–267.

Haule, J.R. (1984). From Somnambulism to the Archetypes: The French Roots of Jung's Split with Freud. *Psychoanalytic Review*, 71 (4), 635–660.

Heidegger, M. (1976). On the Being and Conception of *Physis* in Aristotle's Physics B, 1. *Man and World*, 9, 219–270.

Hendriks-Jansen, H. (1996). *Catching Ourselves in the Act: Situated Activity, Interactive Emergence, Evolution, and Human Thought*. Cambridge, MA: A Bradford Book.

Hogenson, G.B. (1994). *Jung's Struggle with Freud*. Wilmette: Chiron Publication.

Hogenson, G.B. (2001). The Baldwin Effect: A Neglected Influence on CG Jung's Evolutionary Thinking. *Journal of Analytical Psychology*, 46, 591–611.

Hogenson, G.B. (2002). From Silicon Archetypes to Robot Dreams: Evolutionary Psychology and Jung's Theory of Archetypes. *Harvest*, 58, 7–21.

Hogenson, G.B. (2004a). Archetypes: Emergence and the Psyche's Deep Structure. *Analytical Psychology: Contemporary* (pp. 44–67). London: Routledge.

Hogenson, G.B. (2004b). What are Symbols Symbols of? Situated Action, Mythological Bootstrapping and the Emergence of the Self. *Journal of Analytical Psychology*, 49, 67–81.

Hogenson, G.B. (2005). The Self, the Symbolic and Synchronicity: Virtual Realities and the Emergence of the Psyche. *Journal of Analytical Psychology*, 50, 271–284.

Hogenson, G.B. (2007). From Moments of Meeting to Archetypal Consciousness: Emergence and the Fractal Structure of Analytic Practice. In A. Casement (Ed.), *Who Owns Jung*.

Hogenson, G.B. (2009a). Archetypes as Action Patterns. *Journal of Analytical Psychology*, 54, 325–337.

Hogenson, G.B. (2009b). Synchronicity and Moments of Meeting. *Journal of Analytical Psychology*, 54, 183–197.

Hogenson, G.B. (2014). Are Synchronicities Really Dragon Kings. In H. Atmanspacher & C.A. Fuchs (Eds.), *The Jung-Pauli Conjecture and its Impact Today* (pp. 201–216). Exeter: Imprint Academic.

Hogenson, G.B. (forthcoming). The Tibetan Book of the Dead Needs Work: A Proposal for Research into the Geometry of Individuation. In Hogenson, G.B., & Stevens, A. (2003). Debate: Psychology and Biology. In *Cambridge 2001: Proceedings of the Fifteenth International Congress for Analytical Psychology* (pp. 367–377). Einsiedeln: Damon Verlag.

Hogenson, G.B. (1983). *Jung's Struggle with Freud.* South Bend: University of Notre Dame Press.

Jung, C.G. (1960a). The Psychology of Dementia Praecox (R.F.C. Hull, Trans.). *CW*, 3.

Jung, C.G. (1960b). On Psychological Understanding (1914) (R.F.C. Hull, Trans.). *CW*, 3. Princeton: Princeton University Press.

Jung, C.G. (1967). *Symbols of Transformation. CW*, 5. Princeton: Princeton University Press.

Jung, C.G. (1969). Instinct and the Unconscious (R.F.C. Hull, Trans.). In H. Read, M. Fordham, G. Adler, & W. McGuire (Eds.), *The Structure and Dynamics of the Psyche* (pp. 129–138). Princeton: Princeton University Press.

Jung, C.G. (1970a). On the Psychology and Pathology of so-called Occult Phenomena (1902) (R.F.C. Hull, Trans.). *CW*, 1, 3–88. Princeton: Princeton University Press.

Jung, C.G. (1970b). *Psychiatric Studies. CW*, 1. Princeton: Princeton University Press.

Jung, C.G. (1970c). On the Nature of the Psyche (1927, 1931). *CW*, 8, 159–234. Princeton: Princeton University Press.

Jung, C.G. (1912). *Wandlungen und Symbole der Libido: Beiträge zur Entwicklungsgeschichte des Denkens.* Leipzig: F. Deutiche.

Jung, C.G. (2001). *Psychology of the Unconscious: A Study of the Transformations and Symbolisms of the Libido.* (Supplement B). Princeton: Princeton University Press.

Jung, C.G. (2014). *Dream Interpretation Ancient and Modern: Notes from the Seminar Given in 1936–1941 (Philemon Foundation Series).* Princeton: Princeton University Press.

Kamin, L.J., Lewontin, R.C., & Rose, S. (1984). *Not in Our Genes: Biology, Ideology, and Human Nature.* New York: Pantheon.

Karmiloff-Smith, A. (1996). *Beyond Modularity: A Developmental Perspective on Cognitive Science.* Cambridge, MA: The MIT Press.

Kerslake, C. (2006). Insects and Incest: From Bergson and Jung to Deleuze. *philpapers.org.*

Kerslake, C. (2007a). *Deleuze and the Unconscious.* London: Continuum.

Kerslake, C. (2007b). The Somnambulist and the Hermaphrodite: Deleuze, Johann Malfatti de Montereggio and Occultism. *Culture Machine.* Electronic, not paginated.

Kerslake, C. (2007c). *Deleuze and the Unconscious.* London: Continuum.

Kitcher, P. (1985). *Vaulting Ambition: Sociobiology and the Quest for Human Nature.* Cambridge, MA: The MIT Press.

Kitcher, P. (1995). *Freud's Dream: A Complete Interdisciplinary Science of Mind.* Cambridge, MA: The MIT Press.

Knox, J. (2001). Memories, Fantasies, Archetypes: An Exploration of Some Connections Between Cognitive Science and Analytical Psychology. *Journal of Analytical Psychology*, 46, 613–635.

Knox, J. (2003). *Archetype, Attachment, Analysis: Jungian Psychology and the Emergent Mind*. London: Routledge.

Knox, J., Merchant, J., & Hogenson, G. (2010). Responses to Erik Goodwyn's 'Approaching Archetypes: Reconsidering Innateness'. *Journal of Analytical Psychology*, 55, 522–549.

Kundu, A., & Ji, C. (2012). Swarm Behavior of Intelligent Cloud. *arXiv pre-print arXiv:1203.1395*.

Lloyd Morgan, C. (1973). *Habit and Instinct*. New York: Arno Press.

Lothane, Z. (1997). The Schism between Freud and Jung over Schreber: Its Implications for Method and Doctrine. *International Forum of Psychoanalysis*, 6, 103–115.

Malone, T.W., & Bernstein, M.S. (2015). *Handbook of Collective Intelligence (MIT Press)*. Cambridge, MA: The MIT Press.

Maloney, A., & Hogenson, G.B. (2003a). Archetype Theory, Evolutionary Psychology and the Baldwin Effect. A Commentary on Hogenson's Paper (October 2001, JAP, 46, 4). *Journal of Analytical Psychology*.

Maloney, A., & Hogenson, G.B. (2003b). Reply to Hogenson (JAP, 48, 1, January 2003). *Journal of Analytical Psychology*.

Marion, J.-L. (2003). *The Crossing of the Visible*. Stanford: Stanford University Press.

McDowell, M.J. (2001). Principle of Organization: A Dynamic-Systems View of the Archetype-as-Such. *Journal of Analytical Psychology*, 46, 637–654.

Merchant, J. (2006). The Developmental/Emergent Model of Archetype, its Implications and its Application to Shamanism. *Journal of Analytical Psychology*, 51, 125–144.

Nagy, M. (1991). *Philosophical Issues in the Psychology of C. G. Jung*. Albany: State University of New York Press.

Panksepp, J., & Panksepp, J.B. (2000). The Seven Sins of Evolutionary Psychology. *Evolution and Cognition*, 6 (2), 108–131.

Pilard, N. (2015). *Jung and Intuition: On the Centrality and Variety of Forms of Intuition in Jung and Post-Jungians*. London: Karnac Books.

Roesler, C. (2012). Are Archetypes Transmitted More by Culture than Biology? Questions Arising from Conceptualizations of the Archetype. *Journal of Analytical Psychology*, 57 (2), 223–246.

Saunders, P., & Skar, P. (2001). Archetypes, Complexes and Self-Organization. *Journal of Analytical Psychology*, 46, 305–323.

Saunders, P.T. (2003). Bricks Without Straw: Darwinism in the Social Sciences. *Theoria: An International Journal for Theory*, 18 (3), 259–272.

Scarfe, A.C. (2009). James Mark Baldwin with Alfred North Whitehead on Organic Selectivity&58; The "Novel" Factor in Evolution. *Cosmos and History*, 5 (2), 40–107.

Schreber, D.P. (1955). *Memoirs of My Nervous Illness*. New York: New York Review of Books.

Schürmann, R. (1987). *Heidegger on Being and Acting: From Principles to Anarchy*. Bloomington, IN: Indiana University Press.

Shapiro, L., & Epstein, W. (1998). Evolutionary Theory Meets Cognitive Psychology: A More Selective Perspective. *Mind & Language*, 13 (2), 171–194.

Stevens, A. (1983). *Archetypes: A Natural History of the Self*. New York: William Morrow & Co.

Stevens, A. (2015). *Archetype Revisited: An Updated Natural History of the Self (Routledge Mental Health Classic Editions)*. London: Routledge.

Sulloway, F. (1992). *Freud, Biologist of the Mind: Beyond the Psychoanalytic Legend*. Cambridge, MA: Harvard University Press.

Tresan, D. (1996). Jungian Metapsychology and Neurobiological Theory. *Journal of Analytical Psychology*, 41, 399–436.

Tresan, D. (2013). A Commentary on 'A Structural-Phenomenological Typology of Mind-Matter Correlations' by H. Atmanspacher and W. Fach. *Journal of Analytical Psychology*, 58 (2), 245–253; discussion 254.

Valsiner, J. (1998). *The Guided Mind: A Sociogenetic Approach to Personality*. Cambridge, MA: Harvard University Press.

Vandermeersch, P. (1991). Unresolved Questions in the Freud/Jung Debate. *On Psychosis, Sexual Identity and Religion. Anm. av Hans Åkerberg*.

Vogt, P. (2004). Minimum Cost and the Emergence of the Zipf-Mandelbrot Law. *Artificial Life IX: Proceedings of the Ninth International Conference on the Simulation and Synthesis of Living Systems*, 214–219.

Vogt, P. (2005). *Meaning Development Versus Predefined Meanings in Language Evolution Models*. Proceedings from Proceedings of IJCAI-05.

Vogt, P. (2012). Exploring the Robustness of Cross-Situational Learning Under Zipfian Distributions. *Cognitive Science*, 36 (4), 726–739.

Zipf, G.K. (1949). *Human Behavior and the Principle of Least Effort: An Introduction to Human Ecology*. New York: Martino Fine Books.

Chapter 3

Jung and the Mind–Body Problem

Erik D. Goodwyn

Introduction

According to Jung:

> Since psyche and matter are contained in one and the same world, and moreover are in continuous contact with one another and ultimately rest on irrepresentable, transcendental factors, it is not only possible but fairly probable, even, that psyche and matter are two different aspects of one and the same thing.
>
> (Jung, 1954, para 418)

With this quote it appears Jung leaned toward a non-physicalist and non-reductive metaphysical system; more specifically others have noted he appeared to argue from an unstated position of neutral monism with respect to the philosophy of mind, though he never explicitly identified a preferred metaphysical framework for his psychology (Atmanspacher, 2012; Cambray, 2014). But all psychology operates under metaphysical assumptions of some kind whether they are explicitly stated or not. Moreover, underlying any psychological theory will (more specifically) lurk the Mind–Body Problem (MBP)—the problem of exactly what are minds and bodies, and how do they relate. It makes a difference: a physicalist, for example, may look for archetypes in some brain region or another, whereas for a non-physicalist doing so might be a category error. For Jung this question is especially important because of the way in which Jung formulated the archetype as a metaphysical entity later in life—this definition needs a metaphysical analysis, but Jung never provided one, and the lack of an explicit metaphysics has dogged the discussion of archetype in particular over the years. Thus it behooves us to look at Jung's theory from a metaphysical standpoint, particularly with respect to the MBP and the archetype. Since Jung never explicitly committed to any particular metaphysics of mind, tidying up this issue is one of the goals of this chapter. Neutral monism is but one type of the three broad approaches to the MBP I will discuss[1] with the goal being to briefly explore what the implications of each of them are for Jungian theory.

Physicalism

Under this mostly reductive monistic metaphysics, mind is viewed as entirely dependent upon and ontologically derivative from matter. Here, matter is typically considered the only real substance. Varieties of physicalism vary in how reductive they are, and include eliminativism (the mind does not exist and is an illusion—the most reductive physicalism), identity theory (mind exists but is exactly equivalent to and reduces to various brain states),[2] epiphenomenalism (mind is irreducible but merely a side effect of brain activity with no causal efficacy on the brain), and varieties of non-reductive physicalisms that evoke the concept of emergence (mind is an irreducible emergent property of the brain that has causal efficacy, but mind is ultimately still created by matter and its properties). More on emergentism below. Popular defenses of various brands of physicalism include those of Dennett (1988, 1992) and Churchland (1996), among many others (see Chalmers, 2012, *passim*).

Dualism

Under this non-reductive dual ontology, the mind is an entirely separate substance from matter, and neither are given ontological priority. Descartes (1985) is the most well-known defender of this metaphysical system. Though substance dualisms are not as popular as the physicalisms, there are defenders of it, a number of which can be found in Corcoran (2001).

Dual-Aspect Theory

Under this ontology, mind and matter are actually of one substance, which appears differently depending upon one's viewpoint. In simplified terms, from an objective standpoint, this substance appears as brain, but from the subjective viewpoint, this substance appears as mind. This is different from identity theory because identity theory reduces mind to brain/matter, whereas dual-aspect theory views both mind and matter as primary in themselves, with neither derivative of the other. One variant of this is neutral monism, wherein mind and body are both secondarily derived from a single, more fundamental pre-existent neutral substance that is neither body nor mind, and this neutral substance cannot be observed directly. Well-known defenders of dual-aspect monisms and neutral monisms include Spinoza (Morgan & Shirley 2002), David Chalmers (1996), William James (1950), and David Bohm (2010).[3]

The Hard Problem, the Binding Problem, the Interaction Problem, and the Combination Problem

Metaphysical systems are not chosen necessarily as a result of empirical research. They are chosen based on their overall coherence and on which conceptual problems they may have. As it turns out, each metaphysical system has a typical problem associated with it that will impact interpretations made on any psychological system situated within it, Jungian or not:

- Physicalism has the *hard problem of neuroscience* (Chalmers, 1996), or HPN: how does scattered neural activity create a unified conscious experience, complete with subjective feeling, quality (or qualia), and coherence? A related problem is the *binding problem* (or BP): how do the various scattered perceptive systems in the brain "bind" together to form the unitary, coherent sensory experience of the world we all have every day? This problem arises because physicalisms propose that mind is created by matter and its properties. The HPN and BP therefore come as a natural consequence of this supposition. For Jung, physicalism renders the concept of an *a priori* psychological archetype as mover of the psychological realm of questionable necessity, since mind is supposedly created by matter, hence the archetype would need to depart from Jung's formulation somewhat to accommodate this system, either by making it emergent somehow or by eliminating it as an explanatory device altogether.

- Substance Dualism does not have the HPN or the BP since mind is an entirely separate substance from matter and therefore not dependent upon it to exist. Archetypal images in this system could be entirely mental and therefore not derivable from neurons or matter, avoiding the above quandary. This keeps the archetype immune to any needed reformulation in physicalist terms, but this ontology instead has the *interaction problem* (IP): if mind is a fundamentally independent and separate substance from matter— and hence neither creates the other—how is it possible that they can nevertheless affect one another so intimately as they appear to do? How can a purely mental archetype affect physical matter if they are of entirely different substances?
- Dual-aspect monism and neutral monism both avoid the IP by stating that mind and matter are actually the same substance or are derived from a neutral substance, and there is no HPN either, since this ontology does not require that mind be derived from matter, as mind and matter are both already two aspects of the same thing. Both are either aspects of the same substance or they are both derived from an *a priori* neutral substance. Stated differently, all matter has a pre-existent mentality or proto-mentality to it, rather than matter *creating* the mental. However, in these cases we still can have the *combination problem* or CP (see Chalmers, 2016): if the universe is composed of tiny units of mind or proto-mind, how can they combine to create coherent unified experiences? If we eliminate the HPN by postulating that fundamental particles have, in themselves, a kind of proto-consciousness (or the neutral substance from which particles are derived also have a derivable proto-consciousness), we are still left with the problem of how these proto-experiences combine to create a single, unitary coherent experience. So, even without the HPN, dual-aspect theory has a kind of BP in the CP. In this system, the *a priori* archetype can perhaps remain as an organizer of the neutral substance (Jung obviously has this in mind when grappling with the idea of synchronicity), but we still have the CP to contend with: how do micro-mentalities coalesce into archetypal experiences? The role of the archetype in the reductive system is therefore rather ill-defined because of the CP.

Thus far, the HPN, BP, and CP have no agreed upon solution. Moreover, while physicalism is currently quite popular, from a philosophical perspective it is hardly a settled matter, thus there is no need for us to shoehorn Jung into a physicalist framework if it doesn't fit well—so long as we realize the consequences of shifting it out of that paradigm. In any case, situating Jung's theory within one of them purchases an unsolved metaphysical problem to go with it, which we may have to learn to accept. But we can still narrow down our search by seeing which one of these best fits Jungian theory. For instance, we can eliminate putting Jung's theory into a framework of substance dualism due to Jung's insistence upon mind and matter being "two aspects of one and the same thing." It's obviously a poor fit. Thus, we at least do not need to concern ourselves with the IP. Jung also clearly would not cohere with any reductive type of physicalism—too much of his work requires a recognition of the irreducibility and full reality of the mental, which means only non-reductive approaches will really work. This means possibly only emergentist physicalism and neutral monism can make sense of Jung's theory. We will discuss each in turn to see which fits best.

Emergentism

Emergentist types of physicalism are applied to Jung by some Jungian authors (e.g., Knox, 2009; Coleman, 2016[4]). But we need to understand what this maneuver does for us and what it does not do. Emergentist approaches seek to preserve Jung's ideas of the spiritual and the *reality* of the irreducible psyche while avoiding what they feel are Jung's undue reliance on *a priori* ideas of archetypes (i.e., his Neoplatonic and realist leanings with respect to universals). The avoidance of *a priorism* of mind and hence archetypes is why this approach is physicalist: mind is described as *emerging* from the interaction of physical entities *where there was no mentality originally*, rather than mind being a pre-existent aspect of the systems in question (which would be a dual-aspect or neutral monist approach). Typically, this physicalist ontological assumption goes unstated, but at this point it should be obvious that the debate about whether archetypes are *a priori* or not depends on one's metaphysical stance: the physicalist argues that Jung was wrong and it cannot be, whereas the dual aspect/neutral monist agrees with Jung (more or less) and says it is. That these positions come from entirely different metaphysical assumptions may account for the persistence of the debate, and so it should not be a surprise that those who espouse an emergentist physicalist metaphysics typically argue that the idea of the *a priori* archetype is not necessary or needs major revision. But aligning ourselves with physicalism is what requires this departure from/adjustment to Jung. In other metaphysical systems we don't have to do this.

The Common Element: Reduction

In any case, the emergentist physicalist still has to accept the HPN and BP because of the insistence that the mental is not *a priori* present along with matter (or their neutral originators). Meanwhile a neutral monist that is reductive with respect to mind (i.e., that reduces minds into proto-consciousnesses associated with fundamental particles/neurons/etc.) has to accept the CP. Both of these problems are due to the reductive maneuvers within them. That is, the emergentist physicalist, by insisting on the dependence of the mental on the physical for its existence (however it is conceived) does not evade the HPN or BP. It simply *restates* the problems: *how* and *what causes* the emergence of causally efficacious and irreducible qualia/consciousness, and so forth? No matter how well characterized the systems (brains, AI, etc.) that correlate with consciousness come to be, we will still be at a loss to say how they *cause* unitary subjective mental experiences to emerge. The neutral monist avoids the HPN and BP by stating the mental and physical are two aspects of the same substance—here the mental need not be created by matter *ex nihilo* because it is just as foundational and pre-existent as matter, but nevertheless if one tries to argue that minds emerge from even pre-existent proto-minds, we still invite the CP.

Some of the major problems in these sorts of psychophysical reductions—and recent attempts at solution—are explored in depth by Horgan (1993), Kim (1992) and Koons and Bealer (2010). In his famous essay "What is it Like to be a Bat?," Thomas Nagel (1974) puts the problem thus: "In a sense, the seeds of this objection to the reducibility of experience are already detectable in successful cases of reduction; for in discovering sound to be, in reality, a wave phenomenon in air or other media, we leave behind one viewpoint to take up another, and the auditory, human or animal viewpoint that we leave behind remains unreduced." (p. 223).[5] Thus the HPN, BP, and CP are a result of attempts to reduce the mind to matter or to smaller proto-mentalities.

So where does that leave us? If we are content to accept the HPN, BP, or the CP (perhaps in hope that they may someday be finally solved), we can stop here and choose a reductive metaphysics within which to situate Jung, recognizing that in the case of physicalism we will have to accept the HPN and BP, on top of redefining or eliminating the archetype, or in the case of reductive neutral monism, accept the CP and leave the question of the archetype rather murky. If we are not content with this decision, however, we will have to abandon fully reductive accounts that ask so much of parts and so little of wholes. Since Jung had such a strong Neoplatonic influence (MacLennan, 2005; see also Atmanspacher, 2012a, 2012b, 2014a, and 2014b), this source may provide other options to consider, since it is essentially the *opposite* sort of metaphysical system—it is fundamentally non-reductive: instead of starting with parts and working up to wholes (to include the universe itself), we go the other way, from the whole universe down to all the parts via partitions (or 'emanations'). This position of holistic monism has been prominent for the majority of the history of philosophy until more recent centuries; however, there remain very serious reasons to return to it (reviewed by Schaffer, 2010).

The Mind–Body Problem as a Part–Whole Problem

Viewing the MBP as a problem of excessive reduction is not common, but neither is it new. Recent treatments and discussion can be found in Bohm (2010), who references Jung, Kelly et al. (2000), Atmanspacher (2014a; 2014b) and others. Viewing the MBP as essentially a category problem—which shares similarity with what I am doing here—can be found in Ryle (1949). Yablo (1992) examines the part-whole issue I am discussing from the perspective of mental causation (which I do not have space to explore). Here Yablo argues that considering the MPB as a part-whole problem helps to untangle some of the difficulties involved in the concept of mental causation. Peacocke (1983) points out that the sensory system has a considerable amount of holism that cannot easily be reduced (hence the BP), lending support to the holistic approach we are considering from that point of view. Finally Brentano's (1874) classic definition of *mental contents* as essentially relational (or intentional), which is still relevant over a century later (yet see Churchland, 1981 for objections, and Dennett, 1981 and Chisolm, 1957 for rebuttals), further adds to the plausibility of identifying the mental with the holistic, as anything relational must by definition contain more than itself and thus therefore constitute a type of whole. And of course the Neoplatonism, which so heavily influenced Jung (see MacLennan, 2005), is fundamentally holistic, so it is a logical choice to apply it more directly to Jung.

Of the broad ontologies above, we see that both physicalism and dual-aspect theory (as most commonly found) are typically presented as *reductive* ontologies, in that qualia and mind are thought to be derivable entirely from either atoms and their properties (physicalisms) or micro-proto-qualia of some sort (dual aspect and neutral monisms). As mentioned earlier, emergentism tries to provide conceptual help: the gain of emergentism is that it allows for the manifestly irreducible qualities of mind, self, and qualia to stand unmolested by any proposed possibility of reduction once they appear. But the trick is explaining how and why they appear—obviously this is just a restating of the HPN and BP.[6] Thus, emergentism allows for irreducible aspects of experience (and so is not eliminativism), but as a metaphysical system it does not avoid the HPN or BP because it is still a physicalist system, hence the necessity for such systems to typically require a refiguring of the archetype as an explanatory construct.

But if such issues are a consequence of our metaphysical position, what other options exist? Reductive neutral monism still leaves us with the CP, but we don't have to adopt a *reductive* neutral monism. If, instead, we propose that systems have properties in and of themselves that cannot be derived from the properties of the parts *in isolation*, and that moreover, the whole is *ontologically primary* over the parts (this latter characteristic is what separates it from emergentism), we gain relief from all three of the HPN, the BP, and the CP. This stance is an essential aspect of the Jung-Pauli (Neoplatonic) version of neutral monism that has been developed by Atmanspacher (2014a; 2014b) among others, and it is also unsurprisingly continuous with Jung's description of the psyche. It may therefore be a good choice to situate

Jungian theory metaphysically. So what is the conceptual cost of this maneuver? This we will explore next.

Whence Comes the Unity?

The cost is that we must abandon any hope of building up wholes from parts—by definition this is impossible within a holistic system. In other words, if we begin with the assumption that mental experiences, qualia, and consciousness are irreducible (certainly a fair assumption), then reducing them would lead to a contradiction: the HPN, the BP and the CPs simply restate this fact. Since a holistic ontology does not assert this situation of wholes being created by parts, it does not have these problems, but it still must account for what forms wholes: if not parts, then what? As it stands, the fifteenth century Neoplatonist Marsilio Ficino provides an elegant analysis of this issue in his *Platonic Theology*. We will furthermore see that this formulation has direct application to Jungian theory. In his discussion, Ficino examines what possible things could be *the uniting features* of wholes (like, for our purposes, conscious archetypal experiences).

Adapting Ficino's (2001) analysis (pp. 29–54; see also Plotinus, 1917/ 2007, and Proclus 1963, 2015) to the MBP gives us what appear to be the only four possibilities, ranging from most to least reductive:

1. Unifying features of wholes do not exist and are "illusory," hence the unity does not really exist.
2. The parts themselves unify the whole. Hence the reductionist (with or without help from the concept of emergence) solution is really the best. Physicalist and reductionist dual-aspect theories appear to propose this solution.
3. The whole unites the parts—i.e., wholes create their own unity.
4. Unifying features exist, but neither parts nor wholes are responsible for them. This is the radically holistic Neoplatonic solution (of a type similar to that defended by philosopher Jonathan Schaffer 2010) that Ficino settles upon for reasons given below.

#1 is hardly coherent with Jung, so it need not detain us. It should be noted, however, that this maneuver only trades the HPN for the CP anyway, since it proposes that wholes do not exist but the *idea* of wholes (illusionary though they may be) *do*, therefore we are still left with the question of how that is accomplished.[7]

Which leads us to #2, which argues that the parts "create" the unity of the whole. This is essentially an emergentist sort of position, and again, it does seem reasonable on the surface. #2 proposes that qualia/mind are somehow generated by the properties of the parts in themselves (whether they be atoms, neurons, or proto-consciousnesses associated with such things). As mentioned, this solution faces either the HPN and the BP, or the CP. But by now we can see that the problem is the reductive element.

As Ficino put it, un-unified parts creating the unity of the whole is an absurd condition, since it supposes that unity is being brought about by plurality, which is the opposite of unity. Hence we have Ficino's defense of strong holism. The reductive assumption proposes that the unity of any whole must somehow be divided up piecemeal into each part. But this creates the problem of discerning what combines *them* into a whole aside from just jamming them together—in other words, the CP, HPN, and BP arise. Proto-unities must still be united by something to create unities, and the word "emergence" does not magically dispel this problem or get us out of the game. Saying that combining the parts causes the emergence of a coherent whole is simply observing that as a system evolves it appears to become more unified. That's an observation, not an explanation. We are still missing the essential explanatory entity that must unite all the proto-unities. Thus, *whatever it is that unites parts into wholes must itself be unified already*. And this principle, whatever it is, must be incorporeal, otherwise it would be divisible into parts and we would be back to square one. Thus proposing that wholes have an irreducible quality to them requires that we dispense with even an emergentist account of #2.

The problem with #3 is that it appears to suggest that wholes unify themselves before they exist. Not only that, just from a practical standpoint, we know from physics that each particle (electron, neutron, etc.) that makes up an object could theoretically make up any other object in existence from ice cream cones to nuclear missiles. Fundamental particles don't appear to have any qualitative characteristics to them. There seems therefore to be nothing unique in the parts we know about that make it specific to any particular whole. And in any case, wholes assembling themselves appear to involve backward causation—awkward. So #3 seems insufficient to account for the unity of wholes also.

Which leaves us with the conclusion that in order to avoid the HPN, BP, and CP we must assume #4, our only remaining obvious alternative: not only do wholes contain a pervasive unity to them, this unity does not come from the parts nor the whole itself but from something else entirely. Furthermore, logically, it must be already unified and non-corporeal. It therefore must be *a priori* if we wish to avoid the above problems. And whatever it is, this unifying factor manifests as quale-free particles organize through their countless circular mechanical interactions in such a way that the *holistic and irreducible qualities of the system* become evident. Remember, we are not talking about what organizes the parts in themselves—that is well known and characterized by the laws of physics and chemistry—we are asking what brings their *irreducible perceptual holistic qualities* into being as the parts assemble, whether by self-organization or through the actions of a craftsman possessed with an idea. The physicalist is constrained to keep looking at the parts for the answer to this question. And note that we cannot simply say "the brain" either, because the brain is also a system of interacting parts connected through observation to whatever system is being observed. The HPN, CP, and BP express how this doesn't help account for irreducible holistic qualities. The physicalist must either deny such qualities are real or simply leave it unanswerable since he is constrained to keep looking to the parts to provide an answer. The neutral monist is not so constrained, however, because one says such holistic qualities are pre-existent in the neutral substance, though they still need some factor to manifest them. So what is the needed factor? What mysterious creative force has such power to make manifest the irreducible holistic qualities of aggregates of interacting parts, but is not itself a part or a whole? While other ways of explaining it may exist, for our purposes the holistic and Neoplatonic concept of the archetype works well since Jung borrowed, refined and psychologized the concept to such a great extent.

Archetype

When viewed in this light, we can see that Jung's archetype—in its most mature form—is a natural evolution of the Neoplatonic metaphysical archetype, even if Jung never quite committed himself to that label for whatever reason. But regardless, Jung obviously had something Neoplatonic in mind insofar as he referred to the archetype as "an explanatory paraphrase of the Platonic εἶδος" (Jung, *CW*, 9, para 5). But instead of arguing for the logical necessity of the archetype in terms of a holistic neutral-monist metaphysics of mind as I have done here, Jung proposed the archetype as an empirical concept, to be demonstrated through experimental inquiry. But the insistence that the archetype is a hypothetical entity that should be demonstrable through empirical evidence rather than as a philosophical concept to be defended through metaphysical analysis, Jung clouded the discussion of the archetype unnecessarily. Since the archetype is a foundational metaphysical concept, such a task would be like asking a physicalist to "prove that matter exists." Metaphysical concepts aren't "proven," they are foundational givens. Such concepts are then evaluated for how much they are able to explain without contradiction or quandary.

In any case, our goal was to situate Jung into a metaphysics that best cohered with his psychology, so as to put his ideas into the cleanest and least contradictory conceptual footing. Working through the options, we see that every choice entails a certain number of classic problems. The physicalist faces the HPN, the reductive neutral monist faces the CP. For a classically Jungian theory, the most agreeable metaphysics seems to be holistic neutral monism, which requires the concept of the archetype to be coherent but avoids the HPN, BP, and CP. The archetype in this system becomes a conceptual necessity, rather than a thing constructed by matter or mini-mentalities: having identified that wholes exist and must possess some kind of unifying characteristic that inheres neither in the part nor in the whole, but is incorporeal and pre-existent (lest we tempt the HPN, BP, and CP), we need a foundational given to explain such facts. Since the archetype as Jung defined it fits this bill very well, there is no particular need to "demonstrate" that it exists empirically. We already know it must because of our metaphysical position—that is, unless we wish to shift our metaphysics to a different system that does not require them—a maneuver some theorists, in fact, do. But, whether acknowledged or not, doing this purchases the HPN, BP, and/or the CP. If we don't want those plaguing us, we can defend the archetype as a conceptual move that allows us to avoid the HPN, BP, and CP as an explanation of irreducible wholes, including lived experiences and archetypal (and indeed all other sorts of) images.

All metaphysical systems begin with unexplainable givens; otherwise there would be an infinite regress of explanations (Aristotle, 1960). Because they are part of the metaphysics, the archetypes provide tools for explanation in holistic neutral-monist systems, but in themselves do not require explanation, just as physicalist systems do not need to explain the existence of matter and its properties. Archetypes, in this paradigm of holistic neutral monism, are simply the organizational principles that are behind the formation and behavior of wholes, which includes consciousness, and indeed the mind. They are pre-existent and incorporeal by necessity. In other words, archetypes, not the properties of isolated particles, or micro-proto-mentalities (which would be unexplainable givens in their respective systems) give us unified consciousness, qualia, and so forth. Of course, some theorists have already noticed that the archetype has much in common with mathematical principles of organization,[8] which interestingly enough are also *a priori* and noncorporeal.

In any case, as far as universe building goes, this holistic approach proposes that the unity of wholes must derive not from isolated parts but from archetypes, and parts derive from wholes through partition. But for partition, unlike whole-forming, there is no "hard problem." Parts simply come from breaking up pre-existing wholes. It should be noted, of course, that the adoption of this metaphysical system means that everything in the universe must necessarily be derived through partition (or "emanation") from the ur-archetype that organizes the entire universe as the ontologically first whole: what Plato called The One (Plato, 1996, 2001, 2007; see also Plotinus, 1917/2007, and Proclus, 1963, 2015; but see also Aristotle, 1960, and Loux, 1998). In a holistic system, in fact, micro-particles are shifted from primary unmoved movers to the most derivative things in the universe, arrived at after the One has been partitioned as far as possible, leaving successive and irreducible holistic qualities behind with each partition. Jung, it appears, already intuited the necessity of this situation:

> ...the idea of the *unus mundus* [the single, holistic ontological reality] is founded on the assumption that the multiplicity of the empirical world rests on an underlying unity...everything divided and different belongs to one and the same world.
>
> (Jung, 1955, para 767)

If he had more clearly presented his metaphysical position, this statement might not seem so obscure and mysterious. In any case, as universe building goes, partitioning out the One as opposed to building up the universe from micro-parts comes without any annoying HPN, CP, or BP, but it does require an essentially Neoplatonic metaphysics complete with archetypes as unmoved movers rather than micro-particles. It also situates us on the Platonic side of the classic problem of universals (Loux, 1998). Naturally, some may find this move unpalatable or counterintuitive. Nevertheless, it seems to fit Jung's theory quite well, and one may consider it preferable to the HPN, CP, and BP that results from reductive approaches that also require a redefining of the archetype as a derivative rather than foundational principle.

Conclusion: Neoplatonic Neutral Monism May Organize Classical Jungian Theory Best

This notion of the archetypes as *a priori* neutral metaphysical principles that simultaneously order psyche and matter is coherent with Jung's most mature notion of archetype that he described late in his life, particularly after his long correspondence with physicist Wolfgang Pauli (Atmanspacher, 2012), who like Jung likens the archetype to the Platonic idea (Pauli, 1948). Further coherent with Jung is the idea of a psychophysically neutral and unitary wholeness to the universe that is ontologically prior, from which all parts are derived (rather than the other way around). In his late works, Jung equates this notion with the *Unus Mundus* concept (as we saw) developed by the sixteenth century alchemist Gerard Dorn (Jung, 1955, para 767; see Schaffer 2010 for a modern philosophical defense of the idea of holistic monism), further situating us in the Neoplatonic realm.

Clearly the present chapter merely scratches the surface of how this could all be worked out more thoroughly. Ultimately, however, we can see that these considerations require that Jungians make some potentially impactful decisions about what sort of metaphysical framework we wish to position Jung's theory into. The debate on whether or not archetypes are *a priori* is but one example of how metaphysical assumptions can be at the heart of an issue even when they are not fully addressed or acknowledged. Which metaphysical option is preferable to Jungians should be the subject of subsequent discussion, naturally, in full light of all the options. There may even be an Aristotelian middle ground between top-down archetypes and bottom-up emergence that can be worked out. In any case, each option comes with a number of conceptual consequences that shape the way Jung's theory will develop in the future.

Notes

1 I am not including idealist-monism (i.e., that the mental is the only substance and that the physical world is constituted by the consciousness of an observing agent) such as that of Berkeley (Clarke, 2009) despite its potential validity since, as Chalmers argues (2002), this ontology leaves complex regularities of phenomenal states basically unexplainable. Since Jung had apparently no interest in such a framework, exploring this ontology would detain us unnecessarily.
2 Important contributions to the identity theory discussion can be found in Davidson (1970), Feigl (1958), Kripke (1980), Place (1956), and Putnam (1968, 1973).
3 See Atmanspacher (2014) for a summary of these concepts and Neoplatonic connections and Solms and Turnbull (2002) for an application of it to psychodynamic theory.
4 The physicalism of these authors is implied rather than explicitly stated. Since their metaphysical standpoint is never spelled out it is difficult to say for certain where they are coming from and what they view mind to actually be. Thus, it is possible their intent was not to assume a physicalist metaphysics.
5 Responses to Nagel have been many; some examples are Churchland (1996), Levine (1983), Maxwell (1978), and Rosenthal (2002).
6 McGinn (1989) goes so far as to warn against "magical emergentism."
7 Appleby (2014) points out many other ways in which eliminativism assumes a number of Cartesian dualistic ideas, and therefore inherits the essential problems with the radical reductionism involved in both physicalism and Cartesian dualism. See also Kelly et al. (2000) for many more problems with reductive approaches to the mind.
8 McDowell's (2001) work deserves special attention here; see also Freeman (2000) and Kelso (1995) for details on the brain-oriented complexity theory upon which McDowell's work is based.

References

Appleby, M. (2014). Mind and Matter: A Critique of Cartesian Thinking. In Atmanspacher & Fuchs (Eds.) *The Pauli-Jung Conjecture and its Impact Today*. La Vergne: Ingram Books, 7–36.

Aristotle. (1960). *Metaphysics*. Michigan, MI: University of Michigan Press.

Atmanspacher, H. (2012a). *Dual-aspect Monism a la Pauli and Jung Perforates the Completeness of Physics. Quantum Theory: Reconsideration of Foundations*, 6 (1508), 5–21.

Atmanspacher, H. (2012b). Dual-aspect Monism a la Pauli and Jung. *Journal of Consciousness Studies*, 19(9–10), 1–22.

Atmanspacher, H. (2014a). 20th Century Variants of Dual-Aspect Thinking. *Mind and Matter*, 12(2), 245–288.

Atmanspacher, H. (2014b). Notes on Psychophysical Phenomena. In Atmanspacher & Fuchs (Eds.) *The Pauli-Jung Conjecture and its Impact Today*. La Vergne: Ingram Books, 181–197.

Bohm, D. (2010). A New Theory of the Relationship of Mind and Matter. *Philosophical Psychology*, 3 (2), 217–286.

Brentano, F. (1874 [1995]). The Distinction Between Mental and Physical Phenomena. In Terrell, Rancurello & McAlister (Eds.) *Psychology from an Empirical Standpoint*. New York: Routledge.

Cambray, J. (2014). German Romantic Influences on Jung and Pauli. In Atmanspacher & Fuchs (Eds.) *The Pauli-Jung Conjecture and its Impact Today*. La Vergne: Ingram Books.

Chalmers, D.J. (1996). *The Conscious Mind*. New York: Oxford University Press.

Chalmers, D.J. (2012). Consciousness and its Place in Nature. In Chalmers (Ed.), *Philosophy of Mind: Classical and Contemporary Readings*. New York: Oxford University Press.

Chalmers, D.J. (2016). The Combination Problem for Panpsychism. In Chalmers (Ed.), *Panpsychism*. Oxford: Oxford University Press, pp. 179–215.

Chisolm, R.M. (1957). *Perceiving*. New York: Cornell University Press.

Churchland, P. (1981). Eliminative Materialism and the Propositional Attitudes. *Journal of Philosophy*, 78: 67–90.

Churchland, P. (1996). The Rediscovery of Light. *Journal of Philosophy*, 93: 211–228.

Clarke, D. (Ed.). (2009). *Berkeley: Philosophical Writings*. New York: Cambridge University Press.

Corcoran, K. (2001). *Soul, Body and Survival*. London: Cornell University Press.

Davidson, D. (1970). Mental Events. In Foster & Swanson (Eds.), *Experience and Theory*. London: Humanities Press.

Dennett, D.C. (1981). True Believers. In Heath (Ed.) *Scientific Explanations*. Oxford: Oxford University Press.

Dennett, D.C. (1988). Quining Qualia. In A. Marcel & E. Bisiach (Eds.) *Consciousness in Contemporary Science*. New York: Oxford University Press.

Dennett, D.C. (1992). *Consciousness Explained*. New York: Back Bay Books.

Descartes, R. (1985). *Meditations on First Philosophy*. New York: Cambridge University Press.

Ellenberger, H.E. (1970). *The Discovery of the Unconscious: The History and Evolution of Dynamic Psychiatry*. New York: Basic Books.

Feigl, H. (1958). The "Mental" and the "Physical". In Feigl, Scriven, & Maxwell (Eds.), *Concepts, Theories and the Mind-Body Problem*. Minnesota, MN: University of Minnesota Press.

Ficino, M. (2001). *Platonic Theology*. Cambridge, MA: Harvard University Press.

Freeman, W. (2000). *How Brains Make Up Their Minds*. New York: Columbia University Press.

Goodwyn, E. (2012). *The Neurobiology of the Gods*. New York: Routledge.

Goodwyn, E. (2013). Recurrent Motifs as Resonant Attractor States in the Narrative Field: A Testable Model of Archetype. *Journal of Analytical Psychology*, 58: 387–408.

Hogenson, G.B. (2009). Archetypes as Action Patterns. *Journal of Analytical Psychology*, 54 (3), 325–337.

Hogenson, G.B. (2014). Are Synchronicities Really Dragon Kings? In Atmanspacher & Fuchs (Eds.) *The Pauli-Jung Conjecture and its Impact Today*. La Vergne: Ingram Books, 201–216.

Horgan, T. (1993). From Supervenience to Superdupervenience. *Mind*, 102: 555–586.

James, W. (1950). *The Principles of Psychology*. New York: Dover.

Jung, C.G. (1954). *The Structure and Dynamics of the Psyche. CW*, 8.

Jung, C.G. (1955). *Mysterium Coniunctionis. CW*, 14.

Kelley, E.F., Kelly, E.W., Crabtree, A., Gauld, A., Grosso, M. & Greyson, B. (Eds.). (2010). *Irreducible Mind*. New York: Rowman and Littlefield.

Kelso, S. (1995). *Dynamic Patterns: The Self-Organization of Brain and Behavior*. Cambridge, MA: The MIT Press.

Kim, J. (1992). Multiple Realization and the Metaphysics of Reduction. *Philosophy and Phenomenological Research*, 52: 1–26.

Kripke, S. (1980). *Naming and Necessity*. Cambridge, MA: Harvard University Press.

Koons, R.C. & Bealer, G. (Eds.). (2010). *The Waning of Materialism*. New York: Oxford University Press.

Levine, J. (1983). Materialism and Qualia. In Chalmers (Ed.), *Philosophy of Mind: Classical and Contemporary Readings*. New York: Oxford University Press, pp. 354–361.

Loux, M.J. (1998). *Metaphysics*. New York: Routledge.

MacLennan, B. (2005). Evolution, Jung and Theurgy: Their Role in Modern Neoplatonism. In Finamore & Berchman (Eds.) *History of Platonism: Plato Redivivus*. University Press of the South, pp. 305–322.

Maxwell, G. (1978). Rigid Designators and Mind-Brain Identity. In Savage (Ed.) *Perception and Cognition*. Minnesota, MN: University of Minnesota Press.

McDowell, M.J. (2001). Principle of Organization: A Dynamic-Systems View of the Archetype-as-Such. *Journal of Analytical Psychology*, 46, 637–654.

McGinn, C. (1989). Can We Solve the Mind-Body Problem? *Mind*, 98: 349–366.

Morgan, M.L. & Shirley, S. (Eds.). (2002). *Spinoza: Complete Works*. New York: Hackett Publishing.

Nagel, T. (1974). What is it Like to Be a Bat? *Philosophical Review*, 83: 435–450, quote in Chalmers (ed.), *Philosophy of Mind: Classical and Contemporary Readings*. New York: Oxford University Press, pp. 219–225.

Pauli, W. (1948). Letter to Fierz of January 7, 35: 469–497.

Peacocke, C. (1983). Sensation and the Content of Experience. In Sense & Content. Oxford: Oxford University Press, Chapter 1.

Place, U.T. (1956). Is Consciousness a Brain Process? *British Journal of Psychology*, 47: 44–50.

Plato (1996). *Parmenides*. Whitaker (trans.). Newburyport: Focus.

Plato (2001). *Timaeus*. Kalkavage (trans.). Newburyport: Focus.

Plato (2007). *The Republic*. New York: Penguin.

Plotinus (1917/2007). *The Six Enneads of Plotinus*. New York: Forgotten Books.

Proclus (1963). *The Elements of Theology*. Oxford: Clarendon.

Proclus (2015). *Platonic Theology*. New York: Andesite Press.

Putnam, H. (1968). Brains and Behavior. In Butler (Ed.) *Analytical Philosophy: Second Series*. New York: Blackwell.

Putnam, H. (1973). Psychological Predicates. In Capitan & Merrill (Eds.) *Art, Mind and Religion*. Pittsburgh, PN: University of Pittsburgh Press.

Rosenthal, D.M. (2002). Explaining Consciousness. In Chalmers (Ed.), *Philosophy of Mind: Classical and Contemporary Readings*. New York: Oxford University Press, pp. 406–421.

Ryle, G. (1949). Descartes' Myth. In Hutchinson (Ed.) *The Concept of Mind.* Oxford: University of Oxford.

Schaffer, J. (2010). Monism: The Priority of the Whole. *Philosophical Review*, 119: 31–76.

Solms, M. & Turnbull, O. (2002). *The Brain and the Inner World.* New York: Other Press.

Yablo, S. (1992). Mental Causation. *Philosophical Review*, 101: 245–280.

Chapter 4

Empiricism, Skepticism, and Belief in Jung's Epistemology

Marco Heleno Barreto

Time and again Jung insisted that he was not a philosopher, but just an empiricist, dealing only with facts. He believed that "the empiricist must forswear an intellectual clarification of his concepts such as is absolutely imperative for the philosopher," because the thinking of an empiricist "has to mould itself to the facts, and the facts have as a rule a distressingly irrational character which proves refractory to any kind of philosophical systematization" (Jung, 1935a, p. 770 [*CW*, 18, § 1731]).[1] He believed that the "systematization of thought" was an absolute condition for considering a thought as belonging to philosophy. And, besides the alluded irrational character of the facts, "the unrelieved strain of the psychotherapeutic situation, with its host of impressions and emotional disturbances, [does not] leave us [as psychotherapists] much leisure for the systematization of thought" (Jung, 1943, p. 79 [*CW*, 16, § 181]). Hence, he was convinced that his thought was not philosophical, but rather wholly rooted in "scientific empiricism": "I approach psychological matters from a scientific and not from a philo-sophical standpoint" (Jung, 1938/1940, p. 6 [*CW*, 11, § 2]). In brief: "empiricism" was for Jung the hallmark of a scientific approach.

On the other hand, Jung envisaged psychology as "a knowing of the knower and an experiencing of the experiment" (Jung, 1935a, p. 772 [*CW*, 18, § 1733]), and explicitly acknowledged in this kind of psychology the "indirect influence of the type of mind exempli-fied by Hume, Berkeley, and Kant" (ibid. [*CW*, 18, § 1734]). Leaving aside the suggestion of a simplifying and thus disputable inclusion of Kant within the same empiricist tradition of Hume and Berkeley—that, by the way, reveals the bias through which Kant is appropriated by Jung—it is clear that Jung acknowledges a connection of psych-ology with modern philosophical empiricism. Now, the twin brother of modern empiricism is skepticism—and, as is well known, David Hume, mentioned by Jung, is the accomplished instance of modern skepticism, as the logical outcome of the empiricist tradition. This means that, even granting that psychology is not philosophy, from the standpoint of the theory of knowledge Jung's psychological empiricist stance should be defined as a skeptical one.

However, interestingly enough, there is extremely scarce explicit reference to the skeptical setup of analytical psychology.[2] If one consults the general index of Jung's *Collected Works*, as well as the index of his letters and of the seminars, there is no entry related to "skepticism" and/or its correlates. As far as I know, there is only one explicit passage, in a letter to Bernhard Lang dated 8 June 1957, in which Jung refers to his own epistemological stance as being that of "apparent skepticism":

> One can say of all metaphysical statements that their factuality consists in the fact of their being asserted, but none of them can be proved to be true or untrue. It does not come within the scope of a science like psychology to ascertain the truth or untruth of metaphysical assertions. It is a thoroughly outmoded standpoint, and has been so ever since the time of Immanuel Kant, to think that it lies within the power of man to assert a metaphysical truth....My apparent skepticism is only a recognition of the epistemological barrier.
>
> (Jung, 1976, p. 368)[3]

One should note that, despite Jung's own expression, the skepticism described in this passage is not *apparent*: it corresponds exactly to what in the philosophical tradition is called *metaphysical skepticism*. This is the form that skepticism takes when applied to assertions referred to the domain of reality supposedly transcendent to the realm of empirical phenomena, even when the former is thought of as being the deeper structuring reality underlying the latter. By definition, a metaphysical entity or structure cannot be perceived by the senses: it is supersensible, and thus not reachable by sensory experience alone. Consequently, from the outset its knowledge is ruled out by an empiricist stance, within which reality is defined in terms of sensory data and its correlate experience. What Jung calls "the recognition of the epistemological barrier" is simply a statement of his empiricist conception, which is grounded in a very concrete (not simply apparent) metaphysical skepticism. The adoption of the Kantian interdiction to metaphysical assertions within the realm of science is a constant feature of Jung's epistemological standpoint.

But the skeptical stance in Jung is not restricted to the form of metaphysical skepticism. Leaving aside the delimited field of hypothetical metaphysical entities, Jung's skepticism also encompasses the knowledge related to the realm of objects liable to experience—the phenomenal realm—and here it can be summarized by the statement that human knowledge does not reach the *truth* of any phenomenon whatsoever. Here his stance can be described as being what the philosophical tradition generically calls an *epistemic skepticism*. This form of skepticism is not represented in Kant's theory of knowledge (though there are some interpreters who can object to this).

Jung quotes a maxim by Multatuli (a pseudonym for the nineteenth-century Dutch writer, Edward Douwes Dekker): "Nothing is quite true, and even that is not quite true" (Jung, 1934/1950, p. 344 [*CW*, 9i, § 607]; see also Jung, 1976, pp. 334, 521, and 595).[4] He explicitly subscribes to this maxim: "I have made it a rule to apply Multatuli's wise statement" (Jung, 1976, p. 334). Indeed: Jung bluntly declares that the question of truth "is unanswerable anyway and for epistemological reasons has long since become obsolete. Human knowledge has to be content with constructing models which are 'probable'—it would be thoughtless presumption to demand more" (Jung, 1958a, p. 453 [*CW*, 10, § 853]). Here the overcoming of the Kantian notion of science by Jung is evident, and it is performed along contemporary skeptical lines. Despite his claims of a Kantian epistemological standpoint, Jung updated his conception of science in terms of a non-Kantian *skeptical probabilism*: "science gives us only an average picture of the world, but not a true one" (Jung, 1958b, p. 500 [*CW*, 18, § 1188]). He was attentive to and in tune with the transformations in the theory and in the practice of the contemporary sciences, which had as a result a notion of scientificity—and thus of an epistemological stance—very different from the Newtonian paradigm known by Kant:

> Our science … is based upon the principle of causality, and causality is considered to be an axiomatic truth. But a great change in our standpoint is setting in. What Kant's *Critique of Pure Reason*

failed to do is being accomplished by modern physics. The axioms of causality are being shaken to their foundations: we know now that what we term natural laws are merely statistical truths and thus must necessarily allow for exceptions. We have not sufficiently taken into account as yet that we need the laboratory with its incisive restrictions in order to demonstrate the invariable validity of natural law. If we leave things to nature, we see a very different picture: every process is partially or totally interfered with by chance, so much so that under natural circumstances a course of events absolutely conforming to specific laws is almost an exception.

(Jung, 1950, pp. 590–591 [*CW*, 11, § 967])

Note that in this passage Jung points to a *failure* in Kant's *Critique of Pure Reason*, and this alleged failure refers to the way Kant conceived of both "the axioms of causality" and "natural laws." The "volatilization of our material world" performed by modern physics (see Jung, 1928/1931a, p. 89 [*CW*, 10, § 182]) is at the heart of the non-Kantian skeptical definition of scientific truth in statistical terms, which Jung accepts unreservedly.

Jung's epistemic skepticism is even stronger when it comes to psychology in particular. Due to the unavoidable circumstance that in psychological knowledge the object is the subject himself, so that there is no Archimedean point upon which to build psychology, Jung declares that we have to be epistemologically modest:

Not that I believe for a moment that I am absolutely right. Nobody is absolutely right in psychological matters. Never forget that in psychology the *means* by which you judge and observe the psyche is the *psyche* itself... ... In psychology the observer is the observed. The psyche is not only the *object* but also the *subject* of our science. So you see, it is a vicious circle and we have to be very modest. The best we can expect in psychology is that everybody puts his cards on the table and admits: "I handle things in such and such a way, and this is how I see them." Then we can compare notes.

(Jung, 1935b, p. 126 [*CW*, 18, § 277])

The epistemic modesty is a further sign of Jung's skepticism, and, as the passage above can confirm, through the suggestion of an inevitable *subjective perspectivism* ("this is how I see things") it is intimately connected with his theory of psychological types. As is well known, the skeptical tradition in modern philosophy pays special attention to the essential role of subjective structuring patterns in the production of knowledge. At the origin of Jung's idea of psychological types is his honest admission of the relative validity both of Freud's and Adler's viewpoints. This led him to realize the determining role of the psychological type in psychological knowledge. To Jung, typology does not aim at statistical classification, but is "designed, first and foremost, as an aid to a psychological critique of knowledge" (Jung, 1959, p. 471 [*CW*, 10, § 890]).[5]

The impact of typology on psychology's epistemological profile can be felt in Jung's proposal of a "purely phenomenological point of view" within the field of psychology as "the only possible one and the only one with any prospect of success," due to "the enormous complexity of psychic phenomena" (Jung, 1941, p. 182 [*CW*, 9i, § 308]). Jung's phenomenology is presented in empiricist and typological terms:

> Psychic phenomena occasioned by unconscious processes are so rich and so multifarious that I prefer to *describe* my findings and observations and, where possible, to classify them—that is, to arrange them under certain definite types. That is the method of natural science, and it is applied wherever we have to do with multifarious and still unorganized material. One may question the utility or the appropriateness of the categories or types used in the arrangement, but not the correction of the method itself.
>
> (Jung, 1941, pp. 182–183 [*CW*, 9i, § 308])

This calls to mind not only the theory of psychological types, but especially that of archetypes. In the light of this passage, the theory of archetypes could be considered as a methodological as well as a theoretical device, and thus archetypes would have the epistemological status of those "models which are 'probable'" (Jung, 1958, p. 453 [*CW*, 10, § 853]). "The empiricist," says Jung, "must therefore content himself with a theoretical 'as if'" (Jung, 1936/1954, p. 70 [*CW*, 9i, § 143]).

However, Jung goes far beyond this epistemologically humble position, and resolutely affirms archetypes as objective realities found in experience: the methodological and heuristic standpoint gives way to an ontological claim. This leap is epistemologically problematic, and imposes a further qualification in Jung's epistemic skepticism.

The unconscious dimension of the psyche leads Jung to state that he cannot know what the psyche is: "When I say 'Psyche' I mean something unknown, to which I give the name 'Psyche'" (Jung, 1976, p. 583). "I absolutely don't know what [the psyche] is in itself and know only very vaguely what it is *not*" (Jung, 1976, p. 69). But one should note that, despite the epistemic modesty displayed in such statements, it is clear that an ontological status is given to the psyche: it is *something*. The same ontological attribution is extended to the archetypes: "We do not know what an archetype is (i.e., consists of), since the nature of the psyche is inaccessible to us, but we know that archetypes exist and work" (Jung, 1954, p. 694 [*CW*, 18, § 1567]). Here it is obvious that archetypes are not merely interpretative models for classifying morphological similarities in psychic phenomena: the archetype is presented as a *thing*, a *positivity* or an *entity*—even if this entity is thought of as being unknowable in its nature or essence.

Sometimes Jung tells us that he considers the "collective unconscious," in a certain sense, as analogous to Kant's *Ding an sich*: a negative borderline concept (see Jung, 1973, p. 91). But then he transgresses explicitly his praised Kantian "epistemological barrier," and states that this conceptually negative status of the collective unconscious "cannot prevent us from framing ... hypotheses about its possible nature as though it were an object of human experience. But we do not know whether the unconscious *an sich* is unlimited, whether it is experience-able in part or not at all. It could be absolute, i.e., inexperienceable" (ibid.). The seeming skeptical epistemic caution conveyed in these last statements does not quite match the bold decision to frame hypotheses about a dubious *entity*, whose empirical status is highly disputable, not to say that it is forbidden from the Kantian perspective of the negative borderline concept. It is all too obvious that Jung is speculating about something—the unconscious *an sich*—whose knowledge is not granted by experience alone. In so doing, he transforms the "negative border-line concept" into a "descriptive" or "empirical" concept, and toys with the idea or possibility that it could be "an object of human experience."

After this epistemological leap, Jung can submit that the archetype "is not so much a working hypothesis as something that is found" (Jung, 1973, p. 418). What gives him courage to perform such a bold leap is the "*dynamic* background" (see Jung, 1976, p. 259), which accompanies the psychic experience from which archetypes are inferred—in other words, the perceptible (and even in certain cases experimentally measurable) quantum of energy (psychic energy, libido) characteristic of any psychic activity. This dynamic aspect leads Jung to temper his skeptical stance with the ontological (and fundamental) premise of the *Wirklichkeit der Seele*.[6] This premise is plausible, reasonable, and based on the empirical effectiveness of the psychic activity, but it tends to obscure the fact that there is a *realist hermeneutical decision* involved in the interpretation of the psychic phenomena stemming from that activity—which backs up the positing of the *Wirklichkeit der Seele*—as the manifestation of ontological, substantial entities called "archetypes" (or, for that matter, *the* psyche, *die* Seele).[7] There is a gap between the psychic phenomena and the ontological entities (archetypes, or *the* psyche itself) posited to account for them. And this gap is overlooked in the statement that "we know that archetypes exist and work." This means that Jung's skepticism does not reach the fullest strength and radicalness known in certain lines of the skeptical tradition. Therefore, the most accurate description of his epistemological stance, according to the conventional terms adopted in the scholarship on skepticism, is that of a *mitigated epistemic skepticism*. (What mitigates his skepticism is precisely the premise of an ontological reality called "soul/psyche" which, even being declared unknowable *in itself*, is nonetheless presented as *something* found in experience—but how can one claim to experience something, and then declare that it is "unknowable in itself," without necessarily positing a noumenal metaphysical entity beyond the experienceable, and thus beyond one's alleged empiricism?).[8]

I believe that this is enough to substantiate the thesis concerning Jung's skeptical epistemic stance, as well as to indicate how he mitigates the power of his skepticism by introducing ontological presuppositions not backed up by experience alone. On the other hand, and somewhat in tune with the mitigating attitude exposed above, one can find in Jung an explicit critical stance towards skepticism, considered to be just a manifestation of the "gambling intellect" (see Jung, 1976, pp. 595–596, quoted below). Furthermore, one of the most famous statements ever made by Jung—the astonishing answer to John Freeman's question about whether he believed in God: "I don't need to believe. I know"—at first sight conveys the impression of a strong gnostic stance, diametrically opposed to a skeptical position. And finally, relativism—one of the constant elements of the skeptical form of consciousness—is considered by Jung both as an inevitable feature of modernity and a problem to be overcome.[9] This forces us to examine the issue of Jung's epistemological skeptic stance from a broader perspective, which will allow us to understand why, on that single occasion in which he explicitly mentions his skepticism, he dismisses it as being merely apparent.

In a letter to Vera von Lier-Schmidt Ernsthausen, dated April 25, 1952, Jung declares: "I practice psychology in the first place as a science, in the second place as an instrument of psychotherapy" (Jung, 1976, p. 56). In this statement we can find the two dimensions, which constitute the whole field of analytical psychology: the theoretical and the practical. Jung presents these two dimensions as intrinsically related, due to his claim to a scientific empiricism. His psychological science is supposedly informed by the "facts" or "experiences," which constitute the bulk of the psychotherapeutic situation, focused on the psychic activity. Conversely, the psychotherapeutic praxis will be informed by the theoretical constructs (or alleged "empirical concepts") established in psychology as a science, as the hermeneutic framework which provides some orientation to the psychotherapist in the confrontation with psychic phenomena. "Empirical concepts," says Jung, "are concerned for the most part with the chaos of chance events, because it is their function to produce a provisional order amid the disorder of the phenomenal world" (Jung, 1935a, p. 770 [CW, 18, § 1731]).

Nonetheless, there is a problematic tension between these two levels—science and psychotherapy, theoretical understanding and pragmatic goal (psychotherapeutic healing), from the epistemological standpoint. Though being related, at a closer and critical look they are neither simply coincident nor smoothly articulated in Jung's thought. The skeptical mindset of the scientist/psychologist, who states that "the question of truth ... is unanswerable anyway and for epistemological reasons has long since become obsolete" (Jung, 1958a, p. 453 [CW, 10, § 853]), is not transposed *tout court* to the psychotherapeutic situation, as conceived of by this very same skeptical thinker. Let us see why:

> The intellect can make its profound statement that there is no absolute Truth. But if somebody loses his money, his money is lost

and this is as good as an absolute Truth, which means that he will not be consoled by intellectual profundity. There is a thing like convincing Truth but we have lost sight of it, owing the loss mostly to our gambling intellect, to which we sacrifice our moral certainty and gain thereby nothing but an inferiority-complex.

(Jung, 1976, pp. 595–596).

The denial of an absolute truth is indicative of skeptical relativism, and Jung attributes it to "our gambling intellect"—which is thus a skeptically informed intellect. This skeptical intellect is responsible for the loss not only of absolute truth, but also of its surrogate, which is declared to be as good as absolute truth: *convincing truth*. This calls to mind the final paragraphs of Jung's 1937 Terry Lectures on psychology and religion, where one can see that Jung's absolute/convincing truth is to be found in *experience*: "Religious experience is absolute; it cannot be disputed. You can only say that you have never had such an experience, whereupon your opponent will reply: 'Sorry, I have.' And there your discussion will come to an end" (Jung, 1938/1940, pp. 104–105 [*CW*, 11, § 167]).

From the psychological standpoint established by Jung, religious experience is a particular form of psychological experience at large, a form that has numinosity as its specific distinctive feature. Jung uses the expression "immediate experience" only with reference to religious/numinous experience, as a supposedly immediate experience of "psychological archetypes" (see Jung, 1938/1940, p. 89 [*CW*, 11, § 148]). However, there is no formal or structural difference between a numinous dream, for instance, and any archetypally structured dream: both are direct experiences of the "psychic background"—and not all archetypal psychic events are loaded with the typical numinous feeling described by Rudolf Otto and enthusiastically admitted by Jung. Therefore, we can say that *any* experience of such archetypal background is "immediate," in Jung's sense.[10]

Now, on the one hand, epistemologically and in psychology as a science, Jung subscribes to the skeptical stance, as we have seen; on the other hand, in psychology as an instrument of psychotherapy, he is concerned with the healing power of *convincing* psychic experiences. But he opposes the skeptic "gambling" intellect to the psychotherapeutically precious convincing truth. In other words: we find in Jung a conflict between the skeptic consciousness which produces the psychological knowledge and the psychotherapeutic requirements for psychic healing, based on the convincing truth conveyed by the experience of the "psychic background."

Furthermore, according to Jung the skeptic intellect is responsible for the sacrifice of our *moral certainty*. The ethical dimension is absolutely fundamental in Jung's psychotherapeutic conception (see Barreto, 2018). In a letter to E.L. Grant Watson, dated February 9, 1956, Jung states that a philosophy exclusively based upon natural science "is not realistic but rather an abstract half-truth, which, when applied to living man, *destroys all individual values indispensable to human life*" (Jung, 1976, p. 288, my italics). Well, the effects of such philosophy are indistinguishable from those of Jung's skeptical scientific empiricism. The skeptical intellect of the psychologist who "becomes interested in ... the psychology of the vision-making process" (Sonu Shamdasani, in Hillman & Shamdasani, 2013, p. 106) establishes a difficult relation with the pragmatic standpoint of the psychotherapist who, aiming at psychological healing, counts on persuasion and moral certainty as inalienable healing factors. The last word is given to experience *against* the "intellectual profundity" of the (skeptical) "gambling intellect."

Jung opposes belief to knowledge ("I don't need to believe. I know"); but he equates knowledge with experience: "Modern man abhors faith and the religions based upon it. He holds them valid only so far as their knowledge-content seems to accord with his own experience of the psychic background. He wants to *know*—to experience for himself" (Jung, 1928/1931, p. 84 [*CW*, 10, § 171]).[11] The primacy of experience is also attributed to the "primitive" mindset: "People speak of *belief* when they have lost *knowledge*. Belief and disbelief in God are mere surrogates. The naïve primitive *doesn't believe, he knows*, because the inner experience rightly means as much to him as the outer" (Jung, 1976, p. 5). From this privileged standpoint, it becomes clear that Jung's psychotherapeutic project is that of a restitution of a primitive form of consciousness *within* the critical modern form of consciousness, through the emphasis on the "immediate experience" of the "psychic background," which supposedly corresponds to a postulated primordial experience (*Urerfahrung*), insofar as it is archetypally structured. He aims at a *seconde naïveté*.

At first sight, this is an impossible desideratum, once modern consciousness has become irrevocably *skeptical* and critical of the *naïveté* constitutive of primitive consciousness. Seen from a modern skeptical standpoint, the primitive mythic consciousness is wholly *dogmatic*, inasmuch as it does not reflect upon its own presuppositions. Jung himself knows this quite well: he equates our normal (i.e., non-critical, non-skeptical) everyday mental functioning in explaining things to that of the primitive, once this abstract "primitive," like our commonsensical consciousness, "does not examine his assumptions" (Jung, 1931a, p. 52 [*CW*, 10, § 107]).

However, through his dismissal of the "gambling (skeptical) intellect," Jung subtracts experience itself from the critical rational scrutiny definitional of the modern form of consciousness. He blocks the examination of the assumptions that are inevitably interwoven with any experience. This means that, in the last analysis, one has to perform a *sacrificium intellectus* in order to adhere to the convincing truth of "immediate experience." This sacrifice reduces the legitimate critical activity of the intellect to silence. Now, this sacrifice necessarily (even if only implicitly) brings in *belief* into the psychotherapeutic situation. As a matter of fact, belief is already housed in the apparently innocent notion of a *convincing* truth. Let us stress that an absolute truth (for instance: "2 + 2 = 4") does not need to be convincing: either one is able to grasp it rationally, or one's intellect is simply wrong. If I am only *convinced* of a certain truth, this means that I cannot prove it rationally as a compulsory and universally valid truth (such as is any absolute truth), but am just subjectively persuaded that it is true. Since antique Greek philosophy we know the name given to such "convincing truth": *doxa*, opinion, belief. Hence, Jung's "convincing truth" has the same logical status of belief. Belief is simply the hidden side of an experience from the outset immunized (dogmatically and arbitrarily) against doubt.

But Jung himself is conscious of the problem involved in the overestimation of experience/knowledge as the alternative to belief. Let us analyze one passage of his correspondence, in which this problem comes to light in a crystal-clear way:

> I dislike belief in every respect, because I want to know a thing, and then I don't have to believe it if I know it. If I don't know it,

it looks like an usurpation to say "I believe it," or the contrary. I think one ought to have at least some more or less tangible reasons for our beliefs. One should have some knowledge at least that makes a hypothesis probable. Your experience f.i. is not a convincing reason, since we have no means of establishing whether it is a hallucinated piece of memory or a real ghost. In other words, I would dismiss neither the one nor the other possibility.

(Jung, 1976, p. 445)

Here, after beginning by disparaging belief as usual, Jung admits the relation between (what he considers) "knowledge" or "more or less tangible reasons" and "beliefs", or a "hypothesis": experience should be the *convincing* basis of any legitimate belief, supported by "tangible reasons." But let us examine what follows in the quoted passage. The correspondent had seen a ghost. She had had an immediate experience of a ghost (any such experience, simply on account of being the "experience of a ghost," can be considered an archetypal event, and thus would be an "immediate experience" in Jung's terms, an experience of the "psychic background"). But then Jung is perfectly (and skeptically) sober in his assessment of that experience, and states that there are no means of establishing whether it is a hallucinated piece of memory or a real ghost. This is an admission that experience by itself is not enough to establish the "convincing truth" concerning the experienced object: it does not provide by itself a "tangible reason." And with full skeptical coherence, Jung then performs the *epoché* (suspension of judgment) concerning the two *equipollent* possibilities.[12]

But whereas a skeptic usually has no problems with adopting beliefs—consciously represented as such—as guiding practical elements in the conduct of his/her life, Jung thinks that belief is a usurpation, unless it is backed up by the (alleged) certainty conveyed by experience/"knowledge." Unfortunately for him, as the above example shows, this claim is rationally unjustifiable: there is no element in experience alone that could justify any of the two opposite beliefs. The lady presumably either could be subjectively convinced that she had seen a real ghost, provided the overwhelming nature and intensity of her experience were enough to produce such persuasion—opinion, belief, "convincing truth"; or she could simply had taken her experienced object as a hallucinated piece of memory, if the psychic strength or feeling-tone of her experience was not overwhelming. But, in both cases, experience alone would not be enough to convince *reason*.[13] Thus, the unacknowledged result of "immediate experience" is forcefully the return of belief into (or from) the heart of experience itself. Not only that: this belief requires a *sacrificium intellectus* to be effective. The absolute primacy given to immediate experience (which immunizes it from the critical activity of the "gambling intellect") *is* this very same *sacrificium intellectus*.

This means that the arrogant dismissal of belief by Jung boils down to an intellectual bravado. Were he less arrogant towards the modern skeptical "gambling intellect," he would have admitted belief as an essential ingredient in his account of the healing "immediate experience," instead of saying that he does not need to believe because he "knows" (i.e., experiences) something.[14]

But if we examine still more closely the conflict between psychology as (skeptical) science and psychology as an instrument of (dogmatically experience-based) psychotherapy in Jung, another perspective is disclosed. Concerning the alleged sacrifice of our moral certainty to the skeptic "gambling" intellect, one should remember that at the very center of the ethical dimension of the process of individuation Jung sees "the torment of ethical decision":

> For moral evaluation is always founded upon the apparent certitudes of a moral code which pretends to know precisely what is good and what is evil. But once we know how uncertain the foundation is, ethical decision becomes a subjective, creative act ... Nothing can spare us the torment of ethical decision.
>
> (Jung, 1989, pp. 329–330)

This torment by itself shows that "moral certainty" *is not* produced by any gambling of the skeptical intellect: we should say, with Jung *against* Jung, that moral *uncertainty* is constitutive of the production of consciousness:

> Our psychic processes are made up to a large extent of reflections, doubts, experiments, all of which are almost completely foreign to the unconscious, instinctive mind of primitive man.... It is just man's turning away from instinct—his opposing himself to instinct—that creates consciousness. Instinct is nature and seeks

to perpetuate nature, whereas consciousness can only seek culture or its denial.... As long as we are still submerged in nature we are unconscious, and we live in the security of instinct which knows no problem. Everything in us that still belongs to nature shrinks away from a problem, for its name is doubt, and wherever doubt holds sway there is uncertainty and the possibility of divergent ways.... There is no other way open to us; we are forced to resort to conscious decisions and solutions where formerly we trusted ourselves to natural happenings.... We want to have certainties and no doubts—results and no experiments—without even seeing that certainties can arise only through doubt and results only through experiment. The artful denial of a problem will not produce conviction; on the contrary, a wider and higher consciousness is required to give us the certainty and clarity we need.

(Jung, 1930/1931, pp. 388–389 [*CW*, 8, §§ 750–751])

The "experiment of the unconscious" (="immediate experience of the psychic background") is intrinsically permeated by doubt. Conviction ("the certainty and clarity we need") comes from doubt and experiment. Epistemic uncertainty is constitutive of the practical situation within which one has to take decisions.[15]

Not only that. Even within the psychotherapeutic experience (as a particular form of the production of consciousness), the split between the skeptical intellect and the pragmatic psychotherapeutic concerns cannot be absolute for Jung. For he proposes a *differentiation* of the experiencing subject from the images of the unconscious, which burst forth in the so-called immediate experience. This is absolutely crucial to his therapeutic stance. And this differentiation has as its background a relativizing of the *convincing* power of the images of the unconscious that constitute psychic experience. The confrontation with the unconscious, which is the paradigmatic experience for Jung's psychotherapeutic project, is a double-faced endeavor. As Sonu Shamdasani stressed, while commenting on Jung's foundational experience registered in the *Red Book*, first Jung "allows the figures to work on him. It's not he who works on the figures. He lets them instruct him. The relation shifts. ... He lets them do with him what they will" (Shamdasani, in Hillman & Shamdasani, 2013, p. 165). But, Shamdasani continues, "this is not without struggle, this is not without resistance, this is not without objections, so it's not simply giving himself over. He maintains a *skepticism* and a sense of criticism in his act of engagement" (ibid., pp. 165–166, my italics). This means, according to Shamdasani, that Jung "becomes *skeptical* of his own visions" (ibid., p. 106, my italics).

Hence one could say that, according to Jung's stance toward his own visions, one should be convinced of the truth conveyed in the "immediate experience" of the images of the unconscious, but not quite. The *sacrificium intellectus* is performed, no doubt, but, using to my purposes an image of Jung's dream of his submission to the Highest Presence (see Jung, 1989, pp. 217–220), it is not absolute, due to a (symbolic) mental reservation of "one millimeter."[16] This mental reservation is a further sign that Jung's skepticism is not entirely cancelled in his experience of the unconscious images. The skeptical intellect must not be wholly knocked out by the convincing power of the experience. After being methodologically suspended in order to allow a full and live engagement with the images and visions, it comes back and allows the establishment of the distance required to a differentiation of the experiencing subject from those images, from the vision's *mana*. Subsequently, it also allows the formulation of the psychology of the vision-making process.

All what has been said concerning Jung's mitigated epistemic skepticism, as well as the problematic tension between skeptical intellect and belief in his psychology, can find its conceptual harbor in the epistemologically decisive notion of *symbol*. In Jung's definition, a symbol is "the best possible description or formulation of a relatively unknown fact, which is nonetheless known to exist or is postulated as existing" (Jung, 1921, p. 474 [*CW*, 6, § 814]). In this definition, *consciousness* is implicitly and necessarily implied, as the cognitive pole to which the unknown fact is symbolically expressed. This constitutes the situation of an essentially symbolic experience. Consequently, the alleged "*immediate* experience" of the "psychic background" is in fact and necessarily *mediated* by symbols. The symbol is an irreplaceable cognitive tool, which alone and by definition can grasp and express that "relatively unknown fact," the still unconscious meaning of a given psychological event. However, in contradistinction to the direct experience of symbols (or symbolic images), whose existence does not require any further proof, the existence of this "unknown fact," which supposedly is symbolized cannot be rationally demonstrated, and is not *immediately* experienced. Therefore, it can only be postulated: it is an assumption. And, as we have seen, this assumption has the same logical status of a *belief*. But this (mitigating) belief does not erase the (self)critical stance of consciousness in the symbolic experience, once the very definition of symbol implies that this consciousness is relatively unconscious of whatever symbolized fact is expressed through the symbolizing image. In other words, in the symbolic attitude consciousness is self-conscious of its own unconsciousness (*docta ignorantia*: "I know that I do not know"), and at the same time it assumes that it faces an unknown fact (the symbolic attitude is presupposed in Jung's "confrontation with the unconscious"). This critical self-consciousness is the proof that the symbolic experience is a thoroughly *modern* form of experience.[17]

What renders the symbolized fact *relatively* unknown is the actual possibility of its meaning being interpreted, extracted from the symbol, and thus integrated into consciousness. But once the interpretation is successfully performed, the previously "living symbol" becomes a "dead symbol," inasmuch as the interpretation provides a better formulation of that previously unknown meaning (see Jung, 1921, pp. 474–475 [*CW*, 6, § 816]). On the other hand, Jung firmly *believes* (or *postulates*) that the symbolized "relatively unknown fact" ("the unconscious") is inexhaustible, meaning that its expression through symbols is endless or, to put it another way, it exceeds the realm of particular symbolic expressions. This excess is transposed theoretically to the (highly problematic) difference between archetype in itself and archetypal image, the former being the noumenon of the latter (see Jung, 1921, p. 401 [*CW*, 6, § 659]).[18] The archetype in itself is postulated as the "essentially 'irrepresentable' basic form," whose fundamental meanings "can be grasped only approximately," so that "it does not appear, in itself, to be capable of reaching consciousness" (Jung, 1947/1954, p. 213 [*CW*, 8, § 417]). Jung never admitted that this "hypothesis" is in fact ontological, metaphysical—and thus, according to his own terms (as noted before), a hypothetical belief.

In a letter dated February 11, 1956, to Maud Oakes, Jung assumes the tentativeness of his symbols, and declares that he has no religious or other convictions about them, considering them mere allusions, pointing to "those dim horizons beyond which lies the secret of exist-ence"; he does not take them as metaphysical assertions, but considers them only "futile or dubious attempts at pronouncing the ineffable," "humble attempts to formulate, to define, to shape the inexpressible" (Jung, 1976, p. 290). Here, in the subject who experiences and takes possession of *his* symbols, we find both the modern critical skeptic thinker and the believer (who postulates, without rational justifica-tion and based only in the direct experience of images taken as being symbolic, the existence of "the secret of existence," "the ineffable," "the inexpressible"). In a nutshell: a skeptic who believes in God on the grounds of his personal deep-felt non-rational experience of the unknown "secret of existence." In the end, Jung is demure:

> I am incapable of determining ultimate worth or worthlessness; I have no judgment about myself and my life. There is nothing I am quite sure about. I have no definite convictions—not about any-thing, really. I know only that I was born and exist, and it seems to me that I have been carried along. I exist on the foundation of some-thing I do not know. In spite of all uncertainties, I feel a solidity underlying all existence and a continuity in my mode of being.
>
> (Jung, 1989, p. 358)

Notes

1   On the meaning of "irrational" in Jung, see Jung (1921, pp. 454–455; pp. 458–459 [*CW 6*, §§ 774–777; 785–787]). See also Barreto (2015). In passing, we should stress that Jung's contraposition of empiricism and philosophy is an almost unbelievable statement, coming from a learned man, who had had more than the basic education in philosophical matters. For it conveys the absurd idea that philosophy and "empiricism" (or experience—all the realm of "facts") are at odds, whereas since ancient Greek philosophy, which Jung knew all too well, "empiricism" and philo-sophical reasoning went alongside hand in hand. On the other hand, at times Jung acknowledged the essential kinship between philosophy—at least antique philosophy (see Barreto, 2007)—and the psychotherapeutic praxis: "I can hardly draw a veil over the fact that we psychotherapists ought really to be philosophers or philosophic doctors—or rather that we are already so, though we are unwilling to admit it because of the glaring contrast between our work and what passes for philosophy in the univer-sities" (Jung, 1943, p. 79 [*CW 16*, § 181]).

2   One of the rare Jungian scholars who explicitly mentions Jung's skepticism and names it as such is Sonu Shamdasani. See Hillman and Shamdasani (2013, *passim*). From a different and critical standpoint, Wolfgang Giegerich alludes to Jung's unsatisfactory coming to terms with "doubt" as the intrinsic form of truth in modernity (see Giegerich, 2013b, pp. 348–364). Giegerich rightly considers skepticism as "the special legitimate characteristic of modernity, modernity's own main *merit, talent, achievement, and its particular contribution* to the history of the soul," and charges Jung of trying to "counteract the inevitable skepticism, treating it like a mistake, a faulty development, the modern neurosis, in other words, an enemy to be fought" (Giegerich, 2013b, p. 364). Giegerich unveils Jung's strategy in this fight: "Jung believed he could *take a shortcut* to an alleged immediacy, innocence, and unbroken naturalism of felt experience" (ibid.). Jung's opposition to skepticism will be explained below.

3   Concerning the "power to assert metaphysical truths," it is worth noting that Jung considered that the assertion of a metaphysical truth "is and remains the prerogative of belief. Belief in turn is a psychological fact, though it is far from being a proof. The most it tells us is that such a belief exists, and that the belief meets a psychological need. Since no human need is without a reason, we may also expect that the need for metaphysical assertions is based on a corresponding reason, even if we are not conscious of this reason. Nothing is thereby asserted, nothing denied" (Jung, 1976, p. 368; see also Jung, 1958a, p. 448 [*CW 10*, § 845]; Jung, 1935/1953, pp. 511–512 [*CW 11*, §§ 835–836]; Jung, 1955/1956, p. 390 [*CW 14*, § 558]). From this stance comes the notion of a "psychological truth," as well as the (psychologistic) standpoint according to which metaphysical assertions correspond to a self-revelation of the psychic background, being an expression of "the unconscious."

4   This stance is very similar to how Cicero presented the epistemic stance of Arcesilaus, the well-known skeptic of the Third Academy: "Arcesilaus said that there is nothing that can be known, not even that residuum of knowledge that Socrates had left himself—the truth of this very dictum" (*Academica* I, xii, 45). In brief: Arcesilaus, according to Cicero, sustained that we do not even know that nothing can be known. A radically stronger skeptical stance is alluded to by Cicero: "the Chian Metrodorus, at the beginning of his volume *On Nature*, says: 'I deny that we know whether we know something or know nothing, and even that we know the mere fact that we do not know (or do know), or know at all whether something exists or nothing exists'" (*Academica* II, xxiii, 73–74). Jung would not go that far: he is definitely convinced that the psyche, archetypes, the collective unconscious exist, and this conviction is rooted in the premise of the *Wirklichkeit*

der Seele. See below. (I am grateful to Prof. José Raimundo Maia Neto for drawing my attention to the parallel between Multatuli's and Arcesilaus' standpoints.)

5 On the originally epistemological (and not characterological) intention of Jung's typology, see Shamdasani (2003, pp. 83–87).

6 "The psyche is an extremely complex factor, so fundamental to all premises that no judgment can be regarded as 'purely empirical' but must first indicate the premises by which it judges. Modern psychology can no longer disguise the fact that the object of its investigation is its own essence, so that in certain respects there can be no 'principles' or valid judgments at all, but only *phenomenology*—in other words, *sheer experience*. On this level of knowledge, psychology has to abdicate as a science, though only on this very high level. Below that, judgments and hence science are still possible, provided that the premises are always stated ... The premise underlying my judgments is the *reality [Wirklichkeit] of everything psychic*, a concept based on the appreciation of the fact that the psyche can also be pure experience" (Jung, 1935c, pp. 774 and 775 [*CW 18*, §§ 1738 and 1740]).

7 An activity is real, but is not a substance. The expression *Wirklichkeit der Seele* cannot help suggesting the existence of a substantial entity (*die Seele*) as the referent for that activity. Similarly, Descartes' jump from the cogitating activity to the assertion of a substantial subject (*res cogitans*, or *the* I) was criticized by the empiricist tradition in modern philosophy.

8 The uneven and multiple ways with which Jung conceives the archetypes do not always correspond explicitly to this substantializing stance; for instance, he can say that "the collective unconscious is not to be thought of as a self-subsistent entity; it is no more than a potentiality handed down to us from primordial times in the specific form of mnemonic images or inherited in the anatomical structure of the brain," and these images are presented as categories, "*a priori* ideas, as it were, the existence of which cannot be ascertained except from their effects" (Jung, 1922, p. 81 [*CW 15*, § 126]). But whereas Kantian categories are simply formal, their "effects" being purely formal (in our judgments), Jung's archetypes are here almost biological realities, and their substantial status is transposed either to the brain or to an autonomous *seelische Wirklichkeit*, whose *substantial* existence is unambiguously ascertained. Hence, in the last analysis Jung's caution here is misleading: he *is* linking those effects to a self-subsistent entity, and as a result he is substantializing those "*a priori* ideas," *malgré lui.*

9 Jung welcomes Freud's pitiless unmasking of "our occidental illusions and pettiness" as "an historic and necessary rectification of almost incalculable importance," for "it forces us to accept a philosophical relativism such as

Einstein embodies for mathematical physics, and which is a truth of the Far East whose ultimate effect we cannot at present foresee" (Jung, 1929, p. 65 [*CW 16*, § 146]). In a letter of May 1956, he tells the anonymous correspondent: "Modern man in Europe has lost or given up—getting tired of them—his traditional beliefs and has to find out for himself what is going to happen to him in his impoverished state. Analytical psychology tells you the story of his adventures. Only if you are able to see the relativity, i.e., the uncertainty of all human postulates, can you experience that state in which analytical psychology makes sense" (Jung, 1976, pp. 303–304). But Jung believes that "our mistake lies in supposing that the radiant things are done away with by being explained from the shadow-side" (Jung, 1929, p. 64 [*CW 16*, § 146]), i.e., by being submitted to that relativist "necessary rectification." Elsewhere, in a paragraph of the *Gesammelte Werke* omitted in the *Collected Works*, he summarizes his position: "All relativism, when it is a supreme and ultimate principle, works destructively... ... . The ground of the soul is nature, and nature is creative life. Certainly nature itself breaks down what it builds, but it will build it again. What modern relativism destroys in the visible world, the soul gives us back again" (Jung, 1928/1931b, p. 111 [*CW 10*, § 187ᵇ, my translation]).

10 I will not address here the complex problems involved in Jung's psychological conception of religious experience. In what follows, whenever I mention religious experience I intend only to give a particular illustration of the generic "immediate experience" of the "psychic background" according to Jung. This experience does not have to include necessarily religious elements, does not have to be "numinous." On the other hand, the autonomy of "the" unconscious vis-à-vis consciousness allows one to interpret *any* interference of unconscious drives from a religious perspective, in accordance with Jung's standpoint on "God": "It is an apt name given to all overpowering emotions in my own psychic system, subduing my conscious will and usurping control over myself. This is the name by which I designate all things which cross my willful path violently and recklessly, all things which upset my subjective views, plans, and intentions and change the course of my life for better or worse" (Jung, 1976, p. 525). But I believe that the farfetchedness of this standpoint is all too obvious. Wolfgang Giegerich has duly criticized Jung's concoction of a modern psychological surrogate for traditional religious experiences. See especially two of his essays: "Psychology as Anti-Philosophy: C.G. Jung" and "The Disenchantment Complex: C.G. Jung and the Modern World," in Giegerich (2013a).

11 See also Jung (1976, pp. 522–523). Occasionally, though, Jung gives to "knowledge" the sense of "an intellectual conception of things" and

differentiates it from experience: "the most beautiful truth—as history has shown a thousand times over—is of no use at all unless it has become the innermost experience and possession of the individual. ... The needful thing is not to *know* the truth but to *experience* it. Not to have an intellectual conception of things, but to find our way to the inner, and perhaps wordless, irrational experience—that is the great problem" (Jung, 1931b, p. 558 [*CW 18*, § 1292]).

12 In Aenesidemus' Pyrrohnian form of skepticism, when faced with the opposition of appearances and/or thoughts of equal value (the situation of equipollence or *isostheneia*), one should suspend one's judgment (*epoché*), once reason is unable to decide which one is true. And then the skeptic should lead a life according to the appearances or beliefs most convenient to him/her.

13 And the very circumstance that the lady was submitting her experience to the evaluation of Jung shows unmistakably that she was in doubt: her reason was not convinced by her experience.

14 As a matter of fact, we can point to the unwilling admission by Jung of the need of belief in "immediate experience": he highly values *pistis* (which he interprets as "loyalty to oneself" or "loyalty to one's experience": see Jung, 1938/1940, p. 8 and 43 [*CW 11*, §§ 9 and 74]) as a fundamental factor in the ethical commitment to the "experiment of the unconscious." But this *pistis* is a non-rational adhesion to experience, and as such it is a belief in experience, a belief subtracted to the skeptical inquiry of reason.

15 On this topic, see the truly paradigmatic examination of ethical action in Aristotle's *Nichomachean Ethics*.

16 A truly masterful analysis of this dream, from the methodological perspective of psychology as the discipline of interiority, is offered by Wolfgang Giegerich in his "Jung's Millimeter: Feigned Submission – Clandestine Defiance: Jung's Religious Psychology," in Giegerich (2013b), pp. 3–46.

17 Rigorously speaking, the mythic form of consciousness is not "symbolic," in the sense here used. It is *literalist*. For instance: within the "first naiveté" of mythic consciousness, a lightning is not taken as a *symbol* of an unknown fact, but is the undoubted *sign* of the presence of a well-known god.

18 Momentarily contradicting his own distinction between archetypes and archetypal images, in a famous Eranos conference Jung states that archetypes are

> true and genuine symbols that cannot be exhaustively interpreted, either as signs or as allegories. They are genuine symbols precisely because they are ambiguous, full of half-glimpsed meanings, and in the last resort inexhaustible. The ground principles, the ἀρχαί, of the

unconscious are indescribable because of their wealth of reference, although in themselves recognizable. The discriminating intellect naturally keeps on trying to establish their singleness of meaning and thus misses the essential point; for what we can above all establish as the one thing consistent with their nature is their *manifold meaning*, their almost limitless wealth of reference, which makes any unilateral formulation impossible.

(Jung, 1934/1954, p. 38 [*CW 9i*, § 80])

References

Barreto, M.H. (2007). 'It is Something Like Antique Philosophy': Analytical Psychology and Philosophical Practical Wisdom, in *Spring: A Journal of Archetype and Culture*, 77 ("Philosophy and Psychology"), pp. 69–88.

———— (2015). Remarks on the Meaning of 'Irrational' in Jung, in *Jung Journal: Culture and Psyche*, 9 (1), 31–41.

———— (2018). The Ethical Dimension of Analytical Psychology, in *Journal of Analytical Psychology*, 63 (2), 21–40.

Cicero. (1967). *Academica* (trans. H. Rackham). London: Heineman.

Giegerich, W. (2013a). *Collected English Papers. Volume V. An Analysis of C.G. Jung's Psychology Project*. New Orleans: Spring Journal and Books.

Giegerich, W. (2013b). *Collected English Papers. Volume VI. "Dreaming the Myth Onwards": C.G. Jung on Christianity and on Hegel* (Part 2 of The Flight into the Unconscious). New Orleans: Spring Journal and Books.

Hillman, J. & Shamdasani, S. (2013). *Lament of the Dead. Psychology after Jung's Red Book*. London/New York: Norton.

Jung, C.G. (1921). *Psychological Types. CW*, 6.

———— (1922). *On the Relation of Analytical Psychology to Poetry. CW*, 15.

———— (1928/1931a). *The Spiritual Problem of Modern Man. CW*, 10.

———— (1928/1931b). *Das Seelenproblem des modernen Menschen. CW*, 10.

———— (1929). *Problems of Modern Psychotherapy. CW*, 16.

———— (1930/1931). *The Stages of Life. CW*, 8.

———— (1931a). *Archaic Man. CW*, 10.

———— (1931b). *Forewords to Jung: "Seelenprobleme der Gegenwart." CW*, 18.

———— (1934/1950). *A Study in the Process of Individuation. CW*, 9i.

———— (1934/1954). *Archetypes of the Collective Unconscious. CW*, 9i.

———— (1935a). *Foreword to Mehlich: "J.H. Fichtes Seelenlehre und ihre Beziehung zur Gegenwart." CW*, 18.

———— (1935b). *The Tavistock Lectures. CW*, 18.

———— (1935c). *Foreword to von Koenig-Fachsenfeld: "Wandlungen des Traumproblems von der Romantik bis zur Gegenwart." CW*, 18.

———— (1935/1953). *Psychological Commentary on the "Tibetan Book of the Dead." CW*, 11.

———— (1936/1954). *Concerning the Archetypes, with Special Reference to the Anima Concept. CW*, 9i.

———— (1938/1940). *Psychology and Religion. CW*, 11.

———— (1941). *The Psychological Aspects of the Kore. CW*, 9i.

———— (1943). *Psychotherapy and a Philosophy of Life. CW*, 16.

———— (1947/1954). *On the Nature of the Psyche. CW*, 8.

———— (1950). *Foreword to the "I Ching". CW*, 11.

———— (1954). *On Resurrection. CW*, 18.

———— (1955/1956). *Mysterium Coniunctionis. CW*, 14.

———— (1958a). *A Psychological View of Conscience. CW*, 10.

———— (1958b). *An Astrological Experiment. CW*, 18.

———— (1959). *Introduction to Wolff's "Studies in Jungian Psychology." CW*, 10.

———— (1973). *Letters 1: 1906–1950* (ed. G. Adler & A. Jaffé). Princeton: Princeton University Press.

———— (1976). *Letters 2: 1951–1961* (ed. G. Adler & A. Jaffé). Princeton: Princeton University Press.

———— (1989). *Memories, Dreams, Reflections* (Ed. A. Jaffé). New York: Vintage Books.

Shamdasani, S. (2003). *Jung and the Making of Modern Psychology: The dream of a science*. Cambridge: Cambridge University Press.

Chapter 5

A Critique of C.G. Jung's Theoretical basis for Selfhood

Theory Vexed by an Incorporeal Ontology

Robin McCoy Brooks

> *Paucis natse est, qui populum aetatis suae cogitate.*
>
> Seneca [Epist. 79, 17]

("Whomever in [their] thinking [only] takes note of [their] own age will influence only a few." [tr.])[1]

Introduction

Molly McCully Brown (2017) recently wrote a compelling opinion piece that captures her experience of physical pain amongst the activities of everyday life (*New York Times*, November 15). She opens with a description of the two short shallow flights of stairs that lead to the doorway of the university department chair's home and the annual party she is expected to attend. All of the spaces in this home are inaccessible for wheelchairs and precarious enough when navigated with or without a cane. Mingling with other guests is expected and this occurs while standing and standing, Brown describes is excruciatingly painful throughout her joints and entire body. Her head roars with the efforts of feigning comfort, balancing, and breathing. She can only partially attend to the conversations she engages in. "The truth about pain," she states, "is that it makes you tired." Explaining her discomfort, if she were to do so in such situations only widens "the gulf" between her and the other person she quietly manages. From this background, let us follow Molly McCully Brown's powerful depiction of personhood as inexplicably bound to body/brain/mind and its environment:

> I never forget about my disability – its root system is shot through every part of me. This is true on a basic biological level: It's a feature of my brain and the electrical signals it sends. But I mean it

more deeply than that. It's not just that I'm often in pain, or that I have to think about my body almost all the time, although both of these things are true. It's that I don't exist without my body. Its particular margins, and movements and methods for making it through the world are present, not just in the moments when it causes me hardship but in the best and wildest and strongest stretches of my being. My body isn't standing apart from me holding my life in a vise grip: It is making my life, indivisible from the rest of me. We are walking together through the world, as odd and slow as it looks.[2]

The distress I felt when I first read this short paragraph, and indeed the entire article lingers. Like many of you, I work with patients who are living and dying with debilitating physical pain caused by disease or disability of any kind. Maybe you are or have experienced such physical pain or live with physical disabilities yourselves. Brown's poignant piece can also be understood to view personhood (self, subject, personhood, being) as mediated through our bodies, our minds, our brains, the inter-activity with technologies, *and* the rhythms of the cultural environments (including our history) to which we are all inured. Molly McCully Brown's experience of personhood is out of sync with the prevailing social rhythms that are inscribed by social norms and practices because these norms do not embrace the *reality* of physical alterity. Thus, Brown's experience of physical pain generally remains outside of the world's understanding, recognition, and consideration.

C.G. Jung's project was founded on a core belief that self-relation was fundamental to the health of the individual and the entire human species. In spite of Jung's expansive vision for human kind, there is no place for Molly McCully Brown's experience of personhood in Jung's epistemological basis for selfhood. Jung's almost exclusive fidelity to the objective psyche in his attempt to universalize its significance to all disciplines had the unfortunate effect of minimizing the influences of the biological body and its material environments in the formation of selfhood thereby, more than less creating a body-less self.[3] Brown's bodily experiences, she tells us are "indivisible from the rest of me." In these powerful narrative strokes (unbeknownst to her), she drives a stake through the heart of Jung's psychical biases by embodying her existence (mind, self-reflected experience) amidst the world (environment of things and people) she "slowly walks" or wheels through.

Material processes, as I am using it here may include: mental activity, stress, diet, prenatal and birth conditions, environmental chemical exposure (air pollution), genetic/epigenetic factors, physical disability, disease, brain damage, chronic pain, pharmacological and medical interventions or lack thereof, neuro-diversities, aging processes, technological surrounds (wheelchairs, computers, etc.), climate events, concrete cultural, political, social and economic micro and macro processes (including poverty), to name a few.[4] Understanding human experience, for Jung was predicated on interpreting enigmatic messages via the psychoid (archetype) that were generated from the collective unconscious and dispatched from the Unus Mundus (world soul) whose only contact with corporeality was through the instincts or affects. Jung also failed to grasp the significance of personal unconscious processes on the formation of the subject (such as non-archetypal dream material, transference phenomena and projective processes, *nachträglich* shifts in temporality, and the inter-play of the drives and instincts) that emerge within everyday relationships to one's environment with others and things including one's own organicity such as brain states, personal history (childhood development), the interplay of psychical and physical trauma or physical disability (Brooks, 2013, 629).[5] By disavowing these materialisms, the Jungian self could not believe in its own death as it was trapped within an atemporal nether-land. Indeed, throughout his life, Jung was interested in, thought about, and experienced para-psychological events that would later lead him to contemplate the reality of soul life after corporeal death that would become an impetus to articulate a theory of synchronicity (Shamdasani, 2007). Jung's post-heart attack visions (1944) became the subjective proof for postmortem transcendence and watershed through which later works (*Aion*, *Mysterium Coniunctionis* and *Answer to Job*) materialized. Following Jung's near death experience, Shamdasani notes that Jung re-envisioned the aim of psychoanalysis as "a preparation of the soul for death [i.e. the death of the body]," now entering the realm heretofore occupied by philosophy and religion (Shamdasani, 2007, 24; Jung, 1963, 328). Indeed, Jung referred to his own life as "provisional," –a "transitory prejudice, a working hypothesis for the time being but not existence itself" (*Letters I*, 357–359).[6] In other words, temporal life (existence) or the everyday experiences of personhood amongst other places and things, such as Molly McCully Brown's depiction above, had no place in the self's telos, especially in Jung's later formulations.[7]

In Jung's attempts to save the human soul from becoming written out of what he viewed to be a tendency towards scientific specialization in psychology, he took a generalist approach in his various research designs because he believed there was still too much unknown about the new science of the unconscious (Shamdasani, 2003; Jung, 1935a, para. 236). Jung's generalist approach, through which he engaged the intellectual debates of his day across interdisciplinary lines was a vehicle he often used to articulate his key *concepts* with the aim of establishing the prominence of the objective psyche as foundation to the other sciences.[8] I emphasize the term "concepts" here, as throughout the collected works Jung emphasized that he was no philosopher, that he was not theorizing or engaging in speculative arguments or doctrines about the ideas (concepts) he developed throughout his corpus regarding psychical life (*Letters II*, zl-zlii). He repeatedly claimed that did not engage in the philosophical or positivist approaches to make his arguments except for *when he did*, heralding a kind of hybrid-empiricism that he alone created.[9]

During Jung's era, new and evolving disciplines were embroiled in the effort to resolve their distinct identity crises amidst the rising status of scientific positivism while also attempting to address the immediate and impending crisis of civility in the Western world and its emerging conception of human being. Each discipline sought a new understanding of itself in relation to the question of the natural and social sciences amidst a chaotic transformation of concepts from which Edmund Husserl would become the founder of philosophical phenomenology, metaphysics would be reborn into ontology by Martin Heidegger, Sigmund Freud would conceptualize a science of the unconscious, Jung would develop a novel interpretation of psychical reality, and the theoreticians of the Institute for Social Research (also known as the Frankfurt school) would rally around a desire to create a new kind of critical analysis of modern society birthing what would become critical theory.

If we can have a better understanding of the historical environs from which analytical psychology emerged, we might clarify for ourselves what of Jung's project remains subversive today within a discipline vexed by its own contemporary form of identity crises, a crises that (in part) is rooted by his inability to adequately incorporate (no pun intended) the body and other material realities into his theoretical considerations of selfhood. To this end, I highlight the kinds of historical tensions that contributed to Jung's ambiguous relationship to natural (*Naturwissenschaften*) and human (*Geisteswissenschaften*) sciences throughout his life that led him to rely on neo-Kantian philosophical ideas (a foundational ontology) while disavowing the philosophical phenomenological[10] turn ushered in by the works of Edmund Husserl in 1900, and Martin Heidegger in the 1920s. What is the significance of this turn and why should we (those interested in analytical psychology) care today? The philosophical phenomenological turn widened a perceptual frame from a foundationalist epistemological problematic (as Jung embraced) to a fundamental ontological problematic developed through Heidegger's (1927) major work, *Being and Time*. In an earlier work, I articulated the significance of Jung's inability to comprehend Heidegger's non-foundational ontology that I repeat here:

> Fundamental questions about Jung's analysis of human-ness (and psyche) emerge owing to Jung's failure to grasp Heidegger's epistemological position, leaving him struggling with Cartesian and Kantian assumptions that constrained his thinking. Contemporary Jungian theorists have begun to critically challenge the basic theoretical assumptions in Jung's work. These presuppositions include the validity of a set of *a priori* cognitions that guide understanding of the phenomenal world, subjectivity viewed through the lens of the myth of the isolated mind with its innate structures, conventions of interpretation that privilege the illusion of the analyst's epistemological authority, and the universality and essentialism fundamental to Jung's rendering of the self.
>
> (Brooks, 2011, 494)

It cannot be overstated how crucial the phenomenological turn was in the history of ideas and to future generations of philosophical thought (structuralism, [post]modernism, materialisms, analytical philosophy, post phenomenology, philosophy of history, etc.) including academic circles outside of philosophy (anthropology, critical theory, psycho-analysis, [particularly Lacan], psychology, sociology, history, theology, etc.). Heidegger's radical decentering of the human being from a transcendent foundation located "out there" would tacitly come more into the foreground of contemporary post-phenomenological thought (thinkers who reference phenomenology, whatever designation they are given), that in contrast to traditional psychoanalytic theories of mind are more amenable to a socially constructed self that is grounded in materialisms, including biological life, its history *and* more than matter (Zahavi, 2008; Grosz, 2017; Stiegler, 2013; Malabou, 2016).

I organize this chapter in the following sections to elaborate my aim of highlighting the historical tensions in Jung's era that contributed to his ambiguous relationship to science and the humanities whose epistemological remnants continue to hold contemporary psycho-analytic thinkers in a foundationalist chokehold today. The first section explores the early formative influences in Jung's professional life in relation to the Freudian tide that sheds light on the extraor-dinary tensions of the times against which two distinct visions of what it means to be human emerged. The second section sketches (in broad brushstrokes) the historical context from which the "art of understanding" or hermeneutics emerged prior to the birth of psycho-analysis, philosophical phenomenology and analytical psychology. Jung's theoretical turn away (backwards in time) from these contem-porary developments advanced by philosophical phenomenology that contributed to his entrenched foundationalism are highlighted. The third section contains an overview of the epistemological foundations of analytical psychology that Jung more vigorously elaborated in the development of his key concepts throughout his lifetime, particularly after the split with Freud. The fourth section builds upon the pre-ceding ones with a more direct examination of Jung's place in the debate between the natural and human sciences. My intention is to provide a broad historical exposé of the background of influences that contributed to the theoretical choice points Jung made from his moment in history with the idea that we may be inspired to think the-oretically for ourselves from a critically held position about what of Jung's corpus makes sense today amidst our own biological/techno-logical revolution and crisis of civility.

Formative Early Influences Amidst and Against the Freudian Edifice

As a young psychiatrist beginning in 1900, Jung built his reputation on intensive research with the word association test at Burghölzli hospital in Zurich. In his work with psychotic patients, Jung and Franz Riklin would classify and compare the associative patterns of 400 word stimuli against the baseline results of other hospital staff. In their groundbreaking study they discovered that complexes could be unconscious due to their repression and these complexes were also discernible in the wider population, not just the seriously mentally ill. Thus, they were confirming Freud's hypothesis that repression was ubiquitous, and through this discovery, Jung would eventually form an intensive and collegial relationship with the elder Freud that he would theorize against throughout his life. Much has been written and interpreted about the forging of, duration and demise of, this mutually life shaping relationship.[11] My interest here is to briefly highlight the formative tensions that shaped what became analytical psychology to critique how these decisions may contribute to the question of the viability of Jung's concept of psychic reality in today's world. Jung's widely interpreted break with Freud was based, he said, on fundamental and irreconcilable theoretical differences related to the psyche and what accounted for "psychological facts" generated from ontological perspectives that were divided by differences of "truth as one can see it" about the etiology of neurosis (Jung, 1977, 44, 254–255). Jung's perception of Freud's metapsychology was that it was guided by a positivist certainty and hindered by the reductionisms inherent in scientific materialism while analytical psychology (as his psychology became to be known after their split) was guided through the imminent critique of psychic facts, and therefore under the empirical. Jung's focus would become a quest to retain or repair the one-sided thinking that was wrought by the scientization and mechanization of society that cleaved access to one's psyche (soul, self).

Freud was certainly committed to a biological conception of the psyche and he sought to capture it scientifically through the empiricism of psychoanalysis whose goal was a rehabilitation of the patient's neurotic symptoms via building the autonomy of the ego's reasoning capacity. His interest, contra Jung was a self-conscious ego that was informed by engaging repressive enigmatic material of the personal unconscious located in the body. He did not develop a theory of self-hood, as ego consciousness could not be equated with selfness. Yet, following his break with Jung in 1913 and throughout his remaining career, Freud entered into a series of what can be called speculative historical writings that attempted to extend his biomedical conception of the mind into a broader scope of humanist concerns (Tauber, 2010; Makari, 2008). These interests somewhat thematically paralleled the quest behind Jung's pursuits that ironically preempted their break and generally had to do with the evolution and fate of society and culture, the psychological origins of religion and the unconscious, and a psychodynamic study of historical figures.

Psychoanalysis and Analytical Psychology were both birthed in Europe and deeply influenced by the philosophical and scientific heterodoxy of theory that dominated the rigorous debates of their day including the split between *Geiteswissenschaft* (human science) and *Nauturwissenschaft* (natural science). We can feel the tension in Jung's characterization of the historical surround from which the "new science" of the unconscious, or psychoanalysis, emerged in his interview with Stephen Black in 1955. When asked about the "sharp divisions within psychological medicine" that came about in the first half of the century between Freudian, Jungian and Adlerian philosophies, Jung's cogent retrospective gives us a unique sense of the tensions of the times from which the science of the unconscious was emerging. He stated:

> Always in the beginning of a new science, or when a new problem is tackled in science, there are necessarily many different aspects, particularly in a science like psychology, and particularly so when an absolutely new factor has been brought into the discussion ... in this case, it was the unconscious – the concept of the unconscious. It had been a philosophical concept before – in the philosophy of Carl Gustav Carus and then his follower Eduard von Hartman. But it was a mere speculative concept. The unconscious was a kind of philosophical concept at first, but through the discoveries by Freud it became a practical medical concept, because he discovered these mechanisms or connections... He made of it a medical science... Now, I never got so far as to produce a general doctrine because

I always felt we don't know enough... You feel completely lost in such an enormous field as psychology represents. And then you must have something to cling to, some guidance as it were, and that is probably this kind of psychology set out with almost ready-made theories... theories [were] conceived in a moment when one didn't know enough about the role of the psychology of the unconscious.

(Jung, 1977, 252–253)

While there were *thematic* parallels in both men's investigations into the question of what can account for a realization of human potential, the stark theoretical differences really were as Jung stated it, related to different theoretical orientations from which either man would ground his ontology both landing on opposing sides of the human or nature science solution. We can feel through Jung's remembrances the pressure of the times to create a viable theory ("doctrine") when in his mind there was not enough knowledge about the unconscious to support the "ready-made" theories that were evolving. We can better understand Jung's generalist stance as an avoidance of jumping prematurely into speculative conclusions (that he nevertheless engaged in and denied)[12] in a world that was rapidly being shaped by so-called scientific explanatory models of mind. Jung also reflected on how lost he and his pioneer companions were in the psychology boom. What theories of mind could one "cling on to" in order to make sense of reality in all of its emerging dimensions? It was in this atmosphere that both Jung and Freud would attempt to mediate the polarity with varying degrees of believability throughout their careers by attempting to organize around competing imperatives regarding the limits of knowing, the object of treatment, and modes of investigation amidst a series of catastrophic world events that occurred during their lifetimes but also in response or reaction to the lingering effects of immediate pre-history from which these and other developments occurred.

Intellectual Historical Tensions Preceding the Emergence of Analytical Psychology

After Hegel (1770–1831), German philosophy plunged into an "identity crisis" that was shaped by an understanding of consciousness that did *not* rely on the speculative metaphysics of German Idealism.[13] With

Hegel, philosophy gained an historical consciousness. Prior to Hegel, German philosophy was grounded on the Enlightenment's atemporal speculative metaphysics. The intellectual alienation from the unifying concepts of Hegel's system opened up a vacuum from which a conceptual transformation of history, science, hermeneutics, and philosophy could emerge at the turn of the twentieth century. What had been perceived heretofore as a German cultural uniformity of ideas became destabilized through the rise of scientific positivism and empirical realism as the disciplines began to vigorously differentiate themselves from what had been complete systematic interpretations of reality (Brooks, 2016, 139–140). Thus, the human sciences moved towards the empirical sciences with the idea that history, rather than philosophy, was the basis on which to understand humanity. History and science attempted to disentangle itself from philosophy, and both appealed to the natural sciences for credibility.

Amidst this backdrop, theologian Friedrich Schleiermacher's (1768–1834) development of hermeneutics, particularly the psychological contribution to interpretation through the art of understanding, transposed the supposed meaning of a text into a reproduction—a knowing of what had been known (Gadamer, 2004/1975, 186). He held that every idea in a text, if it was to be fully understood, was to be related to its context in the life of its author. The highest determination of interpretation for Schleiermacher was through understanding the real matter of the text, thus reducing the *"thou"* to an aesthetic facsimile of a production. This reduction subdued reality into the play of intellectual intuition thereby separating what could be known from its subject matter. Prior to Schleiermacher, there was no "subject" in and opposed to a "thou." The text stood alone in its inflated alterity, reducing the interpreter to explanation that was strictly governed by rigid rules held by the privileged few.

Following Schleiermacher, Wilhelm Dilthey's (1833–1911) critical publication in 1883, *Introduction to the Human Sciences*, claimed in its subtitle to be "an attempt to lay a foundation for the study of society and history, for the human sciences, or *Geisteswissenschaften*" (Dilthey, 1989; Gadamer, 1977, 186). He was envisioning a broader epistemological application of hermeneutics that would expand the breadth of the hermeneutic methodology so as to permit the acquisition of all kinds of knowledge through what he called "lived experience." In this, he included the humanities, the social sciences and its disciplines (psychology, anthropology, philosophy, theology, history, etc.), to which he contrasted the natural sciences or *Naturwissenschaften*. The natural sciences dealt with sense-based facts that were analyzed from the causal connections observed in the processes of nature.

Dilthey saw a fundamental distinction between the human sciences and the natural sciences and designated himself a spokesperson (and originator of the term) for the former. Human studies, he believed, needed to develop new models of understanding and interpretation of the facts and phenomena that were relevant to a human being's lived experience. Dilthey could not justify that the knowing subject could simply stand over and against his object, viewing subject and object as part of the same flux (Gadamer, 2004/1975, 507–537; Schmidt, 2006, 38). The methodology appropriate to the study of the natural (outer) objects, he thought was not adequate in its application to the understanding inner phenomena. Dilthey's highest category was "understanding" through an act of inner possession of the object or sign (including historic objects, texts, art, etc.). He struggled with defining psychological phenomena, a domain that would be competed for in an emerging empirical psychology. He saw psychology as the most basic discipline of the *Geisteswissenschaften*, in contrast to other movements that located psychology with a more positivistic scientific status (Gadamer, 1977). By relegating psychology into the humanities, Dilthey was also disavowing the materialisms (such as Molly McCully Brown's neuro-diversities and cultural biases to physical alterity) inherent in subject formation and laying groundwork for later disciplinary biases that fail to engage the indivisibility of body/mind/environments. Only later in his work, and indeed in part influenced by the younger Husserl, did Dilthey extricate himself from his earlier foundational focus on psychology as a form of hermeneutics.[14] Dilthey's reflections on the human sciences, hermeneutics, and the importance of historical contextualization, however, crucially influenced the works of Husserl and especially early Heidegger, although to what degree and how remains a topic of critique today. The debates surrounding what constituted science, philosophy, and psychology, etc. were intensely heating up towards the turn of the twentieth century. Philosophy's dilemma of sustaining its viability as a discipline can be understood as the challenge to claim relevancy for the discipline in the emerging scientific age (i.e. whether or not philosophy was useless regarding the link between thought and action).[15] Phenomenology, as a sub-discipline of philosophy, would emerge at the turn of the twentieth century out of this effort, initially through Husserl who sought a new foundation or rehabilitation of its theories and methods.[16]

I will stress two crucial points about Husserl's phenomenology because of his far-reaching influence as a thinker in the history of ideas and his place in history juxtaposed to Jung's. Critical theory (that emerged from the collective efforts of the Institute of Social Research in 1923 and later became the Frankfurt School) and Heidegger's thought are the "conflicted offspring" of Husserlian phenomenology (Zuidervaart, 2017, 147). Husserl's method involved the reduction (*epoché*) of the physical world to its manifestations *in* and *for* consciousness *and* experience that pragmatically focused on objects as they *were*, not as presupposed.[17] His disciplined phenomenology included an approach that involved a sort of mental leap (or reduction) that called for a disconnection from the individual's *natural attitude* (or uncritically held belief) by bracketing everyday presuppositions. In other words, the *epoché* was a procedure that entailed the suspension of our natural inclinations in order to critically investigate the phenomena at hand within the individual's milieu (Husserl, 2012/1931; Zahavi, 2003). Husserl's project incorporated a rigorous theoretical and methodological immanent critique of oneself in relation to what one is observing.

Jung claimed he was the first to "demand that the analyst should himself be analyzed," which was a crucial insight in the history of psychoanalysis (Jung, 1935a para. 7). In this way, the analyst who has been analyzed would become more aware of his or her own unconscious processes that are evoked in relation to the patient's material and be less likely to merge, defend against or engage in projective activity in their own countertransferential processes. While the analyst may engage in a form of "self-bracketing" amidst the process of critiquing the patient's psychical phenomena together, I do not see an equivalent of Husserl's *epoché* in Jung's method of amplification as Roger Brooke has claimed (Brooke, 2015, 34). Brooke uses a series of arguments that do not consider the fundamental epistemological vice grip to which Jung was bound that prevented him (Jung) from conceptually integrating not only aspects of Husserl's phenomenology but especially Heidegger's foundational ontology that drew from and enhanced Husserl's method.[18] Jung's method of amplification was grounded in a foundational problematic that viewed psychic contents as disbursements from the collective unconscious (itself a hypostasized concept that reified its phenomena) and did not value the concrete materialisms that emerged in everyday life to be worthy of consideration in the formulation of self-awareness. This approach does not consider the experience of everyday pain or how pain and or physical disability is responded to in a social or physical environment, such as Molly McCully Brown's depiction as giving rise to self-formation. Furthermore, while a process of amplification may have been rigorous in practice, Jung's actual written clinical methodology was not rigorously composed or incorporated into a coherent theory. Jung also did not appear to be overly concerned with keeping his own presuppositional biases in check even though he occasionally interspersed general admonitory statements throughout his collected works for others. For example, he cautioned his reader to "lay aside all scientific knowledge etc. in order to adopt a 'completely new and unprejudiced attitude,'" or "make an 'explicit attempt to overcome [ones] theoretical and conceptual prejudices,'" in order to approach the analytical task of "understanding with a free and open mind" (Jung, 1935a, paras. 6–7; Jung, 1957, para. 495). As I argued in another work, Jung retained a stance of epistemological authority and held the patient hostage to his analytical sovereignty particularly when he thought he recognized the presence of an "archetype" in the patient's material (Brooks, 2013, 86–90; Jung, 1935b, para. 190). On the other hand, when working with the contents of a patient's personal unconscious, whose elements were simply forgotten or repressed (versus the archetypal contents dispatched from an all knowing *unus mundus*), Jung assumed a more descriptive method adhering to the principles of the word association experiments by following the *patient's* allegorical associations, thereby respecting the individual's singularity.

We know that Jung's father was a "frustrated" philologist, who after having completed his studies (including a dissertation on the Arabic version of *Song of Songs*) had put his "linguistic talent" behind him to become a country parson (Jung, 1965, 91). Also known, is Jung's grandfather (his namesake), Carl Gustav Jung, had been converted by (the German Protestant) Schleiermacher, whom Jung referred to as one of his "spiritual ancestors" (*Letters II*, 115–116, 528). Although

Jung had apparently never "studied him," he described the man as being "vast, esoteric and an individual" (ibid. 115). Historical patriarchal connections to religious philology might have left Jung with a "spiritual tie" to the discipline but, by his own admission, he lacked a rigorous exposure to Schleiermacher's scholarship. Furthermore, Jung did not understand Heidegger's philosophical projects.[19] Jung used the term "hermeneutics" to loosely embellish how he worked with psychic phenomena within his methodology of amplification and the term "phenomenology" as a communicative device in response to its growing popularity (Spiegelberg, 1972, 130–131). Jung's interpretive method was closer to Dilthey's hermeneutics as applied to the understanding of psychical contents that emerged from the patient's personal unconscious (history and contexts of everyday life). With the emergence of so-called archetypal contents, however, Jung's epistemological authority became inflated, as evidenced by his belief that only he could be the mediating authority between (text) archetype and meaning. He demonstrated this tendency, for example in his commentary in the "crab" dream from the Tavistock lectures (1935b, para. 190). In these cases, Jung's method was more akin to the classical philological approach prevalent in the Enlightenment that Schleiermacher's general method of hermeneutics reacted against.

The second point I will briefly stress is that Husserl and the subsequent thinkers in the phenomenology-existential phenomenological traditions, within varying degrees, viewed the body then and now as playing a significant role in shaping one's experience of reality/existence (Askay, Farquhar, 2006, 344). The minimization of bodily import in Jung's corpus regarding the self's nexus is just as astonishing as his disregard for the philosophical thought that was also emerging within his era. In contrast, key concepts contained within the philosophical phenomenological tradition consider the scrutiny of phenomenal complexities of consciousness, the structures of experience, time-consciousness, intentionality, body and self-awareness, and later with Heidegger, the ontological placement of being-in-the-world through language (which cannot be divorced from thought) and care (that we are constituted by care) (Zahavi, 2003, 1–29).[20] Shamdasani (2008) noted that for Jung, the question of the possibility of the soul's survival after the body's death was central to framing his ethic. Let us contrast this perspective to Heidegger's fundamental ontology that considered time as Being itself.

One of Heidegger's philosophical breakthroughs was the notion of Being (the subject, although Heidegger would not use this term) constituted in time. Being as time was syncopated through originary (or authentic) experience that could only be inaugurated through a diachrony of traumatisms (from anywhere including material impingements from body, brain, giving birth, etc.) that penetrated everyday sensibility from which one could more reflectively grasp a deeper sense of life's significance (Heidegger, 2010 50, 83; Hinton, 2015, 365). As such, Being's experiential movements provided a sort of original unity of the past, the present, and of the unknowable future except for the certainty of corporeal death unlike the progressive telos of the self that Jung envisioned, whose personal development did not end with death.

Heidegger's ontological conceptualization of reality, stemming from his critique of Kant's metaphysical episteme represented by Husserl's transcendental phenomenology radically replaced the epistemological focus on subject and object. This movement from an epistemological position to the inclusion of an ontological one was developed through Heidegger's (1927) major work, *Being and Time*. In this work, Heidegger radically proposed a shift away from the study of phenomena through mental "representations," that he described as a remnant of the isolated ego-mind (head on a stick) of Cartesian thought, towards an ontological investigation of the phenomena which revealed "existence" (i.e. a field of meaning as a dynamic process) and what it is to be human in the concrete embeddedness in history and the everyday world. That is, Heidegger strove to understand being in its enigmatic original (authentic) ground, as it was constituted through crises via the everyday ruptures one encounters amidst other beings (2010, 58–59, 1925/92). In contrast, Jung grounded everyday experience to an underlying *a priori*/transcendent world he called the collective unconscious.

Heidegger combined Husserl's phenomenological research with Dilthey's theory of understanding 'life world' and for the first time brought a revised use of both traditions (hermeneutics and phenomenology) together in such a manner as to transcend the subject/object divide inherent in the foundationalist problematic. Heidegger had the crucial insight that there was no demarcation between our thoughts (concepts, ideas) and our daily lives, so we are left with the challenge of thinking and living without a theoretical meta-ground (Lear, 2000). In other words, "there is no outside the text" or aspect of being human in the world that *does not* give rise (or possibility for) singularity (Žižek, 1994, 8; Derrida 1997, 158; Brooks, 2016).

Because of Jung's generalist approach to theory and practice, it cannot be claimed that he was a hermeneut or philosophical phenomenologist except in the loosest of associations because he did not conceptually make the philosophical phenomenological turn. Jung remained bound to a problematic that adhered to dualisms that he continually sought to bridge through the auspices of an all knowing but unknowable world soul located outside of itself. His use of the term phenomenology was more rooted in his reading Kantian philosophy than from an understanding of the contemporary intellectual movements in his surround.

Epistemological Foundations of Analytical Psychology

Jung tenaciously held onto neo-Kantianism as an epistemological basis for key concepts throughout his lifetime, "devoting his chief efforts ... to the elucidation of [the] unconscious psyche" (1954, para. 1585). He generally did not focus directly on an embodied experience of selfhood except as the receptor site for archetypal experience. Jung conflated the terms instinct and drive in what would become his final reconceptualization of the archetype, the psychoid (1954, Shamdasani, 2003, 258–260).[21] An exception to this statement can be made with regard to earlier researches with the association test around 1902 (already mentioned) and psychological typology (1921/1971b). His typological study was based on clinical or anecdotal observation and includes a more in-depth consideration of the effects on bodily being when encountering archetypal phenomena than most anything else he had or would later write.[22] However, Jung's epistemological verification for his psychological types still bound him to a collective unconscious that disavowed being-constituting material phenomena such as Molly McCully Brown's experience of bodily pain that she describes as indivisible from the rest of her.

Jung instead expanded Kant's use of the term *phenomena* to include representations (dream images, etc.) of the noumenal realm that Schopenhauer had also posited as sensed (therefore empirically known) through the body via the instincts (Schopenhauer, 1958/

1819, 191–200). Jung used the outcome of the Kantian antinomy (that argued for God's existence) to substantiate *esse in anima*, but did not use the antinomic form directly in his own theorizing (Jung, 1921/71a, 43–46). The Kantian antinomy is a concept that does not choose one side of a contradiction over the other. Nor does it conflate or reduce one aspect to the other or "enact a kind of dialectical [therefore illusive according to Kant] synthesis" into a global truth of opposites in an attempt to formulate a resolve (Kant, 2007, A 58–64). Kant's solution was unique in that it grasped and stood by the fundamental aspects of the human condition that were finite, primordial, and could not be reconciled or mediated through a synthesis (Kant, 2007, B 310–312; Žižek, 2006). The gap (borderline concept) between the multiverses of the noumenal and phenomenal realms were, in Kant's mind, insurmountable (Kant, 2007, B 310–311). As argued through the postulates of practical reason, he relied on a "leap of rational faith" to navigate the borderline (Kant, 1956/1788, K 126–127).

Jung borrowed aspects from the arguments in Kant's antinomy and had argued, for example, that the highest soul value (God, self,) was an always already existing reality and real in *esse in anima*, not in mind (*esse in intellectu*; universals having their being in intellect) or matter (*esse in re*; universals having their being in the thing) (Jung, 1921/1971a, 63–67, 77–79; Kant, 1956/1788, 124–125).[23] The self therefore was a "borderline concept," a mediating and unifying force located in between the phenomenal and noumenal realms, yet containing both (Jung, *Letters II*, p. 258). This mediatory stance provided a theoretical closure to the tension between the realms, which circumambulated around the enigmatic core of subjectivity. Similarly, Jung would later create another unifying structure in the psychoid function that authorized a determinant empirical position (Archimedean point) through the instincts, thus wielding a final blow to any remnant of irreducibility in the gap between the noumenal and phenomenal realms (Jung, 1938/40, para. 18, 87, 1947/54, para. 438, 130n).[24] On this point, Wolfgang Giegerich asserts that Jung "did not measure up to his own insight," in that his reflection of psyche remained an external reflection versus an internal or immanent reflection (Giegerich, 2004, 4).

Although Jung claimed to have "stood on Kant," his reading of him was influenced by the common threads that unified German Idealism[25] and included those thinkers whom he cited: Johann Gottlieb Fichte,

Wilhelm Joseph Schelling, Friedrich Hegel, Goethe, Friedrich Schiller, Eduard von Hartmann, Carl Gustav Carus, Schleiermacher, and Schopenhauer (a student of Fichte, Schelling and Hegel) (Jung, 1951/59/68. para. 11, 1947/54, paras. 358–361). While each of these theorists maintained a "particular" reading of Kant that cannot be adequately summarized within a survey of trends, I will nevertheless place Jung within the intellectual milieu in which he was already embedded and one from which his neo-Kantian use of phenomenology/hermeneutics becomes more transparent.

To summarize, Jung took the arguments from Kant that he needed to justify his own theory of the self (a higher mediating synthesis of '*re*' and '*intellectu*'), yet fundamentally changed the epistemological terms of the debate by interspersing his own formulations influenced by some of the German Idealist tenets that were incompatible with Kant's program (Bishop, 2000, 153). Unlike the theoretical rigor practiced in the discipline of philosophy, which would cite and extensively argue "advancements" made to a distinct body of thought, Jung's critiques of philosophers from whom he borrowed ideas were sparsely contextualized (or non-existent) and inconsistently cited. He repeatedly and authoritatively cited Kant and then used aspects of his treatises in an idiosyncratic or unexplicated manner to make a point. For example, he gave the concept of *anima* theoretical "content" by purporting to fill in the blank (borderline between mind and matter) with a fantastical bait (Kantian proposition of reality) and switch (non-Kantian synthesizing of both realms through *anima*) movement of thought. Penetrating the efficacy of his thought, one can detect the desire to substantiate the God concept psychologically, which was not Kant's program at all (Jung, 1921/1971a, para. 67; Kant, 1956/1788, 122–127; Brooks, 2011). In so doing, Jung disregarded the antinomic "form" and the insurmountability of the borderline concept by conflating the noumenal and phenomenal realms and thereby collapsing the antinomy.

Jung's Place in the Debate between the Natural and Human Sciences

Jung was deeply interested in the scientific status of psychology and engaged in descriptive experimental analysis in his early career in Burghölzli hospital, you will recall as a newly vetted psychiatrist with the association test experiments. He soon, however, immersed himself in what he repeatedly referred to as scientific empiricism and eschewed experimental methods, which he claimed produced a "psychology without a psyche" (Jung, 1932, para. 490). Experimental psychology was primarily concerned with establishing general laws of mental functioning, such as occurred in the descriptive investigations into mental imagery by contemporaries Francis Galton, Alfred Binet, and by Victor Henri's experiments into memory, reasoning and imagination. Jung explicitly differentiated analytical psychology from experimental psychology in a lecture he delivered at the International Congress of Education in 1924 by stating the following:

> Analytical psychology differs from experimental psychology in that it does not attempt to isolate individual functions (sense functions, emotional phenomena, thought processes, etc.) and then subject them to experimental conditions for the purposes of investigation. It is far more concerned with the total manifestation of the psyche as a natural phenomena-a highly complex structure, therefore, even though critical examination may be able to divide it up into simpler component complexes.
>
> (Jung, 1926/46, para.170)

The disciplined descriptive analysis of objective phenomena was prevalent, not only in the profusion of emerging psychological work of Franz Brentano and Edmund Husserl, but also in contrast to the empirical methods of a science of subjective psychology to which Jung adhered.

Jung's strong affiliation with the rise of a separate psychology modeled on the natural sciences (association test experiments) was complicated by his predilection for the kinds of experiences that had heretofore been the domain of the human sciences. In an essay he wrote for the *Eranos-Jarbuch* originally titled, "Der Gist der Psychologie" ("On the Nature of the Psyche," 1947/54), Jung portrayed a repressed psychology, one subjugated by the grip of professional philosophers dominating "most universities" (*ibid.*, para. 346). In 1935, in his essay, "Fundamentals of Practical Psychotherapy" (1935a.), Jung reflected on the contradictory theoretical bases within psychology, which focused on universal (general, theoretical, objective) components and the individual (particular, unique, subjective). Within the relativity of human individuality could be found general conformity, he claimed, "up to a certain point" (*ibid.*). Making scientific statements of general validity, he thought, "related only to those parts of the psychic system which [did] not conform, i.e. and [were] amenable to comparison and statistically measurable; they [did] not relate to that part of the system which [was] individual and unique" (*Ibid* para. 1). Science, he posited, could only deal with those areas that could be objectively verified.

In 1945, Jung, while reflecting on the status of psychology stated:

> Nowhere do prejudices, misinterpretations, value-judgments, idio-syncrasies, and projections offer themselves more easily and more unashamedly then just in this field. Nowhere does the observer disturb the experiment more than in psychology. Because of this one can, so to speak, never establish facts sufficiently.
>
> (1926/46, para. 160)[26]

Jung was struggling with the tensions inherent in legitimizing analytical psychology as an empirical science. He had become disillusioned with scientific rationalism. Unlike Dilthey, who viewed psychology as a human science, Jung maintained: "In respect of its natural object and method, modern empirical psychology belongs to the natural sciences, but in respect of its method of explanation it belongs to the human sciences (*ibid.*, para. 166)."[27] Jung was relying on Toni Wolff's position framed in her 1935 paper on the scientific status of complex psychology.[28] In this paper, Wolff found support from neo-Kantian philosopher Heinrich Rickert's theories for a methodological basis of the principles of complex psychology. Wolff used Rickert's distinctions between natural and cultural sciences. She had divided complex psychology into two sides; theory on the side of science and method with that of the individual.

A generalizing (or universalizing) method was used on the side of the individual in dealing with psychic elements or general structures of the psyche, such as typology. An individualizing process came into play when dealing with the processes of individuating and the individuating experience. Referencing Wolff, Jung indirectly was using the ideas of Rickert himself to address his own life long pursuit of bridging the two sciences in support of his mediating notion of the psyche (*esse in anima*), an earlier iteration of what would become Jung's later formulation of the psychoid, or psychoid archetype. Jung's tendency to relativize the distinctions between the disciplines to his own advantage under a cloak of "universality" (his own version of psychologism) alongside his stalwart separatist claims in support of his own version of scientific empiricism, were the ramifications of a thinker held within the foundational problematic. It would not be until Heidegger introduced an ontological analytic that attempted to fundamentally transcend such dualisms that philosophical consciousness could know itself from another perspective.

Concluding Remarks

Jung's extraordinary vision for human kind exceeded the bounds of the psychological disciplines that were forming around him. He was responding to the urgency of the times and through this urgency devoted his lifetime to a form of activism through which he claimed self-relation as first philosophy (although he would not call it that) for all disciplines.[29]

Emmanuel Levinas's (1906–1995) claim that ethics was first philosophy and fundamental to ontology was directed against the assumptions of Husserl and Heidegger's existential philosophy (beginning appositely with Aristotle). Ethics, for Levinas, preceded ontology and was fundamental in order to understand anything else. Levinasian ethics, in short, occurs from the moment the other's gaze (or face) summons me (via my sensorial responses or punch in the gut) through its power to elicit my address so that a dialogue *can* occur (Levinas, 1969). Such a dialogue is fundamental to the possibility of a shared world and cannot occur unless we are brought to our knees in response to alterity. From this perspective, what the philosophical phenomenologists brought to us in the history of ideas at the turn of the twentieth century and throughout was the primacy of inter-subjectivising reality (in its various discrete forms) evoked through the ubiquitous, discontinuous, and often meaningless and random encounters with our biological bodies, our self-disruptive minds, the interactivity with technologies, and our cultural (peopled) material environments from which the meaning or meaninglessness of being could occur and inform our discourse with each other. The ethical relation in this sense does not engage a head-on-a-stick amidst a psychical nether-land, as Jung's disembodied model of selfhood portrays, but relies on an embodied response that is indivisible from its mind amidst the material world. While Jung's ontological assumptions created expansive theoretical possibilities for parapsychological realities, it did so at the theoretical expense of embodied experience embedded in a material world. Jung's theoretical tendency to resolve insurmountable realities by either conflating one reality into the other towards a global truth of opposites (psychoid) or choosing one side of a contradiction (psyche) over the other (everything else, including material reality) as foundational cannot be the standard we use to understand what Molly McCully Brown is telling us about the indivisibility of biological life and the mind in a vast enigmatic world.

Our theories about how personhood is constituted must depend on a more inclusive hermeneutic that regards our interrelatedness as biological and more than biological beings so that possibilities for a future are based on the immanent critique of what is real within our current theories of knowledge from *all* disciplines. These considerations ask what things are from many explanatory models and what the relationships are between things and how these relationships connect or do not connect with each other including those connections that exist beyond our capacities for understanding (Grosz, 2017).[30] The intention is, as was Jung's, to explore what allows for human beings to live productive and generous collective lives on a shared planet.

Notes

1 Schopenhauer, 1958, Vol. II. Title page. I add the word "only" for clarity and changed gender pronouns.

2 The *New York Times*, "Calling Long Distance," Opinion, November 15, 2017. I am grateful to Carrie Griffin Basas for sharing this article with me and for her expertise on disability studies with it.

3 A notable exception to this statement is Jung's association test researches and survey of psychological types that I address later.

4 See Coole and Frost (2010), *New Materialisms Ontology, Agency, and Politics* for a compelling collection of innovative materialist critiques by leading thinkers across the humanities.

5 Jung was also uninterested in childhood development being opposed to child analysis. I use the following example of Jung's psychical obsession

from Michael Fordham's recollections at a dinner party: "Fordham recalls attempting to discuss child therapy at a dinner party with the Jung's." Of Jung he stated: "He was starting on a monologue when Mrs. Jung intervened: "you know very well that you are not interested in people, but [only] your theory of the collective unconscious" (Fordham, 1975, 102–113).

6 Letter to Kristine Mann, following his near-death experience.

7 Ladson's Hinton's chapter in this same volume titled "Jung, Time, and Ethics" elaborates on the ethical consequences of failing to consider temporal states of reality in Jung's conception of the psyche. Teleology, a philosophical doctrine that Jung embraced as central for the self's emergence, attempts to purposively encapsulate the goal of all human desire and cannot account for what is disruptive to the mind in its various materialisms that are random and/or meaningless.

8 Shamdasani (2003) elaborates Jung's often confusing non-linear attempts to reformulate the humanities through his over-arching ideological perspectives. Jung was a quasi-theorist, even if he often conveyed his conceptual arguments in essayist format (Colman, 2017, 16; also see Rowland's, 2005 erudite and creative interpretation of Jung's discursive styles throughout his collective works). While some of Jung's arguments were weak or scientifically unsubstantiated (synchronicity) and leaning towards speculative arguments, they are not just mere hypotheses as Colman asserts, but un-thought out formulations of psychic reality as he saw it (see Brooks, 2013 for a full discussion on Jung's questionable epistemological arguments to which he turns to Kant and Schopenhauer in his formulation of the psychoid, as well as Bishop, 2000 and Huskinson, 2003).

9 Examples of the vast range within Jung's generalist research style include a more concrete phenomenological description of phenomena (as a young research psychiatrist at Burghölzli hospital), a lengthy clinical (anecdotal evidence-based) study of the subjectivity of consciousness (psychology types), or his theoretical attempts to bridge his epistemological claims for synchronicity with the science of the time (in his collaborations with physicist, Wolfgang Pauli). See Jung's letters to and from Pauli for a real sense of what appeared to be a powerful and mutually engaging interdisciplinary scientific/psychological collaboration (Pauli/Jung letters, 1932–1958, 2014). The final efforts of this collaboration failed when the fundamental concept called the "principle of parity" that Pauli was using to substantiate Jung's assertions using physical field theory (see 211) was disregarded in the face of new evidence that shattered prior observations (218–225).

10 The term, *phenomenology* was first employed by the Greeks to refer to "that which appears." Modern phenomenology is derived from philosophical

texts in the eighteenth century, particularly in Johann Heinrich Lambert, Immanuel Kant, Johann Gottlieb Fichte, and G.W.F. Hegel. Kant used the term to signify that branch of science, which dealt with things as they appeared to us, i.e., as an object to my subject. Hegel criticized the dualism inherent in Kant's epistemology that, in his view, failed to develop an understanding of mind other than one that was a static consciousness, in contrast to his claim of an inherent dynamic flow of successive forms of consciousness. Hegel's use of the term was prominently featured in the title of his work in 1807, *Phänomenologie des Geistes* (*Phenomenology of Spirit*). It was not until the first half of the twentieth century that the French phenomenologists began to conceive of Hegel as the filial ancestor of the phenomenological method (Moran, 2000).

11 I direct the interested reader to a variety of historical accounts of the Freud/Jung relationship including their letters by reputable researchers: Makari (2008), *Revolution in Mind The Creation of Psychoanalysis*, a text with Freudian focus; Shamdasani (2003), *Jung and the Making of Modern Psychology*, a formidable text with a Jungian focus; Ellenberger (1970), *The Discovery of the Unconscious: The History and Evolution of Dynamic Psychiatry*, a classic and timeless tome.

12 Jung wrote to his translator Richard Hull in 1951, "Don't forget; I am definitely no philosopher and my concepts are accordingly empirical and not speculative" (Shamdasani, 2003, 167). See footnote 12.

13 See Schnädelbach (1984). Speculative metaphysics or philosophy is generally associated with Hegel and is a form of theorizing that goes beyond verifiable observation. It is a philosophical approach that is informed by an aggressive use of systemic principles of idealism that offered a vision of the unity of the categories of human thought (Kant) as they came into consciousness in and through opposition to each other.

14 Dilthey's psychologism is still a controversial matter. Schnädelbach contends that the manner in which Dilthey retained a psychological understanding was closer to Schleiermacher's psychological understanding (regarding understanding the author and his meaning) and had little to do with Husserl's and others critique of psychologism at the turn of the century. He asserts that the relationship between hermeneutics and psychology was not univocal and more complex than is generally conveyed (Schnädelbach, 1984, 122–129).

15 Richard Askay, personal communication, 12/09.

16 Husserl considered his text *Logische Untersuchungen*, 1900–1901 (or *Logical Investigations*, 1970) to be his breakthrough text into the thought field of what would become philosophical phenomenology and a road map that introduced key concepts that he would develop throughout his

lifetime. Just prior to the onset of the World War II and after his death in 1938, many of his texts were smuggled out of Germany (as he was of Jewish heritage) to a monastery in Belgium and the Husserl-Archives were founded at the Institute of Philosophy in Leuven. Here, the critical 34 volumes of Husserl's works were published, although many of Husserl's manuscripts remain unpublished, as he was astonishingly prolific.

17 Or put another way, Husserl's method focuses on the meaningfulness of the experience of the object (including ideas *and* concrete objects).

18 See Brooks (2011) for a more detailed account of my arguments on this matter.

19 Although Jung found Heidegger's philosophy to be unintelligible we have evidence that he made attempts to understand its basic premises but later erroneously claimed to have some prior theoretical connection to it through his concept of the archetype (Jung, *Letters I*, 273, 331–332; Brooks, 2011).

20 The major figures in the phenomenological tradition to emerge in the twentieth century were Husserl, Heidegger, Jean-Paul Sarte, Maurice Merleau-Ponty, Emmanuel Levinas, and Jürgen Habermas, to name a few.

21 In this newer model, Jung (1954) conceived the drives/instincts as having two aspects that were either dynamic instinctual patterns in human biology and/or could enter into consciousness as images (398–399). While Jung viewed the psychical to overlie the biological order with regard to the genesis of the self, the biological participation is vastly understated. The Jungian self is perceived as a passive receptor of the psychical emanations of a world soul and its embodied participations, such as the role of relational elements from the beginning of life with its others are undeveloped (See Brooks, 2014 for a full discussion on this point).

22 Jung was interested in the ways in which types of consciousness could be singularly characterized when encountering and accessing archetypal reality. Jung's analysis is organized around four main dichotomies including extrovert/introvert, rational/irrational, sensation/intuition, and thinking/feeling.

23 I am grateful to Wolfgang Giegerich's translation of the German to English (personal communication, 9/2009).

24 It must be noted that Jung's theorizing included other dualistic dynamic structures of the psyche not fully developed here but noteworthy, including his key concept of the *"Transcendent Function"* (1916/57) and the *"Coniunctionis"* (1955/56/63/70.)

25 German Idealism was a philosophical movement that emerged at the end of the seventeenth century linked with Romanticism and developed out of Immanuel Kant's transcendental idealism. Under the umbrella of German Idealism emerged divergent classifications of thought such as with Hegel

(absolute idealism), and Eduard von Hartmann (transcendental realism), to name a few. Schopenhauer would roll over in his Frankfurtian grave to be characterized as any kind of an idealist although he was certainly influenced by the transcendental idealism of Kant. He was too much of a "philosophical maverick" (i.e., with the inclusion of Upanishadic, Buddhist, and Romanticist metaphysics in his theorizing) to be historically classified (Richard Askay, personal communication 11/09).

26 Shamdasani states that this quote from Jung came from his personal psychological explorations in the *Redbook* that Shamdasani also edited and translated (2003, 94, 2009).

27 It is interesting to note that empiricism too is a form of philosophy, one that had been appropriated from Kant by Jung, although not recognized in this statement. Kant confronted the epistemological dualism of rationalism and empiricism by not seeking closure via splitting and reductively positioning his doctrines on one side or the other or in seeking a dialectical synthesis to bridge the gap between the irreducible points of view (Kant, 2007, B. 432–611).

28 Wolff (1935), "*Einführung in die Grundlagen der Komplexen Psychologie*," noted in Shamdasani, 2003, 94, Footnote 104, trans. mod.

29 The term "first philosophy" is attributed to Aristotle who designated metaphysics to be the "first philosophy" and by that (although he was not entirely clear) he implied that this topic was fundamental (ontologically independent) to the study of everything else. First philosophy for Aristotle was the consideration of "being *qua* being – both what it is and the attributes which belong to it *qua* being" (Barnes, Ed., 1984, *Metaphysics.* 1026a25-23).

30 See Elizabeth Grosz's compelling text *The Incorporeal Ontology, Ethics, and the Limits of Materialism* (2017). In this text, she investigates the role of the body and thinking in a theoretical movement between materialism and idealism.

References

Askay, R., & Farquhar, J. (2006). *Apprehending the Inaccessible: Freudian Psychoanalysis and Existential Phenomenology.* Evanston, IL: Northwestern University Press..

Bishop, P. (2000). *Synchronicity and Intellectual Intuition in Kant, Swedenborg, and Jung.* Lewiston, NY: The Edwin Mellen Press.

Brooke, R. (2015/1999). *Jung and Phenomenology.* New York: Routledge.

Brooks, R.M. (2011). Un-thought out Metaphysics in Analytical Psychology: A Critique of Jung's Epistemological Basis for Psychic Reality. *Journal of Analytical Psychology*, 56, 492–513.

Brooks, R.M. (2013). The Ethical Dimensions of Life and Analytic Work Through a Levinasian Lens. *International Journal of Jungian Studies*, 5, 188–199.

Brooks, R.M. (2014). Accounting for Material Reality in the Analytic Subject. In L. Huskinson (Ed.), *Behavioral Sciences in Dialogue with the Theory and Practice of Analytical Psychology*, 11–26, Basel: MDPI.

Brooks, R.M. (2016). The Intergenerational Transmission of the Catastrophic Effects of Real World History Expressed through the Analytic Subject. In R. Naso, & J. Mills (Eds.), *Ethics of Evil Psychoanalytic Investigations* (pp. 137–176). London: Karnac.

Brooks, R.M. (2017). Self as Political Possibility: Subversive Neighbor Love and Transcendental Agency Amidst Collective Blindness. *International Journal of Jungian Studies*. DOI: 10.1080/19409052.2017.1384396

Brown, M.M. (November 15, 2017). Calling Long Distance. In *The New York Times*, Opinion, Disability. https://nyti.ms/2hG2qGV downloaded 11/19/17.

Colman, W. (2016). *Act and Image: The Emergence of Symbolic Imagination*. New Orleans, LA: Spring Journal, Inc.

Coole, D. & Frost, S. (2010). *New Materialisms Ontology, Agency, and Politics*. (Eds. D. Coole & S. Frost), Durham: Duke University Press.

Derrida, J. (1997). *Of Grammatology*. Baltimore: Johns Hopkins University Press.

Ellenberger, H. (1970). *The Discovery of the Unconscious The History and Evolution of Dynamic Psychiatry*. New York: Harper Collins Publishers.

Fordham, M. (1975). Memories and Thoughts About C. G. Jung. *Journal of Analytical Psychology*, 20, 102–113.

Gadamer, H. (2004/1975). *Truth and Method*. New York: Continuum.

Giegerich, W. (2004). The End of Meaning and the Birth of Man: An Essay About the State Reached in the History of Consciousness and an Analysis of C.G. Jung's Psychology Project. *Journal of Jungian Theory and Practice* 6 (1).

Grosz, E. (2017). *The Incorporeal Ontology, Ethics, and the Limits of Materialism*. New York: Columbia University Press.

Heidegger, M. (1962/27). *Being and Time*. New York: Harper One.

Heidegger, M. (2008/1929). What is Metaphysics? In *Basic Writings*, New York: HarperCollins.

Heidegger, M. (2010). *The Phenomenology of Religious Life*. (M. Fritsch & J.A. Gosetti Ferencei, Trans.). Bloomington, IN: Indiana University Press.

Hegel, G.F.W. (1952). *Phenomenology of Spirit*. Oxford: Oxford University Press.

Hinton, L. (2015). Temporality and the Torments of Time. *Journal of Analytical Psychology*, 60(3), 33–370.

Huskinson, L. (2003). *Nietzsche and Jung: The Whole Self in the Union of Opposites.* New York: Brunner-Routledge.

Husserl, E. (1970). *Logical Investigations.* 2 vols., Trans. J.N. Findlay. London: Routledge & Kegan Paul.

Husserl, E. (2012/1931). *Ideas. A General Introduction to Pure Phenomenology.* Trans. W.R. Boyce Gibson. London: Routledge.

Jung, C.G. (1953). *The Collected Works of C.G. Jung,* Edited by H. Read, M. Fordham & G. Adler. New York: Pantheon; Princeton, NJ: Princeton University Press. [Hereafter cited as *CW* with volume and page numbers].

Jung, C.G. (1916/57). *The Transcendent Function. CW,* 8, 67–91.

Jung, C.G. (1921/71a). *The Problem of Types in the History of Classical and Medieval Thought. CW,* 6, 8–66.

Jung, C.G. (1921/71b). *The Type Problem in Modern Philosophy. CW,* 6, 273–321.

Jung, C.G. (1926/46). *Analytical Psychology and Education. CW,* 17, 65–132.

Jung, C.G. (1932). *Psychotherapists or the Clergy. CW,* 11, 327–347.

Jung, C.G. (1935a). *Principles of Practical Psychotherapy. CW,* 16, 3–20.

Jung, C.G. (1935b). *The Tavistock Lectures. CW,* 18, 5–182.

Jung, C.G. (1938/40). *The Autonomy of the Unconscious (the Terry Lectures) CW,* 11, 5–106.

Jung, C.G. (1947/54). *On the Nature of the Psyche. CW,* 8, 159–234.

Jung, C.G. (1951/59/68). *Fundamental Questions of Psychotherapy. CW,* 16, 94–126.

Jung, C.G. (1954). *Psychology and Religion. CW,* 18, 645–753.

Jung, C.G. (1955/56/63/70). *The Mysterium Coniunctionis. CW,* 14.

Jung, C.G. (1957). *The Undiscovered Self. CW,* 10, 245–305.

Jung, C.G. (1973). *Jung Letters Volume 1:* 1906–1950.

Jung, C.G. (1973). *Jung Letters Volume 2:* 1951–1961.

Jung, C.G. (1965). *Memories, Dreams, Reflections.* New York: Vantage Books.

Jung, C.G. (1977). *C. G. Jung Speaking Interviews and Encounters.* (Eds., W. McGuire & R.F.C. Hull) Princeton: Princeton University Press.

Jung, C.G. (2014). *Atom and Archetype The Pauli/Jung Letters, 1932–1958.* (Ed. C.A. Meier), Princeton: Princeton University Press.

Kant, I. (2007). *The Critique of Pure Reason.* New York: Cambridge University Press.

Kant, I. (1956). *The Critique of Practical Reason.* New York: Cambridge University Press.

Levinas, E. (1969). *Totality and Infinity.* Pittsburg, PN: Duquesne University Press.

Lear, J. (2000). *Happiness, Death, and the Remainder of Life.* London: Harvard University Press.

Makari, G. (2008). *Revolution in Mind The Creation of Psychoanalysis.* New York: Harper Collins.

Malabou, C. (2016). *Before Tomorrow Epigenesis and Rationality.* (C. Shread, Trans.). Malden, MA: Polity Press.

Moran, D. (2000). *Introduction to Phenomenology.* London: Routledge Taylor & Francis Group.

Rowland, S. (2005). *Jung as a Writer.* New York, NY: Routledge.

Schmidt, L. (2006). *Understanding Hermeneutics.* Evanston, IL: Northwestern University Press.

Schnädelbach, H. (1984). *Philosophy in Germany 1831–1933.* Cambridge: Cambridge University Press.

Schopenhauer, A. (1958/1819). *The World as Will and Representation.* Vol. II. New York: Dover.

Shamdasani, S. (2003). *Jung and the Making of Modern Psychology the Dream of a Science.* Cambridge: Cambridge University Press.

Shamdasani, S. (2008). "The Boundless Expanse": Jung's Reflections on Death and Life. *Quadrant*, 38/1, 9–30.

Spiegelberg, H. (1972). *Phenomenology in Psychology and Psychiatry a Historical Introduction.* Evanston, IL: Northwestern University Press.

Stiegler, B. (2013). *What Makes Life Worth Living on Pharmacology.* Cambridge: Polity.

Tauber, A. (2010). *Freud the Reluctant Philosopher.* Princeton: Princeton University Press.

Zahavi, D. (2003). *Husserl's Phenomenology.* Stanford: Stanford University Press.

Zahavi, D. (2008). *Subjectivity and Selfhood.* Cambridge, MA: The MIT Press.

Žižek, S. (1994). Introduction. In *Mapping Ideology.* London: Verso.

Žižek, S. (2006). *The Parallax View.* Cambridge, MA: MIT Press.

Zuidervaart, L. (2017). *Truth in Husserl, Heidegger, and the Frankfurt School: Critical Retrieval.* Cambridge, MA: MIT Press.

Chapter 6

Phenomenological Practices and Philosophical Insights in Jung

Cecile T. Tougas

My brother-in-law Joe rode into Washington DC each workday, waiting at a curb until the right car, needing to become a High Occupancy Vehicle, stopped for him to join the other commuting passengers before speeding off into the fast lane. Fred was riding to his little table at the Library of Congress where librarians helped him collect data for a book on the philosophies of India, so detailed and complex that its Table of Contents was including and distinguishing eighteen philosophical groups, with twenty-eight subcategories under Buddhism.

Joe died of cancer. My sister gave me the published book with Fred's handwriting on the title page, "To Joseph for his human concern and expression of success in my work F.L. Kumar." Even small parts of the book indicate a sense of the whole. Fred himself summarized "Specific Contributions of the Book" on an introductory page:

> The essential quest of Indian thought is the search for the individual self—to understand and explain it. While material possessions are not ignored, the central interest by far was directed toward self-realization which involved understanding of oneself. For this reason, the individual practiced concentration and inwardness. This inwardness was a kind of spiritual experience which gripped the person and guided him to insights and experiences beyond anything physical.
>
> This work places much emphasis upon man's search for a satisfying self-experience independent of any religious practice and belief. Such a self-experience was specifically characteristic of the Munies who practiced and cultivated the self with single-minded attention. These men were spiritually realized individuals who stood out as supreme examples, who searched for the self, understood it, and thus became models, guiding lights to be followed.

In essence for the self is a kind of spiritual experience contained within the human self itself.

(Kumar, 1991, xii)

For several years I read these paragraphs instead of early morning coffee, just before going into the fast lane of the workday. I did not learn from this book that I was an individual self. I was one before I knew it, which is a funny thing to write. I remember as a child getting on a small bench to see my face in the bathroom mirror. When I was sixteen, Paul David Benson invited me to ride on the back of his motorcycle. At that time I was hearing of Platonic forms, and I knew they existed. There was no question of their evidence or their dependence on the effect of hormones or drugs. As Professor Kumar writes, "There are no gray areas where physical brain cells break down and then emerge as mental experiences" (Kumar, 1991, xiii).

The distinction between "ego" and "self" did not appear to be a problem, as I felt and recognized there was more to me than I knew, particularly when I talked to my doll outdoors on the front lawn by the tree or cried indoors in a small room. I lived with what came up, what guided and sometimes scared me.

The difficulty was, and is, with the word "the." Robert Katz, the first mathematician I had as a teacher, said that "one" means "one and only," as engaged couples, but not married couples, mean. He stood on his desk once. Yet he led me to notice difficulties in speaking about "one" and "the one," particularly in relation to saying "the self." If the self is individual and there are many individuals, then "the self" means both "this one" and "many particular ones" in general. For self is not only this unique individual, among many unique individuals, but as one commonality is also the form, the essence, the idea "self," like the number "3" or the ideal "equal."

I was making my slow way through Plato's *Meno* and I loved numbers. I readily saw that there was only one number 3 and that each unique number related to all the others. And the equal as essence had to be one, because if there were many distinct equals different from one another, they would not be equal to each other, and so the equal would not be equal, but it is. Besides, the equal itself is necessary for understanding the unequal. So if "3" and "equal" are each one distinct form, is "self" one distinct form for everyone?

In grief I asked, is my whole existence and all this trouble just a generality, a common human form as essence? Then I studied Aristotle, who did field studies in Asia Minor for twenty years before attending Plato's Academy. He observed long and concluded that a natural being, such as an acorn, had a cause within it besides its material cause, one that was not material but rather formal, tending to form that individual to become itself over time, for that was what the acorn actually did over a long period of time: it was becoming a full tree (see Aristotle, 192a16–195b30). A purely material cause was not enough to account for the activity of its coming to be what it was as this particular tree.

A non-material cause is not a ghost, an electron, a gene, or a projection of the scientist; rather, it is nature as a forming cause for an individual being as aiming towards and becoming itself, what it is in its *individual essence* as "this one." Thus, each self has an individual essence, tended toward in actions expressing and fulfilling the meaning of that self's being, a meaning that becomes evident over time. For human beings, and maybe even for acorns, becoming self involves concentration and inwardness as a kind of spiritual experience which, as Professor Kumar says, grips and guides a person to insights and experiences deeper than what appears physically.

Jung suffered, noticed, and explored such a forming cause in himself and others, calling its process "individuation." Like Aristotle and Professor Kumar, he too was gripped with experiences of a non-material aspect of being. Not only philosophical, Jung was also phenomenological, for he came to insight by continuing reflection on the phenomena, the given appearances, of lived experience.

Nélida Rose Simard, my mother's mother, studied piano at the New England Conservatory of Music, performed concerts with Dr. Jeffries, her teacher, and received so many roses afterwards that some had to be placed in the bathtub. At some time after the birth of my mother, an only child, arthritis set into her hands and she no longer played. She slept in her upholstered chair in the living room, sometimes until 2:00 a.m., before lying down in bed. She had many dreams and spoke of them. We lived nearby and my mother spoke to her every day. She and P'père took care of us after school. She lived to be eighty-six.

Eugène Letendre Tougas, my father's father, studied a classical French program for late high school and college at l'Université de Lavalle in Montréal, being away from his family in Rhode Island for six school years. He served in both world wars, taught high school French, and died of a heart attack at the age of sixty. The first time I saw my father cry was when his father died. Later I found out that, when my father's father received the news on a Sunday morning that his father had died, he still went out with my father to deliver the Sunday newspapers before coming in to eat breakfast and feel affected by the death.

As a very young child, I cried at first when visiting my father's family. Yet I felt their rigorous energy in thinking and wondered at my aunts as I heard their heeled shoes clacking on the wooden floor on their way to ask their father a question about grammar. I advanced academically to the utmost and felt that this P'père would have loved to write a book.

Studying Jung's *Psychological Types*, I easily recognized distinctions between sensation and intuition as ways of perceiving, feeling and thinking as ways of judging, and introversion and extraversion as attitudes towards existence. For my mother's family exemplified the former, and my father's, the latter, of each pair. Like my mother's mother, I too dreamed a lot, and Jung affirmed the importance of dreaming. Jung not only made possible for me a new attitude towards my personal experiences but also affirmed the basic activity of phenomenology.

In graduate school I had felt liberated in hearing Husserl express in words the importance of noticing and describing lived experience as happening, remembered, and anticipated. Doing phenomenology involved reflecting on what I was living, had lived, and even hoped to live, as a way to know both myself and others. Subjectivity was as important as objectivity. Husserl wrote:

> *whatever presents itself in 'intuition' in primordial form* (as it were in its bodily reality), *is simply to be accepted as it gives itself out to be,* though *only within the limits in which it then presents itself.*
> (Husserl 1958: 92, emphasis in original)

For Husserl, "intuition" meant a beholding of anything at all, from the Latin word *intueor*, "look at, watch; contemplate, consider; admire" (Kidd, 1961: 179), with the widest sense of the word "thing," including non-spatial entities such as acts of perceiving, judging, and dreaming.

Studying such acts, along with the objects they make present, is phenomenology. Its basic principle is: whatever is given as itself present, as evident in some way, is to be accepted as evident, to the degree and within the limits of the ways in which it is present, and as open to further experience and questioning (Tougas, 2013: 11–12).

Jung noticed and described different acts of perception, judgment, and attitude, as well as dreaming and imagining, and he accepted each activity as providing some degree of evidence, within its limits and with possible subsequent correction. He saw that science and objective thinking were not the only ways of knowing, as music and subjective feeling too gave their own kinds of evidence. Jung practiced basic phenomenology, even though the glossary of Jung's works does not mention Husserl, nor have I ever read Jung's name in Husserl's writing. The practice was evident to Jung himself as an obvious and felt necessity.

Less than an hour after writing about Aristotle last week, I took up the February 27, 2017 issue of *The New Yorker* and came upon a review by Alex Ross, entitled "Singing Philosophy: Kate Soper's Theatre of the Mind" (Ross, 74–75). Soper's masterpiece of theatre is "*Ipsa Dixit*", Latin for "She Herself Said" as feminine form of a legal term meaning a claim without proof. Ross describes it as "philosophy-opera" in which works of Aristotle, Plato, Sophocles, Freud, Wittgenstein, and others are put to sound, sung, played with, and contradicted. Near the end, a movement called "Metaphysics" asks, "What is the nature of being?" Ross (2017) writes:

> Amid an analysis of the distinction between matter and form, she disassembles instruments mid-performance, detaching the body of the flute from the head piece and removing the rim of a drum; the ensemble goes on making music from the remnants. Instruments, or pieces of them, are then handed around: the violinist blows into part of the flute; the soprano strums the violin; the violinist bows a crotale; the percussionist thumps the violin with a soft mallet. In one glorious moment, Soper and Modney play the violin simultaneously. This ballet of musical objects not only illustrates Aristotle's notion of a fundamental form outside the empirical realm--as matter decays, the spirit persists--but also celebrates the sonic diversity of avant-garde composition. Laughter gives way to

wonder as a cosmic coda makes audible Aristotle's ideal of self-sufficient contemplation... ... the final bars feel uncertain, provisional, questing. A twenty-first-century masterpiece could end no other way. (75)

What are the odds that, just after writing about Aristotle and individual essence, I should find public mention, not only of this philosopher but also of his distinction between matter and form? His spirit seems to persist, despite the questing of our century. Moreover, a woman takes it up as part of her presenting herself originally. Indeed, what are the odds that I should find both a combining and a contrasting of music and philosophy, when a central problem of my life has been to distinguish and relate musical feeling from my mother's mother and logical thinking from my father's father?

Jung called such coincidence "synchronicity" and thought of it as "an acausal connecting principle" in the sense that no material cause is given or even possible to sufficiently account for the experienced connection (Jung, 1981, 816, 866). Exact detailed meaning hits, weighty, clever, scary, funny, amazing, worrisome, all at the same time, connecting moments of time, near or far, and parts of space, near or far—now stretching beyond Aristotle's thought about causality even while affirming it, as both *Ipsa Dixit* and the event of my hearing about the performance show me.

Meaning itself seems alive, as it attracts us and draws our attention. Meaninglessness itself is experienced as a sore or boring lack, sometimes denied in fear or grief, when nothing interests. Where does meaning live? Husserl (1970) described acts of awareness as seeking, aiming at, and tending toward meaning, and as fulfilled by the presence of what is meant. For him, "intuiting" was beholding in the widest sense of the term, as the activity of experiencing the presence of something or someone or some state of affairs. Jung, though, meant "intuition" in a more limited sense, as a contrast and complement to sense perception, often accompanying hearing, seeing, touching, tasting, and smelling.

For Husserl, any awareness is an activity of meaning-intending, whether noticed and reflected upon or not, while an awareness that gives the presence of something, even just a limited presence, is an activity of meaning-fulfillment, as it gives much more than just the aiming and fulfills it to the degree that the intended is present. Through intuiting or beholding of some sort—sense perceiving, dreaming, remembering the just past, for example—we experience that something or some state of affairs, at least partially, but maybe never fully.

Intended meaning and fulfilled meaning may find expression in acts of speaking, writing, singing, drawing, moving, gesturing, pressing forth in many ways. Husserl sees the range of meaning-expressing acts as wide but not so wide as the range of meaning-intending acts. Awareness is in general an aiming at meaning, but it is not the case that each activity of awareness provides the presence of what is thought about or longed for. And much awareness is not even expressed—the current running-on of thoughts, feelings, images, memories, hopes does continue, mostly without words, language, advertisement. Yet this too is intending and meaningful awareness.

In a synchronistic event, we experience that meaning exists not only in subjects, but also in material objects given as present in some way, and we feel that matter has meaning of itself. But modern science does not consider present and active meaning—never mind formal cause— as existing in a physical thing, inasmuch as it holds that molecules, atoms, quanta in motion are sufficient to constitute spatial objects. Jung participated in this modern scientific point of view. At the same time, he had tremendous evidence from other ways of knowing— dreaming, imagining, hoping, reflecting, philosophizing—that material objects themselves have meaning that draws our attention and affects us dynamically. Pondering such evidence leads to a basic phenomeno-logical insight: both material objects and activities of awareness are phenomenal, appearing as themselves in the continuum of awareness as a tending toward meaning.

I go to the book, *Man and his Symbols*, conceived and edited by Jung, as I remember that the words I am aiming to see are on the left side of the page, although it has been years since I have opened this book. There are many pages that have papers in them, but somehow I open immediately to page 56, the one I was hoping for. I feel a little scared. There before me are the words: "mentally my hitherto greatest spiritual adventure had been to study the philosophies of Kant and Schopenhauer" (Jung et al., 1964, 56). In these pages Jung is describing a dream he had and the "phoney" solution of it he gave to Freud in order to avoid Freud's forced interpretation. For at that moment Jung felt overwhelmed by an intuition about the role that the subjective factor plays in psychological understanding ... ... (an) insight into the fact that my dream meant *myself, my* life and *my* world, my whole reality against a theoretical structure erected by another, strange mind for reasons and purposes of its own.

(57)

Jung concludes: "The individual is the only reality" (58).

Jung does not then raise the philosophical question, How is it possible for an individual to know and be known by another? But having studied Kant and Schopenhauer as a great spiritual adventure, he had some sense of their phenomenological attitude. Kant observed awareness critically at length and noticed that appearances constitute our experience. Things, people, the world, and even self, are known as existing only insofar as they are present, given, evident to awareness in some way, as phenomena.

Radically, Kant wrote: "Space is nothing but the form of all appearances of outer sense. It is the subjective condition of sensibility, under which alone outer intuition is possible for us... ... It is, therefore, solely from the human standpoint that we can speak of space, of extended things, etc." (Kant, 1963, A26, B42). Similarly, Kant wrote: "Time is nothing but the form of inner sense, that is, of the intuition of ourselves and of our inner state... ... Time is the formal *a priori* condition of all appearances whatsoever... ... It has objective validity only in respect of appearances, these being things which we take *as objects of our senses*" (Kant, 1963, A33, B49--A35, B51).

Jung (1976) confirms in *Psychological Types*:

> We must not forget--although the extravert is only too prone to do so--that perception and cognition are not purely objective, but are also subjectively conditioned. The world exists not merely in itself, but also as it appears to me. Indeed, at bottom, we have absolutely no criterion that could help us to form a judgment of a world which was unassimilable by the subject.
>
> (621)

The world lived in and understood as "in itself" is the world as appearance to awareness, but considered, thought, presumed, imagined—inadequately so—as the totality of what is given actually or possibly, to any and all awareness. This understanding of world is transcendental, as a glimpse of what is fundamental to experience; it is not a transcendent understanding that is beyond experience. Immersed in experience every day, we might, but rarely do, notice that the world is fundamentally phenomenal, even as it is present as itself, real and shared. The world is given as lived and participated in by each part or member; the tree and the squirrel as seen just now, as well as the molecules and the atoms just thought about, are not independent of awareness. Both Kant and Jung noticed phenomenality. But Jung's sense of synchronicity expands upon the insight that awareness is constituted by phenomena, inasmuch as a sense of synchronicity builds on a sense of fundamental interconnection and mutuality in awareness.

We too can have this sense as we notice that phenomena occur as moments of lived, suffered, endured time to which we are subjected, whether giving us the presence of spatial objects or non-spatial objects such as numbers or feelings. We can also turn our attention to space and time as forming or providing order in awareness. In doing so we may notice awareness itself as a continuum, an ongoing whole of inseparable parts (Husserl, 1970) that includes both what we experience as outward and what we experience as inward.

Awareness exists as a continuum constituted by everyone or everything that has even the least bit of meaning. In a continuum each part is related to every other part, the way numbers are related to one another, and such fundamental relation makes possible the experience of self, others, things—whatever may be given, within the limits within which it is given. We may be attracted to and moved by the meaning of any part, near or far, as ordinary or as synchronistic, in a mutuality that is much more than a mere collection.

Accordingly, Jung's negative terms, "the unconscious" and "the collective unconscious," fall far short in aiming to describe a felt sense of whole constituted by distinct yet inseparable parts, with each part having its particular forming, though little known, cause in relation to the others—little known, yes, but suffered, as James Joyce writes: "we wail, batten, sport, clip, clasp, sunder, dwindle, die … … in the like way is all hidden when we would backward see from what region of remoteness the whatness of our whoness hath fetched his whenceness" (Joyce, 1961, 386–387/394).

Socrates, you agreed with Crito that there is a part of us that is "mutilated by wrong actions and benefited by right ones" (Plato, 1963, 47e). You asked Thrasymachus, "what about living? Shall we not say that it is the work of a soul?" (Plato, 1968, 353d) You concluded that living well comes down to the soul doing its work well. But what does "living well" mean? You spent much time with your associates conversing about what is good and what is just but did not come to a clear definition. Moreover, you led the conversation away from considering the justice of an individual to considering the justice of a whole city, saying "perhaps there would be more justice in the bigger and it would be easier to observe closely" (Plato, 1968, 368e-369a).

Oh ironic man, you had experienced the resentment of men who, when questioned about their opinions, angrily discovered their ignorance, particularly about themselves. You did not cease examining life as the work of souls with respect to being good or just, and your asking questions led to your condemnation and death. What a joke to imply that, because the city is bigger spatially, it may have more justice in it, when it was the city of Athens that condemned you!

Nevertheless, you turned attention to five possible regimes: kingly, timocratic, oligarchic, democratic, tyrannic (Plato, 1968, 580b). At great length you agreed—though you did not teach anyone, insofar as each one has to see individually—that the best and happiest life is being king of oneself, while the worst and most wretched life is being tyrannic, as tyrant of both self and city (Plato, 1968, 580b-c).

You noted that the tyrannic man "didn't blame himself for the evils but chance, demons, and anything rather than himself" (Plato, 1968, 619b-c), though he may have participated in virtue "by habit, without philosophy," being inexperienced and unreflective as if from heaven, "unpracticed in labors" that people from the earth well knew (Plato, 1968, 619c-d). Your practice of conversation and argument is still needed today.

Jung reflected as you did, though mostly in his writing. His long studies, observations, therapeutic work, travels, imaginings, dreams, qualify him as both "philosophical," in your sense of "loving wisdom," and as "practiced in labors" that people from the earth well know. Like you he was crucially aware of the central importance of soul. He too noticed how touchy we become when our ignorance, ineptitude, or immaturity comes to our attention. In describing psychological types, he found opposition throughout, inasmuch as habitual perceiving by the five senses leads to undeveloped intuiting, habitual thinking leads to undeveloped feeling, and diehard extraversion leads to blind introversion—and *vice versa*.

Recognizing and bearing one's weakness, even as one matures, is a daily task and on some days may be excruciating. Trying to find an easy way out of difficulty, we, as Jung said, "project the shadow side" onto others. If we start to discover that what we observe in others really belongs to ourselves, we may become angry and resentful, just like the Athenians who murdered you, Socrates. Yet if, as you agreed, there is a part of us that is "mutilated by wrong actions and benefited by right ones" (Plato, 1963, 47e), and this "part" is our soul or life, we are destroyed and become tyrants if we do not open up to self-knowledge and recognize the shadow as our own.

Jungian analysis, like Socratic examining, is a study of soul that aims not only to question but also to act. Such work is philosophical, phenomenological, and existential.

Kumar and Indian thought: self-realization and inwardness. Aristotle: forming cause in material object. Jung: evident psychological acts. Husserl: tending toward meaning. Kant: spatio-temporal appearances. Jung: reality as phenomenal. Husserl: continuum of awareness. Socrates: examining of soul.

Wanting to glimpse and describe philosophical insights in Jung, I reflect and write from my experience as personally lived, following phenomenological practices: aiming at the meaning hoped for, attending to evidence, performing different acts—noting sensate details, listening to intuitive twinges, thinking with increasing clarity, feeling ranges of value, imagining another as present, waking up after dreaming and scribbling, having the task in mind day and night.

To recognize a philosophical insight in Jung, I need to have the insight myself, at least partially, and to see it in some relation to insights of others. From my own perspective I try to experience theirs, albeit inadequately. During the process a commonality, maybe even an essence, begins to appear, and I pause to review what I have found so far: self, individual form, psychological acts, meaning-intending of phenomena or appearances, awareness as a continuum, soul as life. These all may be the same reality.

Besides his descriptions of typical psychological acts, Jung's most important and unique contribution to phenomenology and contemporary philosophy is his original work on *anima* and *animus*. Revolutionary in the twentieth century, it was liberating to many, though it subsequently incited riots of criticism and alternative interpretations. Recently the introduction of just the two words themselves with brief definitions led to outrage in young people who insisted that the concepts were sexist, prejudiced, gendered, discriminatory, and unacceptable. Some meaning had hit them profoundly, even as they denied its validity.

The Latin noun *animus* is masculine and means "mind, soul; consciousness; reason, thought, opinion, imagination; heart, feelings, disposition; courage, spirit, pride, passion; will, purpose; term of endearment" (Kidd, 1961: 21). The Latin noun *anima* is feminine and means "wind, air; breath; life; soul, mind; ghost, spirit" (*ibid.*). Obviously there is overlapping meaning. The masculine term offers seventeen distinctions in English; the feminine has only eight, with "wind, air; breath" standing out as particular to *anima*.

Jung chose a term with two genders in Latin but did not mean to say that a woman is *anima* and a man, *animus*, inasmuch as the former term refers to an aspect of a man, and the latter, to an aspect of a woman. For Jung observed that a person is both feminine and masculine, with the meaning and expression of these as related to the individual.

Moreover, *anima* and *animus* do not refer to opposing psychological actions or attitudes, like ones he distinguished in his work on psychological types, for their relation is complex. Both mean both soul and spirit. At the same time, they are transcendental—fundamental—forms of soul and spirit, the way space and time are transcendental forms. They give degrees of importance and intensity to phenomena, as though ranking them in order of value. Jung did not officially add them to the Kantian table of forms, but he did see them as fundamentally constituting experience as lived and suffered. For the meaning-intending of awareness is not simply a passionless "aiming" at meaning, but rather, a desiring and seeking instinct that Schopenhauer called "Will" and Freud called "libido."

Jung is original in speaking of spirit, soul, awareness as an erotically connected pair existing in each person: *animus* in a woman and *anima* in a man. Together in the individual they are a creative erotic force mothering and fathering new life. Thus, philosophically, "human" no longer means "man," as it did for centuries in the Western academic tradition, but now, rather, means a pair. Moreover, natality comes to the fore. "All men are mortal" in the model syllogism now has a partner: "All humans are born." Original relation to the feminine as mother is undeniable, even as it had been obscured because of embarrassment at being dependent. Ethics comes to light as grounded in recognition of our primal dependency and consequent gratitude for our caregivers. And erotic interest opens up to a wide variety of possible expressions.

Indeed, the continuum of awareness, considered as a whole of distinct yet inseparable parts like the number continuum, now may be understood as a mutually lived reciprocity, in which each is born and shares life with others, near and far. Ancestors may breathe intentions forward to their progeny as a question and a hope for some fulfillment of what Jung called "the unlived life." Children may feel drawn to accomplish particular tasks, the significance of which they recognize only later in life. Married partners may have called to each other's heart over a vast gulf of interracial hatred or gender bias. The erotically connected pair constituting an individual makes possible other relations of caring, even as war, famine, plunder, pillaging continue to exist. An ethics of caring, like Socratic self-questioning and Jungian analysis, is a work in progress.

Many Jungian analysts observed the feminine/masculine pair and described how the pair was appearing, particularly during experiences of human suffering. Sylvia Brinton Perera studies the myth of Inanna-Ishtar and Ereshkigal, and writes:

> The implication for modern women is that only after the full, even demonic, range of affects and objectivity of the dark feminine is felt and claimed can a true, soul-met, passionate and individual comradeship be possible between woman and man as equals.
>
> (Perera 1981, 94)

The same may be said for men and the dark masculine. Individual self-relation founds relations between two people.

Marie-Louise von Franz at great length describes the phenomena of evil as shown in fairy tales. When the utmost horrible evil happens, soul and spirit seem doomed. Yet von Franz speaks of "the deepest nucleus of the psyche, the Self" as behind an instinct which is felt as the "life-force of the horse" that ordinarily carries one along day to day. In truth, the horse is the Self, "travestied, or covered up, or only appearing as an unconscious urge" (von Franz 1983, 259) that, nevertheless, has a deeper instinct underlying. She affirms:

> The urge towards individuation is in our view a true instinct, probably the strongest instinct of all... ... But it needs the sacrifice, or the having it out with this force, to find out the deeper forms and go beyond experiencing it as a kind of divine carrying impulse.
>
> (von Franz 1983, 259–260)

In a fairy tale about the utmost evil, a king's son and the devil's daughter try to use the devil's own workers to escape from her father, then they run, then become a church and a parson, then an alder tree and a bird, then a horse and rider, then a rice field and a quail, and finally she becomes a big pond of milk and he, a duck always to swim right in the middle "and keep his head under the milk and never look out" but finally the devil becomes furious, loses patience, and "changed himself into an enormous goose, swallowed the whole pond with the duck and waddled home" (von Franz, 1983, 263).

Then there is the experience of losing everything. Psychological facts are cruel. But the milk begins to ferment in the devil's stomach and he can hardly move. Suddenly there is a loud crack and he bursts open. There the erotic pair stand "in their youthful beauty" (von Franz 1983, 264); they marry and inherit the kingdom. Personal feeling for the individual, called "love," thus may suffer devilish totalitarian power, but the pair is not swallowed forever, inasmuch as there is an innermost center of the psyche, "a very profound, mystical solution offered by this fairy tale" (271), von Franz says on the last page.

In her book, *The Stepmother in Fairy Tales: Bereavement and the Feminine Shadow*, Jacqueline M. Schectman (1993) describes the mind and heart of "the wicked stepmother," discovering and shining light on "feelings, behavior and responses which belong not only to mothers and stepmothers, but to all of us," as David Hart says in the preface (xii). Insofar as Schectman characterizes "what is in essence a state of mind" (xii), she is phenomenological.

For many years, much of Schectman's therapeutic work was with poor, abused, and neglected children. Their favorite story was "Hansel and Gretel." In that fairy tale, a cold-hearted, depleted mother abandons her children, and then a gingerbread-house reveals a candy-coated witch eager to devour them. These mothers are not replacements for a good mother who died, but rather "have always been part of the story, a part of the milieu of poverty" (Schectman 1993, 52). To an alone, overburdened, adolescent mother, a child might appear like "the Kleinian vision of the child as an innately sadistic, murderous being" (53) who becomes greedy in face of scarcity.

In the story Hansel and Gretel are wary, vigilant, and streetwise. "Survivor that he is, Hansel has the ability—the hermetic consciousness—to perceive value in apparently ordinary objects" (Schectman, 1993, 56). In the book Schectman interweaves brief descriptions of mothers and children she worked with, noting that the therapist "feels a great pull to be the Good-and-Understanding, All-Giving-Mother, to compensate such patients for their loss" (66). But such a sweet persona is difficult to sustain, and it masks an intent to devour the energy of the young. Perceptively, Schectman notes that any woman who infantilizes her grown child may hold an offspring "very close, but not without his full cooperation" (71).

But Hansel and Gretel do not cooperate with the sweet witch. While Hansel leads much of the pair's actions, Gretel has to do grueling work, face the witch, keep her eyes open, and trick the trickster, in order "to come into her own, to feel her strength" (71). While taking responsibility, both have inner resources, with a bit of good luck or grace. Schectman describes both children up to the end, when they become independent of each other.

Using a myth, fairy tales, and therapeutic data, three woman analysts thus observe and describe, respectively, woman in relation to herself and to man, the couple in relation to the innermost center of self, and the stepmother and her children in reciprocal relation—all in the face of evil and intense human suffering. In distinguishing *animus* and *anima*, while emphasizing erotic relation within a person, Jung initiated a new direction in phenomenological work that inspired these women and others. Such work needs to continue today.

Acknowledgments

I wish to thank John D. Scanlon for being my Husserl teacher at Duquesne University, Pittsburgh, PA, and for his translation of Edmund Husserl's lectures entitled *Phenomenological Psychology*. I also wish to thank the University of Massachusetts Lowell, the University of Southern Maine, and the North Carolina School of Science and Mathematics for my teaching opportunities; and to Routledge for publishing my book, *The Phenomena of Awareness: Husserl, Cantor, Jung.*

References

Aristotle (1941). *Metaphysics* and *Physics* in R. McKeon (Ed.) *The Basic Works of Aristotle*, New York: Random House.

Husserl, E. (1958). *Ideas: General Introduction to Pure Phenomenology*, trans. W.R.B. Gibson, New York: The Macmillan Company.

———— (1970). *Logical Investigations, 2 vols*, trans. J.N. Findlay, New York: Humanities Press.

———— (1977). *Phenomenological Psychology: Lectures, Summer Semester, 1925*, trans. J. Scanlon, The Hague: Martinus Nijhoff.

Joyce, J. (1961). *Ulysses*, New York: Random House.

Jung, C.G. (1966–1992). *The Collected Works of C. G. Jung, 20 vols*, trans. R.F.C. Hull, ed. H. Read, M. Fordham, & G. Adler, Princeton: Princeton University Press.

———— (1976). *Psychological Types, CW,* 6. trans. H.G. Baynes, rev. R.F.C. Hull.

———— (1981). *The Structure and Dynamics of the Psyche. CW*, 6, trans. R.F.C. Hull.

Jung, C.G. et al. (1964). *Man and His Symbols*, New York: Doubleday & Company Inc.

Kant, I. (1963). *Immanuel Kant's Critique of Pure Reason*, trans. N.K. Smith, London: Macmillan and Company Ltd.

Katz, R. (1964). *Axiomatic Analysis: An Introduction to Logic and the Real Number System*, Boston: D. C. Heath and Company.

Kidd, D.A. (ed.) (1961). *Collins Latin Gem Dictionary*, London: Collins.

Kumar, F.L. (1991). *The Philosophies of India: A New Approach*, Lewiston, NY: The Edwin Mellen Press.

Perera, S.B. (1981). *Descent to the Goddess: A Way of Initiation for Women*, Toronto, Canada: Inner City Books.

Plato (1963). *Crito* in E. Hamilton & H. Cairns (Eds.) *The Collected Dialogues including the Letters*, New York: Random House, Inc.

———— (1968). *The Republic of Plato*, trans. A. Bloom, New York: Basic Books, Inc.

Ross, A. (2017). Singing Philosophy: Kate Soper's Theatre of the Mind, *The New Yorker*, February 27, 2017, 74–75.

Schectman, J.M. (1993). *The Stepmother in Fairy Tales: Bereavement and the Feminine Shadow*, Boston: Sigo Press.

Schopenhauer, A. (1958). *The World as Will and Representation, 2 vols*, trans. E.F.J. Payne, New York: Dover Publications, Inc.

———— (1974). *On the Fourfold Root of the Principle of Sufficient Reason*, trans. E.F.J. Payne, La Salle, IL: Open Court Publishing Company.

Tougas, C. (1993). Correspondence with Roger Brooke, *The San Francisco Jung Institute Library Journal*, 12 (2), 54–60.

————(1996). Distinct yet Inseparable: Edmund Husserl, *Logical Investigations*, *The San Francisco Jung Institute Library Journal*, 15 (2), 49–76.

———— (1997). Correspondence: Phenomenologists Reading Jung, *The San Francisco Jung Institute Library Journal*, 15 (4), 67–74.

———— (1999a). How Rejection of Essences Expresses Despair, *Journal of Analytical Psychology*, 44 (3), 309–329.

———— (1999b). Reply to Polly Young-Eisendrath, *Journal of Analytical Psychology*, 44 (3), 337.

———— (2000). What is the Difference between Spirit and Soul? Jungian Reflections, *Harvest: Journal for Jungian Studies*, 46 (1), 52–66.

———— (2009). Opposition and Postmodernism, *Jung Journal: Culture & Psyche*, 3 (1), 68–77.

———— (2013). *The Phenomena of Awareness: Husserl, Cantor, Jung*, London: Routledge.

———— (2014a). Causality as individual essence: its bearing on synchronicity, *Journal of Analytical Psychology*, 59, 411–421.

———— (2014b). *Q.E.D.*, *Jung Journal: Culture & Psyche*, 8 (2), 78–82.

———— (2015). Attentive notice to a reply of Harald Atmanspacher, *Journal of Analytical Psychology*, 60 (1), 126–128.

Tougas, C.T. & Ebenreck, S. (Eds.) (2000). *Presenting Women Philosophers*, Philadelphia: Temple University Press.

Von Franz, M.-L. (1983). *Shadow and Evil in Fairy Tales*, Dallas, TX: Spring Publications, Inc.

Willeford, W. (1987). *Feeling, Imagination, and the Self: Transformations of the Mother-Infant Relationship*, Evanston, IL: Northwestern University Press.

Witt, C. (1989). *Substance and Essence in Aristotle: An Interpretation of 'Metaphysics VII-IX'*, Ithaca, NY: Cornell University Press.

Chapter 7

Jung's *Answer to Job*
Toward a "Sensible" Mysticism

Garth Amundson

When considering how to approach Jung's view of religion, I immediately felt that I must write about *Answer to Job*. I say "must" because this essay has had a powerful psychological hold on me since age nineteen, when I first stumbled on it in an anthology of Jung's writings in my college bookstore. At that time, I was another one of those spiritually confused young adults, no longer able to accept the simple faith of my conventional Lutheran upbringing. But neither could I shake the feeling of something profound in the idea that God felt compelled to become a man, a militant rabbi whose brief life reflected an Absolute overflowing with both tender love and terrible wrath (though few Christians that I knew spoke of this latter attribute of the deity, and those that did swiftly qualified it as understandable righteous indignation). I immediately took to Jung: here was another disillusioned Lutheran boy, but one who had come to terms with the contradictions in his faith. His weirdly appealing vision of God was closer to the pulse of life in the world as I was coming to know it: an unlikely paradox of stunning beauty and excruciating loss.

So this chapter is a kind of homecoming for me, a return to the faith of my childhood, though bearing the fruits of years of contemplation about spirituality from diverse perspectives like those in *Answer to Job*. Philosophically and theologically, Jung's work is implicitly mystical. As such, it exists far outside the limits of any taken-for-granted doctrine, such that members of the three main Western religions invariably find it hard to read without reflexive resistance. To them I should say that I haven't set out to rattle anyone's faith. Rather, I have tried to modestly emulate Jung's example of freely exploring the "dark," hidden dimensions of Western religious feeling, knowing as I do that new life usually springs from underground.

Answer to Job (1958) proposes what for Western faith traditions is a heretical twist to our cultural religious narrative. Put inelegantly, Jung asserts that God Himself is in need of psychotherapy: specifically, and predictably, analytic therapy. *Answer to Job* frames humanity's relationship to the Creator as an epic, eons-long dialogue: an intense, variously loving, testy, and ominously disturbing give-and-take between the eternal and temporal that theologian Martin Buber (1937) defines as an intimately "I and You" form of relation to the Absolute (in the original German, *Ich und Du*, and later rendered in the English printing as *I and Thou*). The concept of a dialectic with the divine, first appearing in ancient Hebrew myth, is basic to conventional Judeo-Christian theology. Despite the often harshly contentious nature of God's contribution to this dialogue, all mainstream Western faiths insist on His ultimate virtuousness. Should this seem absent, it is because we have not humbled ourselves before the Lord's inscrutable ways, goes the argument.

It is here that Jung, in *Answer to Job*, makes a rancorous departure from orthodoxy, starting with his biting analysis of the "dark side" of God's personality. Specifically, Jung asserts that our dialogue with the Eternal may, and in fact *must* become the conduit through which we confront what he sees as the destructive aspects of the Creator's unconsciousness; an infantile and narcissistically self-indulgent, often ruthlessly violent aspect of the divine psyche. In this context, the concept of an I-You dialectic must be expanded to include its function as the arena in which we courageously attempt to expand God's self-awareness. For Jung, it is of the essence that we rise to the occasion of offering this gift to the Godhead, given that He is unable to generate it for Himself. To shrink back from this task is to miss a critical opportunity to insist on our inherent dignity in the face of indifferent Being, and, in doing so, progress toward greater consciousness, individually and collectively. Jung uses the Book of Job as a poetic platform through which to analyze the emergence of a decisive change in the God imago. This evolution is instigated by humanity's demand that the deity grasp the nature of our time-bound world, and show compassion for the suffering inherent in our "thrownness" into this realm. Specifically, Jung posits the need for a revitalized symbology that closes the gap between the human world with a God who, due to the enormous influence of Renaissance and Enlightenment rationalism, has now largely lost His standing as a compelling existential presence. In *Answer to Job* (1958) he argues that this is an urgent undertaking for the West, noting that "a situation has arisen within Christianity which removes it further than ever from the sphere of world understanding" (p. 104), and warns that believers "cannot afford to remain rigid and impervious to the spirit of the age" (p.105).

Jung sees the characteristic angst of modern persons, and the rise of inhuman, fanatical contemporary social movements, as reflecting a pervasive alienation from the emotionally healing and ennobling experience of the transcendent. Until quite recently, reverent awareness of the extra-mundane was a normal part of human group life, he argues, acting to ground individuals and societies in the conviction—and, in certain cases, the ecstatic experience—of unity with Being itself. But there is no returning to earlier eras, he declares: such symbols are bygone or fading fast into what Nietzsche (1889) famously calls the "twilight of the idols."

Spiritual Symbols

The symbol is a palpable manifestation of one or more of the immaterial archetypes, unconscious psychic dynamisms expressing recurring, compelling common human circumstances, such as falling in love, childbirth, life in society, suffering, and death. Archetypal patterns are the doorway to the collective unconscious (Jung, 1929), an ineffable, transcultural, and transpersonal core of the personality— sharing similarities with the Buddhist concept of "storehouse consciousness" —which emits an unending stream of "primordial images" (p. 112), and whose presence in the psyche is not explainable by socialization. Symbols of the transpersonal, while often spellbinding, are fragile. An "adequate" symbol is finicky; it must fit its surroundings just so. Its power to compel is parochial, that is, conformed rather precisely to the unique qualities of life in specific human groups, and this for only limited time spans. The symbol mediates our engagement with a hypothesized Absolute, being as close as we may come to touching on the actual essence of the metaphysical object. It tends to clothe itself in images or unbidden ideas that are at least faintly recognizable to ego-consciousness (although its uncanniness becomes greater at the "deeper" levels of the psyche). Symbols retain their emotional power only as long as they are taken-for-granted phenomena, "hidden in plain sight" within daily life. When they become objects of analysis, they are already long dead.

But new symbols, relevant to our communal experiences and dilemmas, arise naturally from the heart of the universe, acting to illuminate the present nature and possibilities of our human condition. Jung's essay, *Answer to Job*, suggests a new God imago that is relevant to disillusioned, self-enclosed modernity. It forwards an experiential spirituality of "inwardness" to replace what he sees as anxious, obsolete clinging to doctrine, intellectual persuasion, or its close relation, "faith." In what follows I describe the emergent new symbolism of *Answer to Job* as "sensible." By this I mean that it presages a spirituality of God's embeddedness in the tangible here-and-nowness of the world, something that I argue is an essential collective need of modern persons, mired as we are in cynicism about anything transcendent or absolute.

I try to clearly separate terms like "sensible," "sensate," and "tangible" from their conventional definitions, which are informed by the modern assumption that something cannot be a palpable object of sense experience *and* a living metaphor of immaterial spiritual reality. Rather, I side with neo-Jungian James Hillman's (1975, p. 137) view that the fullness of concrete experience unfolds in what he calls "psychologizing" or "seeing through" mere literalisms (an idea he also applies to metaphysical propositions about reality, such as the nature of the mind or God, that seek to literalize abstractions in static "isms"). So Jung's evolved God imago has a concrete vitality because it speaks to the actual spiritual dilemma of the present human condition. This dilemma is an unavoidable side effect of the dawn of what Philip Rief (1961) calls "psychological man." Humanity thus defined is constructed on an *ethos* of the applied use of linear reason, cultural and moral relativism, and, perhaps most significantly, the idealization of individuality. Jung's resuscitated God imago folds our contemporary insistence that religion conform to the dictates of logic, a stance he insists is fully legitimate, into a larger, synthetic supra-logical framework. In doing so, he skirts the literalist pursuit to "demythologize" religion and instead becomes an ironist, in Kierkegaard's (1841) sense of this term: systematically using reason to demonstrate its own limitations and final insufficiency to embrace life.

Unsurprisingly, Jung is ambivalent about institutional religion. On the one hand, he affirms its singular value in transmitting the notion of the transcendent to human communities in what we may call psychologically "manageable" forms. Implied herein is his perception of the Absolute as a volatile, possibly dangerous energic field: in shielding us from directly apprehending its true nature, culturally-ensconced ritual also protects us from what would otherwise be an overwhelming and traumatizing encounter with its uncontained potency, he says (Jung, 1938, pp. 59–60). On the other hand, Jung sees the "socialized" ego that attaches itself to ritual as inherently and ultimately problematic, since it is formed and maintained by disavowing the very mystical consciousness that is also the well-spring of all human vitality. Shoe-horning subjectivity into socially accepted moulds necessarily narrows our field of awareness, constricting our primal intuition of being situated as distinct, conscious points of view along what F.C.S. Northrop (1946, p. 82) calls the "aesthetic continuum" of Being. But we may become genuinely "sensible" when the paradoxical inner coherence of life's diverse expressions foregrounds itself to us, a realization that is essentially mystical.

For Jung, the symbol points toward the wholeness of Being, intimating the delicately intertwined nature of what ego-bound common sense tells us are unbridgeable differences. Hence, for example, across different cultures living symbols are often defined as simultaneously and fully material and immaterial: that is, "meta-physical." This is seen, for example, in the Roman Catholic and Eastern Rite communion ceremonies, in which the sensate wafer and wine is said to be transformed into the actual body and blood of the deity. Jung sees *Answer to Job* as a contribution toward the full realization of this incarnational theodicy, one hinted at in the Job story, and which still awaits its complete unfolding (Jung, 1958, p. 52).

Here I want to expand our appreciation of *Answer to Job* by analyzing its themes in light of select trends in Western philosophy defining prereflective experience of our immersion in the world as foundational to an authentic spiritual sensibility. I apply a select few philosophical angles that have occupied my attention over the years, some derived from Jung's essay, others imported so as to tease out its implications. In all this I seek to illuminate why Jung settled on the Book of Job as an archaic platform for addressing modern Western spiritual problems.

The Evolving God Archetype

To Jung, the God archetype is inherently incomplete. In *Answer to Job* he casts this incompleteness as a function of the deity's failure to grasp the agonizing dilemmas and conflicts that He has set into motion in creating the temporal dimension. *Contra* William Blake, who writes that "Eternity is in love with the productions of time," Jung states that the elevated perspective of the Godhead begins as a profound *obstacle* to His understanding, much less loving our time-bound, material world. This existential condition renders God insensitive to this world, and humans unable to make "sense" of him. This is an unusual idea to Westerners: we presume that the Almighty's omniscience and omnipotence is naturally accompanied by the assurance of His empathy. But Jung (1958, p. 49) argues that this presumption of divine goodwill is arbitrarily "tacked on" to the image of the deity, in the face of vast evidence to the contrary; a rationalizing defense against our unconscious dread that we are in the hands of a cosmic psychopath.

Jung asserts that God's omniscience and omnipotence actually *prevent* the achievement of certain kinds of knowledge, in this case of the suffering contained within a human condition that, ironically, *He* created. To be clear, the Book of Job does not portray God's remoteness from humanity as a wrathful punishment for our wrongdoing. In fact, in this Biblical text God's callous neglect of humanity is remarkable for its *lack* of passion, either negative or positive. Rather, the Creator is cast as an oblivious child, lacking the differentiated consciousness needed to devise genuinely unjust acts (Jung, 1958, p. 10). Jung's prose even brings out a certain preposterousness in God, who is cast as an oafish toddler, bewildered, like Inspector Clouseau, by catastrophes He can't fathom having caused.

While the Immortal's gross indifference to His creation reflects His incompleteness, this imperfection is not intrinsic to His being, says Jung. Rather, he sees the Divinity's narcissism as reflecting a lack of integration of the qualities constituting His nature, which, because He is Being itself, include all possible ways of envisaging and engaging existence. God is "all in all," the archetypal sum of all that is or can be. But there's a catch: crucial features of this primary archetypal psychic unity have been split off from the deity's awareness. Deprived of the synthesizing action of an observing ego, these exist in an embryonic state of unconsciousness, unavailable to enlarge God's empathic grasp of humanity. This renders Him childishly one-sided and cruel in certain circumstances, particularly when His competence is questioned, as we shall see in the Job story. Commenting on this aspect of the divine, an archaic, psychologically unevolved, preconscious expression of its nature called *Yahweh*, Jung notes, "Morality presupposes consciousness. By this I do not mean that Yahweh is imperfect or evil...He is everything in its totality...total justice, and also its total opposite." He continues, "From the way the divine nature expresses itself we can see that the individual qualities are not adequately related to one another, with the result that they fall apart into mutually contradictory acts" (1958, p. 10). It is this splitting of the divine psyche that is behind the Creator's shocking "senselessness," as portrayed in scripture.

The Tale of Job

The Book of Job is one of the most ancient of all Biblical texts. Its original sources are uncertain, with some analysts suggesting the presence of non- or pre-Hebrew sources, though there is modest agreement that the text is indeed fully Hebrew in origin, and that it appeared in roughly its present form between 400 to 1,300 B.C.E. (Harris, 1972, pp. 3–9). The text's editorial emendations are also a topic of controversy. Yet here too there is moderate agreement that the manuscript is essentially a unity, though at one point the story line becomes illogical, indicating that some lines of dialogue have gone missing or were inaccurately transcribed (Harris, 1972, pp. 14–17). The text consists of two sections of prose, between which is an extended poetic account of a theological debate occurring between Job and three companions.

Textual criticism aside, it is the psychology of the deity Yahweh, as presented in the final canon of the Book of Job, that is of central interest to Jung. "Yahweh" is the imprecise Latinate pronunciation of the letters of the Hebrew acronym for the deity, יהוה, called the tetragrammaton, written in Latin as YHVH. The tetragrammaton is essentially code for the deity's actual identity, which cannot be uttered because it is ineffable, according to the mystical Kabbalist tradition, or because doing so is arrogant, according to mainstream Judaism. It is often translated in Hebrew as "I am," though the epithet has no exact meaning. A rabbi once told me that "Yahweh" may be an arbitrary extension of ꞌ, "yaw," the first character in the tetragrammaton, which he thought is used as a stammering exclamation of bewilderment— like the English *huh?*. And there is much about this immortal to provoke such reflexive shock. As Jung suggests, Yahweh is unreflective and without self-critical capacities; hence, not immoral, but *amoral*, and therefore unpredictably moody, capricious, and sometimes violent. With this in mind, the meaning of "I am" may also be liberally interpreted as reflecting the deity's profound self-involvement: "*only* I am." It is surprising that the Book of Job was allowed into the Jewish, Christian, and Islamic canons at all, given its withering critique of the deity. Jung supposes that certain of the ecclesiastical fathers of these traditions perhaps unconsciously intuited that maintaining a one-sidedly "all good" canonical image of the Creator would ultimately delegitimize their faith traditions, since there can be no compelling experience of God's radiance without the conscious understanding that all bright light casts a correspondingly black and impenetrable shadow.

In the first part of the poem, a member of the heavenly court called the Accuser, or *Satan* in Hebrew, challenges Yahweh's boastful claim that the man Job is a perfectly devoted servant of Heaven. He ruthlessly jibes the creator about his estimation of Job's faithfulness: Job only keeps the faith because Yahweh has blessed him with a prosperous and secure life, he mocks. Angered by this dig, Yahweh proposes a wager: he will allow Satan to decimate Job's livelihood, kill his family members and servants, and, finally, ruin his physical health, betting that, even after this ghastly treatment, Job will continue to obediently serve Heaven, thus proving that his worship has substance. Satan agrees, and proceeds in step-wise fashion to rain misery on the blameless man. In Hebrew mythology, Satan is not evil, but an irreverent provocateur serving to goad the Creator out of sedate unawareness. He is a disintegrate of the Almighty's total self, a vitally important, albeit dissociated, hence undeveloped self-observing function within the deity's being (Jung, 1958, p. 21). This explains Yahweh's baffling lack of insight into how human motives and behavior may be influenced by personal gain, a rudimentary aspect of adult judgment. But, having been projected outward from the deity's mind, this elementary understanding of things interpersonal becomes embodied in the figure of Satan, who begins to gleefully make sport with this giant flaw in His thinking.

So, with Yahweh's blessing, Satan systematically destroys all that is dear to Job: family, servants, property, and health. Initially, Job accepts his fate, piously intoning that "God gave and God took away; blessed be God" (Job 1:21). This is his attempt to pay homage to the ineffable nature of the deity's actions, in accord with Hebrew tradition. But his resentment grows and finally gets the better of him. Convinced that this catastrophic turn of events is unjust, he confronts three friends who have arrived to comfort him, challenging them over the course of an extended dialogue to explain why the good suffer, and why he should not deem Yahweh to be cruelly unfair in this regard. Job's plea for a "sensible" deity is an argument that God be reasonable, though it is more than just that. Fundamentally, it is an appeal for the appearance of a God that is consciously and empathically attuned to the gritty hardship of our material existence, from which both our bodies and interior lives evolve and in which they participate. Job's discourses with his friends are long and unfruitful. The three present their objections to Job's complaints against the divine, presenting different arguments exonerating Yahweh of blame, some of which suggest that Job must have sinned unknowingly. But Job, convinced of his innocence, will have none of it.

From His heavenly dwelling, Yahweh listens to their unproductive debate, and is increasingly enraged by Job's sharply-worded criticisms. Finally, unable to tolerate any more, Yahweh appears to Job in the form of a whirlwind. In a lengthy monologue He blasts his responses to Job's challenges. There is no pretense of dialogue here, merely a display of terrible might expressing Yahweh's psychological immaturity. Mired in unconsciousness, the deity explodes in a crude outpouring of hyperbolic boasts and threats from inside the funnel. Jung sees Yahweh's tantrum as reflecting unconscious guilt: secretly aware that He cannot match the moral legitimacy of Job's argument, Yahweh instead resorts to intimidation, bellowing of His omnipotence in a numinous display meant to overwhelm the man with dread. Despite Yahweh's apparent indifference to humanity, in the above we see that the deity is actually inordinately attached to humans and their opinions of Him, seeking not simply their tribute, in the manner of the Greek gods, but also their admiration. It is this unconscious narcissism and associated dependence on His human creations that forms the possibility that He may be influenced to reflect more critically on His actions, if steadfastly and bravely opposed by a reasonable interlocuter.

As noted earlier, an aspect of Yahweh's infantilism is His alienation from the qualities of tender-heartedness, concern, and fellow feeling. These are dimensions of what Jung describes as *eros* and which he identifies as expressions of the feminine principle. He infers this quality in eros, in part because of its personification in the Greek mythic figure of Sophia, what Jung calls a "coeternal and more or less hypostatized (sp) pnuema of feminine nature that existed before Creation" (p. 24). Hence, for Jung, eros is a form of wisdom rooted in the eternal feminine principle; a way of knowing that is achieved through the emotions, particularly in moments of empathic identification with another. At one point in his fruitless argument with Yahweh, Job asks rhetorically, "Where is wisdom?" (Job 28:12). Jung understands this as a plea for this very same, feeling-toned feminine archetype to emerge from its hiding place in the shadow of Yahweh's overblown male ego. He infers that the feminine principle enters the conflict between Job and Yahweh as a supportive advocate for humanity, seeking to soften Yahweh's heart with subtle seductions.

To support this textual analysis Jung plays fast and loose with what can be reasonably inferred from both the text of the Book of Job and historical data, I believe. Specifically, he mentions in an aside that the verse points to the infusion of the Greek mythological account of the transcendent feminine spirit Sophia into the text and proposes that this *mythos* was known to the author(s) by way of its transmission through Alexandria (p. 24). This hypothesis may be correct, though the huge variance in estimates of the Biblical text's conception leaves much room for doubt. Jung's motive for this perhaps dubious assertion is clear: he devotes much of the remainder of *Answer to Job* to an exegesis upon this single, brief verse, incorporating further historical associations to Western cultural images of femininity as he goes along. Whatever its objective accuracy, this tact culminates in his prescient outlay of a comprehensive, proto-feminist vision of a gender-integrated Western God imago.

Answer to Job defines Yahweh's encounter with this personification of wisdom as a *déjà vu* experience for Him, as He dimly recalls His primordial state of union with the feminine. Jung refers to the marriage of masculine and feminine principles as the *hieros gamos*. This prehistoric experience of completeness has been forgotten by Yahweh, displaced by His thundering demands for perfection, a symptom of a hyper-masculine consciousness unmoderated by feminine feeling. In contrast, the archetypal feminine aims at wholeness: Sophia overcomes the clash of opposites, not through the either/or of judicial logic, but through an erotic embrace of all that is. This leads not to a rational "solution" of the debate, but to its transcendence, a state that both encompasses and moves beyond its seemingly warring elements.

Despite its protagonist's (alleged) appeal to feminine wisdom, the Book of Job records no decisive change in Yahweh's stance. By literary and moral standards the poem's ending is deeply flawed: the traumatized Job relents, insincerely professing that Yahweh's kingly might is the sole measure of truth. Yahweh is pleased by this outcome and subsequently doubles up on his material blessings to Job, supplying him with new children, servants, property, and, we suppose, renewed health. This conclusion allegedly vindicates God morally and rebuilds His bond with humanity.[1] But such a half-baked ending is not really the end, suggests Jung. Rather, it is a new beginning for the God imago: in this poem we find the groundwork for the later incarnation of the Creator in Jesus, the Christ, an expression of Yahweh's resolve to assuage His newly-discovered capacity for guilt by achieving a more conscious, integrated understanding of the human condition. And, over time, He does so, the culmination of which occurs in the momentous act of Himself becoming a man, an ordinary laborer's son who chooses life as a wandering rabbi.

In the remainder of *Answer to Job* Jung presses home his point that we must continually confront and integrate the Western deity's shadow. For example, even with the coming of Christ and its gospel of love, we find the Creator's capacity for blind cruelty reappearing on a regular basis, as in the final New Testament book, The Revelation of Jesus Christ (also called the Book of Revelation and the Apocalypse of John) he argues. Hence, Jung's religious vision calls for a more synthetic and intellectually rigorous understanding of the deity. This is one that rejects defensive insistence on ideas of God's goodness, suggesting that we instead nurture trust in our sensibilities to inform our comprehension of the Almighty's nature. This is not a retreat into the adulation of human reason. Rather, it is a fresh affirmation and continuation of the West's emotionally-charged "I-You" relation to the Absolute, one that, influenced by our historically recent ennoblement of individual experience, now pivots to recognize the need for humanity's critical faculties to take a proper place in this dialogue.

Spiritual Culture and Practical Morality

First-world Westerners often see metaphysics and spirituality as irrelevant to their personal lives and the practical business of society, relics of intellectually childlike bygone eras. But all societies are embedded within what theologian William Dean (2002) calls a "spiritual culture," one that is often, to use his term, "noncognitive." A spiritual culture contains a people's essential shared values, understanding of the existential import of its heritage, and grasp of the transgenerational continuity of their relation to the Absolute. Dean cites American pragmatist John Dewey's (1958) view that social coherence is rooted in, as Dewey writes, a "sense of an extensive and underlying whole" (p. 194). This sense of the whole may not be explicitly based on a metaphysical Absolute. Yet even here it functions as a *de facto* spiritual template, in that, like religiously-inspired action, its authority rests on moral ideals aiming toward practical ends deemed incontrovertibly superior to all others. Says Dean (2002):

> Dewey argued that, in any particular instance, no society truly knows how to react to its local environment unless it has a vision of its total environment (its "universe"). This vision of the totality enables a society to interpret its particular environment – much as, say, a parent's theory of the whole family enables him or her to discipline a particular child.
>
> (p. 20)

Arguably, Jung's exegesis on Job places him among the ranks of what Dean calls "religious public intellectuals," that is, those social critics who judge communal ideological trends from the perspectives of their faith traditions. Exemplars of this group include Mahatma Gandhi, Dr. Martin Luther King, Jr., the Dalai Lhama, and, less consistently, various Popes. They have contributed to our corporate health by challenging what they deemed immoral and/or deluded social orders. Clearly, Jung's ominously brooding, dark prophesies lack the appealing humanism of these individuals. However, his critique of

Western religion provides a real social benefit, for those with ears to hear. This is so because, left unanalyzed, the "shadow side" of the God imago lapses into the unconscious nether realm of the social psyche. From there it may reappear publicly in varied forms; given the right circumstantial "stressors," these may be unmoderated and hence ferociously one-sided. Examples of this include the alarming absolutisms of some modern political movements, such as fascism and, more recently, certain xenophobic populisms, all of which Jung sees as energized by what are unrecognized spiritual strivings applied to "this worldly" realities in secular forms (Jung, 1965, pp. 328–329). So a spiritual culture is *real*, because it creates *actual* effects.

Jung's concern with the sensate makes perfect "sense" as an historical development. Underway since the Reformation, it is part of a cultural transition from an "other-worldly" to "this-worldly" or, if you like, "inner-worldly" religion. Sociologist Max Weber (2013, p. 155) sees this as symptomatic of our modern "disenchantment" with the spiritual ideal of a distant Heaven, under the influence of Protestant inwardness and hyperindividualism. Perhaps it is Jung's genius to have discovered its primeval fount in the tale of Job. This-worldly faith is, in fact, maybe not "faith" at all, as usually understood, inasmuch as faith looks beyond immediate experience, aiming to attach to, as Paul wrote, "things unseen." Recalling his youthful disdain for his Lutheran minister father's beliefs, Jung (1965) says, "It seemed to me that the arch sin of faith was that it forestalled experience" (p. 94). So perhaps the word "faith" is misapplied in this context, and should be replaced by "experience," implying its status a prereflective encounter with life, the existential underpinning of our rapport with life's here-and-nowness. Hence, modernity's essential need of an embodied, "in-carnate" ("in-the-flesh") deity, one compelling to sensibilities.

The Contributions of Rudolf Otto

There are a number of ways in which *Answer to Job* can be understood as advocating for an embodied, experiential spirituality. Foremost is Jung's extensive use of the work of Protestant religious scholar Rudolf Otto, contained in his treatise *The Idea of the Holy* (1958), to lay the conceptual foundation for *Answer to Job*. Otto's work defines even the most intellectually sophisticated religious praxis as rooted in an ancient, usually unexpected personal encounter with a transcendent deity that is "wholly other," as he puts it: Moses' shock at being addressed by a god contained within a burning bush, or Paul's stupefied collapse on the road to Damascus, temporarily blinded by the radiance of the risen Christ. Says Otto, the fact that we lack any preformed mental categories or language through which to understand this ineffable "other" is evidence for its ontological reality ("ontological" being derived from the Greek *ontos*, meaning roughly, "having authentic being"), as opposed to reducing such an event to an elaboration upon something already known, consciously or unconsciously. The disorienting, shocking foreignness of the metaphysical object, and the unprecedented nature of its appearance, leave us solely dependent on our raw emotional responses with which to form a preliminary impression of its nature. Otto argues that *only* such an essentially mystical-affective apprehension of the divine, one that momentarily negates thought, can compel surrender to the impulse for redemptive meaning that is at the heart of the religious quest.

Otto (1958) refers to this state as, in part, a revival of our sense of "creature-consciousness" (pp. 9–10). By this term he means our immediate, sensuous experience of having emanated from the womb of the physical world, and the profound sense of dependence on Being that accompanies this. It is just then, when we are reduced to a sense of either absolute or relative awareness of our insignificance and helplessness, that we may access something deeply expressive of our humanity. For Jung, such moments are needed to subvert our identification of ourselves with the ego and its insatiable drive for mastery. At the beginning of the tale of Job we find him, apparently a settled, middle-aged patriarch, living a charmed life. We may infer that consciously he feels that he knows himself and his place in the world and has charted an undisturbed course for his remaining days. Important here is an early passage noting Job's recurring obsessional fear that his children will displease Yahweh by entertaining evil thoughts (Job 1:5). This neurotic preoccupation implies someone whose idea of the divine remains childlike, and, more generally, whose relationship to life has stultified at its summit by clinging to ideals of "normalcy." The psyche does not tolerate the persistence of such defensively conventional attitudes, beyond their normal life span in development. So, in Jungian terms,

Job's meticulously ordered, socially "proper" life means he is ripe for a fall.

Hence, Job's self-satisfied illusion of command is shattered by the intrusion of multiple catastrophes that, together, force him to face the wholeness of the deity's nature, and, by extension, his own. From a Jungian perspective, psychic disasters erupt as unconscious compensations for such psycho-spiritual banality. These are the psyche's attempt to repair the individual's disconnection from the source of Being. They do so by plunging him or her ungraciously into an engagement with what Jung refers to as the *numinosum*, a concept he borrowed from Otto. It is a term indicating the dynamic, transcendent, and spell-binding ambiance surrounding the wellspring of existence. The majesterial and impersonal "otherness" of the numinosum transcends and thwarts intellectual understanding, provoking a reflexive experience of awe when encountered (Otto, 1958, pp. 25–30). What we call "God" is a term for the West's culture-specific rendering of the *numinous*: creeds, concepts, rituals, and artistic renderings rooted in a primary, awe-ful experience of what Otto (1958, pp. 13–24) calls the *mysterium tremendum et fascinans*, a mystery before which we experience both dread and fascination.

Two Sources of Human Dignity: Gut Instinct and Reason

Jung identified a poverty of deeply-felt spiritual symbols available to contemporary Westerners. In our era, we are instead beckoned by offensively dull, self-serious fundamentalisms, and their relations, cheaply-bought, self-congratulatory liberal humanisms. In *Answer to Job* Jung stridently insists upon the necessity of attending to another competing avenue of approach to this problem. It is one that he saw as reliant on the only subjectively authoritative source of knowledge about our place in eternity left to the industrialized West: what is loosely called "inner experience." This is an idea with ancient roots in the Western tradition. It started with Augustine of Hippo, arguably the first Western thinker to explain systematically how one locates the presence of God within oneself, through an "inward turn," rather than in the interpersonal or communal realms (Cary, 2000). This notion continues to exist in the modern era, minus the idea that God awaits us in the psychic inner sanctum. Rather, what we find within are private germinating desires that form the bedrock of our humanity. These are emblems of what D.W. Winnicott (1965, pp. 140–157) calls the "true self," an affective core of spontaneous strivings often expressed via unpremeditated interpersonal "gestures."

I suggest that the ancient precursors of this idea appear in the Book of Job, where at one point in the story we find the protagonist wheeling about emotionally, as it were, driven by an unprompted, fierce inner resolve to face Yahweh. But first something happens within Job's inner world that makes this confrontation possible. As one reads the text a shift in its emotional tone can be detected, as Job experiences an unbidden inrush of self-certainty about the correctness of his position. He spontaneously looks within, reconsiders his tortured state, and, minus any discernible change in his dire circumstance, suddenly and quite simply *feels* that the time has come to demand that Yahweh act in accord with a moral standard. Thereupon, the disgusted Job spontaneously issues a sarcastic and blistering address to Heaven: "Does it seem good to you that you should oppress, that you should despise (and) reject the work of your hands?" (Job 10:8).

In following his "gut instincts" Job implicitly affirms the dignity of immediate, unpremeditated emotional experience as a guide to life. That is, Job does not reason that his position is logically superior, and then act on the basis of this conclusion. After all, the best, most cogent ideas cannot provide sufficient motivation to confront a dangerously wild deity. Rather, he responds to (and from) his sensibilities, as it were. Job confronts God on the basis that He is unfair because He acts unreasonably; though he finds the strength to do so, not because he sees his assessment as logical, but because he experiences some compelling movement in his *feeling* about himself that emboldens him to challenge Heaven. Ironically, here both Job and God act from a self-same, logically inexplicable drive for self-expression: Job counters the bellicose behavior of the god called "I am" with "But I am, *too.*" In avowing the worth of his subjectivity, Job adds insult to God's injured narcissism by attaining a radiant godlikeness himself, inasmuch as he is suddenly in the position of knowing God better than God knows Himself. "Job realizes God's inner antinomy, and in the light of this realization his knowledge attains a divine numinosity," says Jung (1958, p. 15).

The most awe-ful depths of the encounter with the deity cannot be articulated, eluding capture in all language. However, in *Answer to Job*, Jung insists that while initially we may stand in stunned, reverential silence before the divine, this does not mean that we will have nothing to say to or about it, eventually. As noted earlier, he goes beyond this, insisting that we fail our humanity by not doing so. The Judeo-Christian tradition exhorts us to prayerfully dialogue with Heaven. And it is arguably an expectation of the faithful that they do so about all of life, and not only about things that are "easy." But the prejudice against voicing heartfelt disillusionment with the Divine is deeply rooted, a symptom of what my fellow traveller the rabbi, mentioned earlier, calls "five-year-old religion." Though mysticism arguably offers something more comprehensive and philosophically cogent than this, it is often branded negatively, as Alan Watts (1972) humorously protests: "anyone who speaks as a mystic...is expected to behave as a non-entity...Strength of personality – even though you yourself know very well that it is a big act – is always taken for an 'ego-trip,' and, in the mystic, for a contradiction of everything you are saying" (p. 322). And Otto (1958) points out that the irrationality of the metaphysical object "does not mean that nothing can be asserted [about it]...otherwise, mysticism could only exist in unbroken silence, whereas what has generally been a characteristic of the mystics is their copious eloquence" (p. 2). Our human capacity to devise concise, conscious interpretations of experience, so as to selectively resist and alter Being's imperious demands, is essential to our creatureliness. In the Job story we see this aspect of our humanity expressed in Job's act of confronting the deity with a logical, compelling moral argument. In doing so, he declares himself an entity (from the Latin *esse*, "to be") who in some ways is rightfully Yahweh's equal. This is later underscored in Jesus' appeal to God in the Garden of Gethsemane prior to his arrest and execution, "Why have you abandoned me?" (Matthew, 27:46), a further step in our comprehension of God's shadow side. Across history, such addresses to the Absolute are guided by the cardinal importance that Nature places upon the fact of self-reflective consciousness, and the archetypal drive toward personal existence hidden within this.

Thought provides the marvellously intricate, nuanced contemplations on life, which are absolutely necessary to make us fully and genuinely human. The Book of Job provides us with a view of the natural routes and sequences by which our thoughts about God emerge: first—and always first—in a sensuous immersion in some mysterious moment of contact with Otto's "wholly other." Over time we look back on the encounter and begin to extract ideas and their redemptive meanings from the mire of unselfconscious immersion in our creatureliness. Reason can never lead the way: but reason *must* arise, after all, from the elements of our affective experiences, to then speak bravely into the horrifying whirlwind that inevitably invades all human lives. Those who do not develop a conscious viewpoint on this primary experience, one allowing some freedom from the consuming numinosum and a point of view from which to engage its power more deliberately, remain psychically stunted, unfree proto-humans, says Jung (1958, pp. 97–99).

The Trojan Horse of Jung's "Empiricism"

How does Jung justify his claim to know these things? Presenting *Answer to Job* as a literary interpretation would avoid the need for such explanation: in this form, he could simply say "it's only a narrative exposition." But Jung presents his insights as derived first and foremost from his meticulous survey of both his own and patients' inner experiences, such as dreams and fantasy states, what he deems authoritative sources of factual datum about the mind's nature. While he regularly reminds us that his conclusions are posed as opinions, it means something that he consistently understands and presents these as *scientific* opinions, which is why I think he insists that his views be accorded credibility as "hard science" in ways that would never be granted to literary interpretations. This greatly complicates "epistemological" questions related to his analysis (from the Greek *episteme*, knowledge, and *logos*, logic), that is, the application of theories of knowledge to clarify how we know what we say we know.

Throughout his life Jung boldly proclaimed his research methodology to be an application of the empirical method, implying that his conclusions are passionless, hence truly scientific, and so dependable by modern standards. For example, in a late interview he stated, "I have no system, no doctrine, nothing of that kind. I am an empiricist, with no metaphysical views at all" (Jung, 1977, p. 419). Empiricism is a systematic means of encountering and making sense of phenomena that looks first to the raw data of one's senses. Here he references the selfsame epistemological stance that one finds buried in the philosophical foundations of Western science, with its claims to unbiased objectivity and emotional neutrality. This appeal to empiricism is startling, coming from someone often criticized—with some justification, I think—as a weirdly obtuse thinker prone to highly speculative inferences. Yet, such is the case: here we find that very same Jung, suggesting in all seriousness that he derives conclusions about the psyche, including its religious function, from the datum of his senses; that is, empirically. Hence, when asked during a 1959 television interview if he believed in God, Jung replied, "I don't have to believe. I know." The comment was soon thereafter repeated by Jung biographer Frieda Fordham (1959) in a brief article in the British magazine *The Listener*. Scrambling to quell the ensuing public uproar about this provocative thought, which he might have known would not be understood with anything like the subtlety that went into forming it: Jung penned a clarifying letter to the editor of *The Listener*. This was published early the next year. In it he wrote that the comment "means that I am confronted with a factor unknown in itself...This is the name by which I designate all things that cross my willful path violently and recklessly, all things which upset my subjective views...and change the course of my life for better or worse" (Jung, 1960, p. 133). What to make of this? Jung had a lifelong fear of being dismissed as promoting a magical, pre-scientific worldview, a charge Freud heaped on him following Jung's revision of his prized libido theory. Fear of such critiques motivated Jung to dress up his private religion in the gray tweed suit-and-tie garb of a neutral, fact-finding scientific mission. Doing so was a strategy to make him less threatening to button-up mainstream rationalism and materialism, freeing him to pursue his speculative interests by saying, in essence, "You may disagree, but I'm looking at this objectively, and the data is in."

This is disingenuous, of course; though I, for one, can forgive him, given that even Jesus played politics to avoid useless confrontations with the authorities. Beyond Jung's purely political motives for this assertion, however, I infer the presence of another, well-established philosophical position in his claim to be employing an empirical outlook. This position is widely known as the *phenomenological* approach to knowledge. It is a term that Jung also uses on occasion to describe his approach, as evident in the title of his important later work *Aion:*

Researches Into the Phenomenology of the Self (Jung, 1969). Not being a formally trained philosopher, he sometimes conflates the perspectives of phenomenology and empiricism. (Later we will see how Jung's self-described "empiricism" also fits the criteria for what American pragmatism calls "*radical* empiricism.") Of course, whatever terminology he uses, the essential thing to bear in mind is his wish to underscore the primacy of interior experience as the methodology of choice for exploring the psyche.

That said, unlike Jung, our task here *is* philosophical, and terminology is important in philosophy. Hence, we should tease out the defining qualities of these two systems—phenomenology and empiricism—as doing so provides a context in which to better understand Jung's radical insistence on personal visions of reality as dependable guides to life. Phenomenological philosophies are not uniformly equivalent to empirical approaches. The two are intellectual second cousins, similar enough to enable Jung to credibly describe his approach to religion as the latter, though I think that he was unconsciously making a *de facto* appeal to something along the lines of the former. The central difference between these two epistemologies is that empiricism claims (incorrectly, as I will argue) to employ an objective approach to reality. As a theory of knowledge, it imagines itself to be dispassionately observing recurring patterns in the material world and assembling these systematically for use in the construction of logical strategies for improved, what it considers "real world," adaptation. The empirical attitude assumes a more or less exact correspondence between the perceiving mind and the environmental phenomena that it encounters. Consequent to this is the emboldening conviction that one may grasp the true nature of existence once distorting subjective biases are eliminated.

This is a simple, forthright theory of the mind's nature. It enjoys huge popular appeal in the modern era, and with good reason: the empiricism of the scientific model has lifted humanity out of slavish dependence on a world whose natural patterns it did not fathom in earlier eras. However, to a great extent, this freedom from external constraints has been purchased at the cost of our hard-won, Enlightenment and Romantic-era reverence for human interiority. In principle, empiricism posits that we gain knowledge of the world via the five senses, a view that *seems* to assume that we are tangibly integrated into that world. However, it is fatally flawed when it seeks to neutralize the relevance of the experiencing subject to our wish to know the world. In practice, this leads to a form of methodological dualism (Chomsky, 1979), one that proceeds as if reality exists "out there" in pristine form, waiting to be comprehended veridically by an uninterested, data-gathering mind. But desire and imagination are not opposed to seeing things object-ively. On the contrary, they are *essential* to our ability to interpret *any-thing* objectively, since interpretation is an act occurring in intimate relation to a circumstance that moves us emotionally. Considering this problematizes the relation of subjective and objective realms.

In contrast, the phenomenological approach begins with the prop-osition that mind and world are an interdependent, mutually-defining pair. This view asserts that something viewed in a *purely* objective manner, were such a thing even possible, could not be called "real," since reality requires human subjectivity to warrant the name. That is, in the act of contemplating reality we also literally create it. This does not mean that we author existence *per se*, or that Being is solely a product of our minds, as solipsism would have it. Rather, it means that by observing and thinking about Being we facilitate its appearance in specific forms that would not occur otherwise. To put it differently, by engaging Being in this way, we *elicit* certain possibilities inherent though as yet undisclosed in its structure. This is an implicitly mys-tical worldview, of course. Its philosophical legitimacy is supported by modern physics, in the logic-defying quantum theories of Max Planck, Albert Einstein, Niels Bohr, and others (see Stenger, 2000). As the research of these theoretical physicists implies, Being "needs" us in order to embody certain physical qualities, just as, in the tale of Job, God also needs us so that He may realize certain potentialities in His own being.

At times Jung takes this idea to its limit, explicitly stating that nothing exists without an observing human consciousness (Jung, 1965, p. 256). This is a knotty idea, to put it mildly, and nowhere does he try to explain the logic behind it. Jung is an impressively astute and nuanced thinker, so it seems incredulous to say that in this alone he resorts to a naive solipsism. Perhaps here we encounter the limits of language to explain causality, including Jung's assertion that humans evoke Being in the act of observing it. This limitation is particu-larly evident in the structure of our English tongue, which artificially divides reality into subjects and objects, with the former said to act on the latter in linear fashion. Hence, dilemmas about causality may simply be illusory artifacts of word-magic: the tendency of language to seduce us into experiencing the unified, co-creating whole of reality as merely an assemblage of discrete units. Buddhist philosophy offers an appealing alternative vision of causality: a pillar of its ontology refers to the "dependent origination" (Lopez, 2001, p. 29) or "mutually arising" nature of all expressions of Being (Harvey, 1990b, p. 54), meaning that the diversity of all phenomena is, paradoxically, derived from their underlying ontological unity, an aspect of which is that nothing literally "causes" anything else. Beyond this Buddhism sees logic as insufficient to convey the actual structure of reality, and so simply tells us to bracket discrimination and take in the "gestalt" of each moment, a stance resonating with Jung's intuitive attitude.

In phenomenology, what is "real" is less clearly defined than in objectivism, though "map-able," so to speak, in the way a cartographer works in sensible relation to the contours of a particular landscape. In this view, we correctly navigate our way through reality because of the interpenetration of mind and world. Were such interpenetration absent, we would lack the most basic relation to the sensate environment around us, and so could not comprehend and move coherently— if at all—within its strictures. Hence, in most phenomenological approaches mind and world are not essentially different, but points along an ontological continuum. We are both our private or "interior" experience, and the "outer" world that we encounter, positions on the spectrum of existence that define and playfully co-create one another. I believe this comes closer to what Jung means when he insists that he is an empiricist. This description also has affinities with his neo-Platonic-nee-Hindu account of subjectivity as the seat of mystical phenomenal experience. Specifically, Jung cautiously speculates that interiority may be linked to a larger, autonomous metaphysical reality, one giving rise to archetypal images and other experiences of the collective unconscious. Hence, his "subject" is not the private, self-enclosed entity of secular humanism: one that "has" experiences in the way one has a car, good time, or the flu. Rather, a liberal understanding of Jung's subject is that it springs from mystical immersion in the very mind of God, though he is always careful to note that this is not objectively verifiable, but an inference derived from the presence of recurring archetypal patterns in consciousness.

Job, Individuation, and the Archetypal Nomad

As noted earlier, in *Answer to Job* Jung embraces a prophetic role, attempting to ready us for the unprecedented upheavals of modernity. This relates directly to his theory of individuation, the innate tendency of every organism to achieve the fullest possible expression of its being. Jung (1958, p. 98) says that the story of Job is foremost a symbol of this archetypal process, implying certain changes in human consciousness that, together, serve to affirm its independence and worth. Individuation occurs in all creatures as a natural bio-genetic phenomenon. However, under certain circumstances it may also occur as a dramatic expansion of self-understanding. This is a statistically rare event, and one that never occurs fully, as no individual can sanely incorporate the limitless potential of an archetype. Such accelerated self-awareness is usually only initiated by a severe personal circumstance. If the person survives their misfortune they may partly transcend the normally unreflective course of human life, to partake of the aura of "godlikeness" that Job evidenced in his newly found understanding of Yahweh.

Individuation is not strictly "individual"; any movement toward a genuinely personal existence also relates one to the larger life of the group. The process of individuation in America has its own, distinct qualities and forms relating personal life to the life of the group. As in all societies, this development is embodied in symbols revealing its progressive, enlightening, as well as darkly regressive aspects. Here I want to explore how the experiential emphasis of the philosophical school of American pragmatism is an important "local" symbol of this evolution, one embodying the changes in modern selfhood. In turn, I will relate these to what I coin as the archetype of the nomad implied in *Answer to Job*.

From early in our history, observers of American social psychology note a characteristic, vigorously assertive, and optimistic quality to Americans' interpersonal styles and habits. This is a uniquely "New World" variety of ego consciousness. Its historical roots are old and tangled, though analyzable. Such a form of consciousness reflects an *ethos* of intuitive, improvisational action that developed naturally from the early European immigrants' responses to the challenges of American wilderness life. Getting by in an unknown frontier, minus dependable foreknowledge with which to anticipate its demands, immigrants learned to "make it up" as they went. This has a distinctly Biblical background, and one that is uniquely American. Dean (2002) says that the first European colonists, overwhelmingly religiously conservative Protestants, found their own circumstances mirrored in scripture accounts of the ancient Hebrews, who millennia before were also despised, uprooted, frightened wanderers seeking hope in a new land. These early New World migrants consisted of Anabaptists, Calvinists, and other "non-conforming" Protestants, a term referring to their radically inward spirituality and defiance of both dominant ecclesiastical and worldly authorities, which they saw as ungodly. Their concept of the divine was "proto-pragmatic" (Delbanco, 1999, p. 35), in that they located God's presence first and foremost in concrete, historical events. This is a "hands on" historical theology, heir to the Hebrew concept of the Lord's will as tangible in the ebb and flow of human events. Says Dean, "The most ambitious expression of the Israelites' pragmatism lay in their belief that God was real not because God was rational, sublime, or otherwise fit for divinity, but because God acted in Israel's history" (p. 62). Such a uniquely here-and-now spirituality is one we might expect to find in any human group that can no longer understand its present by looking to the past, and so has become "ahistorical."

The foundational premise of the first American Pragmatists, Charles Pierce (1878), William James (1907), and John Dewey (1934; 1934/ 1958), is that "truth" is something worked out in one's daily interactions with the world, and not by reference to abstract, *a priori* conceptions. Perhaps as no other philosophy in history, pragmatism springs directly from its cultural "grass roots": the daily struggles of poor, often uneducated, yet impressively inventive colonists just cited. It is a philosophy of lived experience, one that remains central to the peculiarly American construction of selfhood. Hence, like any Dakota farmer, pragmatism defines truth as that which impresses itself on us as palpably altering the world. Or, using idiomatically American action-oriented language, "truth" is that which "works," "pays off," or "delivers," a stance toward life that boldly, and at times recklessly, proclaims it "can do."

In its crude forms, this is exactly the intellectually lazy utilitarianism that many see it as. However, philosophical pragmatism also teases out a highly synthetic, implicitly mystical epistemology of entanglement in Being from within this homespun *credo*. It does so by putting into formal philosophical terms this worldview's conviction that navigating reality occurs, not primarily by analysis of its component parts, but by first intuiting a sense of the "whole" nature of a given circumstance, in Dewey's use of this term. It is in this emphasis on the prereflective, synthetic nature of our encounter with Being that pragmatism intersects with phenomenology. Prereflectiveness is a general property of mystical knowing, yielding conclusions that are not formed deliberately, but appear as numinous inner revelations of the "total" nature of one's involvement in life; the "ah-ha" experience in which one suddenly sees through a baffling conundrum or, in religious practice, an ultimate mystery.

Of all the early American pragmatists, James' thought is the most preoccupied with this phenomenon. His most widely-known work, *The Varieties of Religious Experience* (James, 1902) is a dense catalogue of experiential religion. It is one whose research methodology he occasionally, like Jung, calls "empirical," though, also like Jung, he too means a method favoring the datum of subjectivity, making it a *de facto* phenomenology. (He later modified this term, calling his approach "radical empiricism" [James, 1912], whose focus is a metaphysical "pure experience" that he believes underlies mind and matter.) *Varieties* is guided by the prototypically American maxim that, as James writes, "God is real because He has real effects" (pp. 406–407). Throughout this volume he echoes Jung's argument that the sense of the Absolute is potentially accessible to human subjectivity (to recall Jung's comment, "I don't have to believe. I know"). Specifically, James argues that if we take in the full scope of our experience, suppressing natural prejudices, we may be left with the impression of an overarching whole that is larger than its parts, a "more" that exists simultaneously within and just beyond the horizon of ordinary awareness. In lines that could have been lifted directly from *Varieties*, Jung (1938) as much as repeats verbatim the pragmatist adherence to sensate experience, including its conviction that a difference in words alone is not a "real" difference at all, and must yield to the phenomenology of consciousness as engaged with the world:

> The thing that cures a neurosis must be as convincing as the neurosis; and since the latter is only too real, the helpful experience must be of equal reality. It must be a very real illusion, if you want to put it pessimistically. But what is the difference between a real illusion and a healing religious experience? It is merely a difference

in words...Nobody can know what the ultimate things are. We must, therefore, take them as we experience them. And if such experience helps to make your life healthier, more beautiful, more complete and more satisfactory to yourself and to those you love, you may safely say, "This was the grace of God".

(p. 114)

Put simply, Jung, like James, is saying that we can and should trust ourselves to discern the unspeakable, embedded within the folds of ordinary life. And if our instincts or "hunches" direct us toward certain ideas, agendas, and acts, we will likely do best to obey them.

Although pragmatism's views are usually presented in secular terms, the pervasive, if veiled influence of America's Protestant "can-do" heritage on its themes is plain to see. In Jungian terms, pragmatic thought is a living symbol of important developments in modern consciousness, wrought by the archetype behind this historical evolution. Jung identifies a certain nervous creativity at the heart of the Protestant construction of self, which has now become the general template for the modern Western temperament. It is one sustained by the qualities of self-assertion, practical accommodation, and innovation that Weber (2013) identifies as key hidden religious pillars of modern Western free-market capitalism, for example. In *Answer to Job* Jung says:

Not only did [Protestantism] develop...from an encounter with the worldly spirit of the times, but it continues this dialectic with the spiritual currents of every age; for the pneuma, in keeping with its original wind nature, is flexible, ever in living motion...In order to fulfill its task, the Protestant spirit must be full of unrest and occasionally troublesome; it must even be revolutionary, so as to make sure that tradition has an influence on the change of contemporary values.

(p. 104)

Individuation is a process transcending linear time, forever reappearing in discrete parochial cultural symbols. In Jungian parlance, both the Book of Job and American philosophical pragmatism epitomize a consciousness specific to the archetype of the nomad, and the distinctively energetic, inventive construction of self associated with this psychic dynamism, one that came into its own in the New World. Job's uprootedness is not geographical. Yet, like the first American settlers, he too enters a mysterious, in his case, metaphoric "new world," in which his prized presumptions about reality are undermined. Disoriented and psychologically adrift, the nomad is thrust back upon a native ability to spontaneously assess their total circumstance, and pivot, prereflectively, to meet its demands. Jung's analysis of the Job myth intimates and prefigures the unfolding of this archetype, one continually reflected throughout later scripture in the saga of the wanderings of the Israelites with which colonial America so closely identified.

The character of Job embodies a certain hardscrabble, plainspoken tenacity that is likely familiar to most Americans. Like any freedom-loving, bereft migrant, Job, with little left to lose, refuses to yield until the last act of the poem. But Jung suggests that here the story of this man's quest for what in America we might call "the right of free speech" is merely interrupted, to be continued in the further evolution of the archetype found in the Jesus myth, who, like Job, also bravely resolves to "speak truth to power." What Jung calls the "revolutionary" face of the Protestant psyche, inheritor of the historical legacy first hinted at in Job, is of a dual nature. In America, still unconsciously steeped in its Pilgrim worldview, this is embodied in both a forward-looking defiance of convention, and a regressive insistence on "being oneself" that is often simple childish egoism. Arguably, it is America's collective task to reconcile these tendencies in new personal and social forms.

The Dissociated Feminine in Job

Finally, I want to briefly examine Jung's interpretation of the meaning of the figure of the feminine Sophia (in Greek, "Wisdom") in the Book of Job. As noted earlier, Jung maintains that the Book of Job introduces the idea of eros into its narrative structure, a development in the story line evident in Job's lament that wisdom is nowhere to be found. As we have seen, he explains the nature of eros by reference to the Greek allegorical figure Sophia, a symbol of a specifically feminine wisdom rooted, not in the static dictates of abstract reason, but in a heartfelt, empathic grasp of the terrors and promise of the human condition. She represents a dissociated, loving and doting aspect of Yahweh's total personality, argues Jung, one split off before the dawn of time, in the same way that Satan was conceived. Sophia defends Job, opposing Yahweh's amorality, and thus stoking the internal conflict simmering within His undeveloped consciousness. But unlike Satan, she does not do so by openly challenging the already narcissistically injured god. Rather, Sophia operates by an erotic appeal to the unconscious dimension of the divine psyche.

Jung writes that her unexpected appearance in the Job story signals the hope that the tantruming hyper-masculine god may be enticed to have concern for His creatures. One of Sophia's key functions is to prevent humanity from falling into despair over the brutality that inheres in Yahweh's nature and His creation: "Taking a highly personified form that is clear proof of her autonomy, Wisdom reveals herself to men as a friendly helper and advocate against Yahweh, and shows them the bright side, the kind, just, and amiable aspect of their God" (Jung, 1958, p. 34). As noted above, Jung identifies the reunification of male ego-consciousness with its disavowed feminine dimension as the hieros gamos. This is a term derived from his fascination with the symbolism of Alchemy. Medieval alchemical science is a mystical practice that developed around the concept of transformation. Alchemists write in deceptively concrete terms of such things as turning base metals into gold. However, there is a hidden symbolical subtext to their efforts: the metamorphosis of consciousness, toward the realization of the underlying unity of all seemingly opposed elements of Being (Jung, 1965, pp. 212–213). A seamless rejoining of Yahweh and Sophia will not be achieved. Nor is it even desirable, as consciousness requires differentiation, notes Jung. But greater unity-within-diversity, the rapprochement of immaterial spirit and carnality, is both possible and necessary. It is preceded by Sophia's role as midwife, preparing the conditions for the physical incarnation of God in the person of Jesus, the Christ. Says Jung (1958): "she realizes God's thoughts by clothing them in material form, which is the prerogative of all feminine beings" (p. 35). As foreshadowed in the Book of Job, one of these immaterial thoughts is to become the rabbi Jesus: the deity regenerated as flesh, in a redemptive marriage of God and humanity.

This concept of God has direct relevance to modern life. Take our careless destruction of the natural world in the service of "progress". This is an idea rooted in a macho, triumphalist aspect of Protestantism that is secretly contemptuous of nature, which is seen as impeding the march toward an other-worldly, non-sensate paradise in which matter, understood as a hateful obstacle to omnipotent control of reality, is overcome. The etymological root of "matter" is the Latin "mater," meaning "origin," "source," and "mother." With this in mind, our exploitation of the physical world is arguably linked to a deeper collective misogyny, expressed in a metaphoric contempt for "Mother Nature" that figures in the ominous advent of global warming. While the Sophia figure in Job is benevolent, she is also whole. Hence, her beneficence simultaneously casts a deep psychic shadow, this being the "dark side" of her particular numen. One wonders if it is this "dark feminine," an offended maternal World-Spirit, that is "turning up the heat" on us through dangerous warming of the climate, revenge for our rape of the earth. Such a cataclysm handily meets Otto's description of an awe-some, dreadful confrontation with a numinous feature of Being: it is unanticipated, uncontrollable, and indiscriminately destructive.

Concluding Thoughts: Inventing God

In *Answer to Job* Jung describes the archaic unfolding of a prerequisite for the development of an emotionally mature humanity: that we shed our childish terror of the numinosum in which Being is enshrined, and claim our proper role as indispensable co-participants in shaping the nature of the God imago. For this reason, perhaps the most important contribution of Jung's essay is his thesis that, in trusting the evidence of our felt experience, we actively and *actually* evoke the carnal—that is, "sensible" —dimension of what would otherwise remain a remote, internally divided World-Spirit. As we have seen, this means that Being needs us to become itself. Or, put differently, we call forth certain qualities of existence with which we are then confronted: so, for example, the Hebrews personally "invented" ontologically real properties of the God of history that they then worshiped and engaged as an objective reality. This understanding transcends a number of what I have come to see as false dichotomies: that something cannot be simultaneously and fully subjective and objective; that our religious instincts are either psychological fantasies projected onto reality, or evidence of the objective existence of a Creator; and so on. *Answer to Job* sidesteps the bugaboo of these dualisms. As perhaps we may too.

Acknowledgment

Special thanks to my cousin Naomi Sheggeby of Clarkfield, Minnesota, USA, who gave me a home following my migratory exodus from Chicago, complete with a kitchen table upon which to complete this manuscript. She unknowingly enhanced my sense of the universal nature of the human quest for freedom in a "new land," literal and metaphoric, about which I have written here in the subsection entitled "Job, Individuation, and the Archetypal Nomad."

Note

1   Years ago an undergraduate religion professor of mine, Gary Stansell, Ph.D., told me that he was convinced that this ending is a later editorial insertion penned by nervous ecclesiastics, their fumbling, post-hoc attempt to salvage Yahweh's character. Try as I might, I find no support for this view in any of the Biblical textual criticism, leading me to the depressing conclusion that this faux-resolution reflects craven cowardice toward social convention rather than loyalty to the spirit of fearless inquiry into unpleasant truths characterizing the Book of Job.

References

Buber, M. (1937[1977]). *I and Thou*. New York: Scribner's.

Cary, P. (2000). *Augustine's Invention of the Inner Self: the Legacy of a Christian Platonist*. New York: Oxford.

Chomsky, N. (1979). *Language and Responsibility: Based on Conversations with Mitson Ronat*. (Trans. John Viertel.) New York: Pantheon.

Dean, W. (2002). *The American Spiritual Culture and the Invention of Jazz, Football, and theMovies*. New York: Continuum.

Delbanco, A. (1999). *The Real American Dream: A Meditation on Hope*. Cambridge: Harvard University Press.

Dewey, J. (1934). *A Common Faith*. New Haven: Yale University Press.

Dewey, J. (1934/1958). *Art as Experience*. New York: Capricorn.

Harris, R. Laird (1972). The Book of Job and Its Doctrine of God. *Grace Theological Journal*, 13 (3), 3–33.

Harvey, P. (1990). *Introduction to Buddhism: Teachings, History and Practices*. Cambridge: Cambridge University Press.

Hillman, J. (1975). *Re-Visioning Psychology*. New York: Harper and Row.

James, W. (1902[1985]). *The Varieties of Religious Experience*. Cambridge: Harvard University Press.

James, W. (1907[1977]). Pragmatism's Conception of Truth. In L. Menard, Ed., *Pragmatism: A Reader*. New York: Vintage, pp. 112–131.

Jung, C.G. (1927[1980]). *The Structure of the Psyche. CW*, 8. Ed. and Trans. G. Adler and R.F.C. Hull. Princeton: Princeton University Press.

Jung, C.G. (1929[1980]). *The Significance of Constitution and Heredity in Psychology. CW*, 8. Ed. and Trans. G. Adler and R.F.C. Hull. Princeton: Princeton University Press.

Jung, C.G. (1938[1966]). *Psychology and Religion*. Binghamton: Vail-Ballou.

Jung, C.G. (1958[2011]). *Answer to Job: Fiftieth Anniversary Edition* (Trans. R.F.C. Hull). Princeton, NJ: Princeton University Press.

Jung, C.G. (1960). Letter to the Editor. *The Listener*. January 21, 1960 issue.

Jung, C.G. (1965). *Memories, Dreams, Reflections*. (Ed. A. Jaffe, Trans. R. & C. Winston) New York: Vintage.

Jung, C.G. (1977). *C.G. Jung Speaking: Encounters and Interviews*. (Ed. W. McGuire & R.F.C. Hull.) Princeton, NJ: Princeton University Press.

Jung, C.G. (1969). *Aion: Researches into the Phenomenology of the Self*, 2nd Ed. Trans. R.F.C. Hull. *CW*, 9, Part 2. Princeton: Princeton University Press.

Kierkegaard, S. (1841[2004]). *The Concept of Irony, with Continual Reference to Socrates: Notes of Schelling's Berlin Lectures*. (Trans. H.V. Hong.) Princeton: Princeton University Press.

Lopez, D.S. (2001). *The Story of Buddhism*. New York: HarperCollins.

Nietzsche, F. (1889[1977]). *Twilight of the Idols*. (Trans. R.J. Hollingsdale.) London: Penguin.

Northrop, F.S.C. (1946[1979]). *The Meeting of East and West: An Inquiry Concerning World Understanding*. Reno: Oxbow.

Otto, R. (1958). *The Idea of the Holy* (Trans. J. Harvey.) London: Oxford.

Pierce, C.S. (1878[1997]). How to Make Our Ideas Clear. In L. Menard, Ed., *Pragmatism: A Reader*. New York: Vintage, pp. 26–48.

Stenger, V. (2000). *Timeless Reality: Symmetry, Simplicity, and Multiple Universes*. Buffalo, NY: Prometheus.

Winnicott, D.W. (1965). *The Maturational Process and the Facilitating Environment: Studies in the Theory of Emotional Development*. Ego Distortions in Terms of True and False Self. New York: International Universities Press.

Watts, A. (1972). *In My Own Way: An Autobiography*. New York: Vintage.

Weber, M. (2013). *From Max Weber: Essays in Sociology*. London: Routledge.

Chapter 8

Jung, the Numinous, and the Philosophers

On Immanence and Transcendence in Religious Experience

John R. White

Introduction

Religious experience plays a substantial role in Carl Jung's psychological and clinical theories. In contrast to his mentor, Sigmund Freud, who considered religious belief to be a symptom of neurosis, Jung treated religion as a potentially positive source for psychological health and investigated religion and religiously-relevant themes throughout his career. Jung frequently lamented what he viewed as the Christian Church's ineffectiveness in the twentieth century, something he considered one of the great psychological tragedies of the age.

Despite the high value he placed on religion and religious experience, Jung's understanding of religious experience often seems inadequate to his purposes. Jung was, for example, often accused by his readers of reducing religious experience to a purely psychological phenomenon. Though Jung denied this accusation, sometimes vehemently, his responses to those objections tend to be inadequate from a philosophical point of view, suggesting that Jung did not understand the potential force of those objections. Jung especially seems unable to entertain that there might be an inherent intentionality to religious experience, such that the latter cannot be analyzed as a phenomenon purely immanent to the psyche but must also be understood in terms of the transcendence that it claims.

In the following chapter, I attempt to clarify Jung's understanding of religious experience in terms of immanence and transcendence. I will then turn to Jung's main philosophical source for his analysis, Rudolf Otto, and show how Otto's similar tendencies may have influenced or at least confirmed Jung's view. I will then contrast both Jung's and

Otto's view to an older philosophical tradition, that of natural theology, highlighting how modern philosophical approaches to religion, Otto's included, seem to misunderstand ancient and medieval metaphysical thinking about God and its experiential basis, consequently misunderstanding their own contrasting projects. Finally, I will suggest that many of Jung's views are, if anything, closer to that older tradition of natural theology than he thinks.

Jung and the Numinous

Generally, when Jung describes religious phenomena, he turns to Otto's notion of the numinous. We need not speculate on the importance of the numinous for Jung's understanding of psychology: he speaks freely of the primacy of the numinous in his books and his letters.

> ... the main interest of my work is not concerned with the treatment of neuroses but rather with the approach to the numinous. But the fact is that the approach to the numinous is the real therapy and inasmuch as you attain to the numinous experiences you are released from the curse of pathology. Even the very disease takes on a numinous character.
>
> (Letter to P. T. Martin in Jung, 1973: 377)

Passages of this kind highlight both the primacy of the numinous in Jungian psychology as well as the healing power that Jung and Jungians as a rule attribute to it. Such passages also give the impression of a specifically religious orientation to Jung's thought, something many Jungians take for granted.

This last assumption is perhaps more problematic than it might appear, however. One set of issues revolves around Jung's tendency to treat the numinous as coextensive with the religious. If Jung accepts Otto's analysis at face value, as he seems to do, that assumption would not be accurate. Otto's understanding of the numinous is substantially broader than his understanding of the "holy," the latter alone being the numinous phenomenon properly pertaining to religion (Huskinson, 2006). Ironically enough, what Otto takes to be one of the primary features of the numinous—that it is a category of *value*—seems completely lost on Jung, though Jung defines the "feeling function" in terms of value (Jung, 1923; Jung, 1923a) and seems primarily interested precisely in the affective dimensions of Otto's analysis. Hence, either Jung incorrectly identifies the numinous specifically with the religious or else he is purposely deviating from Otto by treating all numinous phenomena, just by virtue of their being numinous, as religious.

The latter option has been taken up by many Jungian practitioners and authors. Lionel Corbett, by way of example, treats the numinous as in principle coextensive with the religious and takes Jung to be intending just that identification (Corbett, 1996; 2006). According to Corbett, this identification is part and parcel of Jung's project to offer a way to be religious outside of traditional religious forms, as well as to facilitate the development of "personal" religious symbols, free of a no longer effective religious tradition (Corbett, 1996). Ann Ulanov substantially concurs with Corbett, noting that Jung frequently bemoaned the fact that the traditional churches and religious forms of the West no longer spoke to modern humanity, but that Jung's own psychology could help people understand their individual religious experiences outside traditional forms, a trope Jung himself also often repeats (Ulanov, 1997).

This Jungian view is interesting, in that it suggests analytical psychology could in some measure function as a surrogate for religion, something which seems far-fetched. The way a scientific psychology might "explain" symbol formation does not seem at all parallel to the way religions "explain" symbols, the former focusing on the psychological genesis of symbols, the latter on the symbols' existential meaning. Furthermore—and this I would suggest is the rub—religions, especially those traditional to the Western world, claim to offer a grand narrative in terms of which to understand one's own individual life narrative, one that connects the individual to the movements of history, to the structure of the cosmos, and offers a link to ultimate sources of meaning. Psychological explanation of symbol formation and numinous experience hardly function as religious phenomena themselves, any more than, say, theories of the Oedipus complex could substitute for the pity and fear evoked by the Oedipus tragedies and the religious transformation evoked thereby.

Jung's religious convictions about his psychology derived from his sense that numinous experiences are operative throughout psychic life. At rock bottom, Jung believed that, by taking the numinous seriously, psychology can give what traditional religions once gave, namely, the feeling that there is a kind of meaning and calling to life, the process Jung calls "individuation." In the final analysis, for Jung, the numinous is associated with "the Self," the image of the divine in the psyche, which Jung believes leads or draws the person to a fuller individuation, rather like Aristotle's final cause draws all things to itself—with the exception that Jung's "Self" is immanent to the individual psyche.

This is, in fact, a somewhat confusing point in Jung and one that raises questions about the genuinely religious character of his psychology. On Jung's account, not only the Self but also numinous experiences are purely intrapsychic phenomena. Jung appears quite confident that his notion of the numinous correlates to Otto's, as when he writes:

> In speaking of religion, I must make clear from the start what I mean by that term. Religion, as the Latin word denotes, is a careful and scrupulous observation of what Rudolf Otto aptly termed the *numinosum*, that is, a dynamic agency or effect not caused by an arbitrary act of will. On the contrary, it seizes and controls the human subject, who is always rather its victim than its creator. The *numinosum* – whatever its cause may be – is an experience of the subject independent of his will. At all events, religious teaching as well as the *consensus gentium* always and everywhere explain this experience as being due to a cause external to the individual. The *numinosum* is either a quality belonging to a visible object or the influence of invisible presence that causes a peculiar alteration of consciousness.
>
> (Jung, 1989: 7)

As far as it goes, this is an adequate description of the numinous according to Otto, though it leaves out the specifically religious, the holy, and focuses only on the immanent experience of being impacted by something from without.

Yet, at the same time, Jung also insists that psychological phenomena of any sort, including the numinous, are purely immanent to the psyche. For example, regarding the experience of the Holy Spirit, Jung writes "Psychology's concern is with psychic phenomena alone and with nothing else" (Jung, 1989a). Jung suggests that anything transcendent to the psyche is outside psychology's interests and knowledge, except as a hypothetical source of the experience extrinsic to the psyche. A few lines down, in fact, Jung speaks of the doctrine of the Holy Spirit as a *numen* but suggests that anything numinous is reflecting unconscious processes, evidently reducing the apparent independence of the cause of numinous experience to an intrapsychic experience of the unconscious.

Lurking behind Jung's considerations of the numinous is a central philosophical problem, namely, whether religious experience can be understood in terms purely immanent to the psyche. If an immanent analysis is adequate, then Jung's psychology and Corbett's and Ulanov's treatment of Jung and religion would sufficiently explicate religion. If, on the other hand, there is also an intrinsic transcendent claim in religious experience, one can doubt that the Jungian solution is adequate.

Otto and Religious Experience

This issue was brought to Jung's attention more than once and Jung's reactions were strong and at times vehement (Ulanov, 1997). Jung insisted that, just like the sociologist or the historian, he can assume hypothetically that religious experience originates in the divine, though he equally admits there is no way to know that to be the case. Jung never seems to question this methodological approach. Rather, when it comes to questions transcendent to the psyche they fall outside his discipline. Hence there is a certain methodological immanentism that Jung adheres to, though it wasn't news in Jung's time that phenomenologists like Edmund Husserl and Max Scheler each considered psychic activities and functions intentional ("operative intentionality").

Jung's interest in Otto in part consisted in the latter's breaking with certain rationalist philosophical traditions as well as his development of the "non-rational," emotional experiences associated with the numinous. Yet the way Otto poses his understanding of the numinous appears to influence and potentially confirm Jung's immanentist trend and appears questionable philosophically. Otto begins his analysis in *The Idea of the Holy* by contrasting his position with that of the "rationalist" approach to God: an approach which consists in speaking about God through rationally clarified concepts. In contrast,

Otto posits a "profounder" religious conception, which relates qualities of the divine to affective or emotional reactions in the human person.

This latter approach appears to me an important advancement in the philosophical understanding of the divine as such and also something of psychological importance; this should be granted to Otto and to Jung. However, it also seems to pose a set of false alternatives regarding the understanding of God, which also Jung seems to adopt without question. For example, what Otto calls the "rationalist" approach is a deductive approach to God bereft of experiential sources, whereas the numinous is an experiential-based understanding of the divine. Further, the former, by being deductive and supposedly not based on experience, also seems to talk about the divine in exclusively *transcendent* terms, as if it can list characteristics of the divine "in himself," a somewhat suspicious undertaking in post-Kantian philosophy and of little value in the pulpit as well. Otto's approach, in contrast, offers an experience-based approach to the divine and further illuminates that set of experiences by looking at the Old Testament and other religious documents, to illustrate his views.

Nonetheless, though Otto's approach has definite values that the "rationalist" tradition lacks and though he offers phenomenologically valuable descriptions of the numinous, the later chapters of the book also dissolve his experiential and phenomenological analyses into an immanentist approach, through his assumption of neo-Kantian epistemological explanations. After his subtle descriptive analyses of numinous experience, Otto uncritically reduces the numinous to a purely a priori category, a "disposition" of the mind. I say "uncritically" because I see nothing in his descriptive analyses of the numinous or the holy that implies or even suggests that their justification must be found in mental structures; this assumption is merely imposed on the descriptive analyses.

In this respect, Otto and Jung do not greatly differ, except that Otto's immanentism is in principle more pronounced than Jung's, while simultaneously having no clear justification for it, thereby leaving us with a philosophically ambiguous notion of the numinous. Is the holy in fact an experience of the Wholly Other, or is it in the end merely an appearance of Otherness?

I believe Otto's text suggests a number of reasons for his immanentist assumptions. One is that he was put off by the rationalist tendency simply to list divine perfections as if God is no different from,
say, some visual object: a thing-like entity I can simply describe. Otto
was also troubled by the fact that a specifically religious approach to
the divine must in some way move the human person, which the rationalist approach cannot do, because it is purely intellectual. But another
reason we need to pursue in more detail is that Otto counteracts
excesses in the rationalist tradition by defending the opposite extreme.
While one can sympathize with his concerns, Otto lacks an adequate
diagnosis of the problems of the rationalist tradition. Rationalism
in the philosophy of God is less a tradition than a deformation or
derailment of a tradition. Had Otto undertaken a sufficient historical analysis of the origins of the rationalist tradition, he might have
recognized where his allies were.

The Ancient Roots of Natural Theology

What Otto terms the "rationalist" approach to God, we might call,
following post-Wolffian practices, "natural theology." Though Otto
offers a brief statement of this tradition in the first chapter of his
book, some understanding of its historical background is important.

Problems associated with the experience of the divine extend, in principle, to ancient philosophy. Already Xenophanes implicitly recognizes
this problem by critiquing the myths philosophically, in terms of what
can and cannot be properly said of the divine. His approach implies
that the philosopher has cognitive access to what medieval philosophers
called "pure perfections" (*perfectiones simpliciter*), i.e. perfections
properly said only of the divine, in order to have a standpoint from
which to criticize the myths. Xenophanes' approach also suggests a
close connection between the ancient philosophers' experience of
reason and their experience of the *divine*. Later ancient philosophers,
such as Plato, Aristotle, and some Stoics, went further by recognizing
that the immediacy of experience implies principles beyond the sensory (e.g., the Ideas of Plato, final causality, etc.) and thus that we
can, through experiences of world-immanent and consciousness-
immanent phenomena, transcend to something beyond the world. The
achievements of the ancient philosophers in this regard require some

extra consideration, in part because those achievements are often cast into oblivion in our own time.

It may be difficult at the beginning of the twenty-first century to imagine a time when "reason" in the philosophical sense was not consciously exercised. Though traditionally reason is understood to be a faculty or power intrinsic to human nature, its conscious articulation and effective use is an event in history, an event that was recorded in the work of the ancient philosophers (Voegelin, 1978). Following Voegelin, we can say that the ancient philosophers used certain sets of symbols to articulate the new experience, symbols which illuminate the problem of immanence and transcendence in the experience of the divine. It is worth underlining that the philosophers expressed these experiences in *symbols* rather than *concepts*, because they recognized they were not speaking of thing-like realities, easily susceptible to conceptualization. Rather, the ancients used symbols because they recognized the experience of the divine in a non-objectifying yet intentional experience.

Speaking schematically about the ancient philosophers, Voegelin notes that the notion of reason was developed on the background of a perceived disorder, both in individual psyches and in social reality, the latter being, as Plato put it, "the soul writ large." Hence, the articulation of the original experiences of reason was not abstracted from their historical context, as, for example, in the manner of formal logic, but was understood as an experience of *resistance* to disorder in the soul and the polity. Reason therefore has a decisively existential component in the ancients and, especially in Plato, an index of urgency, as the latter bears witness to the growing corruption of Athens. Plato symbolizes the experience and exercise of reason as the *health* of the soul and its disordered use or nonuse as *nosos* or disease of the soul (a practice also followed by Cicero), and Plato further analyzes the polity in those same terms of the healthy or unhealthy ("feverish") city, for example in the *Republic*.

Plato's conception of reason is a movement of the soul characterized first and foremost by tensions, not only the above tension between health and illness, but broader tensions between life and death, time and eternity, past and future, all symbolized by the *metaxy*, or the "In-between" of the *Symposium* and *Philebus*. Hence Plato recognizes a set of tensions that function as both the context of reason and also, like the marionetteer in the *Laws*, as forces impacting reason—forces which it is reason's task to analyze and put into balance. For example, the tensions between eternity and time are *meant* to be a tension in the psyche. If one loses the tension, one tends toward "mortalizing" passion, i.e. toward the "temporal" side of the tension, living in disorder. Plato's analysis of tensions continues in other forms, as in Aristotle's analysis of the virtues in terms of the deformations of deficit or excess.

As Voegelin notes, reason is differentiated (already in Heraclitus) into *nous*, that which intuitively grasps Ideas or essences or, in other words, understands a rational order in being, and *logos*, the ability to articulate the experienced order in terms of specific language symbols. Among the most central symbols for the ordered use of reason—philosophy—are two sets, one associated with "wondering," "seeking," and "searching," i.e. symbols of the experience of recognizing one's tendency toward ignorance and disorder and, on the other side of the tension, sets associated with "pulling," "drawing," and "being moved," i.e. the responsive seeking for order, experienced as originating in the divine. Several of these symbols are used in Plato's Parable of the Cave, where the restless wondering of the released prisoner, leads to the recognition of the disease of those locked in the Cave and the experience of an invisible force drawing the liberated yet still seeking philosopher, up the difficult path out of the Cave.

This invisible force should not be missed in the Parable. As Voegelin puts it:

> In the Platonic-Aristotelian experience, the questioning unrest carries the assuaging answer within itself, inasmuch as man is moved to his search for the ground by the divine ground of which he is in search. The ground is not a spatially distant thing but a divine presence that becomes manifest in the experience of unrest and the desire to know. The wondering and questioning is sensed as the beginning of a theophanic event that can become fully luminous to itself if it finds the proper response in the psyche of concrete human beings – as it does in the classic philosophers. Hence, philosophy in the classic sense is not a body of "ideas" or "opinions" about the divine ground dispensed by a person who calls himself a "philosopher," but a man's responsive pursuit of his questioning unrest to the divine source that has aroused it.

This pursuit, however, if it is to be responsive indeed to the divine mover, requires the effort of articulating the experience through appropriate language symbols; and this effort leads to the insights into the noetic structure of the *psyche*.

(Voegelin, 1978: 95–96)

Several points are important here. First, we notice that the numinous experience refers neither to a thing-like transcendent God nor to a merely immanent experience. It is rather given in the experience of the *metaxy*, in the existential tensions between immanence and transcendence. Furthermore, the experience is "intentional," in the phenomenological sense, because of the meaningful relationship between the experience of the divine and the tensions engendering the experience. Third, the articulation of the experience of the divine is simultaneous to the articulation of its meaning for the psyche, the implication being that the experience of the divine pole of the tensions illuminates also one's place in the cosmos and the rational order of being, expressed for example in Aristotle's notion of "nature" or the Stoic "Logos" permeating the universe.

The Medieval Inheritance

The medieval scholastics not only systematize the achievements of ancient philosophy but retain certain assumptions about what it is to be a philosopher. As we have seen, the philosopher on the ancient model is not simply a rational knower—a more or less contemporary notion of the philosopher—but one with a direct awareness of the divine as one of the tensions in the *metaxy*, which in turn expresses one's participation in a pre-given rational order. This expressed itself in the Middle Ages in meditative processes, which purported to awaken one to an ultimate reality beyond appearances and to the rational order of the cosmos. Bonaventure makes this point explicitly in Question One, Article One of his *Disputed Questions on the Mystery of the Trinity*, where he claims that the so-called "proofs for God's existence" are not so much proofs as exercises of the intellect, designed to articulate what is known previously through meditation (Bonaventure, 2000). The philosopher is therefore one who experiences a movement in the soul toward an ultimate reality beyond what is sensuously given, in turn illuminating how the philosopher can *also* articulate rational proofs for God's existence based on an understanding of the cosmic order. This approach is sometimes infelicitously called "divine illumination theory," a term giving the impression that God illuminates the mind, rather than that the philosopher, by means of a meditative process, experiences the tensions in existence, making consciousness luminous to itself (White, 2002; White, 2008; White, 2009). Historians such as Pierre Hadot, Etienne Gilson, and Voegelin have underlined elements of the meditative and mystical basis of philosophical understanding in the ancient and medieval philosophers and we find some recent philosophers re-articulating these ancient views in terms of their own philosophizing, for example, Max Scheler in his *On the Eternal in Man* (Scheler, 1960).

The medieval philosophers both inherited and reformulated ancient philosophical traditions, setting forth a "doctrine" of knowledge of God which dominated Western philosophy through the time of Christian Wolff in the eighteenth century—precisely the era which Otto refers to as "rationalist." Yet this latter tradition is "rationalist" not because it is natural theology, but because it lost the numinous pole of the tensional experience inherent to the tradition and imagined it could produce something other than empty concepts without meditative experiences in the *metaxy*.

A few features characterize pre-rationalist natural theology. First, medieval ruminations on the divine were guided by Dionysius the Areopogite, whose analysis implied that all knowledge of God is "more false than true," a formulation meant to capture the ambivalent nature of such knowledge: on the one hand, it is actual knowledge and yet, on the other, its claims entail extreme limits both on human understanding and on the adequacy of human language. Thus, philosophical knowledge of God—in contrast to its numinous basis—was primarily propositional knowledge based on analogy. For example, one could know through meditative experiences that God is good; however, articulating this point philosophically required that one understand God's goodness through analogy with the goodness of the world and that one recognize the limits of statements such as "God is good," since one could not actually understand what that goodness looks like in God "in himself," how goodness "inheres" in

God, how this goodness relates to other divine perfections, and so on. Hence one's formulation is always more false than true. It is *not* that the philosopher had no experience of God, but that epistemological and linguistic limits significantly qualified the sense and value of one's statements about the divine.

Second, due to these limits, rational knowledge of God was a largely deductive process, whose premises were derived from experiences of the finite world. Duns Scotus is explicit on this point when he states that though Being qua Being is the *subject matter* of metaphysics, God is the ultimate *object* of metaphysics (Scotus, 1975). This approach allowed the medieval philosophers to honor Aristotle's dictum that metaphysics studied Being qua Being, while simultaneously holding to a basically Christian view that God is the ultimate telos of human thinking and acting.

Third, this approach supposed that all empirical knowledge in philosophy is sensuous, usually including an ambiguous "inner sense" as one of those sources. This might appear in contradiction to my claim that natural theology is rooted in numinous knowledge. The resolution to this apparent problem, however, is that the order of evidence in *proofs* requires sensuous experience since it is intersubjective and general, whereas it cannot be guaranteed that others have the mystical experience of the (genuine) philosopher. Hence, though the primary access to the divine is mystical, the rational proofs for God's existence are and ought to be articulated in terms of standard rules of philosophical reasoning and explanation of the time, beginning in sense experience, according to the medievals.

Otto tends to discount natural theology as a whole because he assumes it is rationalist, an understandable assumption if it is based on eighteenth century Wolffian styles of thinking. Furthermore, it should be granted that longstanding philosophical traditions tend to forget their experiential basis with the overlay of accepted theory, something definitely characteristic of rationalist natural theology. However, a comparison between Bonaventure's *The Mind's Journey to God* and Gottfried Leibniz' *Metaphysics* is instructive here. Bonaventure believes, through a process of negation of limits on concepts, he can develop concepts predicable of God that are more or less expressive of his numinous experience of the divine, but nonetheless "more false than true." Bonaventure carefully derives his concepts of God from experience, while insisting he can only approximate an ineffable experience and cannot know how exactly they exist in God—classical natural theological thinking within the Dionysian constraints. In contrast, Leibniz simply begins with talk about God, even to the point of simply positing God non-problematically as a substance and without any of the Dionysian constraints on his thinking. Lost in the rationalist tradition is the consciousness of the tensions of opposites in the *metaxy* so characteristic of the more traditional natural theology.

While Otto quite rightly understands his work as a break from the "rationalist tradition," he seems mistaken in thinking that the numinous as an experiential basis for religious knowledge did not exist in the older tradition. Otto's work on the numinous and the holy should be interpreted less as a contrast to, than a working out of, that mystical basis which the precursors to the rationalist tradition assumed, before its derailment in the modern period, though it should also be admitted that Otto captures only one pole of what was conceived of as a tensional experience, linking both immanent and transcendent experiences. Nonetheless, recognizing the extent to which there is a contrast between Otto and the rationalist tradition underlines one of the problems of Kant and post-Kantian philosophy, including Otto.

Otto and the Critique of Experience

For it is at the endpoint of the rationalist tradition, in the middle of the eighteenth century, that the notion of "experience" itself becomes a central concern for Western philosophy, as evidenced by Kant's first *Critique*. Kant seems to have understood Hume's critique of human knowledge of efficient causality as potentially a universal problem for philosophy, because it suggested that purely empirical experience could not yield the knowledge of any of the sorts of (necessary, universal, and certain) principles that made philosophical and universal knowledge possible, including philosophical or rational knowledge of God. Kant's *Critique* was intended to describe the limits of experience, so that Kant could, in turn, reimagine the nature of philosophy, in a way consistent with the limits of experience. Kant himself consistently treats of anything not explicitly sensuous as arising from the transcendental realm of the mind. Though later Idealists did not always agree with that assessment, one can nonetheless read much of German philosophy from Kant to the death of Schelling as revolving around the issue of what is the nature and range of human experience and to what extent can what "appears" in experience be justified as genuine knowledge.

This trend in fact appears to be one of the decisive differences between modern philosophy and the older traditions, which especially impacts issues associated with the experience and knowledge of the divine. Medieval philosophers, for example, did not consider experience a problematic concept at all: Aristotle's analysis of experience as both sensuous but expressive of intelligible essences and multiple causes seemed both adequate and more or less beyond question to medieval thinkers. With the Humean critique of experience and its relationship to philosophical knowledge, experience itself becomes problematic and thus the locus of a good deal of philosophical thinking.

Otto writes on the background of these shifts in philosophical epistemology in general, and of the philosophy of God in particular. *The Idea of the Holy* is in essence part of a broad movement in German-language philosophical thinking that attempts to resolve at least some of the problems surrounding the critique of experience. One aspect of this movement that Otto specifically exemplifies is the attempt to clarify the basic issues of experience by means of a largely descriptive analysis of the characteristics of experience, both the subject- and object-sides of the experience. Very much in the spirit of early phenomenology, which at times Husserl characterized as "descriptive psychology," Otto offers a descriptive analysis of the essence of both the numinous and the Holy and of the experience in which it is given.

Nonetheless, Otto falls back on neo-Kantian categories to justify the phenomenological descriptions he offers, rather than entertaining the possibility that his descriptions of experience in no way entail a purely immanent justification and in fact might offer another access to an experience of the divine. In principle, Otto's recognition of descriptive characteristics on both the subject and object side of the intentional relationship might suggest something of the tensions in existence that the ancients saw. After all, the Dionysian constraints on the ancient and medieval conceptions of natural theology were themselves born of the sense of divine holiness and ultimacy, experiences that presumably yielded something like a sense of the *mysterium tremendum, fascinans*, and so forth and, emotionally, the shuddering and other experiences that Otto describes. If one conceives of natural theology in purely rationalist terms, it is indeed fundamentally a contrast to Otto. But rooted in its more traditional experience, natural theology and philosophy of religion a la Otto are ultimately harmonious, as Max Scheler's *On the Eternal in Man* demonstrates (Scheler, 1960). Scheler proposes what he calls the "system of conformity," whereby natural theology and philosophy of religion are coworkers in the same project, correcting the excesses to which each is susceptible.

Returning to Jung

Jung's acceptance not only of Otto's notion of the numinous, but of also of its immanence is in part born of Jung's own notion of the unconscious. The notion of the unconscious in the modern period arises from the work of early German Idealism, especially Fichte and the early Schelling, and was already in the air when Freud and the early psychoanalysts were attempting to understand the psychic processes they termed "unconscious" (Ellenberger, 2006). Jung's own notion of the unconscious, though on much richer than Kant's "transcendental," nonetheless continues the Kantian construal of the latter by treating the unconscious as a dark, mysterious root of all that is not given empirically and by often adopting a largely Humean epistemology of the senses, as if sense impressions are all that is "given." Similar patterns of thought are present in Otto, as we have seen, and Jung appears to adopt not only Otto's conception of the numinous but also its immanence—for Jung immanence to the unconscious, for Otto immanence to the a priori category. Indeed, Jung's being a fellow traveler with Otto in a basically neo-Kantian framework, along with his ignorance of the older natural theological tradition, inhibit his recognition of some his own real achievements regarding religious experience.

Several of the central ideas from the ancient philosophers actually find resonances in Jung's psychology. For example, Plato's symbol of the *metaxy* as the locus of tensions in the psyche is familiar to Jung in the form of the "tension of opposites." Jung in fact often defines neurotic symptoms in terms of a "one-sidedness," one which requires tension from the opposite side. Further, Jung recognizes that the balance of consciousness in his notion of the "transcendent function" (Jung,

1972), a notion that suggests that the right balance of tensions brings a "higher" consciousness, an idea both Plato and Aristotle would recognize. However, true to the immanentist tendencies in Jung, one side of the tension always gets subsumed into the unconscious and, since Jung's notion of the unconscious seems to collect both primitive "subconscious" and potentially transcendent "superconsciousness" (to use Schelling's distinction), there is no way to express a tension between immanence and transcendence. Jung's incapacity or unwillingness to entertain phenomenological intentionality or to differentiate the vast strata of reality contained in his notion of the unconscious excludes the possibility of a more adequate understanding of the numinous: Jung's numinous experience can be "transcendent" only to the conscious ego, but not to the psyche as a whole.

A similar set of problems arises with Jung's concept of the "Self." Though the latter is put in strongly non-psychological language—*das Selbst* being better translated as "the Itself" rather than "the Self" (Ellenberger, 2006)—and though Jung consistently uses symbols for the divine to describe the Self, such as Bonaventure's description of the divine as both "the Center and the Circumference" and symbols of "pulling" on the ego that closely parallel the ancient descriptions of being drawn by the divine, Jung nonetheless seems once again so constrained by a quasi-Kantian model of the unconscious that he cannot imagine a non-sensuous reality that is not in some fashion a product of the psyche. From a descriptive standpoint, Jung is often very close to the ancient philosophers on these points yet always resorts to a self-enclosed psyche and to an immanentist reading of data that often suggest the opposite.

Without some conception of transcendence in relationship to the divine, it is difficult to understand why Jung thinks the numinous to be healing. The model we drew from ancient philosophy articulated the problem of disorder and how recognizing the tension between the divine and divine order, on the one hand, the disorders of both the soul and the polity on the other, give us a glimpse of possible healing, precisely because there one can consciously partake of that transcendent order, even if only within the limits of finite human experience. Jung's immanence offers nothing equivalent, at least that I can see, leaving open what might actually heal.

If this story is to some extent a tragedy, it is because Jung's descriptive investigations of religious phenomena might have led him to a

more consistent psychology of religion, one which neither takes immanence as its sole possibility nor falls into the trap of transcendental
rationalism, free of the constraints of human experience. Nonetheless,
Jung's treatment of these issues may well lead to a richer understanding
of numinous experience into the future, if those of us who work with
it can begin to remember and re-articulate some of the achievements
of the past.

References

Bonaventure, S. (2000). *Disputed Questions on the Mystery of the Trinity*
(Vol. 3). (Z. Hayes, Trans.) St. Bonaventure, NY: Franciscan Institute, St.
Bonaventure University.

Corbett, L. (1996). *The Religious Function of the Psyche.* London: Routledge.

Corbett, L. (2006). Varieties of Numinous Experience: The Experience of
the Sacred in the Therapeutic Process. In A. Casement, *The Idea of the
Numinous. Contemporary Jungian and Psychoanalytic Perspectives* (pp. 53–
67). London: Routledge.

Ellenberger, H.F. (2006). *The Discovery of the Unconscious. The History and
Evolution of Dynamic Psychiatry.* New York: Basic Books.

Huskinson, L. (2006). Holy, Holy, Holy: The Misappropriation of the
Numinous in Jung. In A. Casement, *The Idea of the Numinous. Contemporary
Jungian And Psychoanalytic Perspectives* (pp. 200–212). London: Routledge.

Jung, C.G. (1923). *Psychological Types, CW,* 6. (R.F. Hull, Trans.) Princeton:
Princeton University Press.

Jung, C.G. (1923a). *Psychological Types. CW,* 6 (R.F. Hull, Trans., pp. 510–
523). Princeton: Princeton University Press.

Jung, C.G. (1972). The Transcendent Function. *CW,* 8 (R.F. Hull, Trans., Vol.
8, pp. 67–91). Princeton: Princeton University Press.

Jung, C.G. (1973). *Letters.* (R.F. Hull, Ed.) London: Routledge.

Jung, C.G. (1989). A Psychological Approach to the Dogma of the Trinity. In
C.G. Jung, *Psychology and Religion: West and East* (R.F. Hull, Trans., Vol.
11, pp. 107–200). Princeton: Princeton University Press.

Jung, C.G. (1989a). Psychology and Religion. In C.G. Jung, *Psychology and
Religion: West and East* (R.F. Hull, Trans., 2nd ed., Vol.11, pp. 3–105).
Princeton: Princeton University Press.

Otto, R. (1976). *The Idea of the Holy.* (J. Harvey, Trans.) London: Oxford
University Press.

Scheler, M. (1960). *On the Eternal in Man.* (B. Noble, Trans.) New York:
Harper & Bros.

Scotus, J.D. (1975). *Philosophical Writings.* (A.B. Wolter, Ed., & A.B. Wolter, Trans.) Indianapolis, IN: Bobbs-Merrill.

Ulanov, A.B. (1997). Jung and Religion: The Opposing Self. In P. Young-Eisendrath, *The Cambridge Companion to Jung* (pp. 296–313). Cambridge: Cambridge University Press.

Voegelin, E. (1978). Reason: The Classic Experience. In E. Voegelin, & G. Niemeyer (Ed.), *Anamnesis* (G. Niemeyer, Trans., pp. 89–115). Colombia, MO: University of Missouri Press.

White, J. (2001). The Illumination of Bonaventure. Divine Light in Theology, Philosophy And History According to Bonaventure. *Fides quaerens intellectum*, 1 (2), 201–223.

White, J. (2008). Divine Light and Human Wisdom: Transcendental Elements in Bonaventure's Illumination Theory. *International Philosophical Quarterly*, 48 (2), 175–185.

White, J. (2009). Illuminating Josef Seifert's Theory of a priori Knowledge in Back to Things in Themselves. On What – and How – We Learn from St. Bonaventure's Illumination Theory. In *To Love All Truth and in All Things* (pp. 113–156). Santiago, Chile: Ediciones UC.

Chapter 9

Jung on Myth

Robert A. Segal

Nineteenth- and Twentieth-Century Approaches to Myth

The nineteenth century saw myth as about the physical world. The most famous nineteenth-century theorists were the English anthropologist E.B. Tylor, whose chief work, *Primitive Culture*, first appeared in 1871, and the Scottish classicist and anthropologist J.G. Frazer, the first edition of whose main opus, *The Golden Bough*, was published in 1890. Both Tylor and Frazer take for granted that myth is part of religion. For both, myth serves to explain physical events. The explanation is always a decision by a god.

For Tylor, myth explains physical events as an end in itself. For Frazer, myth explains physical events as a means to controlling them. For both, myth is the "primitive" counterpart to science, but to theoretical science for Tylor and to applied science for Frazer. For Tylor, myth explains why it rains. For Frazer, myth either brings rain or ends rain. For Tylor, the explanation is a decision by a god. For Frazer, the explanation is the physical condition of a god. If the god of rain is ailing, the rainfall will be limited. If the rain god is incontinent, there will be flooding.

As the commonplace way of both explaining and effecting physical events, science for Tylor and Frazer is wholly modern. Myth and science do not merely duplicate each other but are incompatible. One cannot consistently accept both. Because moderns by definition have science, they cannot logically also have myth. "Modern myth" is a contradiction in terms. By science is meant natural science, not social science. The events explained or controlled by myth are primarily external ones like the falling of rain, though also human events like birth and death. Explanations of customs, laws, institutions, and other social phenomena ordinarily fall outside myth.

In the twentieth century Tylor's and Frazer's theories have been spurned by fellow theorists of myth on many grounds: (1) for pitting myth against science and thereby precluding both traditional myths and modern ones; (2) for subsuming myth under religion and thereby precluding secular myths; (3) for deeming the function of myth explanatory; (4) for deeming the subject matter of myth the physical world and not the social world; and (5) for deeming myth false. Nevertheless, Tylor's and Frazer's theories have remained central to the study of myth, and subsequent theories can be taken as rejoinders to them.

The overarching twentieth-century rejoinder to Tylor and Frazer has been the denial that myth must go when science comes. Twentieth-century theories have defiantly sought to preserve myth in the face of science. Yet they have not done so by challenging science as the reigning explanation of the physical world. They have not taken any of the easy routes: "relativizing" science, "sociologizing" science, or "mythicizing" science. Rather, they have recharacterized *myth* as other than a literal explanation of the physical world. Sometimes myth has been severed from religion, so that myth is free of conflicts between religion and science. In short, myth for twentieth-century theories is compatible with science because of a reconfiguration of myth, not because of any reconfiguration of science.

I divide twentieth-century theories into three groups: (a) those which maintain that myth, while still about the physical world, is not or not primarily an explanation, in which case its function runs askew to that of science (Bronislaw Malinowski, Mircea Eliade); (b) those which maintain that myth is not to be read literally, in which case myth is not even referring to the physical world (Rudolf Bultmann, Hans Jonas, Albert Camus); and most radically, (c) those which maintain both that myth is other than an explanation of the physical world and that myth is to be read symbolically. I place both Freud and Jung in this third camp.

Freud and Jung on Myth

For Freud and Jung alike, the subject matter of myth is the human unconscious and so anything but the physical world. The function of myth is to enable one to encounter the unconscious. Myth does not make the unconscious conscious. On the contrary, it ordinarily operates unconsciously and for Freud must operate unconsciously. Freud and Jung differ sharply over the nature of the unconscious and over the reason that myth is needed to express it.

Because the Freudian unconscious is composed of repressed, antisocial drives, myth releases those drives in a disguised way, so that neither the myth maker nor the reader of the myth ever confronts its meaning and thereby the myth maker's or the reader's own true nature. Myth, like other aspects of culture, serves simultaneously to reveal and to hide its unconscious contents. Myth is a "compromise formation." The classical Freudian approach takes myth as wish-fulfillment. Focusing on myths of male heroes, Freud's one-time disciple Otto Rank, in *The Myth of the Birth of the Hero* (1914, 2003), sees the myths as providing a partial fulfillment of, above all, Oedipal drives. By unconsciously identifying oneself with the named hero, the reader of the myth gains a vicarious, mental fulfillment of the reader's own lingering desires. Hero myths serve neurotic adults fixated at their Oedipal stage.

Spurred by the emergence of ego psychology, which has broadened psychoanalysis from a theory of abnormal personality to a theory of normal personality, contemporary Freudians like Jacob Arlow (1961) see myth as contributing to psychological development and not just to neurosis. For them, myth helps one grow up rather than, like Peter Pan, remain a child. Myth abets adjustment to society and the physical world rather than childish flight from them. Myth may still serve to release repressed drives, but it serves even more to sublimate them and to integrate them. It serves the ego and the superego, not merely the id. Moreover, myth serves everyone, not only neurotics.[1]

For Freudians, myths project human nature onto the world in the form of gods—for Freud himself, largely father-like gods. To understand the world is to withdraw those projections. The world really operates according to mechanical laws rather than according to the wills of a divine family. There is no symmetry between humans and the world. There is a disjunction. Even myths about heroes involve projection: the plot of hero myths is the fantasized expression of family relations, with the named hero playing the role of the idealized myth maker or reader. In the real world there are no comic-book heroes, only some human beings better than others.

For Jungians as well as for Freudians, myths project human nature onto the world in the form of gods and of heroes. To understand the world is, similarly, to withdraw those projections and to recognize the world as it really is. Jungian projections are more elusive than Freudian ones because they cover a far wider range of the personality. After all, there is an endless number of sides of the personality, or archetypes. Almost anything in the world can be archetypal—that is, can provide a hook for the projection of an archetype.

Unlike Freudians, Jungians have taken myth positively from the outset. For them, the unconscious expressed in myth is not a repository of repressed anti-social drives but a storehouse of innately unconscious archetypes that have simply never had an opportunity at realization. Myth is one means of encountering this unconscious. The function of myth is less that of release, as for classical Freudians, than that of growth, as for contemporary ones. But where even contemporary Freudians see myth as a means of adjustment to the demands of the outer world, Jungians see myth as a means of the cultivation of the inner world. The payoff is not adjustment but self-realization. Myth is a circuitous, though still useful, means of self-realization because it involves projection: one encounters oneself *through* the world. Ordinarily, projections are recognized and thereby withdrawn only in the course of analysis—a point that holds for Freudians as well. If, for either Freudians or Jungians, myth can still be employed once the projection has been recognized, then the middle man—the world—has conveniently been eliminated.

Both Freudians and Jungians bypass the power of myth at the conscious, usually literal, level. While both appreciate the need to be moved by the life of the named hero or protagonist, that figure can be fictional. One does not have to accept the historicity of Oedipus to be moved by his saga, which means to imagine oneself as Oedipus. As Freud writes, "Oedipus' destiny moves us only because it might have been ours—because the oracle laid the same curse [i.e., the Oedipus complex] upon us before our birth as upon him" (Freud 1953, p. 262). Jung would concur. For both, a story that can never be imagined as happening to oneself will not work. In short, myth for Freudians and Jungians alike never takes one outside oneself. No theory of myth is more solipsistic than theirs. Jung's is much more solipsistic than Freud's because myth for him is a means of encountering other sides of one's own personality rather than other sides of one's feelings toward others.

It is conventionally assumed that Jung, on myth as in general, is arguing against Freud, just as it is conventionally assumed that Freud or Freudians on myth are arguing against Jung and Jungians. But in fact both are arguing at least as much against nineteenth-century theorists like Tylor and Frazer. Both must first show that myth is not about the physical world before they can debate each other over what myth is about psychologically.

Jung cites Frazer repeatedly but cites Tylor only occasionally. For Jung, both Tylor and Frazer wrongly intellectualize myth and religion, which they attribute to conscious reflection rather than to the unconscious: "So this idea [of god] has been stamped on the human brain for aeons. That is why it lies ready to hand in the unconscious of every man. Only, certain conditions are needed to cause it to appear" (Jung 1966 [1953], p. 69). The experience of the external world provides the "condition" for the appearance of the unconscious, which is always experienced as extraordinary rather than ordinary, as sacred rather than profane, as divine rather than human.

Like many others, Jung turns to Frazer for example after example of myths worldwide, but he always psychologizes whatever examples he uses. Above all, he cites examples of Frazer's own key myth, that of the death and rebirth of the god of vegetation. In contrast to Tylor, who stalwartly reads myth literally, Frazer sometimes reads this myth as symbolic of the course of vegetation itself. Thus

> the story that Adonis spent half, or according to others a third, of the year in the lower world and the rest of it in the upper world, is explained most simply and naturally by supposing that he represented vegetation, especially the corn, which lies buried in the earth half the year and reappears above ground the other half.
> (Frazer 1922, p. 392)

True, Frazer, like Tylor, assumes that "primitives" themselves take their myths literally and must do so for their myths to explain and control events in the world. But Frazer breaks with Tylor in asserting that myths are in fact, albeit unrecognized, symbolic descriptions of natural processes themselves.

Against Frazer, Jung offers his own symbolic rendition of these myths: the myth of the death and rebirth of a god is a symbolic description of a process taking place not in the world but in the mind. That process is the return of the ego to the unconscious—a kind of temporary death of the ego—and its re-emergence, or rebirth, from the unconscious:

> I need only mention the whole mythological complex of the dying and resurgent god and its primitive precursors all the way down to the re-charging of fetishes and churingas with magical force. It expresses a transformation of attitude by means of which a new potential, a new manifestation of life, a new fruitfulness, is created.
>
> (Jung 1971, p. 193)

Jung does not deny that the psychological process of the death and rebirth of the ego *parallels* the physical process of the death and rebirth of vegetation. He denies that the physical process *accounts for* the psychological one, let alone for the mythic one.

For Frazer, as for Tylor, the leap from vegetation to god is the product of reasoning: "primitives" observe the course of vegetation and hypothesize the existence of a god to account for it—even if, again, for Frazer the god is a mere symbol of vegetation itself. For Jung, the leap is too great for the human mind to make. Humans generally, not merely "primitives," lack the imagination required to concoct consciously the notion of the sacred out of the profane. They can only transform the profane into a sacred that already exists for them. Humans must already have the idea of god within them and can only be projecting that idea onto vegetation and other natural phenomena:

> This latter analogy [between god and natural phenomenon] explains the well-attested connection between the renewal of the god and seasonal and vegetational phenomena. One is naturally inclined to assume that seasonal, vegetational, lunar, and solar myths underlie these analogies. But that is to forget that a myth, like everything psychic, cannot be solely conditioned by external events. Anything psychic brings its own internal conditions with it, so that one might assert with equal right that the myth is purely psychological and uses meteorological or astronomical events

merely as a means of expression. The whimsicality and absurdity of many primitive myths often makes the latter explanation seem far more appropriate than any other.

(Jung 1971, pp. 193–194)

It is not only allegories of physical processes that Jung rejects as the real subject matter of myth. It is also literal interpretations of myth like Tylor's, which still makes the subject matter outer rather than inner. For Tylor, myths are actual *explanations* of natural phenomena and not merely, as for Frazer, colorful *descriptions* of them.

Jung conflates Tylor's theory with Frazer's in stating that "People are very loath to give up the idea that the myth is some kind of explanatory allegory of astronomical, meteorological, or vegetative processes" (Jung 1969a [1960], pp. 38–39). The phrase "explanatory allegory" equates Tylor's theory—myth as explanation—with Frazer's—myth as allegory. Jung asks rhetorically "why," if myth is really about the sun, "the sun and its apparent motions do not appear direct and undisguised as a content of the myths" (Jung, 1971, p. 444). But the question is rhetorical for Frazer's theory only. For Tylor, a myth describes the sun god and not merely the sun because the myth is about the sun god and not merely about the sun. Yet even if Jung were to distinguish Tylor's view from Frazer's, he would still invoke his fundamental claim that human beings are incapable of consciously inventing gods and can only be casting onto the world gods already in their minds.

Yet for Jung, myth is no more about gods than about the physical world. It is about the human mind. Myth must be read symbolically, as for Frazer, and the symbolized subject is a process, as likewise for Frazer, but the process is an inner rather than outer one. If on the one hand Jung would doubtless prefer Frazer's symbolic reading of myth to Tylor's literal reading, on the other hand he would surely prefer Tylor's appreciation of the divine referent of myth to Frazer's reduction of it to something natural, which psychologically means the reduction of the unconscious to consciousness.

Jung takes as projections not only nature myths but all other kinds of myths as well. He states that "in fact, the whole of mythology could be taken as a sort of projection of the collective unconscious... Just as the constellations were projected into the heavens, similar figures were projected into legends and fairytales or upon historical persons"

(Jung 1969b [1960], pp. 152–153). Once Jung decouples myth from the natural world, he is no longer confined to myths that at face value are about the external world—for example, myths of creation, floods, the seasons, paradise, and the end of the world. He can now fix his psychological gaze on myths that at face value are about human beings—for example, myths about children, old persons, kings, and queens.

Hero myths, of which Jungians are especially enamored, are projections onto mere human beings of a quasi-divine status: "the hero myth is an unconscious drama seen only in projection, like the happenings in Plato's parable of the cave. The hero himself appears as a being of more than human stature" (Jung 1967 [1956], p. 391). Moderns, even while often professed atheists, still create myths by projecting onto their fellow human beings exaggerated qualities that turn them into superhuman figures—not only into heroes but also into saints, demons, and stereotypes.

For Jung, traditional myths, to which Tylor and Frazer limit themselves, have been religious myths. They have been either about gods acting in the world (Tylor) or about the world as symbolized by gods (Frazer). The decline of religion in the wake of science has obliged moderns to seek secular myths, such as myths about heroes, who, if superhuman, are still not quite gods. The decline of religion has also spurred moderns to forge their own, private myths, of which Jung is particularly appreciative.

Once Jung differentiates a psychological interpretation of myth from a non-psychological one, he turns to differentiating his particular psychological interpretation from Freud's. Jung grants the Freudian claim that there exist "fantasies (including dreams) of a personal character, which go back unquestionably to personal experiences, things forgotten or repressed, and can thus be completely explained by individual anamnesis [i.e., recollection]" (Jung 1968b [1959], p. 155). But he vaunts his own claim that, in addition to these manifestations of the personal, Freudian unconscious, there exist "fantasies (including dreams) of an impersonal character, which cannot be reduced to experiences in the individual's past, and thus cannot be explained as something individually acquired" (Jung 1968b [1959], p. 155). These fantasies must emanate from a different unconscious, which, rather than the creation of an individual, must be inherited. Jung insists that myths are always the product of this distinctively Jungian, or collective, unconscious: "These fantasy-images [of an impersonal character] undoubtedly have their closest analogues in mythological types" (Jung 1968b [1959], p. 155).

The Puer Archetype

In contrast to Freud, whose writings on myth are sparing and who left it to Otto Rank, Karl Abraham, and others to apply the theory systematically to myths, Jung himself writes continually on myths.[2] He writes on myths worldwide—on myths from Eastern as well as Western religions, from "primitive" as well as "higher" religions, and from the classics as well as from the Bible. He writes essays on the I Ching, on Zen Buddhism, and on Yoga. He writes an essay on Gnosticism and three whole books on alchemy. He writes not only on past myths but also on the revival of past myths, such as the revival of the worship of Wotan in German-speaking lands in his own day. And he writes as well on modern, secular myths, most famously on what he titles "Flying Saucers: A Modern Myth."

Jung does write far more on biblical myths than on classical ones. One reason is that he is preoccupied with Jewish and, more, Christian theology, which for him are illustrated by myths but encompass more than myths. The volume of his Collected Works on "Psychology and Religion: West and East" is divided into sections on Western and Eastern religions. The section on Western religions is almost exclusively on Christianity.

Jung is exceedingly attracted to myths from anywhere, not least the classics. The myth that best illustrates his approach is that of Adonis. True, Jung himself mentions Adonis only in passing,[3] but he mentions him as an instance of one of his best-known archetypes: that of the eternal child, or *puer aeternus*.[4] Jung devotes even more attention to an allied archetype, that of the Great Mother.[5] Marie-Louise von Franz, one of Jung's closest disciples, wrote a book (1981 [1970]) on the puer archetype.

From a Jungian point of view, the myth of Adonis functions not merely to present the archetype of the puer but also to assess it. The myth serves as a warning to those who identify themselves with the archetype. To live as a puer, the way Adonis does, is to live as a psychological infant and, ultimately, as a fetus.[6] The life of a puer in myth invariably ends in premature death, which psychologically means the death of the ego and a return to the womb-like unconscious.

As an archetype, the puer constitutes a side of one's personality, which, as a side, must be accepted. A puer personality simply goes too far: he makes the puer the whole of his personality. Unable to resist its spell, he surrenders himself to it, thereby abandoning his ego and reverting to sheer unconsciousness.

The reason a puer personality cannot resist the puer archetype is that he remains under the spell of the archetype of the Great Mother, who initially is identical with the unconscious as a whole. Unable to free himself from her, he never forges a strong, independent ego, without which he cannot in turn resist any smothering female he meets. His surrender to the puer archetype means his surrender to the Great Mother, to whom he yearns only to return. A puer "only lives on and through the mother and can strike no roots, so that he finds himself in a state of permanent incest." Jung even calls him a mere "dream of the mother," who eventually draws him back into herself (Jung 1967 [1956], p. 258).

Biologically, a puer can range in age from late adolescence to middle or even old age. Psychologically, however, he is an infant. For Freud, a person in the grip of an Oedipus complex is psychologically fixated at three to five years of age. For Jung, a puer is fixated at birth. An Oedipus complex presupposes an independent ego "egotistically" seeking to possess the mother for itself. A puer involves a tenuous ego seeking to surrender itself to the mother. A puer seeks not domination but absorption—and thereby reversion to the state prior even to birth.

For Freud, attachment to the mother at any stage means attachment to one's actual mother or mother substitute. It means attachment to the person herself. For Jung, attachment to the mother means attachment to the mother archetype, of which one's actual mother or mother substitute is only a manifestation. For Freud, a boy should free himself of his yearning, infantile or Oedipal, for his own mother. For Jung, a boy should free himself of his inclination to identify himself with the mother archetype. For Freud, the failure to free oneself means eternal attachment to one's own mother. For Jung, it means the restriction of one's personality to the mother archetype within. For Freud, the struggle for freedom is between one person and another: son and mother. For Jung, it is between one part of a person and another: ego and unconscious, which, again, the mother archetype first symbolizes.

"[T]he mother corresponds to the collective unconscious, and the son to [ego] consciousness" (Jung 1967 [1956], p. 259). Approached properly, the puer archetype provides an ego that has managed to sever itself from the unconscious re-entry into it. Taken rightly, the puer dimension of a person evinces itself in moments of playfulness, creativity, and spontaneity—moments that complement the rationality and sobriety of the ego. Taken to excess, the puer personality amounts to nothing but these moments.

Although the puer personality arises in infancy, it manifests itself most dramatically at adolescence. A puer personality is even called an eternal adolescent. A puer is impulsive, dreamy, irresponsible, and self-centered. He dreams of accomplishing great deeds but never does them. He makes great plans, but they never materialize. He may work hard, but only sporadically and only when interested. A puer avoids commitments and refuses to be tied down. He craves excitement and seeks risks. Scornful of the mundane, everyday world, he waxes spiritual and otherworldly. Sexually, he is promiscuous. He dreams of a perfect mate but, never finding her, scorns anyone else. He refuses to become attached. He may be a Don Juan. According to an older, no longer assumed Jungian view, he may turn to homosexuality. The difference between a puer personality and a normal adolescent is that a puer remains an adolescent for life. In fact, it is normally at adolescence that the son finally breaks away from the mother. Still, the puer personality is infantile. It arises in infancy, not adolescence, and at adolescence merely expresses its infantilism in adolescent form.

A puer can be either an actual person, such as Casanova and Aleister Crowley, or a symbol, such as Peter Pan and the Little Prince. Famous historical pueri can become symbols themselves. While a historical puer is biologically an adult, a symbolic one may never grow up. These symbolic pueri exemplify exactly the eternally young life that actual puer personalities strive to emulate.

The opposite of the puer archetype is that of the hero.[7] The hero is the opposite precisely because he succeeds where a puer fails. Strictly, there are two stages of heroism. In the first half of life an ego is heroic in managing to liberate itself from the unconscious and establish itself in society. A hero manages to secure a fulfilling mate and job. A puer fails to do either. In the second half of life a now independent ego is heroic in managing to break with society and return to the unconscious without thereby falling back into it. Where a hero in the first half of life establishes himself in the conventions of society, a hero in the second half defies those conventions. But a hero is consciously defiant. A puer is only unconsciously so. Where a hero risks everything for whatever he has committed himself to, a puer has committed himself to nothing and so risks nothing. Because a puer never establishes an independent ego, he never faces the possible loss of it. Where a real hero is like Daedalus, a puer is like Icarus. Because a puer is a failed hero in the first half of life, he is necessarily a failed hero in the second half as well. Indeed, for him there is no second half.

Adonis as a Puer

Adonis is a quintessential puer because he never marries, never has children, never works, and dies young. He simply never grows up. His puer personality spans the period from infancy to adolescence. He must first break out of a tree in order to be born. His mother, transformed into the tree, is reluctant to let him out. Like any other mother, she may be overjoyed at his conception; but unlike normal mothers, she wants to hoard him. In Ovid's version, Adonis himself has to find an exit.

Adonis' mother has herself proved unable to break out of her father, the only male who ever arouses her. Even if her incestuous desire results from a curse, the curse is punishment for her indifference to other men, for which a prior attachment to her father is likely the latent cause. In any event her desire is not really for intercourse with her actual father but for absorption in the father archetype. For she, too, has never severed herself from the unconscious and therefore has never grown up. Not coincidentally, she is incapable of raising Adonis, whom others, whatever their motives, must raise instead. She is a puella.[8]

No sooner does Adonis emerge from the tree than, in Apollodorus' version, Aphrodite thrusts him back—not, to be sure, into the tree but into a chest. She thereby undoes the birth that had proved so arduous. She tells no one, for she wants Adonis all to herself. When Persephone, to whom Aphrodite has entrusted the chest without revealing its contents, opens it, she likewise falls in love with Adonis and refuses to return him. Each goddess, just like his mother, wants to possess him exclusively. Though Zeus' decision leaves Adonis free for a third of the year, Adonis readily cedes his third to Aphrodite. Never, then, is he outside the custody of these archetypal mother figures.

Adonis has no conception of reality. He knows the world only through manifestations of the smothering mother archetype, which means that he knows them and not the world. He has no conception of hunting or of its dangers. He lives in a fog.

Seemingly, a Jungian interpretation of the myth faces the same contradiction as Frazer's: that Adonis' annually breaking free of the mother does not go on forever but, as Frazer himself recounts, ends in eventual death—permanent death. A Jungian might dismiss Adonis' final death as an aberration and stress his perennial liberation from the mother. In that case Adonis would be a hero rather than a puer.

Yet a Jungian interpretation can reconcile Adonis' final demise with his recurrent revival. For the annual cycle of death and rebirth can symbolize not Adonis' annual liberation from the mother but the opposite: his annual return to the mother. Where a normal child needs to be born only once to liberate himself from the mother, Adonis, as a puer, continually returns to the mother and so must be born again and again. To quote Jung: "The corn-god of antiquity was Adonis, whose death and resurrection were celebrated annually. He was the son-lover [i.e., puer] of the mother, for the corn is the son and fructifier of the earth's womb" (Jung, 1967 [1956], p. 343 n. 79). His final death is simply his permanent rather than temporary return to her. It is the culmination of his past returns rather than a break with them. Previously, he had been strong enough to resist the mother temporarily. Now he can no longer do so. Put another way, Adonis' cycle of death and rebirth constitutes neurosis: his weak ego compulsively returns to the mother. His final death represents psychosis: in returning forever to the mother, his ego dissolves altogether.

To be sure, this negative interpretation of the puer archetype and of Adonis represents only the classical Jungian view. The post-Jungian, or "archetypal," view of James Hillman (1979) interprets the puer archetype positively and would therefore applaud rather than castigate Adonis for his identification with that archetype. Where for Jung and von Franz the life of a puer ends tragically, if not pathetically, in premature death, for Hillman it ends triumphantly, in a refusal to compromise with the everyday world. The behavior that for Jung and von Franz is childish would for Hillman be childlike.

Archetypal psychology faults classical Jungian psychology on multiple grounds. By emphasizing the compensatory, therapeutic message of mythology, classical Jungian psychology purportedly reduces mythology to psychology and reduces gods to concepts. In espousing a unified self (or "self") as the ideal psychological authority, Jungian psychology supposedly projects onto psychology a Western, specifically monotheistic, more specifically Christian, still more specifically Protestant, outlook. The Western emphasis on progress is purportedly reflected in the primacy that Jungian psychology accords hero myths and the primacy that it accords the ego, even in the ego's encounter with the unconscious: the encounter is intended to abet development.

As a corrective, Hillman advocates that psychology be viewed as irreducibly mythological. Myth is still to be interpreted psychologically, but psychology is itself to be interpreted mythologically. One grasps the psychological meaning of the myth of Saturn by imagining oneself to be the figure Saturn, not by translating Saturn's plight into clinical terms like depression. Moreover, the depressed Saturn represents a legitimate aspect of one's personality. Each god deserves its due. The psychological ideal should be pluralistic rather than monolithic—in mythological terms, polytheistic rather than monotheistic (see Miller 1981 [1979]). Hillman takes his mythic cues from the Greeks rather than from the Bible, however simplistic his equation of Greece with polytheism and of the Bible with monotheism may be.

Insisting that archetypes are to be found *in* symbols rather than outside them, Hillman espouses a relation to the gods in themselves and not to something beyond them. The ego becomes but one more archetype with its attendant kind of god, and it is the "soul" rather than the ego that experiences the archetypes through myths. Myth serves to open one up to the soul's own depths. The payoff is aesthetic rather than moral: one gains a sense of wonder and contemplation, not a guide to living. The most apposite myths for the archetypal school are those of the playful puer and of the receptive anima rather than, as for classical Jungians, those of the striving hero and of the fully integrated wise old man.

Notes

1   Bruno Bettelheim (1976) says much the same, but of fairy tales *rather than* of myths, which he continues to interpret in a classically Freudian way.

2 For an overview of Jung on myth, see Segal (1998), pp. 3–45.
3 On Adonis, see Jung 1967 [1956], pp. 219, 223 n. 32, 258–259, 343 n. 79; 1969 (1958), pp. 442–443.
4 On the archetype of the puer aeternus, see Jung 1967 [1956], pp. 257–259, 340; 1968 [1959]), p. 106. See also Neumann 1970 [1954], pp. 88–101. Neumann himself using the term "son-lover" for puer.
5 On the archetype of the Great Mother, see Jung 1968 [1959], pp. 75–110; 1967 [1956], pp. 207–444. See also Neumann 1972 [1955]; 1970 [1954], pp. 39–101, 152–169.
6 The Freudian, or breakaway Freudian, counterpart to the focus on the work of Otto Rank, who claimed that the key trauma is not the Oedipus complex but birth. The title of Rank's book says it all: *The Trauma of Birth* (1924 in German, 1929 in English).
7 On the hero archetype, see Jung 1967 [1956], pp. 171–444; 1968b [1959]; 1968 [1953]), pp. 333–339. See also Neumann 1970 [1954], pp. 131–256; 1972 [1955], pp. 203–208. On Jungian heroism, see Segal 1990 [1987], chs. 2–3; Segal 1998, pp. 145–173. On the hero as the opposite of the puer, see Segal 1998, pp. 122–145.
8 On the puella archetype, see von Franz 1981 [1970], pp. 81–84, 150–151, 152–154.

References

Arlow, J. (1961). Ego Psychology and the Study of Mythology. *Journal of the American Psychoanalytic Association*, 9, 371–393.

Bettelheim, B. (1976). *The Uses of Enchantment*. New York: Knopf.

Frazer, J.G. (1890). *The Golden Bough*. 1st ed. 2 vols. London: Macmillan.

——— (1922). *The Golden Bough*. Abridged ed. London: Macmillan.

Freud, S. (1953). *The Interpretation of Dreams. Standard Edition of the Complete Psychological Works of Sigmund Freud*, eds. and trans. J. Strachey et al. Vols. 4–5, 339–627. London: Hogarth Press and Institute of Psycho-Analysis.

Hillman, J., ed. (1979). *Puer Papers*. Dallas: Spring.

Jung, C.G. (1967 [1956]). *Symbols of Transformation. CW*, 5, eds. Sir H. Read et al., trans. R.F.C. Hull, 2nd ed., Princeton, NJ: Princeton University Press.

——— (1971). *Psychological Types. CW*, 6. Princeton, NJ: Princeton University Press.

——— (1966 [1953]). On the Psychology of the Unconscious in *Two Essays on Analytical Psychology, CW*, 7, 2nd ed., pp. 3–119. Princeton, NJ: Princeton University Press.

—— (1969a [1960]). On Psychic Energy in *The Structure of the Psyche*, *CW*, 8, 2nd ed., pp. 3–66. Princeton, NJ: Princeton University Press.

—— (1969b [1960]). The Structure of the Psyche in *The Structure and Dynamics of the Psyche*, *CW*, 8, 2nd ed., pp. 139–158. Princeton, NJ: Princeton University Press.

—— (1968a [1959]). Psychological Aspects of the Mother Archetype in *The Archetypes and the Collective Unconscious*, *CW*, 9, pt. 1, 2nd ed., pp. 75–110. Princeton, NJ: Princeton University Press.

—— (1968b [1959]). The Psychology of the Child Archetype in *The Archetypes and the Collective Unconscious CW*, 9, pt. 1, 2nd ed., pp. 151–181.

—— (1969 [1958]). Answer to Job in *Aion CW* 9, pt. 2, 2nd ed., pp. 355–470. Princeton, NJ: Princeton University Press.

—— (1968 [1953]). Religious Ideas in Alchemy in *Psychology and Alchemy CW*, 12, 2nd ed., pp. 225–483. Princeton, NJ: Princeton University Press.

Miller, D.L. (1981 [1979]). *The New Polytheism*. 2nd ed. Dallas: Spring.

Neumann, E. (1970 [1954]). *The Origins and History of Consciousness*, tr. R.F.C. Hull. Princeton, NJ: Princeton University Press.

—— (1972 [1955]). *The Great Mother*, tr. R. Manheim. 2nd ed. Princeton, NJ: Princeton University Press.

Rank, O. (1914). *The Myth of the Birth of the Hero*. 1st ed. Trs. F. Robbins & S.E. Jelliffe. New York: Journal of Nervous and Mental Disease Publishing.

—— (2003). *The Myth of the Birth of the Hero*. 2nd ed. Trs. G.C. Richter & E.J. Lieberman. Baltimore, MA: Johns Hopkins University Press.

Segal, R.A. (1990 [1987]). *Joseph Campbell: An Introduction*. Rev. ed. New York: New American Library/Penguin.

—— (1998). ed. *Jung on Mythology*. Princeton, NJ: Princeton University Press; London: Routledge.

Tylor, E.B. (1871). *Primitive Culture*. 2 vols. 1st ed. London: Murray.

Von Franz, M.-L. (1981 [1970]). *Puer aeternus*. 2nd ed. Santa Monica, CA: Sigo.

Chapter 10

What's the Matter—with Alchemical Recipes?

Philosophy and Filth in the Forging of Jung's Alchemical Psychology

Stanton Marlan

Prelude

What matters in filth and endures in ashes is at the heart of alchemical recipes, but is often rejected and even despised. As some spiritually oriented alchemists began their work of sublimation and purification, the cry was: Out with the foul, the obscene and unclean, the garbage, grit, dirt, and grime. In the mind and under fire, feces and falsehoods are all refined; demons burn as flesh is roasted, basilisks and blood also calcined, and in a flash all foolishness undermined. As the volcano cools and leaves behind a blackened earth for us to find, all ash is left within the mind; blackness cools, but will they find, the lava goddess left behind?

Jung as Philosopher

The *Mysterium Coniunctionis* was Jung's last great work, a summative treatment and final account of his alchemical reflections. As a book and as the central image of the *coniunctio*, it is essential to understanding his psychology. The problem of the relation of opposites is a central issue in Jung's understanding of alchemy, which comes into sharp focus in the *Mysterium*. The book describes the opus of alchemy in scholarly and psychological depth and is organized around images that illuminate the archetypal psyche and the individuation process. In spite of this major and innovative accomplishment, there remain important issues that require philosophical reflection.

While Jung often considered his work to be an empirical science, he also saw alchemy both as a form of religious philosophy and as a precursor to his psychology of the unconscious. The relationship between natural science, philosophy, and religion remains an ongoing tension throughout his work. The question of whether Jung can be considered as a philosopher who has made ontological and metaphysical claims has been opened up by Jon Mills (2012; 2014) in two important papers. In both, Mills contends that Jung does make such claims, and he raises a number of traditional criticisms of his work. Such criticisms have haunted Jung's ideas in both academic and psychoanalytic circles, often in a biased and uninformed manner. Critics of Jung have rarely sought out dialogue and engagement with Jungian analysts and Jungian scholars. Mills (2014), while raising several important and difficult issues concerning Jung's ideas, does so with integrity and as an explicit call to Jungians and other specialists to engage in an evaluation of Jung's ideas. He notes: "I wish to open a permissible space to question Jung's major concepts not as a polemic, but as a genuine search for meaning in his philosophy and with respect to his textual word" (p. 16). This book opens such a space in which philosophical implications of Jung's thought can be explored in a genuine, open, and scholarly manner. Mills (personal communication, October 8, 2017) describes what he has in mind: "Through analyzing Jung philosophically, new vistas emerge for enhanced explication, theoretical refinement, revision, and shifts in emphasis that lend more proper cohesion to Jung's philosophy." And in a recent article, he notes: "After all, we are drawn to Jung's theories for a reason. Why not improve them?" (2014, p. 14). Mills sets out to do just that.

Mills' initiative, while welcome, is difficult in light of Jung's style of thinking. Jung speaks of

> our understandable desire for crystal clarity, but we are apt to forget that in psychic matters we are dealing with processes of experience, that is, with transformations which should never be given hard and fast names if their living movement is not to petrify into something static. The protean mythologem and the shimmering symbol express the processes of the psyche far more trenchantly and, in the end, far more clearly than the clearest concept; for the symbol not only conveys a visualization of the process but—and this is perhaps just as important—it also brings a re-experiencing of it, of that twilight which we can learn to understand only through inoffensive empathy, but which too much clarity only dispels.
>
> (Jung, 1967, ¶199)

Given Jung's symbolic style, any effort seeking philosophical clarity has to take into account Jung's differences in intention and approach.

While Mills' style of criticism begins with strong and dismissive judgments, he also seems genuinely drawn to and attracted by Jung's ideas. He makes a sincere effort to think through, develop, and improve on what he feels is lacking, problematic, or confusing in Jung's formulations. He then proposes how one might philosophically reformulate Jung's concepts. One of Mills' contributions is to consider Jung as a philosopher. Whether Jung's ideas legitimately can or should be understood as philosophical and/or metaphysical is of particular interest. The importance of philosophy in Jung's work and in developing an alchemical psychology is both clear and problematic. By following a thread in this development, the reasons for Jung's lack of clarity will become more explicit. While I support Mills' call for more philosophical clarity in Jung's psychology of the unconscious, philosophy is but one aspect of a complexity of thought that involves religion and science, images and symbols, a mix that amplifies consciousness, while at the same time deconstructing it.

The legitimacy of seeing Jung as a philosopher and metaphysician has already raised an important controversy within Jungian circles. Jungian analyst Mark Saban (2014) has pointed to Jung's frequent denials that he is a philosopher or that he intended his theories to be taken as ontological or metaphysical claims. While Saban (personal communication, November 12, 2017) criticizes Mills for having gone too far in considering Jung as a philosopher, metaphysician, and ontologist, he also wonders if, in defense of Jung, he himself has gone too far in entirely rejecting Mills' claim and making too sharp a distinction between philosophy and psychology. While Saban offers many citations where Jung makes it explicitly clear that he considers his work to be psychological in nature and specifically not metaphysical,[1] there are moments when Jung himself was careful not to draw psychology and philosophy, and for that matter religion, too far apart. Jung notes:

> I can hardly draw a veil over the fact that we psychotherapists ought really to be philosophers or philosophic doctors—or rather that we already are so, though we are unwilling to admit it because of the glaring contrast between our work and what passes for

philosophy in the universities. We could also call it religion *in statu nascendi*, for in the vast confusion that reigns at the roots of life there is no line of division between philosophy and religion.

(1966, ¶181)

And, I would add, psychology.

Jung's sentiments are echoed by philosopher and Jungian scholar Edward Casey (2017) who has claimed that while philosophy and psychology have been thought of as two different exclusive enterprises, they may be more closely related than typically imagined. In fact, for Casey, they may show themselves not simply needing to be brought into relationship, but as "already conjoined" (1991/2004, p. xi).[2] The idea that philosophy and psychology are connected is complicated insofar as both disciplines are in themselves complex and highly differentiated fields. There are many varieties of philosophy and psychology, and there are philosophical dimensions of psychology and psychological dimensions of philosophy.

Just what is meant when we speak of philosophy in terms of metaphysics? Traditionally, metaphysics as a branch of philosophy was divided into ontology, cosmology, and epistemology. Ontology is concerned with first principles and the fundamental nature of reality. It asks the question, 'What is real?' Cosmology is concerned with the origin, nature, and structure of the universe. And epistemology is concerned with knowledge and asks the question, 'How do we know what we know? How do we know what is real?' There are philosophical ontologies grounded in a metaphysics of nature and matter, and others in a metaphysics of spirit or soul. In either case, such philosophical/psychological considerations play an important role in an attempt to understand Jung's alchemical psychology.

As Jung moved toward his idea of a psychology of alchemy and away from its simply literal, material practices, he recognized the importance of philosophy for understanding it and its goal: the Philosophers' Stone. In *Psychology and Alchemy* (1968), he cites Richardus Anglicus, who states: "Therefore all those who desire to attain the blessing of this art should apply themselves to study, should gather the truth from the books and not from invented fables and untruthful works. There is no way by which this art can truly be found … except by completing their studies and understanding the words of the philosophers" (Jung, 1968, ¶362).

Likewise, he notes Raymond Lully who "says that owing to their ignorance men are not able to accomplish the work until they have studied universal philosophy, which will show them things that are unknown and hidden from others. 'Therefore, our stone belongs not to the vulgar but to the very heart of our philosophy'" (Jung, 1968, ¶365), to what Jung called the *aurum non vulgi* or *arum philosophicum*, a philosophical gold (1963a, p. 210, fn11). The emphasis on alchemy's true goal in the minds of Anglicus and Lully reflected a religious Christian view that was quite critical of the materialist, mundane, and so-called demonic practices of those alchemists whom they considered foolish and vulgar. For Jung, the emphasis on the philosophical dimension of alchemy helped to dispel the literalism of many alchemical operations and recipes, which were seemingly nothing more than a 'witch's brew' of vile ingredients that sometimes led to chemical discoveries, but more often than not ended in no value—or worse in poverty, sickness, and/or the death of the alchemist.

As Jung notes, Anglicus rejected all the assorted 'filth' with which the alchemists worked in typical alchemical recipes: "eggshells, hair, the blood of a red-haired man, basilisks, worms, herbs, and human feces." Anglicus stated: "Whatsoever a man soweth that also shall he reap. Therefore if he soweth filth, he shall find filth…Turn back, brethren, to the way of truth of which you are ignorant; I counsel you for your own sake to study and to labour with steadfast meditation on the words of the philosophers, whence the truth can be summoned forth" (Jung, 1968, ¶365).

In contrast to the misguided and materially-oriented alchemists, Dionysius Zacharias relates his experience of turning away from such degrading practices. He "relates that a certain 'religiosus Doctor excellentissimus' advised him to refrain from useless expense in 'sophisticationibus diabolicis' and to devote himself rather to the study of the books of the old philosophers, so as to acquaint himself with the *vera materia*," the true material. Jung relates Zacharias' process as reviving from a "fit of despair" with the help of the Holy Spirit and applying himself "to a serious study of the literature," which he "read diligently and meditated day and night until his finances were exhausted. Then he worked in his laboratory, saw the three colors appear, and on Easter Day of the following year the wonder happened: 'Vidi perfectionem'—'I saw the perfect fulfillment,'" the quicksilver was converted into pure gold before his eyes. Jung states that "[t]here is an unmistakable hint here that the work and its goal depended very largely on a mental condition" (Jung, 1968, ¶365). Here Jung is building his case for a psychological understanding of alchemy, but the call for philosophy and the "mental condition" in these passages is an expression of the religious philosophy of Zacharias and Anglicus whose work served to help Jung recognize the importance of mind and spirit for understanding his psychological approach to alchemy, but it also degraded the importance of matter and nature.

Jung's close follower Marie-Louise von Franz (2006) has noted that in both Arabic religiosity and Western Christianity the idea of matter became more and more 'spiritualized.' She points out that the "masculine element of logos slowly prevailed over matter," to the extent that there was a "loss of the dimension" of materiality, to which she ultimately ascribed the highest value by calling it "Divine Matter" (2006, p. 29).

Jung's Reclaiming of the Filth

While spiritual philosophy was a stepping stone to Jung's recognition of the importance of the mental aspect of the alchemical opus, it also was a rejection of the shadow of what it called "filth." Spirituality split off and turned away from worms, feces, blood, and basilisks,[3] from what the religious doctrines called diabolical—but Jung was not one to turn away from the daemonic, the darkest, most repulsive aspects and deepest roots of the repressed and unknown dimensions of nature. In fact, alchemy's attention to the *nigredo* and nature in all of her aspects was one of its important responses to Christian religious philosophy.

While for Jung Christian philosophy was central to the development of the Western psyche, it fell short of adequately resolving the split between spirit and matter. Thus, alchemy with its emphasis on nature and the material world was an important compensation to the over spiritualization of religious philosophy.[4] In contrast to a metaphysical ontology of spirit, Jung spoke of the significance of the shadow of materiality and of the daemonic. At a 1952 Eranos Conference, religious scholar Mircea Eliade interviewed Jung, who spoke of the serious problem of integrating the opposites. Jung notes that in *Psychology and Alchemy* (1977), he "had the occasion to interest [himself] in the integration of Satan," noting that to the extent Satan was "not integrated, the world is not healed and man is not saved." The alchemists' ideal of the Philosophers' Stone "was to save the world in its totality" (p. 227). The very things rejected from alchemical recipes by religious philosophers were included by Jung in his formulation of the alchemical work. He states: "The work is difficult and strewn with obstacles; the alchemical opus is dangerous. Right at the beginning you meet 'the dragon,' the chthonic spirit, the 'devil' or, as the alchemists called it, the 'blackness,' the *nigredo*" (p. 228).

By confronting the chthonic and the demonic, Jung plunges into a witch's brew of his own and struggles to come to terms with the unconscious, and with what he called the 'shadow' that is just below the surface of our civilized and often pious identities. Jung goes on to describe this alchemical and psychological work with the often repulsive 'prima materia': "The prima materia is 'Saturnine,' and the malefic Saturn is the abode of the devil, or again it is the most despised and rejected thing. 'Thrown out into the street,' 'cast on the dunghill,' 'found in filth.'" (Jung, 1967, ¶209). For Jung, the central mystery of alchemy comes in the linking of conscious and unconscious in a *coniunctio* that aims at "synthesis" and "assimilation," but he also notes that this process of linking above and below produces suffering and intense struggle. The soul finds itself in the throes of melancholy in which "matter" itself is said to "suffer" (Jung, 1977, p. 228). For Jung, the coming together of conscious and unconscious, Sol and Luna, masculine and feminine, spirit and matter, the pure and the impure, often has "undesirable results to begin with: it produces poisonous animals such as the dragon, serpent, scorpion, basilisk, and toad" (1963b, ¶172).

Struggling with such creatures is working with the unconscious and with those elements of it that were rejected by spiritual philosophy, but nevertheless are essential to the development of Jung's psychology. As Jung discovered and engaged the symbolic life of the unconscious, he found ouroboric dragons, suffering matter, the peacock's tail, alembics and athanors, red and green lions, kings and queens, fishes' eyes and inverted philosophical trees, salamanders, hermaphrodites, black and white earth, and *sol niger*, the black sun, and all of the "chthonic filth" of materiality that had been rejected and fallen into the shadow or that had not yet become conscious. It would be too easy to consider these images as psychological and symbolic fantasies that were projected onto the reality of the material world, and Jung has demonstrated that the withdrawal of such projections can yield profound insights into our subjectivity. But is there something more to an ouroboric dragon or a philosophical tree that remains unknown and unappreciated?

Typical of Jung's style, he defines a symbol as the best possible expression of an as yet unknown fact, which is "none the less known to exist or is postulated as existing" and "cannot be differently or better expressed" (1971, ¶814). In this definition, the symbol points both to and beyond itself to a mysterious presence/absence, both to the flesh of a visible mystery and to the mystery of an invisible arcane substance. The archetype-in-itself is an unconscious absence not unlike the notion of God or the Philosophers' Stone. Both have multiple divine and symbolic names, but as Jung points out, just what the philosophers meant by the arcane substance has never been quite clear. In a 1946 letter to a pastor, Jung wrote: "The concept of the unconscious *posits nothing*, it designates only my *unknowning*." (1973, p.411) Still, for Jung, we can proceed 'as if' we know something by virtue of the filth and flesh of archetypal images, as our best expressions and manifestations of psychic reality without taking this reality literally in traditional metaphysical terms.

James Hillman, a Jungian analyst, writes:

> The work of soul-making requires corrosive acids and heavy earth, ascending birds; there are sweating kings, dogs, and bitches, stenches, urine, blood .... I know that I am not composed of sulfur and salt, buried in horse dung, putrefying or congealing, turning white or green or yellow, encircled by a tail-biting serpent, rising on wings. And yet I am! I cannot take any of this literally, even if it is all accurate, descriptively true.
>
> (1978, 37 and 39)

Hillman describes the soul, which includes filth, sweat and stench, urine, blood, and horse dung, etc., and resists translating these images into psychological (or philosophical) abstractions that leave these images behind. For Hillman, it is not adequate to translate the "White Queen and Red King" into "feminine and masculine principles," "their incestuous sexual intercourse" into "the union of opposites," or "the freakish hermaphrodite and uniped, the golden head," into "paradoxical representation of the goal, examples of androgyny symbols of the Self" (2010, p. 15). For Hillman, keeping the image alive requires the offense and stench, the preservation of the flesh, the vital quality bypassed by spiritual purification where what's the matter with alchemical recipes is that the matter was rejected and thrown out. By refusing to translate images into concepts, Hillman preserves the mysterious, often bizarre and repulsive but vital quality of psychic reality, resonant with Gerhard Dorn's challenge to: "Transform yourself from dead stones into living philosophic stones" (Eliade, 1971, 158). Finally, for Hillman it is not a matter simply of image versus concept, a literal move, but of keeping the metaphoric vision of the alchemical imagination alive as it returns the soul to the world.

The self for Jung and soul for Hillman were radical ideas that recognized "the identity of *something* in man [self/soul] with *something* concealed in matter [body/world]" (Jung, 1968, ¶378; emphasis added). In the last chapter of the *Mysterium*, Jung analyzes Dorn's alchemical recipe to achieve the magnum opus, a conjunction which is the goal of the alchemical work. It is an operation that involves the relationship between the mind/spirit, soul, body, and world that takes place in stages and begins with the creation of the *unio mentalis*, the union of the soul with the mind, separated from the body and the natural world. The importance of this separation was to "establish a spiritual position supraordinate to the turbulent sphere of the body" (1963b, ¶671) and to create "a state of equanimity transcending the body's affectivity and instinctuality" (1963b, ¶470).

Psychological development requires not being controlled by instincts and/or bodily emotions—but leaving our natural vitality behind cripples life, creates dissociation, can be too pure, too literal, and ultimately a condition that limits the fullness of life. Something more is required, another step, namely, the reintegration of the *unio mentalis* (soul and mind) with the body. This second conjunction is particularly important, since it moves from an intellectual/philosophical and abstract spirituality to a more fully developed existential life.

The question for Jung was, How does this further integration happen? Following Dorn, Jung sees that only part of the process takes place in the 'psychological' sphere. The rest of the procedure requires the use of magical substances said to be hidden in the body. Dorn called it the '*caelum*' or 'sky stuff,' that was to be prepared to serve as a medium for the unification of the *unio mentalis* with the body. It would be a quintessence that would hold together opposites and binaries. "Beginning with the *caelum*, other ingredients are added to make a robust 'arcane substance' that will hold the body and spirit together in a *coniunctio*. .... Jung finds an analogy between this stage of Dorn's *coniunctio* and the creation of the Jungian *self*. The *self* repairs the dissociation that is both individual and collective" (Power, 2017, pp. 46–47).

Dorn describes the ingredients of his alchemical recipe as requiring a mixture of the *caelum* with honey, chelidonia, Mercurialis, rosemary, red lily, and blood. These complex ingredients are rich with symbolic resonances, which render understandable at the psychological level why they would be valuable in promoting a reunification of body and soul. Honey, for instance, includes the qualities of purification, cleansing, and sweetness along with the capacity to unify body and soul. "With the honey the pleasure of the senses and the joy of life went into the mixture, as well as the secret fear of the 'poison,' the deadly danger of worldly entanglements" (Jung, 1963b, ¶704). Chelidonia, a golden flower, was seen as a kind of philosophical gold and was said to protect against "outbursts of affect" and thunderstorms (1963b, ¶687). It cures eyesight and draws humidity (soul) out of Mercurius as the supreme chthonic spirit—linking both spirit and body. The plant Mercurialis contributes the attractive power of sexuality "favorable to the coniunctio" and is a mediator between the microcosm and macrocosm (1963b, ¶688). Rosemary (Ros marinus) contributes the quality of "sea-dew ... the *aqua vita* ... divine water," divine grace, "the great sea over which the alchemist sailed ... guided by the 'heart' of Mercurius" (1963b, ¶688). This water is also said to be a bath of generation, a spring rain which brings forth vegetation. Dorn's recipe also includes the red lily, the male part of an alchemical pair, the female aspect of which is represented by the white lily. Together, they express the energy of the *hierosgamos*, the divine sexual connection; eternal nature, "the quintessence itself" said to be "the noblest thing that human meditation can reach" (1963b. ¶689). The lily is considered a true gamonymus (hierogamus of light and darkness), an energy of bringing together what is disparate. Finally, and possibly, according to Jung, the most important ingredient is human blood, the red tincture, "seat of the soul" (1963b, ¶690) and considered "a preliminary stage of the lapis." Blood has long been seen as "a magic charm ... binding the soul to God or the devil" (1963b, ¶690). The addition of human blood, according to von Franz, means "a complete devotion to the work" (von Franz, 1979, p. 113). For her, the result of Dorn's recipe leads to the secret of the Philosophers' Stone. The stone:

> is identical with the God-image in the human soul. The whole procedure is like an active, imagination performed with symbolically meaningful substances .... The end result is also described as a four-petaled yellow flower, exactly as in the Chinese text of *The Secret of the Golden Flower*. The whole recipe runs: Take the inner truth, add your *elan vital* to it, the inspiration of the Holy Ghost, and the capacity to link opposites. Put into this mixture heavenly and earthly love (sex) and then you have an essence with which you can unite heaven and earth. All ingredients assemble round the four-petaled yellow flower, i.e., the Self.
>
> (pp. 113–114)

In the above ingredients, one finds material support for the second conjunction linking the *unio mentalis* to the body. In addition, Jung's amplifications also address the shadow and the archetypal bipolarity of these ingredients that can interfere with, poison, negate, and blacken the *coniunctio*. The process and production of the second *coniunctio* requires careful consideration of the *pharmakon*—both the healing and poisonous dimension of the recipe, whether literal or symbolic.

It is not easy to define the meaning of the *caelum* which, like the Philosophers' Stone, has many names—"the quintessence, the 'philosophical wine,' a virtue and heavenly vigor, ... the 'truth' ... the panacea .... the *imago Dei*," etc. (Jung, 1963b, ¶681). Jung was able to understand these descriptions in a psychological and symbolic way as images of the self and the individuation process, but he was also aware that "[t]he production of the caelum" took place for Dorn as "a symbolic rite performed in the laboratory"—perhaps as an alchemical form of active imagination (1963b, ¶705). How can a philosophical position account for these phenomena?

For Jung, the engagement with this elusive and mercurial materia requires unusual concentration, religious fervor, meditation, and imagination. Meditation, as Jung describes it, is used when we have "an inner dialogue with something unseen ... The engagement is *not mere cognition*, but explicitly an inner dialogue and hence a living relationship to the answering voice of the 'other' in ourselves, i.e., of the unconscious" (1968, ¶390). But, as Jung has described it, the unconscious is not simply 'in us.' It is as much, and perhaps more, outside us (see 1968, ¶396). Such ambiguity is captured by Martin Heidegger, who noted that the call of conscience summons us. It is a call that "comes from me and yet from beyond me" (BT, pp. 271/316). What is this "outside"? What is this "beyond me"? What are we summoned to? Is there any there there, as they say?

For Paracelsus and Ruland, it is the imagination that sees into the beyond and is an "astrum" or "star in man, the celestial or supercelestial body" (Ruland, quoted in Jung, 1968, ¶394), a quintessence which should not be conceived as "immaterial phantoms," which "we readily take fantasy-pictures to be, but as something corporeal, a 'subtle body,' semi-spiritual in nature" (1968, ¶394). Jung explains the subtle body as:

> a hybrid phenomenon .... half spiritual, half physical; .... The *imaginatio*, or the act of imagining, is thus a physical activity that can be fitted into the cycle of *material changes* that brings these about and is brought about by them in its turn. In this way the alchemist related himself not only to the unconscious but directly to the very *substance* which he hoped to transform through the power of imagination. .... Imagination is therefore a concentrated extract of the life forces, both *physical and psychic*. .... But, just because of this intermingling of the physical and the psychic, it always remains an obscure point whether the ultimate transformations in the alchemical process are to be sought more in the material or more in the spiritual realm.
>
> (1968, ¶394, emphases added)

The strange middle ground and ambiguity of Jung's psychological/ philosophical position received criticism from both sides of the divide between material and spiritual orientations. Actually, for Jung, it was not a question of either-or, but of "an intermediate realm between mind and matter, i.e., a psychic realm of subtle bodies whose characteristic it is to manifest themselves in a mental as well as a material form" (Jung, 1968, ¶394). The symbolic, magical, mythological, and alchemical meanings of the substances are amplified by Jung. Still, Jung is not completely convinced that it is adequate to interpret these ingredients only symbolically or whether and to what extent it is important to acknowledge their literal or magical importance.

Critiques of Jung: Idealist and Naturalist

The tension between the symbolic and the literal places Jung between two alternative philosophical orientations: idealism and naturalism—and he is criticized from both perspectives. From an idealist position, Jungian analyst Pamela Power (an adherent of Wolfgang Giegerich) has claimed that the *Mysterium* is no longer relevant to today's soul and is of historical interest only (Power, 2017). Following Giegerich, Power is critical of Jung's reading of Dorn's alchemical recipe arguing that Jung remains too attached to a symbolic understanding and does not go beyond it into thinking proper. She holds that given Giegerich's notion of absolute negative interiority all such symbols and substances, images and imagination, must be surpassed, negated, cut through over and over again, aiming at a purification approaching a more sophisticated version of the Christian philosophers' view of purity and a homeopathic distillation that leads to a logical level such that "it no longer contains any molecules of ... specific ingredients at all" (2017, p. 47). For Giegerich and Power, any trace of a remainder of natural substances in Jung's formulation disqualifies his psychology from becoming the highest expression of the soul's logical life.

Power's description of Giegerich's system of "applying negation after negation, negating highly sensuous ingredients" as parallel to homeopathic remedies is apt (p. 47), but I do not see this level of purification as achieving the potency of Jung's grittier spagyric formulations. "Homeopathic remedies are created by extracting a substance" to such an extent that it leaves only a "vibrational signature of the original material ... with none of its physical characteristics. ... [This] total annihilation of the substance's physical being is ... [the homeopathic character of] Hahnemann's work" (Nilsson, 2006).

Jung's approach is more like Paracelsus' spagyric formulas: "Paracelsus repeatedly stressed the importance of [not eliminating or surpassing the sensuous reality of materials that still contain] deep color, intense flavor, and low dosage ... The difference between ... spagyrics and any homeopathics, then, is ... apparent to the ordinary senses" (Nilsson, 2006). In a similar manner, it is the presence and importance of the imagistic subtle body and sensate dimension of Jung's work that gives it its healing power.

From a nearly opposite perspective, chemists and natural science historians Lawrence Principe and William Newman (2006) reject Jung's psychological and symbolic understanding of alchemical recipes as not literal enough, noting that all the ingredients, the "alien," "strange," "bizarre" (p. 418), and "outlandish" (p. 417) are not symbolic in Jung's sense, but are rather signs and code names (Decknamen) for *natural substances* used by al-chemysts in the laboratory. For them, there is no need to explain alchemy in any way that exceeds the metaphysical worldview of 'natural philosophy.'

Following the actual notebooks of the alchemist George Starkey (aka Philalethes), Principe unmasks the seemingly symbolic processes by creating a chemical version of " 'animated' Philosophical Mercury" and its production of a "philosophical egg" out of which, over time and with proper heating, there emerged a glittering and fully-formed tree in a laboratory flask (p. 165). For Principe, this was "the 'Tree of Hermes,'" the philosophical tree, which for the alchemist would have been "vivid and unquestionable proof that he had found the 'entrance to the palace of the king,' that is, the crucial threshold leading to the Philosophers' Stone" (p. 165). Principe reflects that "[f]or the historian, the reality of this Philosophical Tree indicates unambiguously that at least some of the imagery of chrysopoeia [gold-making, seeking the Philosophers' Stone], bizarre as it might seem, stems from the literal appearance of reacting chemicals" and must be taken literally (p. 165). For Principe, the results of such experiments must have served to encourage the alchemists in pursuit of their goals. Yet, while this discovery is indeed very provocative, it is also interesting that "Starkey's continued experimentations apparently did not lead to the Philosophers' Stone; otherwise, it is doubtful he would have ended up in debtor's prison. The failure finally to obtain the stone, despite encouraging results such as gold's volatilization or its germination into a glittering tree," (p. 166) raises for me the question: Why were there so many alchemical failures to produce the Philosophers' Stone? From my perspective, the reason for this is that limiting the philosophical tree to a naturalistic perspective reduces it to a literal, chemical phenomenon.

It is interesting to compare Principe's version of the philosophical tree with the way Jung imagined it. Jung acknowledges "that the adept [can literally see] branches and twigs in the retort" (1967, ¶374). However, for Jung, the tree is an archetypal image with broader-ranging meaning. What Principe did not do in his experiment was what the alchemists advised: to "contemplate [the tree's] growth, that is, to reinforce it with active imagination." According to Jung, for the alchemist Senior, "[t]he vision was the thing to be sought" (1967, ¶374). Recognizing this, "[h]ermetic philosophy had for its goal an explanation that included the psyche in a total description of nature. The empiricist [e.g., Principe] succeeds in avoiding archetypal explanatory principles, that is, the psychic premises that are a *sine qua non* of the cognitive process, or to repress them in the interests of 'scientific objectivity'" (Jung, 1967, ¶378). Jung points out that:

> The Hermetic philosopher regarded these psychic premises, the archetypes, as inalienable components of the empirical world-picture. He was not yet so dominated by the object that he could ignore the palpable presence of psychic premises in the form of eternal ideas which he felt to be real. The empirical nominalist, on the other hand, already had the modern attitude towards the psyche, namely, that it had to be eliminated as something "subjective," and that its contents were nothing but ideas formulated *a posteriori*, mere *flatus vocis*. His hope was to be able to produce a picture of the world that was entirely independent of the observer. This hope has been fulfilled only in part, as the findings of modern physics show: the observer cannot be finally eliminated, which means that the psychic premises remain operative.
>
> (1967, ¶378)

Thus, for Dorn and Jung, the philosophical tree is far more than the literal chemistry of the flask. It is "a metaphorical form of the arcane substance, a living thing that comes into existence according to its own laws, and grows, blossoms, and bears fruit like a plant. ... Dorn ... makes a distinction between the 'living things of nature' and those of matter. ... But it is not so clear what the former are meant to be." They don't seem to be "'vegetabilia materiae' nor are they found in nature, at least not in *nature as we know it*, though they may occur in that more comprehensive, Platonic nature as Dorn understood it, that is, in a nature that includes psychic 'animalia,' i.e., mythologems and archetypes" (Jung, 1967, ¶382; emphasis added).

Active Imagination and the Forging of Jung's Psychology of the Unconscious

From the beginning, Jung felt that the goal of his psychology was to make a contribution to the science of modern psychology, but a powerful experience of the archetypal psyche led him to enlarge and deepen the course of his work: "But then, I hit upon this stream of lava, and the heat of its fires reshaped my life. That was the primal stuff which compelled me to work upon it, and my works are a more or less successful endeavor to incorporate this incandescent matter into the contemporary picture of the world" (1963a, ¶199). It is this experience of psyche that opened Jung to a vision of reality beyond the natural science of his day. Jung's dreams and active imagination helped him move beyond fantasy to psychic reality and to the signature of things, to an embodiment not simply logical (Giegerich and Power) or literal (Principe), but mysterious and hard to define. For Jung, the imaginal is not simply a mental process, but also a subtle body, corporeal yet semi-spiritual, not unlike the alchemist's idea of Mercurius: it is said "sometimes Mercurius is a substance like quicksilver, sometimes it is a philosophy" (1959, ¶240). Mercurius is both "material and spiritual" and "the process by which the lower material is transformed into the higher and spiritual, and vice versa" (1967, ¶284).

Likewise, active imagination is a mercurial process, an embodiment of imaginal life incarnating the spiritual and psychizing nature. Typically in active imagination, it is of value to begin with a dream, an event, a memory, or a fantasy, and fixing it in writing, painting, sculpture, then engaging with its embodiment, honoring it, dreaming it onward, imagining it forward, and dialoguing with it. Over the years of working with this process, I have found it of value to help patients expand the process in such a way as to suggest the value of pursuing memories, dreams, and images by enactments, an acting in and out that sometimes leads beyond typical ways of getting at what the psyche presents—not unlike enacting magical rituals or practicing alchemical recipes in a laboratory. Such enactments often lead to a deepened and expanded sense of a psychic experience and to moments of mythical and magical realism that set the stage for synchronistic occurrences, and open to a world beyond our everyday experience.

The following active imagination is of a patient who had many losses and an extremely difficult family life. He was in a marriage that was not working. His inner life was an intense struggle and one might alchemically characterize his life as being in a state of *nigredo*, of blackness and burnout. He is highly intelligent and a person who has worked with his dreams, active imagination, and magical enactments that have helped to activate a deep psychic process. He reports a vision of entering into a space where the earth is pitch black, burnt, and crusted, like volcanic rock and ash. He is looking at the landscape when he observes a movement of the earth taking shape in the contour of the voluptuous body of a woman who emerges from the blackened ground. Her skin is extremely dark and smooth.

My patient decides that he wants to get to know this woman better and so he begins another active imagination. Engaging the black woman is hot, with pools of lava, molting and flowing in circular patterns. He sees her torso and breasts. She's heating up from the inside out. Her black skin glows red beneath the surface. She has an animal ally standing with her, a large, hooded falcon. When the hood is removed, the falcon looks directly at my patient. He holds out his hand with a gift offering—a mirrored stone, silver and shiny, like a drop of mercury reflecting light. The falcon extends its wings and claws, grabbing the mirrored stone, and in a flash of light the stone becomes an egg, brightly glowing with intricate, iridescent triangles that appear in the egg, overlapping in a complex design, like some kind of code like DNA. The triangular lines are made of beads of light, strung together, cellular.

Another active imagination begins with the intent of further exploring the egg. He reaches inside with two fingers and a thumb, and something grips him. Pulling out a long snake or eel, he shakes it off, violently waving his arm, terrified! The creature lets loose but moves toward him, mouth open. Frightened, he evades contact and it moves away over his shoulder. Once again, my patient reaches into the egg and a glowing human skull emerges and also terrifies him. He now recognizes that what he is doing is dangerous and he needs to protect himself. Carefully, reaching down again, he pulls out a handful of orange powder. He rubs his hands together. The substance coats his palms like chalk. He holds his hands up to the sky and the cosmos attaches to them like gloves made of purple, black, and glittering light. No longer apprehensive, he experiments by pressing his hands together and pulling them apart, creating an energy-field between them. He is able to manifest forms, but cannot control what he manifests. He can only choose how to interact with what emerges. Taking a breath and reaching down inside the egg once more, he sees a large beam of light that begins to grow into the form of a pillar, arrow-like and erect, pointing towards the sky. He feels an affinity with this energy and good about interacting with it. As this happens, he looks down in the midst of the blackened earth, volcanic rocks, and ash. He is surprised to see very green plants and grasses growing. The air becomes humid, but only around the pillar. It's like a rainforest drizzle. Branches begin to grow out of the pillar of light that is now also a tree—a single verdant light-filled growth on the blackened earth.

The emergence of moisture, rainforest air, humidity,[5] and the growth of a tree of light in the midst of rocks and ashes was a transformative image that spurred a further active imagination with the intent to nourish and care for the tree, now glowing brightly with yellow-white light. As my patient walks toward it, he feels the warmth of the volcanic landscape underneath his bare feet. As he approaches the tree, he sees that the branches have grown and are now full and golden. They look almost like neurons. From a distance, the full branches on the tree look like a large, radiant brain, with glowing filaments of light. In a final moment, my patient realizes that the tree is sentient, fleshy. He looks at it and it looks back at him. Its eyes are deep and very ancient. The tree is a living presence and he wants to talk to it and share his pain, and he begins to cry. The sparks of light gather together in a swarm and congeal into an image of his son illuminated in the trunk of the tree. He feels overjoyed and embraces his child. He feels complete.

While I will not elaborate all of the personal meanings and developments in my patient's process, it is interesting to revisit some of the archetypal images and moments that emerged in the process: the blackened earth of hardened lava, the ash, the energizing volcano goddess, the shine of darkness itself, the incandescent lava fires and crystal stone, the mirror and mercury, flashes and sparks of light, the gift, the transformation from bird to egg, and the emergence of a poisonous snake or an eel as electrifying irruptions he tries to shake off. He came to see the glowing skull as the light and illumination that comes from death, and beyond it there is a starry cosmos, the sky stuff like the *caelum*, the towering phallus and the philosophical tree, the blessed greenness, moisture, humidity, and growth in the most burnt and dried out ground of the soul. It is a tree that continues to glow and grow full and golden. It is sentient or super-sentient. It looks back and is a living presence that hears and reaches out to the patient. The fertile waters are also tears that soften and smooth. It mirrors his inner and outer child in sparks of light and heals his wounds, opens his heart and senses, and leaves my patient feeling complete.

In the above active imagination, there is a profound transformation from the deep *nigredo*, the filth and the dirt of the blackened earth, to a vital renewal symbolized by the growth of an archetypal and Philosophical Tree of life and light. It is interesting to compare the notions of the philosophical tree created by the chemist Principe in the context of natural scientific philosophy and the ones elaborated by the dreams and active imaginations of my patient, the alchemists, and Jung. For all of them, the tree requires the 'true imagination'[6] of the alchemists if the tree is to flower as a philosophical tree—an illuminated tree of light.

In an archetypal image of the philosophical tree, as reported by Jung in *Memories, Dreams, Reflections* in his now famous Liverpool dream, Jung reports finding himself in Liverpool, "in a dirty, sooty city" (1963a, p. 197). He was walking

> through the dark streets. .... The various quarters of the city were arranged radially around the square. In the center was a round pool, and in the middle of it a small island. While everything round about was obscured by rain, fog, smoke and dimly lit darkness, the little island blazed with sunlight. On it stood a single tree, a magnolia, in a shower of reddish blossoms. It was as though the tree stood in the sunlight and were at the same time the source of light.

... I was carried away by the beauty of the flowering tree and the sunlit island. ... Then I awoke.

(p. 198)

Jung comments:

> The dream represented my situation at the time. I can still see the grayish-yellow raincoats, glistening with the wetness of the rain. Everything was extremely unpleasant, black and opaque—just as I felt then. But I had had a vision of unearthly beauty, and that was why I was able to live at all. Liverpool is the "pool of life." The "liver," according to an old view, is the seat of life—that which "makes to live."
>
> This dream brought with it a sense of finality. I saw that here the goal had been revealed. One could not go beyond the center. The center is the goal, and everything is directed toward that center. Through this dream I understood that the self is the principle and archetype of orientation and meaning. Therein lies its healing function.
>
> (1963a, 198–199)

A final question remains about the nature of the subtle body and the images of active imagination. In the alchemical sense, these were a mixture of psyche, soul, body, and what the alchemists considered to be matter and the nature of the world. However, at one point, Jung suggested that what the alchemists projected onto matter had nothing to do with matter as we know it today. What can the crazy images of psyche have to do with our knowledge of scientific reality?

Unus Mundus as a Philosophy of the Integration of Self and World in Jung's Psychology

Gary Sparks (2007) gives an example of the importance of heeding dreams, images, and emotions for scientific discovery. He elaborates the discovery of the benzene ring by Kekulé who demonstrated how dreams helped him to develop insights into the structure of matter. Kekulé shows how in his dream vision a snake seized hold of its own tail, leading him to have an intuition about the scientific structure of the benzene ring. The snake biting its own tail is an archetypal symbol of the Ouroboros of the Greek alchemists, "one of the central, recurring symbols representing the structure of the psyche" (p. 81).[7]

> In the case of Kekulé we can clearly see the relation between an archetypal image and the form in which matter is constructed, an example of the psychoid dimension of the archetype that [Wolfgang] Pauli [the world-renowned physicist] felt could be constructively applied to our understanding of how scientific creativity works—in the way both outer matter and inner psychology overlap. The archetype pertains to both psyche and matter and is what allows the former to see into the structure of the latter. Thus, Pauli was keenly interested in the influence of archetypal images on the development of science.
>
> In conclusion the hypothesis of the psychoid archetype spoke to both Jung and Pauli with respect to the parallel structures of matter and psyche. Both saw that continued research in their respective fields might shed light on the psychoid archetype.
>
> (Sparks, 2007, p. 81)

It is provocative to imagine that other archetypal images, 'dragons of the mind,' may lead to discovery of material realities as yet unknown. The movement from the *ouroboros* to the benzene ring is a one-way direction, but all forms of matter also contain denizens of the deep that reflect unknown aspects of the psyche waiting to be discovered, a chemistry of the depths, an alchemy of the soul beyond our laboratory products. The play between psyche and matter is itself ouroboric, and awaits a new alchemical recipe, a psychoanalysis and a philosophy that can do justice to the circular movement of the soul.

Such a connection between the soul and material reality was also a part of the vision of Dorn's third *coniunctio* "in [which the] conjunction [of] the combined spirit-soul-body now merges with the universal ground of being" (Mather, 2014, p.163). Mather (2014) points out that this union with the *unus mundus* is described by Jung as the *mysterium coniunctionis*. The perplexity of this psychoid union was important to both Jung and Pauli, each of whom took up the question from his own perspective. Pauli continued to seek for a rational, scientific explanation, as Jung also did, but Jung's perspective was enlarged by his discovery of the archetypal layers of the psyche, which played an essential role in his conception of reality.

The philosophical issue of psychoid reality has also been considered by Mills (2014) in his development of a psychoanalytic metaphysics. I believe Mills is on the right track by insisting on the importance of philosophy as essential in improving our understanding of Jungian psychology. For me, philosophy is an important part of the mix, which can add to more clarity to our understanding of Jung's ideas and the forging of his psychology.

If we are to consider Jung a philosopher, it is as an alchemical and philosophic doctor of the soul—Paracelsian and spagyric, intent on coming to terms with the unconscious and with saving the phenomena. As a thinker, Jung allowed himself to be shaped by volcanic, incandescent fires and their lava, and by illuminated, philosophical trees of light found in the midst of darkness and soot. For Jung, psyche's serpentine and ouroboric revelations spoke to the depths of reality, both visible and invisible, intertwined in a chiasm,[8] and manifested in the flesh of images and symbols. As a philosopher of psychic depths, Jung was led by these images to resist static formulations and to develop a philosophical and creative way of thinking that requires doing justice to what he called 'the protean mythologem and the shimmering symbol'— with the recognition that filth and images are not left behind.

Notes

1　Jung's separation between psychology and metaphysics runs throughout his work and is a particular focus in the last sections of the *Mysterium Coniunctionis* (1963b). See particularly pp. 544–553, *The Self and the Bounds of Knowledge.*

2　The issue of the relationship between philosophy and psychology has been specifically taken up in a major Jungian journal guest-edited by Casey and David Miller (2007), also a Jungian scholar and Professor Emeritus of Religion.

3　Basilisks are mythical creatures often related to lizards and are considered kings of the serpents. They are feared because of their power to cause death with a single glance.

4　For a fuller discussion of these points, see Marlan, 2006, p. 270.

5　"For the alchemists the prima materia was the *humidum radicale* (radical moisture), the water, the *spiritus aquae*, and *vapor terrae*; it was also called the 'soul' of the substances, the *sperma mundi*, Adam's tree of paradise with its many flowers, which grows on the sea" (Jung, 1967, ¶173).

6 "True imagination" is a term the alchemists used as having to do with the intimate connection between psyche and matter. "Jung understood 'true imagination' as the creation and evocation of images which have a life of their own and which develop according to their own logic ... [and] which grasps inner facts and portrays them in images true to their nature" (Salman, 2006, p. 176).

7 The question if the relationship of archetypal images and the structure of matter is genuine in Kekulé's case has been raised by the chemist John Wotiz, who accused Kekulé of fabricating his dream interpretation in order to obscure the fact that others had discovered the structure of the benzene ring before he did. What Wotiz doesn't consider is the possibility that Kekulé's account is both true and it is also the case that there were earlier renditions of the structure of the benzene ring. His view that Kekulé simply lied is an assumption for which I have not seen any conclusive evidence (cf. Browne, 1988).

8 Chiasm and flesh, refer to Maurice Merleau-Ponty's, *The Visible and the Invisible*.

References

Browne, M.W. (1988). The Benzene Ring: Dream Analysis. *The New York Times*. Retrieved from: www.nytimes.com/1988/08/16/science/the-benzene-ring-dream-analysis.html.

Casey, E. (1991/2004). *Spirit and Soul: Essays In Philosophical Psychology* (Second, expanded edition). Putnam, CT: Spring Publications.

Casey, E. & Miller, D. (Eds.) (2007). Spring 77: Philosophy and Psychology. *Spring Journal: A Journal of Archetype and Culture*.

Eliade, M. (1971). *Forge and Crucible: Origins and Structures of Alchemy*. New York, NY: Harper & Row.

von Franz, M.-L. (1979). *Alchemical Active Imagination*. Dallas, TX: Spring.

von Franz, M.-L. (2006). Psychological Commentary. In *Corpus Alchemicum Arabicum: Book of the Explanation of the Symbols, kitāb ḥall ar-rumūz* by M. Ibn Umail & T. Abt (Eds.). Zurich, CH: Living Human Heritage Publications.

Giegerich, W. (1999). *The Soul's Logical Life: Towards a Rigorous Notion of Psychology*. Frankfurt am Main: Peter Lang.

Heidegger, M. (1962). *Being and Time*. (J. Macquarrie & E. Robinson, Trans.) New York, NY: Harper & Row.

Hillman, J. (1978). The Therapeutic Value of Alchemical Language. In R. Sardello (Ed.), *Dragonflies: Studies of Imaginal Psychology*, 1(1). Irving, TX: University of Dallas.

Hillman, J. (2010). *Alchemical Psychology, Uniform Edition of the Writings of James Hillman (Vol. 5)*. Putnam, CT: Spring Publications.

Jung, C.G. (1959). *Aion, CW*, 9. G. Adler (Ed.). (R.F.C. Hull, Trans.). Princeton, NJ: Princeton University Press.

Jung, C.G. (1963a). *Memories, Dreams, Reflections*. A. Jaffé (Recorder & Ed.). (R. & C. Winston, Trans.). New York, NY: Pantheon.

Jung, C.G. (1963b). *Mysterium Coniunctionis. CW*, 14. G. Adler (Ed.). (R.F.C. Hull, Trans.). Princeton, NJ: Princeton University Press.

Jung, C.G. (1966). *The Practice of Psychotherapy*, *CW*, 16. G. Adler (Ed.). (R.F.C. Hull, Trans.). Princeton, NJ: Princeton University Press.

Jung, C.G. (1967). *Alchemical Studies*, *CW*, 13. G. Adler (Ed.). (R.F.C. Hull, Trans.). Princeton, NJ: Princeton University Press.

Jung, C.G. (1968). *Psychology and Alchemy*, *CW*, 12. G. Adler (Ed.). (R.F.C. Hull, Trans.). Princeton, NJ: Princeton University Press.

Jung, C.G. (1971). *Psychological Types. CW*, 6. G. Adler (Ed.). (R.F.C. Hull, Trans.). Princeton, NJ: Princeton University Press.

Jung, C.G. (1973). Letter to Pastor Max Frischknecht. In G. Adler (Ed.) in collaboration with A. Jaffe. (R.F.C. Hull, Trans.), *C.G. Jung: Letters, Vol. I: 1906–1950*. Princeton, NJ: Princeton University Press, pp. 408–412.

Jung, C.G. (1977). *C.G. Jung Speaking: Interviews and Encounters*. W. McGuire & R.F.C. Hull (Eds.). Princeton, NJ: Princeton University Press.

Marlan, S. (2006). Alchemy. In R. Papadopolous (Ed.), *The Handbook of Jungian Psychology: Theory, Practice and Applications* (pp. 263–295). London, UK: Routledge.

Mather, M. (2014). *The Alchemical Mercurius: Esoteric Symbol of Jung's Life and Works*. New York, NY: Routledge.

Merleau-Ponty, M. (1968). *The Visible and the Invisible*. Evanston, IL: Northwestern University Press.

Mills, J. (2012). Jung's Metaphysics, *International Journal of Jungian Studies*, 5(1): 1–25. Also online at: www.processpsychology.com/new-articles2/Jung.pdf.

Mills, J. (2014). Jung as Philosopher: Archetypes, the Psychoid Factor, and the Question of the Supernatural. *International Journal of Jungian Studies*, 6 (3), 227–242. doi: 10.1080/19409052.2014.921226.

Nilsson, M. (2006). Spagyrical Homeopathy. *Alchemy Journal* 7 (1). Accessed online at: www.alchemylab.com/AJ7-1.htm#Spagyrical_Homeopathy [unpaginated]

Power, P. (2017). 'The Psychological Difference' in Jung's *Mysterium Coniunctionis*. In J.M. Sandoval & J.C. Knapp, *Psychology of as the Discipline of Interiority: "The Psychological Difference" in the Work of Wolfgang Giegerich* (pp. 43–54). London, UK: Routledge.

Principe, L. (2013). *The Secrets of Alchemy*. Chicago, IL: University of Chicago Press.

Principe, L. & Newman, W. (2001). Some Problems with the Historiography of Alchemy. In W.R. Newman & A. Grafton (Eds.), *Secrets of Nature: Astrology and Alchemy in Early Modern Europe* (385–431). Cambridge, MA: MIT Press.

Saban, M. (2014). A Response to Jon Mills' Paper, 'Jung's Metaphysics.' *International Journal of Jungian Studies*, 6(3), 205–216. Available online at: www.tandfonline.com/doi/abs/10.1080/19409052.2014.921224?journalCode=rijj20.

Sparks, G.J. (2007). *At The Heart of Matter: Synchronicity and Jung's Spiritual Testament*. Toronto, CAN: Inner City Books.

Chapter 11

Jung, Time, and Ethics

Ladson Hinton

Introduction and Genealogy

The connection of time and ethics is ancient, but not familiar to most contemporary thinkers. A reflection on Jung and time and ethics is even less common. I will begin with some perspectives on temporality in order to orient the reader, and then focus on Jung's theories in that context. I will begin in our beginnings, with a brief genealogy of temporality and the emergence of the human.

It is temporality that most clearly distinguishes *homo sapiens* from the higher primates. Leroi-Gourhan points out that the great break between our human ancestors and other mammals came with bipedalism—erect posture (Audouze, 2002, p. 298). This freed the hand and mouth, and opened room in the brain case for more complex motor structures, including areas involving language and memory. Recent studies have shown the crucial importance of diet in the increase of hominids' brain size. Bipedal posture and tools and weapons facilitated a richer, meatier diet that stimulated brain development (DeCasien, Williams & Higham, 2017).

Bernard Stiegler describes technics, as a process of *exteriorization*: the pursuit of life by means other than pure biological life (Stiegler, 1998, pp. 16–17).[1] *Anticipation*, and the stimulation of foresight, is embodied by tools, which functioned like mirrors of memory. Stiegler asserts that the relation of being and time only developed within the horizon of technics (ibid., pp. 134–135). 'Internal' and 'external' were comingled from the beginning of culture.

The first clear sign of awareness of temporality was the appearance of intentional burial practice in the Middle Paleolithic (Lieberman, 1991, pp. 162–164). The corpses were coated with red ochre, which was strongly connected with pregnancy in the later cave art. The trauma and mystery of death and the hope for a future was evident.

Cave art began to appear around 40,000 BC. It was clear that there was a *future* expectation of return to the scene for rituals of some kind—clearly a horizon of temporality. In that sense, creative imagination was directed toward an unknown future, employing a potent collaboration of tools and images. Technology and cave art were highly interrelated. The various pigments, the lamps and torches used for working deep into caves, and the technique used by the artists showed a sophistication that would have taken a long time to develop—gifts and memories from an unknown past of unknown ancestors.

Time and space are crucial to the organization of who we are (Blommaert & De Fina, 2006, p. 1). Culture stems largely from the awareness of future times with all their possible dangers and opportunities, along with the need for creating provisions for the safety and well-being of the group. It is difficult to know when spoken language developed, but written language came forth during the Neolithic period of settled farming around 8,000 years ago. A form of exteriorized memory emerged for cataloging stored items, and then expanded. This was a mode of taking care of the future, of planning for a rainy day! Written memory was basic in cultural development, and our growing dependence on technology for memory is part of the crisis of our times (Audouze, 2002, p. 293).

Developmental psychology lends credence to a view that time sense is basic to both speech and interpersonal memory. The development of speech may be dependent on the emergence of a rudimentary temporal sense (de Diego-Balanger et al., 2016). In addition, it has been consistently found that the capacity to retain past events as interpersonal and specifically temporal seems to emerge around four to five years of age. Before that consciousness is mainly spatial (Tulving, 2005, p. 32).

An increasing capacity to remember interpersonal events is crucial to the development of ethical awareness—the effect of our actions upon others, the capacity to recall and take responsibility for what we have done and how we have been—our traumas and triumphs. One would assume that this developed on the grounds of pre-existing practical habits of care and survival such as one sees in other animal species that lack a developed sense of time (Cortina, 2017).

After a slow development over 2–3 million years, there was a profound acceleration of culture and technics in the Upper Paleolithic. It is important to note that *technics evolves more quickly than culture* (Stiegler, 1998, p. 15). Upon such a basis, Stiegler has developed a theory of *epiphylogenesis*, which is the idea that increasing retention of the past by means of early technics had the effect of strongly accelerating the process of technological and cultural evolution. That is, such 'retentions' became, in turn, a reflexive stimulus for evolution, constituting a dramatic break from the simpler manifestations of mere biological and cultural evolution (ibid., pp. 139–140; pp. 175–177).

Both neuroscience and psychoanalysis have demonstrated the constant augmentations and revisions of memory that are part of expanding human identity (Edelman, 2005, p. 99; Green, 2017, pp. 77–82). A sense of conscience, of debt to unknown ancestors, is part of the human condition, a part of our thrownness into the world (Stiegler, 1998, pp. 258–259). We emerge into the world in debt to those on whose shoulders we ride. This contributes to a sense of care for our world, the basic ethical stance for being-in-the-world (ibid., pp. 46–47; Heidegger, 1967, p. 274). If we evade our debt to our ancient heritage, we suffer the fate of Narcissus, who could only survive if he never knew himself, only took from life and never immersed himself in time, never accumulated memories. He could only be echoed in the present.

Phronesis: The Ethic of 'Practical Wisdom'

In this reflection on Jung and ethics, I will favor the lens of 'virtue ethics,' an approach that emphasizes personal character and that tends to become more apparent with time (Hursthouse & Pettigrove, 2016).[2]

The most common way that one falls short of virtue is through lacking *phronesis*, or practical judgment (Colman, 2013). One may reflect on Jung's life and ideas in multiple ways, and those ways often seem contradictory. However, the practical effect he had on people's lives, and the inspiration he provided for both individuals and the broader culture, make his life and ethos significant. Early on, he advocated immersion in experience along with a deeply ethical dedication to the quest for consciousness, and he maintained that stance throughout his life. A temporal perspective is most useful in reflecting upon how all the dimensions of his ethos emerged.

For Plato, speaking through the words of Socrates, it often comes across that, to live well ethically, one should base one's decisions on *epistêmê*, or 'scientific' knowledge, grounding one's actions on an intellectual grasp of the Idea of the Good itself (Kirkland, 2007, p. 127). This provoked Aristotle to bring a charge of intellectualism against Platonic ethics (ibid.). The implications of that approach to ethics could put a preference for the Good above existence itself, including the life of the body; at the extreme, one could see that as an apprenticeship for death (Goodchild, 2010, p. 24)! Aristotle attacks not only Plato's view of the role of the abstract and general idea of the Good, but also what he sees as an attempt to ground ethical judgment solely in *epistêmê*. He systematically distinguishes the *practical* region of human understanding from the *theoretical*.

According to Aristotle, character, not intellect, is the core of ethical virtue. It is a matter of prudence or practical wisdom, not knowledge (*epistêmê*), for it is concerned with the particular, the singular character of the thing having to be done in any situation. In contemporary terms, one would say that the life of the mind and body escapes representation (Goodchild, 2010, p. 25). For Aristotle, *epistêmê* is a way of conceiving universals—absolutes that are *actually everywhere and always the same*, and thus *atemporal* (Kirkland, 2007, p. 128). He tells us that *phronesis* attends principally to the particular available means, which are *within time*, the basis being provided by the agent's quality of character. *Phronesis* derives its enigmatic power from its complete immersion in time, in the past, present and future (ibid., p. 130). This complexity lends a basic imprecision to ethics.

In the ethical context, Aristotle asserts, one must look to the *kairos*, 'the right or opportune moment.' This is *the good that manifests in time*. However, the *kairos* in any situation cannot be judged with absolute precision because it reflects the desire to bring about this or that result *in the future*. However, the future is hidden from us. "*Phronesis* must therefore be understood as a power by which one looks properly toward *what does not appear*, toward what remains hidden because [it is] in the future, and makes good ethical decisions precisely by doing so" (ibid., 131). Ethics, and life itself, both have a strongly future-oriented quality.

Temporality is a kind of intrinsic limitation, emphasizing the finitude of ethical judgment, situated between a past that can never be totally known and a future that can't be predicted. That is, one cannot overcome these temporal limits because we must acknowledge that *phronesis* is bound both to a particular past and particular future possibilities that we can only partly know (ibid., p. 134).

Deliberation with others is crucial in the process of 'looking to the *kairos*.' Thinking in itself is a virtuous act, in Aristotle's view (Goodchild, 2010, p. 30). This process would be endless, except that *kairos* appears in a fleeting moment that cannot be anticipated, but when action must be taken. To await that moment requires courage (Kirkland, 2007, p. 136). One could, with Deleuze, call this a 'transcendence in immanence,' or a kind of 'transcendental empiricism' (Smith, 2012, p. 153). To attain the necessary virtue requires grounding in everyday life (Kirkland, 2007, p. 137).

On the one hand, *Phronesis* seems to describe an intensely dialogical process, and that is sometimes present in Jung's approach. On the other hand, he often seems to value *epistêmê*, the archetype or archetypal. Sometimes that attitude is pronounced, and comes across in an authoritative pronouncement of 'truth,' the archetype as 'truth', in contrast to the murkiness of everyday life. Jung had a great curiosity about ideas and cultures, and he often conveyed a generous and dialogical spirit. That seemed to increase with age, as manifested in his interest in alchemy. This dichotomy in his thinking between *epistêmê* as archetype and *phronesis* with its richly dialogical spirit can be confusing, and this confusion often seems to derail Jungian discourse and its underlying ethos.

The Emergence of Jung's Ethical Orientation

Given the above contexts, I want to focus more specifically on some dimensions of the ethical perspective that the human being, Carl Gustav Jung, developed within his own time, experience, and reflection. I will provide some lengthy quotes because I think that is crucial in gaining a real sense of his presence and ideas. From early on in his career, he foregrounded the 'moral factor' in his thought, and that strongly differentiated his approach from Freud's. In fact, he held that the moral factor was innate (Merkur, 2017, p. 17). Whatever Jung's vicissitudes, his commitment to self-understanding was profoundly ethical, and one could call it religious in the broader sense of the word (Barreto, 2013). He was determined to live and to think about his experience.

In 1910, the 35-year-old Jung wrote a letter to Freud, expounding critically about the possibility of supporting a new "International Fraternity for Ethics and Culture" (Jung, 1973, pp. 17–18):

> I cannot muster a grain of courage to promote ethics in public, let alone from the psychoanalytic standpoint! At present, I am sitting so precariously on the fence between the Dionysian and the Apollonian...The ethical problem of sexual freedom really is enormous and worth the sweat of all noble souls. But 2000 years of Christianity have to be replaced by something equivalent. An ethical fraternity, with its mythical Nothing, not infused by any archaic-infantile driving force, is a pure vacuum and can never evoke in man the slightest trace of that age-old animal power that drives the migrating bird across the sea...I think we must give it time to infiltrate into people from many centers...ever so gently to transform Christ back into the soothsaying god of the vine, which he was, and in this way absorb those ecstatic, instinctual forces of Christianity for the *one* purpose of making the cult and sacred myth what they once were--a drunken feast of joy where man regained the ethos and holiness of an animal. That indeed was the beauty and purpose of classical religion, which from God knows what temporary biological needs has turned into a Misery Institute! Yet how infinitely much rapture and wantonness lie dormant in our religion, waiting to be led back to their true destination!

Just prior to the time of this youthful, exuberant, iconoclastic letter, Jung had been involved in a 'mutual analysis' with Otto Gross, a creative and troubled pioneer in psychoanalysis who was an admirer of both Nietzsche and Freud. He was an advocate of 'free love,' and felt that psychological problems were due to sexual repression. At times, Jung referred to Gross as his 'twin brother" (Heuer, 2001). This early letter is an example of Jung's experimental attitude toward life and practice as a young analyst. It was also a precursor to his later involvement with female patients.

Fifty years later, a young student studied the letter to Freud, and wrote to Jung, questioning him about his remarks. Jung reflected (Jung, 1973, p. 19):

Best thanks for the quotation from that accursed correspondence. For me it is an unfortunately inexpungable reminder of the incredible folly that filled the days of my youth. The journey from cloud-cuckoo land back to reality lasted a long time. In my case, Pilgrim's Progress consisted in my having to climb down a thousand ladders until I could reach out my hand to the little clod of earth that I am.

There are many things one could consider here about this thoughtful and honest reply, but the crucial thing to me is the ethical perspective gained through time and memory, "The better part of a lifetime." The profound subjective tension with which Jung had lived, and his fierce commitment to reflect and create amidst that turbulence, was remarkable. Whatever his vicissitudes, a sense of ethical commitment to consciousness seemed to always be there: "where Kant insists on the consciousness of duty, Jung emphasizes rather the duty to be conscious" (Colacicchi, 2015, p. 43).

Jung's 'Seven Sermons' and Temporality

I will now focus on some of the specific fluctuations and evolutions of Jung's ideas over a broad length of time, the process that emerged in the decades between his sojourn in 'cloud-cuckoo land,' and the moving letter he wrote toward the end of his life, embracing that 'clod of earth' that he was.

Jung himself did not construct a focused analysis of temporality, but Angeliki Yiassemides (2014) has written a valuable elaboration of his views, employing the text, *Septem Sermones Ad Mortuos* (The Seven Sermons to the Dead). This was a philosophical poem written in 1916, but not published until 1961 when it appeared as an appendix to some editions of *Memories, Dreams, Reflections* (Jung, 1963, pp. 378–390). It was later found in the closing pages of *The Red Book*, and was the only part of that work published during Jung's lifetime. He employs several voices in this work, and they can seem a bit strange and esoteric if you are not accustomed to that mode of expression. I will use them because it seems important to capture the intensity and uncanniness of his process.

In the *Seven Sermons*, the Gnostic 'Basilides' is the narrative voice of the poem. The distinction between 'Pleroma' and 'Creatura' is a core element of the text. Pleroma indicates the totality of the divine, a *timeless* dimension which cannot be grasped by humans, whereas Creatura is the realm of the human (Yiassemides, 2014, p. 6). Creatura has qualities and is subject to change, whereas in Pleroma there are no distinctions, that is, Creatura is *embedded in temporality*.

This is the first emergence of the temporal perspective in Jung's work (ibid., p. 10). A division, more like a chasm, lies between time and timelessness. According to the text, Creatura foments differentiation in the universe by projecting its (temporal) inner reality on (timeless) Pleroma. One can see how this sets the stage for the development of Jung's major ideas. There are hints of the Kantian division of phenomenon and noumenon, or Platonic Ideas versus being a prisoner in the Cave (Plato, 1992, para. 514–541).

It would seem that the Pleroma was later expressed by the idea of the Self, or more abstractly, even metaphysically, as the Unus Mundus, whereas Creatura encompassed everyday, time-bound consciousness, ego, etc. (Yiassemides, 2014, p. 10). In Yiassemides' view, "Jung provided a detailed account regarding the process by which the differentiated ego strives to *return to the original wholeness of psychic reality*" (ibid.; italics added). This 'original wholeness' was timeless. Creatura must accept its time-bound nature, and in addition, seek 'participation in the...eternal reality of the universe,' and 'return to [its] true nature' (ibid.). This is a process of individuation, seen as the *interplay of time and timelessness*. In this view, there is an Eternal, timeless ground to which Creatura may return: an ultimate, underlying foundation. In the view of Baretto (2014), such vestiges of timeless bastions ultimately undermined the integrity of Jung's process, as well as analytical psychology in general, because such bastions constitute a means of 'escape' from an ultimate kenosis, a deeply dialectical emptying that could lead to a new level of life.

Another Gnostic entity named 'Abraxas' appears later in the poem. This is "The deity that rules over the totality of time and in whose power time is both made and unmade," and is thus "the sum of and the liberator from the cycle of necessity, freeing man from the cycle of time and in whose power time is made and unmade... freeing man from the cycle of necessity... [Abraxas] is the eternally available timeless moment, the eternal now... which brings freedom from time in both its linear and its cyclic aspects. That is, for the Gnostics, the ultimate goal is the return to the Pleromatic state, which is timeless. '*The object of salvation is to deliver us from the lie of time*'" (Yiassemides, 2014, p. 11, italics added).

In this view, liberation from time is a repeatable event in the present. "The atemporal and eternal power of Abraxas is the key to the soul's deliverance, which can be obtained repetitively at the present moment. This seems to imply that the 'atemporal' can dominate the flow of temporality: *When time is tamed and subdued*, psychic salvation is attainable" (ibid.; italics added).

This privileging of the 'timeless' had a powerful effect on Jung's theorizing, especially during the middle period of his life. The 'personal unconscious' became a lesser thing, deserving only moderate interest, that Jung often looked upon it with a somewhat condescending tone. He often mentioned disparagingly that Freud and Freudians found their meaning only in the everyday and in the personal past. When the ground of existence is timeless, everyday life—the personal unconscious—comes across as inferior, as opposed to the 'eternal' archetypes or the collective unconscious. Strangely, there are only two papers in the *Journal of Analytical Psychology* that seem to specifically address this question, although it is touched upon throughout the Jungian literature (Zinkin, 1974; Williams, 1963). The most common Jungian theorizing has concerned various relationships, dimensions, and manifestations of archetypes, or the adoption of an object-relations perspective that largely bypasses these issues.

Wolfgang Giegerich and Michael Whan speak of the Jungian focus on myth and symbol as the "Neurosis of Psychology" (Giegerich, 2005, pp. 1–17; Whan, 2015, pp. 3–7 & 2017, pp. 242–260). They hold that the myths of the past are largely dead, while pointing out that Jung wanted to 're-mythologize' the world, and that many Jungians still have hope for a return to a mythical, timeless place. However, they see this desire to reverse history creating a neurosis of its own, due to the strain of sustaining a simulated reality. Ascribing this simulation to a defensive denial, Giegerich says that our childish dependency on dead myths must end for us to be fully present in the everyday, to have a kenotic attitude, an openness to the temporal processes of our own times—as opposed to a defensive quest to re-create the past, to escape, like a child wanting to return to a fantasy of eternal delight (Giegerich, 2008; Mogenson, 2010).

The tormenting richness of our everyday trauma and turmoil, the endless process of elaborating the enigmatic core of our memories through *Nachträglichkeit*, tends to get lost in an assumed teleology that privileges the timeless as the goal. A more complex view of temporality is required: "The past is not the passive container of things bygone. The past, indeed, is our very being, and it can stay alive and evolve; the present is the passage where the retranscription and recontextualization of our past continually occur, in line with Freud's [1895] concept of *Nachträglichkeit*"[3] (Scarfone, 2006, p. 814).

It is memory and reflection on the past that makes ethical reflection possible. Jung's memories of being in 'cloud-cuckoo land' had enabled him to reflect in depth on his past, and reply so authentically to the student who wrote to him. It is reflection upon what we have done, and what we have thought, that provokes ethical awareness. The past is not static, and does not imply a reductionistic approach to the psyche. It lies at the heart of ethical awareness. If clinical work has ethics at its core, as Jung was wont to say, then the past is also at the core—and not 'archetypal' potentials.

This contradiction pervades much of Jung's writing, but evolved somewhat after he became involved in alchemy, which seems to privilege process more than concept. In some respects, he began to more closely approach the mode of *phronesis*, a processual view that seems closer to phenomenology. This process may commence with the most basic primal stuff (*prima materia*) of life: excrement (Jung, 1956, para. 276.)!

The Personal Unconscious and the Collective Unconscious

Warren Colman powerfully and critically describes the impact of Jung's disownment of everyday reality and temporality as a Kantian/Cartesian view of a mind " 'shut up in its own sphere,' apart from the living world" (Colman, 2017, p. 36). What was left to Jungian psychology was a view of the world "as the expression of archetypal forces, somehow apart from the realities of geography, climate, competition for resources, and social and political conflict... [that] not only fails to address the complex interrelation between states of mind and the state of the social world but reduces the latter to a kind of ghost-life as if it is merely a screen for psychic projections" (ibid., p. 37). In a convincing way, Colman's ethical purview of Jung's theory describes how privileging a set of 'archetypes' that seem 'inner,' and are 'timeless,' can deeply undermine ethical concerns about everyday human needs and activities, as well as larger temporal/historical/cultural contexts and events. Expositions of alchemical process still retain some sense of a mind isolated in its own subjectivity, as Colman elaborates.

To elaborate upon these thoughts, reviewing some of Jung's specific remarks about time and the "timeless" is very useful. In speaking about the progression of a case, Jung describes the emergence of a 'transpersonal control point' (Jung, 1966, para. 216–217):

> I saw how the transpersonal control-point developed--I cannot call it anything else--a *guiding function* (sic) and step by step gathered to itself all the formal personal over-valuations; how, with this afflux of energy, it gained influence over the resisting conscious mind without the patient's consciously noticing what was happening. From this I realized that the dreams were not just fantasies, but self-representations of unconscious developments which allowed the psyche of the patient gradually to grow out of a *pointless personal tie* (italics added).[4]
>
> This change took place, as I showed, through the unconscious development of a transpersonal control point; a virtual goal, as it were, that expressed itself symbolically in a form that can only be described as a vision of God.

What is notable to me here is how quickly Jung attributes 'guidance' or change to the transpersonal. The personal is deemed 'pointless,' and any meaningful subjective fantasies are deemed self-representations of 'deeper' unconscious developments, via the 'transcendent function,' 'the Self,' or 'God.'

That perspective would seem to undermine a sense of ethical agency or personal responsibility, of change born from the sweat and toil of everyday life. It is as if only something 'special' can save us, and that is a pre-existing religious or transpersonal factor, not immanent in the everyday.

Later, he gives a similar description of psychological life (Jung, 1944/1968, para. 329–330):

we are dealing here with an a priori 'type,' an archetype which is inherent in the collective unconscious and thus *beyond individual birth and death. The archetype is, so to speak, an 'eternal' presence, and the only question is whether it is perceived by the conscious mind or not*...the increase in the clarity and frequency of the mandala motif is due to a more accurate *description of an already existing 'type,' rather than that it is generated in the course of a dream series.* In practice...it is met with in distinct form in a few cases, though this does not prevent it from functioning as *a concealed pole around which everything else revolves* (italics added).

Again, the 'archetype' is behind the scenes at all times, seemingly directing the action. It is 'eternal,' that is, timeless, not 'generated' from experience, but on a different plane from temporality and the everyday. It does not seem too much of a leap to imply, with regard to ethical perspectives, that 'the archetype did it.' This would seem to reflect and even encourage an abdication of personal responsibility.

Jung mentions an affinity for Platonic ideas (*epistêmê*) in other writings (Jung, 1960, para. 274–275):

Just as it may be asked whether man possesses many instincts or only a few, so we must also raise the still unbroached question of whether he possesses many or a few primordial forms, or archetypes, of psychic reaction...In Plato, however, an extraordinarily high value is set on the archetypes as metaphysical ideas, as 'paradigms' or models, while real things are held to be only copies of these model ideas...St. Augustine, from whom I have borrowed the idea of the archetype...still stands on a Platonic footing in that respect.

Here, Jung references archetypes as resembling Platonic entities, leaving 'real things' as only copies, or perhaps simulacra (Whan, 2015). These seem set apart from time, and *phronesis.* The 'personal unconscious,' the everyday, our temporal life, is then only a copy of these eternal forms. Archetypes begin to sound almost classificatory, like a mythological version of *Psychological Types* (Jung, 1936).

Further (Jung, 1959, para. 3–5):

A more or less superficial layer of the unconscious is undoubtedly personal. I call it the *personal unconscious*...But this personal unconscious rests upon a deeper layer, *which does not derive from personal experience but is inborn.* I call this the *collective unconscious...'Archetype' is an explanatory paraphrase* of the Platonic *eidos*...it tells us that so far as the collective contents are concerned we are dealing with archaic or--I would say--primordial types, that is, with *universal images that have existed since remotest times* (italics added).

The reference to Plato is repeated, and the 'personal unconscious' is obviously viewed as inferior by comparison (see pages 5–6 of this writing). That would seem to be the position of the inmates of Plato's Cave! Archetypes are the 'deeper' part of psychological life. Again, the real action is not in the realm of personal experience.

And, finally (Jung, 1968, para. 81): "This 'personal unconscious' must always be dealt with first, that is, made conscious, otherwise the gateway to the collective unconscious cannot be opened." Here, the 'personal unconscious' is an apprentice-piece at best, only a preliminary gateway on the path to the 'real stuff' behind the scenes. Everyday life, to repeat Colman's rich description, becomes a sort of ghostly presence, an inferior sort of reality. From this perspective, *temporality*, the realm of the human, pales in comparison to the *timeless* archetypal dimension. The everyday world of temporality, in its messy fascination, its wars, its loves and hates, is not the true scene of action. This negates the ethical point of view.

Jung sometimes discussed archetypes as hypothetical, "irrepresentable" factors that were also, perhaps, elements of brain structure (Jung, 1960, para. 29). However, many of his pronouncements carried the ring of an authority that 'knew' when those elements were present in psychological life. A notable—and regrettable— instance of this attitude was his essay, "Wotan," published in 1936. In this essay, he portrayed the phenomenon of Nazism as a manifestation of the "Wotan archetype" (Jung, 1936, paras. 389 & 385). This seems to undermine consideration of real-time historical events and responsibilities (Colman, 2017, p. 36). His views appear especially poignant in the face of the sufferings that the Nazis were, as Jung to some degree notes, already inflicting on Jews and other minorities in nearby Germany. Even more alarmingly, he also stated that those evil excesses, though dangerous and regrettable, might actually represent a *reculer pour mieux sauter*, a sort of cultural regression in the service of cultural evolution.

I don't think that Jung was a Nazi sympathizer, but I do believe that 'archetypal' thinking can at times result in a dulling of ethical vision. How can an 'archetype' express the reality of a concentration camp, or the lesser evils that abound in life? Such a view all too easily serves as a lofty resistance to the very necessary "thick description" of the brute reality of personal and historical suffering—the torments of everyday life, whatever the setting (Hinton, 2015; A. Hinton, 2016).

Oedipus and Time

Sophocles' *Oedipus Rex*, probably the best-known story in the psychoanalytic world, is a moving and multi-dimensional depiction of the connection between ethical awareness and time. John Manoussakis (2017) has written a thought-provoking set of reflections on Oedipus (see pp. 68–75). In his view, ethical stories are clearly based on the intricacies of time, but he points out that, in most discussions, interpretations are modified to sound as if they are simple before and after events. The substance of the everyday is redacted. Manoussakis' perspective on Oedipus reveals the many layers of ethical situations that require time to unfold, time for the reflection on the past that is necessary in revealing their truth.

In the opening of the play, there is an awful plague affecting the city of Thebes, where Oedipus has become the ruler. Sophocles implies that it is a political disease, a moral disease. Something is rotten in the city of Thebes. The city is sick, and the spectator of the play knows that, beneath appearances, Oedipus is also sick. The devastating crisis is the result of a history of multiple expulsions of otherness, of enigma: first Oedipus himself expelled as an infant, due to the dire prophecy that he will murder his father and marry his mother; then his accidental killing of his father; and finally the expulsion of the Sphinx through Oedipus' clever use of reason. Oedipus strongly identifies with his role as the man who vanquished the Sphinx, and had thereby become the ruler of the city. He publicly preens himself for his exploit.

Very insightfully, Jung pointed out in 1916 (Jung, 1956, para. 264), "Little did he know that the riddle of the Sphinx can never be solved directly by the wit of man." However, he then seems to adopt a rationalistic view of Oedipus' dilemma.[5] Jung speculates that, "*those tragic consequences...could easily have been avoided* if only Oedipus had been sufficiently intimidated by the frightening appearance of the 'terrible' or 'devouring' Mother whom the Sphinx personified" (ibid., p. 181, italics added). He discusses the symbolism of the Sphinx, usefully differentiating his own theories from what he saw as Freud's emphasis on the narrower dimensions of sexuality and the incest taboo (Jung, 1961, para. 565).

In 1958, Jung returned to the question of the Sphinx, pointing out that, "Oedipus did not use his intelligence to see through the uncanny nature of this childishly simple and all too facile riddle, and therefore fell victim to his tragic fate, because he felt he had answered the question. It was the Sphinx itself that he ought to have answered and not its façade" (Jung, 1936, para. 714). This was a profound insight into the enigma of the Sphinx, but he then proceeds to connect it to the 'anima,' a "mediatrix between the unconscious and the conscious." The goal of justifying his theory overrides the raw truth and necessity of the process of time, the humility of realizing that hindsight is not foresight. There is even a hint of arrogance in Jung's depiction, when he criticizes Oedipus' naïveté vis à vis the Sphinx. As is so common with Jung, he describes an enigmatic dimension of life, but then obscures its impact with a profusion of amplifications which seem to privilege 'knowing.'[6]

To continue the story: Oedipus had ostensibly liberated the city from the Sphinx's enigmatic presence, from her otherness. This is ironic because he had himself been a terrifying enigma that had to be extruded from the city, because of the dire prophecy that he would kill his father and marry his mother. He had been put out to die as an infant—but he only comes to know that with time. The expulsion of otherness, out of fear of chaos, dominated the history of Thebes.

Typically fearing instability, the chorus begs Oedipus, their ruler, to always remain the same, apart from time and change.

Clinging to recurring sameness, otherness is excluded, and there is no diachrony that could disrupt, but also renew life. Within synchrony, time does not flow—there is stagnation and pollution in the form of a plague. Ethical taint creates a mood of miasma. The past cannot be past without truth and reflection. As a result, there is only a recurring present, and a mood of monotonous, deathlike synchrony pervades the city.[7]

The Sphinx, in her enigmatic presence, had been a reminder of the uncanny nature of transitions, which usually involve acknowledgment of primal loss as well as new and unknown horizons. What is crucial for the Oedipal drama is ethical re-reflection on the past that is not past, that has remained an 'Unpast' polluting the present and future (Scarfone, 2006, pp. 807–834).[8] Vanquishing the Sphinx's enigmatic reality resulted, paradoxically, in the re-emergence of the massive, unacknowledged "dim past" of Oedipus and Thebes in the form of a plague, mightily disrupting and terrifying the city (Manoussakis, 2017, p. 71).

The sage, Teresias, enters the stage exactly where Oedipus will later exit it. He is blind, led by a child, and knows the truth. As this thread to the future appears, Oedipus asks the terrifying question about his past, about his parentage: "Who are my parents?" Tiresias answers, "This day shall be your parent and your destroyer" (Sophocles, 1994/429 BC, p. 367). The crucial, diachronic question could not be articulated until Teresias had appeared in the present as the harbinger of a possible future (ibid., p. 72). The question about Oedipus' beginnings signals the traumatic end to his imaginary, narcissistic self. At first he violently rejects Teresias, banishing him from the city. But the seed of truth has been planted, and the progression toward knowing terrible truths soon follows.

Oedipus had been a rationalist, a man who could think the enigma but not live it. His illusion had been to believe that thinking the enigma would solve it: *Cogito ergo sum*. The truth of time proves otherwise. It is only after he has fulfilled the original Delphic prophecy that he can know his criminality, through time and reflection (ibid., p. 74). The Unpast can then become truly past, and wisdom can emerge, born out of terrible truth.

The Oedipus story is a dramatic instance of how living an engaged life can enable a re-collection of the self from the Unpast, through time and narrative memory (Manoussakis, 2017, p. 83). We lack foreknowledge, and that fact is intrinsic to the human condition. Our dearly-won wisdom comes through *phronesis*, not only through clever logic and reason. Oedipus is not merely a man who killed his father and married his mother, but something more profound that penetrates to the core of the human condition. It requires time to reveal the nuances and multi-dimensional truth of human actions. The good is a temporal process, a complex process that is never complete (ibid., n. 25, p. 181).

Some Later Thoughts: Alchemy

At age 79, Jung still held firmly to the idea that the unconscious is timeless, although his attitude had mellowed to some degree, and there is less of a sense of a tormenting division between archetype and everyday (Jung, 1976, para. 1572):

> Through the progressive integration of the unconscious we have a reasonable chance to make experiences of an archetypal nature providing us with the feeling of continuity before and after our existence. The better we understand the archetype, the more we participate in its life and the more we realize its eternity or timelessness.

Alchemy grew in importance for him. In 1954, he describes a transition from the 'personal unconscious' to archetypal symbols, but he described the relationship between the personal and the collective unconscious as a dissociation, more fluid, and seemingly closer to a relationship of equals (Jung, 1967, para. 480–481):

> *the symbol is not reduced...but is amplified by means of the context which the dreamer supplies...*the unconscious can be integrated and the dissociation overcome...[through] an experience of a special kind, namely, the recognition of an alien 'other' in oneself, or the objective presence of another will. The alchemists, with astounding accuracy, called this barely understandable thing Mercurius...he is

God, daemon, person, thing, and the innermost secret in man; *psychic as well as somatic. He is himself the source of all opposites*, since he is *utriusque capax* ('capable of both').

'Mercurius' describes a general process, involving not merely an 'archetypal' realm but seemingly involving embodiment. In any case, he seemed to shift away from the perspective of an overexciting, somewhat inflated, 'archetypal' realm that contrasted with the seemingly lesser dimension of the everyday, the personal. Edinger notes that the spirit Mercurius is a "peacemaker, the mediator between the warring elements and the producer of unity" (Edinger, 1995, p. 31).

In mythology, Mercury was unique among the gods because he could transit between the worlds of divinities and men, and is concerned with everyday shopkeepers as well as gods (*Oxford Classical Dictionary*, p. 962). The end stage of the alchemical process is most often depicted in everyday, 'chop wood and carry water' terms, not a dramatic transcendence (Henderson & Sherwood, 2003, pp. 159–169).

Jung saw the Unicorn as a symbol of Mercurius, and the end plate of the Unicorn Tapestries at the Cloisters in Manhattan clearly shows, in the background, a symbolic 'royal couple' in jail, even as a lively marital festivity takes place. Perhaps this is a warning that there is danger in a too confident view of 'unity' (Cavallo, 2010, p. 70). In the hands of the 'Spirit Mercurius,' the thread of life is always in the move!

This presents a view of a process that is experimental and inventive, in endless movement, yet remaining the same. "Mercurius is a psycho-logical concept [that] contains both reality and our subjectivity within itself" (Giegerich, 2008, p. 137). This is an evolution beyond an excited discovery of "the archetype," and represents a process that cannot be bottled up in the form of static mythic entities and symbols. Now, "the history of the soul has entered a stage with which the stage of mythology is once and for all superseded" (ibid., p. 137).

'Mercurius' has a strongly temporal sense of life flowing endlessly in all its strangeness and variations, its past, present and future. Each time and place has its own symbolic realm, its own temporal 'realities,' and this is our fate, our 'thrownness.' We are stuck with whatever our time's real images and temporalities happen to be, and we are stuck with death at the end. It is part of ethics to know this, and to also know that life is change, and the future tends to appear in unexpected, even reviled forms. To disown or obstruct this temporal process is to disown life itself, and that is the essence of evil. This is what Jung seems to have learned from being tossed about, but not fleeing from, the strange and stormy vicissitudes of his many-sided life.

A 1957 letter to Eric Neumann reflects many of his later thoughts, commenting upon how limited we are in our capacity to foretell the effects of our actions: we can only know about it with *time* (my italics) (Jung, 1976, p. 365):

> I know that I do not want to do evil and yet I do it just the same, not by my own choice but because it overpowers me. As a man I am a weakling and fallible, so that evil overpowers me. I know that I do it and know what I have done and know all my life long I shall stand in the torment of the contradiction. *I shall avoid evil whenever I can but shall always fall into this hole...*I am therefore like a man who feels hellishly afraid in a dangerous situation and would have run for his life had he not pulled himself together on account of others, feigning courage in his own eyes and theirs in order to save the situation...for anyone who passes off his shadow as a passing inconvenience or, lacking all scruple and moral responsibility, brushes it off as irrelevant, they offer dangerous opportunities for aberrations in moral judgment, *such as are characteristic of people with a moral defect who consequently suffer from an intellectual inflation.*

This powerfully conveys the perspective of the aging Jung, reflecting on his rich and extensive memories, having been deeply engaged in all the dimensions of temporal existence. It feels very personal and everyday rather than 'archetypal.' He takes no refuge in transpersonal justifications or speculations. His profound honesty conveys a rare depth, an almost excruciatingly painful awareness of the raw truth of experience, and of the human condition. This is the sort of ethical awareness that only comes with time. His profound declaration certainly approaches the Oedipal level of tragic recollection, and the perspective of *phronesis*. It provides a moving summation of the ethical life of an extraordinary man, Carl Jung.

Notes

1 'Technics,' refers here to technical practices as a whole; 'technology' refers to the amalgamation of technics and modern sciences.

2 As an example, a virtuous person would be someone who is kind in many situations over a lifetime because of their character and not because they want to maximize utility or gain favors or simply do their duty. 'Virtue ethics' deal with wider questions such as how one should live, what is the good life, and what are proper family and social obligations (Athanassoulis, 2017). In this writing, I will view 'morals' as normative social customs and practices, and 'ethics' as the philosophy of that realm of human experience, including the broader dimensions of good and evil. In practice, morality and ethics are often not clearly separable.

3 *Nachträglichkeit* refers to the continual revision of memory due to new experiences, as well as the discovery of enigmatic dimensions of pastness that influence—and open up—reconstructions of memory (Boothby, 2001, pp. 198–208). This concept has been developed especially by Lacan and the French school (Green, 2017). In *Wider Than the Sky*, Gerald Edelman has written of a similar process in the neuroscience of memory (2005, p. 99ff.). The point here is that the dimensions of memory and the 'personal unconscious,' are, potentially, almost limitless.

4 There is a footnote here referring to the "transcendent function" in *Psychological Types*, Def. 51, "Symbol."

5 Jung has a deep insight here, but then seems unable to stay with the idea that there is an enigmatic core of life that lies at the heart of human existence, and is ultimately untranslatable (Hinton, 2009).

6 In many ways, Jung was a man of his times. "For the philosophical tradition of the West, all spirituality lies in consciousness, thematic experiences of being, knowing" (Levinas, 1998, p. 99).

7 6 I use 'synchrony' here as describing a unified, unchanging self or culture—something timeless. In the early part of *Oedipus Rex*, both Oedipus and the Chorus equate the stability of his health with the stability and health of Thebes. They ask him to be unchanged, and he reassures them. 'Diachrony' is the intrusion of otherness, of new truth, into the same, offering the possibility of a restoration of the flow of time. The initial picture is of a mood of dread and fear, trapped in a lifeless synchrony, anticipating the diachronic, disruptive events to come—in time. One could call synchrony pre-ethical because without a temporal horizon there is no way to ascribe an ethical value to an act (Manoussakis, 2017, p. 69).

8 By 'Unpast,' Scarfone indicates experiences that have not acquired a quality of pastness, but are not 'timeless' (Zeitlos).

References

Athanassoulis, N. (2017). Virtue Ethics. *Internet Encyclopedia of Philosophy*. www.iep.utm.edu/virtue/

Audouze, F. (2002). Leroi-Gourhan, A Philosopher of Technique and Evolution. *Journal of Anthropological Research*, 10 (4), 4, 277–306.

Barreto, M.H. (2013). The Unity of the Ethical and the Religious in Jung's Thought. *International Journal of Jungian Studies*, 5 (3), 226–242.

Barreto, M.H. (2014). Requiem for Analytical Psychology: A Reflection on Jung's (Anti)Catastrophic Psychology. *Journal of Analytical Psychology*, 59 (1), 60–77.

Blommaert, J. & De Fina, A. (2016). Chronotopic Identities: On the Timespace Organization of Who We Are. *Tilburg Papers in Culture Studies, Paper 153*. www.tilburguniversity.edu/upload/ba249987-6ece-44d2-b96b-3fc329713d59_TPCS_153_Blommaert-DeFina.pdf

Boothby, R. (2001). *Freud as Philosopher: Metapsychology after Lacan.* New York: Routledge.

Cavallo, A.S. (2010). *The Unicorn Tapestries.* New York: The Metropolitan Museum of Art; New Haven & London: Yale University Press.

Colacicchi, G. (2015). *Jung and Ethics: A Conceptual Exploration.* Doctoral Thesis, Centre for Psychoanalytic Studies, University of Essex.

Colman, W. (2013). Reflections on Knowledge And Experience. *Journal of Analytical Psychology*, 58 (2), 200–218.

Colman, W. (2017). Soul in the World: Symbolic Culture as the Medium for Psyche. *Journal of Analytical Psychology*, 62 (1), 32–49.

Cortina, M. (2017). Adaptive Flexibility, Cooperation, and Prosocial Motivations: The Emotional Foundations of Becoming Human. *Psychoanalytic Inquiry*, 37 (7), pp. 436–454, doi: 10.1080/07351690.2017.1362920

DeCasien, A.R., Williams, S.A., & Higham, J.P. (2017). Primate Brain Size is Predicted by Diet but not by Sociality. *Nature Ecology & Evolution*, Volume 1, Article 0112. doi: 10.1038/s41559-017-0112

Diego-Balanguer, R., de Martinez-Alvarez, A., & Pons, F. (2016). Temporal Attention as a Scaffold for Language Development. *Frontiers in Psychology*, 7:44; doi10:3389/fpsyg.2016.00044

Edelman, G.M. (2005). *Wider Than the Sky: The Phenomenal Gift of Consciousness.* New Haven: Yale University Press.

Edinger, E. (1995). *The Mysterium Lectures*. Toronto: Inner City Books.

Giegerich, W. (2005). Introduction. In *Collected English Papers, volume I: The Neurosis of Psychology*, 1–17. New Orleans: Spring Publications.

Giegerich, W. (2008/1986). The Rescued Child, or The Misappropriation of Time: On the Search for Meaning. In *Collected English Papers, volume III: Soul- Violence*, 45–75. New Orleans: Spring Publications.

Giegerich, W. (2008). *The Soul's Logical Life*. Frankfurt: Peter Lang.

Goodchild, P. (2010). Philosophy as a Way of Life: Deleuze on Thinking and Money. *SubStance #121*, 39 (1).

Green, S. (2017). Lacan: *Nachträglichkeit*, Shame, and Ethical Time. In *Temporality and Shame: Perspectives from Psychoanalysis and Philosophy*, pp. 74–100. Eds. L. Hinton. & H. Willemsen. New York & Milton Park, Abingdon, Oxon: Routledge.

Heidegger, M. (1967/1927). *Being and Time*. Trans. J. Macquarrie & E. Robinson. Oxford: Blackwell.

Henderson, J.L. & Sherwood, D.N. (2003). *Transformation of the Psyche: The Symbolic Alchemy of the Splendor Solis*. East Sussex & New York: Brunner- Routledge.

Heuer, G. (2001). Jung's Twin Brother. Otto Gross and Carl Gustav Jung. *Journal of Analytical Psychology*, 46 (4), 655–688.

Hinton, A.L. (2016). *Man or Monster? The Trial of a Khmer Rouge Torturer*. Durham: Duke University Press.

Hinton, L. (2009). The Enigmatic Signifier and the Decentred Subject. *Journal of Analytical Psychology*, 54 (5), 637–657.

Hursthouse, R. & Pettigrove, G. (2016). *Virtue Ethics. Stanford Encyclopedia of Philosophy*, 1–43. Stanford: Stanford University Press.

Jung, C.G. (1936). *Wotan. CW*, 10, para. 371–399. Trans. R.F.C. Hull. New York: Bollingen Foundation.

Jung, C.G. (1956). *Symbols of Transformation. CW*, 5. Princeton: Princeton University Press.

Jung, C.G. (1959). *The Archetypes of the Collective Unconscious. CW*, 9i. Princeton: Princeton University Press.

Jung, C.G. (1960). *The Structure and Dynamics of the Psyche. CW*, 8. Princeton: Princeton University Press.

Jung, C.G. (1961). *Freud and Psychoanalysis. CW*, 4. Princeton: Princeton University Press.

Jung, C.G. (1963). *Memories, Dreams, Reflections*. Ed. A. Jaffé. New York: Vintage Books.

Jung, C.G. (1966). *Two Essays on Analytical Psychology. CW*, 7. Princeton: Princeton University Press.

Jung, C.G. (1967). *Alchemical Studies. CW,* 12. Princeton: Princeton University Press.

Jung, C.G. (1968). *The Unicorn in Alchemy. CW,* 12, para. 518–519. Princeton: Princeton University Press.

Jung, C.G. (1944/1968). *The Symbolism of the Mandala. CW,* 12 para, 329–330. Princeton: Princeton University Press.

Jung, C.G. (1973). Letters I, 1906–1950. Eds. G. Adler & A. Jaffé. Trans. R.F.C. Hull. Princeton: Princeton University Press.

Jung, C.G. (1976). Letters II: 1951–1961. Eds. G. Adler & A. Jaffé. Trans. R.F.C. Hull. Princeton: Princeton University Press.

Jung, C.G. (1976). *The Symbolic Life. CW,* 18. Princeton: Princeton University Press.

Kirkland, S.D. (2007). The Temporality of Phronesis in the Nicomachean Ethics. *Ancient Philosophy,* 27, 127–140.

Levinas, E. (1998). *Otherwise than Being or Beyond Essence.* Trans. A. Lingis. Pittsburgh, PN: Duquesne University Press.

Lieberman, P. (1991). *Uniquely Human.* Cambridge, MA: Harvard University Press.

Manoussakis, J.P. (2017). *The Ethics of Time: A Phenomenology and Hermeneutics of Change.* New York: Bloomsbury Publishing.

Merkur, D. (2017). *Jung's Ethics: Moral Psychology and His Cure of Souls.* Ed. J. Mills. New York: Routledge.

Mogenson, G. (2010). Post Mortem Dei Jungian Analysis. *Spring 84: A Journal of Archetype and Culture,* 207–270. New Orleans: Spring Publications.

Plato (1992/380 B.C.). *Republic.* Trans. G.M.A. Grube. Indianapolis, IN: Hackett Publishing.

Scarfone, D. (2006). A Matter of Time: Actual Time and the Production of the Past. *Psychoanalytic Quarterly,* LXXV, 807–834.

Smith, D.W. (2012). *Essays on Deleuze.* Edinburgh: Edinburgh University Press.

Sophocles (1994/429 B.C.). *Oedipus Tyrannus.* Ed. & trans. H.L. Jones. Cambridge, MA: Harvard University Press.

Stiegler, B. (1998). *Technics and Time,* 1. Stanford: Stanford University Press.

Suddendorf, T., & Corballis, M.C. (2007). The Evolution of Foresight: What is Mental Time Travel, and is it Unique to Humans? *Behavioral and Brain Sciences,* 30, 299–351.

Tulving, E. (2005). Episodic Memory and Autonoesis: Uniquely Human? In *The Missing Link in Cognition,* Eds. H.S. Terrace & J. Metcalfe, 4–56. New York: Oxford University Press.

Whan, M. (2015). The Logic Of Image: Simulating 'Mythic Image'. In *Anselm Kiefer's 'Parsifal II'*. ISPDI Newsletter, April, 2015. http://ispdi.org/index.php/en/newsletter/ispdi-newsletter-april-2015

Whan, M. (2017). Disavowal in Jungian Psychology: A Case Study of Disenchantment and the Timing of Shame. In *Temporality and Shame: Perspectives from Psychoanalysis and Philosophy*, 242–261. London & New York: Routledge.

Williams, M. (1953). The Indivisibility of the Personal and Collective Unconscious. *Journal of Analytical Psychology*, 8 (1), 45–50.

Yiassemides, A. (2014). *Time and Timelessness: Temporality in the Theory of Carl Jung*. New York: Routledge.

Zinkin, L. (1979). The Collective and the Personal. *Journal of Analytical Psychology*, 24 (3), 227–250.

Chapter 12

Jung, Literature, and Aesthetics

Christian McMillan

Introduction: The Encounter

Any cursory glance at a definition of the branch of philosophy associated with aesthetics will usually convey that it is concerned with the nature and appreciation of art, beauty and taste, the term itself deriving from the Greek "aisthetikos" translated "of sense perception." As a system of principles, the term was first used by German philosopher Alexander Gottlieb Baumgarten (1714–1762) in *Aesthetica* (1750). Bishop contends we 'could thus describe aesthetics as specifically German discipline' (2008, p. 126) and, following Baumgarten's definition of aesthetics as 'the science of sensory knowledge' (or 'the quality of sensation'), the sensation of 'beauty' remained a preoccupation of philosophical aesthetics well into the post-Kantian period. Van den Berk remarks that 'Jung remained sensitive to the notion of 'aesthetics' as it was introduced into European culture' by Baumgarten but 'whereas later researchers equated 'aesthetics' with 'art,' Jung persistently took a different course' (2012, p. 58). In *Psychological Types* (1921) Jung reveals what troubles him about aesthetics in his rejection of what he calls 'aesthetism' ('aesthetic view'):

> Aesthetism is not fitted to solve the exceedingly serious and difficult task of educating man, for it always presupposes the very thing it should create – the capacity to love beauty. It actually hinders a deeper investigation of the problem, because it always averts its face from anything evil, ugly and difficult, and aims at pleasure, even though it be of an edifying kind. Aestheticism therefore lacks all moral force, because *au fond* it is only a refined hedonism.
>
> (1921/1971, para. 194; cf. Bishop, 2008a, pp. 139–143;
> Van den Berk, 2012, p. 69)

What Jung means by a lack of 'moral force' is bound up elsewhere with what he refers to as a lack of 'moral obligation' commanded by his own fantasy images if treated as 'art' (1963/1979, p. 212). The 'moral' and the ethical appear to be equated by Jung to the extent that aesthetism is ethically barren. It 'converts the problem into a picture which the spectator can contemplate at his ease, admiring both its beauty and its ugliness, merely re-experiencing its passions at a safe distance, with no danger of becoming involved with them' (ibid., para. 232).

This idea of an easy and safe contemplation, at a distance, is undermined by Jung's own encounter with certain works he classes under the popular label 'modern art.' *Ulysses* (1922) by Joyce (1882–1941) is the subject of a monograph by Jung (1932/1966) in which he finds his 'ill will' aroused. Papadopoulos suggests that this encounter demonstrates Jung's 'epistemological sensitivity' meaning 'Jung's awareness to his own countertransference to Joyce's novel' (2006, p. 12). Gaillard similarly writes that in 'his study of Joyce's *Ulysses*,' Jung 'accepted the *shock* and *destabilisation* he felt when encountering this work' and that his 'attention was deliberately placed on the vivid and violent countertransference that seized and animated him' (2006, p. 338; emphasis added). In terms of the psychological functions (thinking, feeling, sensation and intuition), Gaillard adds that 'Joyce's work decidedly does not place him on the side of thinking and feeling but rather on the side of the exercise of perception, or more exactly sensation' which Jung's 'literary and artistic perusals, the common expectations of his intellectual training, and his moral and aesthetic values had as good as failed to acquaint him with' (ibid.). This encounter is 'ethical' in a way that sits uncomfortably with Jung's determination of 'moral force'.

In suggesting that *Ulysses* has aroused his 'ill will' (1932/1966, para. 167) it could be maintained that Jung had implicitly presupposed a 'goodwill' which was temporarily compromised by the 'shock' and 'destabilisation' of the encounter. Where writers speak of Jung's counter-transference, I see Jung as becoming not 'an individual endowed with a good will and a natural capacity for thought, but an individual full of ill will who does not manage to think, either naturally or conceptually' (Deleuze, 1968/2004, p. 166). Jung attempts a certain 'modesty,' 'not managing to know what everybody knows, and modestly denying what everybody is supposed to recognise. Someone who neither allows himself to be represented nor wishes to represent anything' (ibid., p. 165). The modality of this aesthetic encounter does not recapitulate the cliché of a detached, philosophical contemplation exemplified for example by Cartesian 'doubt,' presupposing a conception of truth and seeking it under the best conditions possible and in a contented state of retirement from the activities of the world. Rather, in a 'fundamental *encounter*' (Deleuze, 1968/2004, p. 176) or *Kairos*, one is *forced* to think.

The encounter transforms Jung into a participant with something that involves him from the 'outside.' It is an involuntary encounter in the Proustian sense: 'The real theme of a work is therefore not the subject the words designate, but the unconscious themes, the involuntary archetypes in which the words, but also the colours and the sounds, assume their meaning and their life. Art is a veritable transmutation of substance' (Deleuze, 1964/2000, p. 47). Jung's criticisms of aesthetics, concerned with a detached and distanced 'beauty,' are based upon epistemological presuppositions. When he asserts that 'beauty does not indeed lie in things, but in the feeling that we give to them' (1912, p. 193), emphasis is placed on a 'subjective viewpoint' (Van den Berk, 2012, p. 60) recapitulated in his suspicions about an artistic interpretation of the *Red Book* fantasies as 'arbitrary inventions.' Yet this view is not always consistent in Jung's thought. In 'Archaic Man' (1931/1969) he asks, 'Is a thing beautiful because I attribute beauty to it? Or is it the objective beauty of the thing that compels me to acknowledge it?' (1931/1969, para. 135). His reflections involve him in a 'thought-experiment' (Bishop, 2008b, p. 510) in which he considers whether the object may actually be said to constitute the subject:

> Does the psychic in general – the soul or spirit or the unconscious – originate in *us*) or is the psyche, in the early stages of conscious evolution, actually outside us in the form of arbitrary powers with intentions of their own, and does it gradually take its place within us in the course of psychic development?
>
> (Jung, 1931/1969, para. 140)

Tentatively I lay stress on the way Jung uses 'outside' in this passage. A valuable interpretation presented by Bishop asserts that 'Archaic Man' 'insinuates the possibility of what might be called a *vitalist-materialist* outlook' (2008a, p. 512).[1] If we couple this with Bishop's recent suggestion that Jung was trying to develop a new kind of 'vitalist aesthetics' (2017, p. 209) we might read his 'encounter' with *Ulysses* as an example of ethical transformation given that it undermines the hegemony of the 'subjective viewpoint' via a form of immanent critique. Likewise it reveals genetic and immanent conditions upon which this viewpoint is constructed.

Synthesis and its (Post)-Kantian Philosophical Lineage in Jung's Aesthetics

Resources which help us to unpack the dynamics of the aesthetic 'encounter' and which are germane to a philosophical treatment of Jung's aesthetics can be found in several of his works. Recognizing the German and post-Kantian origins of aesthetics as a discipline helps us to make sense of Kant's (1724–1804) appearance at an important juncture in Bishop's commentary on the philosophical lineage of Jung's aesthetics. In Kerslake's, *Deleuze and the Unconscious* (2007), we are presented with reading that places Kant's theory of symbolism from his *Critique of Judgement* (1790) within a remarkable synthesis of the thought of Jung, Bergson (1859–1941) and Gilles Deleuze (1925–1995).[2] In Bishop and Kerslake's work it is the role of the imagination and the transcendental schematism in Kant's critical philosophy, which merits consideration.[3] Bishop relates that:

> The psychological process binding objects and concepts which Jung calls 'esse in anima' resembles Kant's transcendental schematism, which combines the universality of a concept with the particularity of the content of that concept, mediates categories and sensory intuition and enables the mind to bring the individual case under a general rule.
>
> (2000, p. 156)

Esse in anima (Jung, 1921/1971, para. 77), or 'being in soul,' *resembles* the transcendental schematism but it is by no means the same. For Kant the schematism is involved in the production of *possible* experience and he attributes a constitutive synthetic role to the productive imagination in this process. Conceptual thought and sensory intuition, the two sources of knowledge for Kant, involve four faculties: sensuousness (*Sinnlichkeit*), understanding (*Verstand*), reason (*Vernunft*), and the imagination (*Einbildungskraft*). Ultimately it is the faculty of the Understanding which takes the lead in coordinating this process of production in Kant's first two *Critiques*.

In the *Critique of Pure Reason* (1781), Kant reserved the power of synthesis for the active 'I think', the activity of the understanding, and he regarded the passive ego as a simple *receptivity* possessing *no* synthetic power. Kant conceived the sensible to be a quality related to an object that sensibility passively intuited. Hence, he determined the transcendental form of space (the condition of outer sense) by geometric extension (pure intuition of objects). For concepts to be applied to intuitions an exterior harmony was required between the faculties of the understanding and sensibility made possible by the *deus ex machina* of the schematism of the imagination, making the spatio-temporal relations of intuitions align with the logical relations of the concept (cf. Smith, 2012, p. 96).

Jung uses the term 'living reality' to denote the 'product neither of the actual, objective behaviour of things nor of the formulated idea exclusively, but rather the combination ... through *esse in anima*' (1921/1971, para. 77). In concert with his use of the term 'fantasy' (ibid., para. 78), Jung alters the role of the productive imagination describing 'imaginative activity' as 'the reproductive or creative activity of the mind in general,' which 'can come into play in all the basic forms of psychic activity, whether *thinking*, *feeling*, *sensation*, or *intuition*' (ibid., para. 722). If we grant that 'the Jungian equivalents to these four faculties are the psychic functions,' acknowledging that they 'do not map directly onto the faculties as classically understood' (Bishop, 2009, p. 100), then it makes sense to situate Jung's aesthetics within the post-Kantian context of Weimar classicism, with its various 'totality' models of the synthesis of the faculties/functions in 'aesthetic contemplation' (see Bishop, 2008a, p. 101).

The question I ask is how might *esse in anima* function as a potential resource to help unpack the dynamics of the aesthetic 'encounter.' In part the question and the answer correspond to a recent objection against Jung's use of *esse in anima* raised by Colman. He claims that 'Jung's ploy here is to take the notion of psyche as the *primary datum*, the only thing which we can directly know, and then suggest that since both the phenomenal and noumenal worlds are experienced psychically, they can be interpreted as functions of the psyche' (2017, p. 35; emphasis added). Another way of stating this objection is to say that all power of synthesis is reserved for the (transcendental) psyche and that conditions of (psychic) experience remain *external* to what they condition resulting in the production of *possible* (psychic) experience. By hylomorphically severing thought and being, this transcendental procedure blocks any attempt to investigate the *genesis* of experience. It is unclear whether Bishop's account of Jung's aesthetics could disarm this objection. 'For Jung,' he says, 'the imagination has both a Kantian dimension, in the form of transcendental apperception, and a neo-Kantian one, when he speaks of the power of the imagination to produce "living" reality' (2008, p. 112). What is at stake is the 'primary datum' or its form as an active synthetic unity of apperception (transcendental subject).

Discounting Colman's own bio-phenomenological solutions to the objection and including comment on the aesthetics of modern art (which Bishop and Kerslake's accounts avoid) I return to Jung's 'encounter' with *Ulysses*. Jung writes a somewhat flippant but no less important remark about this work: 'In its destruction of the criteria of beauty and meaning that have held till today, *Ulysses* accomplishes wonders. It insults all conventional feelings, it brutally disappoints our expectations of sense and content, it thumbs its nose at all synthesis' (1932/1966, para. 77). The "synthesis" that is fractured in the 'encounter' (a process Jung refers to as "shattering,' 1932/1966, para. 186) is an *active* synthesis, fractured by a genetic mode of conditioning Jung calls "visceral thinking" (ibid., para. 166). It undermines an 'image of thought' dominated by object recognition, beginning not with common-sense, but sense itself, something that does a violence to the 'harmony' of the active synthetic unity of the subject. Sense is no longer passive, awaiting an external set of transcendental conditions to transform it. This 'sense' has a passive synthetic power of its own, one that can send the faculties/functions into a *discordant* harmony, a free-play, which Jung experiences as troubling. *Esse in anima* as 'living reality' refers to an aesthetic 'encounter' with the 'outside', one which temporarily destabilizes a one-sided synthetic orientation revealing passive syntheses capable of producing discord and new synthetic relations among the faculties/functions.

The troubling aspects that *Ulysses* and 'modern art' present to Jung partly concern a breaking of the synthesis and symmetry of an organic conception of totality or wholeness. In his "After the Catastrophe" (1945/1970) Jung remarks:

> Whether we like it or not we are bound to ask: What is wrong with our art, that most delicate of all instruments for reflecting the national psyche? How are we to explain the blatantly pathological element in modern painting? Atonal music? The far-reaching influence of Joyce's fathomless *Ulysses*? Here we already have the germ of what was to become a political reality in Germany.
>
> (1945/1970, para. 430)

Apart from these lamentations about the 'pathological' and 'schizophrenic' pathogenesis of 'modern art,' what I find curious about these remarks is how uncomfortably they would sit with the outlook of post-war continental philosophical critiques of the hegemony of representation. Are these 'modern' aesthetics not part of the critique of representation and identity itself? Are they not in some way a critique of the politicised versions of holistic organicism that became embedded in totalitarian ideologies including that of National Socialism? (see Harrington, 1998). Indeed, do Jung's words not betray a "neoconservative ideology, his affinities with those who only a few years later [1932] would coin the slogan of 'degenerate art,' and his own taste for petit-bourgeois, reactionary art" (Hohl, 1983, p. 14). What I think Jung finds difficult to acknowledge is an ethical and creative experimentalism that some of this 'modern art' embodies in the form of a critique of representational foundationalism. It is this foundationalism that converts experience into 'possible' experience and in turn makes experience immanent *to* a subject, or, in Kantian terms, immanent *to* an active transcendental subject (primary datum).

Recalling Jung's reluctance concerning Joyce's 'visceral' style and "cerebration reduced to mere sense-perception" (1932/1966, para. 172), an alternative presentation of such style is offered by Deleuze in his criticisms of "The Image of Thought" as he finds this in the model of object-recognition and constitutive finitude established in Kant's first *Critique*:

> Something in the world forces us to think. This something is an object not of recognition but of a fundamental *encounter*. What

is encountered may be Socrates, a temple or a demon. It may be grasped in range of affective tones: wonder, love, hatred, suffering. In whichever tone, its primary characteristic is that it can only be sensed. In this sense it is opposed to recognition. In recognition, the sensible is not at all that which can only be sensed, but that which bears directly upon the senses in an object which can be recalled, imagined, or conceived...The object of the encounter, on the other hand, really gives rise to sensibility with regard to a given sense. It is not an *aisthēton* but an *aisthēteon*. It is not a quality but a sign. It is not a sensible being but the being *of* the sensible. It is not the given but that by which the given is given.

(1968/2004, p. 176)

The 'object,' in this passage, (or the dream, the archetype, the symbol) is not an object of recognition. But it is curious how Jung's encounter with *Ulysses* draws him to comment on the object in terms of recognition. He writes that *Ulysses* wants 'to be the eye of the moon, a consciousness detached from the object, in thrall neither to the gods nor to sensuality, and bound neither by love nor by hate' (1932/1966, para. 186). He reiterates this theme of 'detachment from the object' (ibid., para. 193; cf. pars. 187, 191, 193) and suggests that the work of Picasso also demonstrates:

a growing tendency to withdraw from the empirical objects, and an increase in those elements which do not correspond to any outer experience but come from "inside" situated behind consciousness – or at least behind that consciousness which, like a universal organ of perception set over and above the five senses, is orientated towards the outer world. Behind consciousness there lies not the absolute void but the unconscious psyche, which affects consciousness from behind and from inside, just as much as the outer world affects it from in front and from outside. Hence those pictorial elements which do not correspond to any "outside" must originate from "inside".

(1932/1966, para. 207)

Whilst this "withdrawal" 'thumbs its nose at all synthesis' (1932/1966, para. 178), i.e. the synthesis of recognition and commonsense, a consciousness 'detached' presents a potentially misleading impression. It is a dissolved self, undergoing a discordant harmony of the faculties, a transcendental exercise of the faculties, a free and indeterminate accord of the faculties that arises when there is no determining concept to legislate (see, Deleuze, 1968/2004, p. 177).[4] The 'outside' is not clearly distinct from an 'inside.'

The Outside: The Form of Exteriority

The problem of inside and outside, interiority and exteriority can be re-framed by appeal to the use of *Gemüt* (affect) in the aesthetics of German poet, dramatist and novelist Heinrich von Kleist (1777–1811). This features in Deleuze and Guattari's twelfth 'plateau,' "Treatise on Nomadology: The War Machine," from *A Thousand Plateaus* (1980). In his lecture, "Thoughts on the Nature and Value of Speculative Enquiry" (1898) from the *Zofingia Lectures*, Jung refers to a letter Kleist wrote to his sister Ulrike in March 1801 outlining his first pained encounter with Kantian philosophy: 'My sole, my highest goal has been lost and I have no other' (para. 180). Jung's sympathy for Kleist as a figure 'genuinely expressive of tragic spirit' (ibid.) relates to his view of truth at this time and what he calls a 'metaphysical longing' (ibid., para. 181) to satisfy the principle of causality (teleological purpose) which Kant had attempted to block as regulative only in the third *Critique*.[5] The response of Kleist to the vertigo induced in him by Kant's epistemology is generative of a frenzied production, which followed in the next ten years during which Kleist produced all his major works. According to Adkins, 'Kant's restriction of the understanding to appearance, rather than things-in-themselves, seems to have created an ontological problem for Kleist' (2015, p. 109). Arguably this 'ontological problem' animates the narrative of Jung's engagement with Kant throughout the *Zofingia Lectures*. Kleist's response to this problem was to create art 'in which expectations are overturned, in which people lose control of their lives, in which affect dominates reason' (ibid.).

In the hands of Deleuze and Guattari Kleist's use of affect can be taken as a 'war-machine' that destabilizes the 'image of thought'; an image that Kant, as a 'state thinker' stabilizes (Goethe and Hegel being other 'state thinkers' that Deleuze and Guattari name, 1980/1987, p. 356; p. 269, 378). As we continue, let us also consider *Ulysses* as an example of an aesthetic 'war-machine' whose *ethical* (as opposed to moral) function also consists in de-territorializing this 'image.' The form of *Ulysses* as a book is not state-like, something Jung finds troubling when he announces that 'in those seven hundred and thirty-five pages no obvious repetitions, not a single blessed island where the long-suffering reader may come to rest; no place where he can seat himself' (1932/1966, para. 164). The idea of *Ulysses* as a 'whole' consisting of coded internal relations is replaced by a nomadic or rhizomatic open-whole. Marlan refers to the work as an 'alchemical book,' which by 'being flexible, like wax or soft gold, *Ulysses* as an image of the Philosophers' Stone defeats logocentrism' (2013, p. 16). Likewise, Deleuze and Guattari argue:

> The State as the model for the book and for thought has a long history: logos, the philosopher-king, the transcendence of the Idea, the interiority of the concept, the republic of minds, the court of reason, the functionaries of thought, man as legislator and subject. The State's pretension to be a world order, and to root man. The war machine's relation to an outside is not another "model"; it is an assemblage that makes thought itself nomadic, and the book a working part in every mobile machine, a stem for a rhizome (Kleist and Kafka against Goethe).
>
> (1980/1987, p. 24)

Curiously, some of the characteristics of this nomadic aesthetic have also been identified in Jung's own style of writing. Rowland for example characterizes "On the Nature of the Psyche" (1947/1954) as a 'net of reflected discourses,' which 'offers many directional paths, multiple cultural positions, a uroborous of discourse' (2005, p. 92). 'With the imperious ego decentred, there is no centre-margin figuring the psyche,' 'the final flattening of the persona into the multiplicity of 'we' leaves the reader as one of many within the web of argumentation of multiple relationships' (ibid., p. 97). We might also compare this with Bishop's indictment against Jung's tendency to privilege the 'mystical' over the aesthetic. Guided by Goethe's poem "Epirrhema" (1818), Bishop relates how this text 'works on a 'horizontal' level of 'inside' and 'outside' rather than the vertical level of 'above' and 'below'; in this case it holds a position that is *immanent*, not transcendent' (2009, p. 105; emphasis added). Consequently, Bishop relates that 'Goethe's immanence offers a truly ethical approach, unlike the evasive mysticism of which Jung became so routinely accused' (ibid.). These detours are of value insofar as the status of the inside and the outside becomes 'flattened' along a 'horizontal level' or immanent plane.

Kleist's (and Joyce's) aesthetics refer us to an 'outside' or 'form of exteriority' by way of affect. Affect opens interiority to the outside like a rhizome, allowing for the construction of immanent heterogeneous connections. A translation of *Gemüt* normally suggests 'disposition,' 'soul,' 'mind' or 'heart.' But, in the words of Adkins, the 'problem with translating the word in this way is the unavoidable connotations of interiority' (2015, p. 116). Alternatively, *Gemüt* translated as 'affect' gestures to the production of new thoughts relating to the notion of being 'forced to think' that I introduced earlier. Affects are 'Impersonal, non-subjective and non-signifying. They are not the possession of a subjective interiority or thought. Affects are external to every interiority and in fact are the conditions for the possibility of interiority' (ibid., p. 117). And in Kleist:

> the secret is no longer a content held within a form of interiority; rather, it becomes a form, identified with the form of exteriority that is always external to itself. Similarly, feelings become uprooted from the interiority of a "subject," to be projected violently outward into a milieu of pure exteriority that lends them an incredible velocity, a catapulting force: love or hate, they are no longer feelings but affects. And these affects are so many instances of the becoming-woman, the becoming-animal of the warrior (the bear, she-dogs). Affects transpierce the body like arrows, they are weapons of war.
>
> (Deleuze & Guattari, 1980/1987, p. 378)

Contra Jung's assertion that *Ulysses* is, among other things, 'bound neither by love or hate' (1932/1966, para. 186), we find that the 'war-machine' of *Ulysses* has converted these into affects of exteriority. The binary Jung erects between a 'non-objective art,' which draws from the 'inside' and the 'object of outer experience' (ibid., para. 206) leads to his assertion that this 'art' exhibits a 'withdrawal' from 'empirical objects.' While the 'empirical object' may precipitate an aesthetic encounter, it is ultimately of secondary importance with respect to the passive syntheses that govern the production of empirical (actual) experience and which make an appearance in the aesthetic encounter. Genetic conditions of experience are unconscious, but not by way of a bordered 'inside.' The danger is that the designation of the unconscious as an 'inside' implicitly carries through a form of conditioning in which the conditions, like Kantian conditions, remain invariant and external to what they condition (partly responsible for the numerous debates concerning the 'Platonic' or 'Kantian' status of the archetype).

With *Ulysses* Jung encounters a genetic account of conditioning which he articulates as 'a stream of time seven hundred and thirty-five pages long which all consist in one single and senseless day in the life of every man, the completely irrelevant sixteenth day of June, 1904, in Dublin' (1932/1966, para. 164). Jung judges this day to be "senseless" relative to subject-centered experience, i.e. to the smooth continuity of day-to-day experience. But as an occasion for an involuntary 'encounter' what is 'senseless' can alternatively be rendered as a passive synthesis, as the condition under which thought is engendered within thinking. Additionally, the apparent 'senseless' nature of the work implies that it lacks method. But it is anti-methodological because it does not presuppose thought to be a voluntary activity that we are free to initiate at will. A concern over method appears to animate Jung's resistance to aesthetics in general, prompting Wojtkowski to deduce an 'art complex' (2009, p. 25). The concern and the response in *Memories, Dreams, Reflections* is well known: 'When I was writing down these fantasies, I once asked myself "what am I really doing? Certainly this has nothing to do with science. But then what is it?" Whereupon a voice within me said, "It is art" .... This time I caught her and said, "No, it not art! On the contrary, it is nature"' (1983, p. 209). Bishop contends that for 'Jung, it was vital to reject the idea his experiences were aesthetic ones,' otherwise Jung would fail to see that 'they would have carried no more conviction than any other 'sense perception,' and he would have felt no 'ethical obligation' towards them' (2009, p. 45). Bishop asks if by 'abandoning art, however, was Jung forced to assign to consciousness [*Verstand*] a superior position to the unconscious (including the senses)?' (ibid., p. 48).

These points are crucial if we are to understand why 'Jung's aesthetics' have been pieced together via secondary literature and why common departures have been advanced in certain key respects. These departures implicitly or explicitly focus on the problem of the 'ethical' in aesthetics as Jung saw it, offering alternative interpretations. For Bishop, it is Goethe and Schiller's models of the *cultivation* of the personality that engenders a being capable of liberating the imagination from its subordination to the understanding (*Verstand*) making it capable of entertaining a 'living reality' via what he refers to following Goethe as a new 'simple empirical intuition' (2009, p. 34), an 'aesthetic perception/intuition/outlook/vision' (ibid., p. 35, 73, 74) and an 'archetypal/aesthetic vision' (ibid., p. 7), which 'properly understood, can be used to view the world as a totality—as a totality of immanence, not a totality of transcendence' (ibid., 2009, p. 73). Viewing 'the world,' can be likened to a sentiment that Deleuze and Guattari raise in their last work, *What is Philosophy?*: 'it may be that living in this world, in this life, becomes our most difficult task, or the task of a mode of existence still to be discovered or our plane of immanence today' (1994, p. 75).

Concluding Remarks: The Depth of this World—A Chaosmos

This is a 'world' of as yet unlived possibilities and the task of believing in it is ethical in the Spinozistic sense; an expansion of what a body can do. This 'ethics' seems to be different from the 'ethical obligation' that Jung considers most aesthetic practices incapable of delivering. This distinction emerges because of a difference between the clinical responsibilities of the therapist (to individual, group, society) and the creative experimentalism of the philosopher and artist. Faced with *Ulysses* and works by Picasso, Gaillard notes that Jung wondered 'how far we can go in such a descent towards the most archaic and dangerously fragmented part of ourselves, and at what price' (2006, p. 345). In my view this distinction is partly generative of the alternatives that present themselves in the secondary literature on Jung and aesthetics. For example, Bishop champions Goethe and Spinoza for their 'aesthetic ethics' or 'ethical aesthetics'

(2009, p. 3). Including Nietzsche and Jung he writes that the 'affirmation of the totality (of the individual) is linked to the affirmation of the totality (of the whole)' (ibid., p. 4). These unique individuals were arguably capable of enduring a great deal. If we take Jung's own confrontation with the unconscious as an example (his 'creative illness,' 1913–1919), he becomes an apprentice of the unconscious largely through his own efforts which are subsequently transmuted into the founding principles of Analytical Psychology.[6] Feats of endurance could be associated with the emphasis that Goethe and Jung placed on 'becoming' in the development of the personality which Bishop describes as 'evoking that aesthetic 'ennoblement' of the human being, which Nietzsche would advance under the rubric of the 'superman' (*Übermensch*), and which Jung would propose as the outcome of the 'individuation process' (2009, p. 93). This is not the 'average' 'human' being and as *Übermensch* suggests, 'becoming' in this context might be akin to going 'beyond the human' (to plagiarize from Bergson).[7] In one of the most powerful passages near the end of *Bergsonism* (1966/1991) where Deleuze elaborates in quasi-hermetic terms on the place of the human being in the universe, he articulates that 'this liberation, this embodiment of cosmic memory in creative emotions, undoubtedly only takes place in privileged souls' (1991, p. 111) and that 'great souls – to a greater extent than philosophers – are those of artists and mystics. ...At the limit it is the mystic who plays with the whole of creation, who invents an expression of it whose adequacy increases with its dynamism' (ibid., p. 112). Such sentiments are not absent in Jung's work. He admitted that the path to personality is 'unpopular' and 'highly uncongenial to the herd' and that for this reason 'only the chosen few have embarked upon this strange adventure... as a rule the legendary heroes of humankind' (1932/1954, para. 298), and perhaps also the 'visionary artist' that Jung details in "Psychology and Literature" (1930/1950/1966, pars. 139, 141, 143, 144–145, 147–148).

Ulysses does not 'thumb its nose at all synthesis,' rather it conveys a different kind (or kinds) of synthesis germane to the experimentalism of 'privileged souls' such as Joyce. We might otherwise refer to different kinds of synthesis as different disjunctive uses of the faculties, different indeterminate accords or different discordant accords. Bishop's interpretation of Jung's aesthetics through Weimar

Classicism argues for a 'highest reason' via aesthetics, a product not of the 'conventional perceptual apparatus' (2009, p. 34) but of the 'productive imagination' involving intuition (*schauen*). Kerslake's interpretation of Jung's aesthetics refers to a 'subterranean *destination* of the imagination, beneath the functions of conceptual representation, in the apprehension of the world as symbol' (2007, p. 111). He claims that 'Deleuze's turn to Kant for a theory of symbolism in fact gives the Jungian theory of symbolism a firmer epistemological grounding' (ibid.). In both interpretations what resonates is Kant's notion of the schematism of the imagination but with its synthetic power drawn 'away from its function in the process of knowledge and empirical perception, towards another destination' (ibid.). How 'deep' is this destination? The question is apt insofar as its answer may offer a reason for the reticence behind Jung's concern for the limited moral/ethical obligation that the aesthetic entails.

This 'depth' concerns what I referred to above (following Deleuze and Guattari) as 'this world.' We visited this point when considering Kleist's 'affect' and the 'outside' as well as Bishop's complaint against the 'transcendence' privileged in Jung's use of the term 'mystical.'

With Spinoza (1632–1677) this 'depth' refers to what a body can do and *not* what its essence is. If 'becoming' in individuation is often associated with a potentiality then it may be presupposed by the question, What *must* you do to realize your essence? By contrast the question that guides Spinoza's ethics asks, What are you *capable* of doing by virtue of your power? This immanent approach to the question of ethics is developed in Nietzsche's philosophy in terms of active and reactive forces, but it also gestures to the kind of 'being,' 'human' or 'beyond the human' that Jung appears to limit with a notion of the 'ethical' that is arguably closer to the transcendence of the 'moral law' in Kantian terms. Jung writes that '[a]estheticism not only lacks completeness; it lacks any real *moral* commitment – reducing its holder to the status of a detached observer, a disguised hedonist, who is entertained by the passing parade but never a real participant in it' (1921/1971, para. 194; emphasis added).

If aestheticism lacks 'moral' commitment in the Spinozist and Nietzschean senses of an immanent ethics, it is because it is occupied not with judgment in terms of transcendent truths or universal values but with an intensified life of becoming. Because *Ulysses* forces Jung to become a 'participant' it involves him in an intensified becoming given that its 'synthesis' is problematic and productive. What I mean by 'problematic' is that it places in question any guaranteed horizon of identity (e.g., Kant's three Ideas; theological, cosmological and psychological), which might constrain what a body can do. Joyce's own term for the affirmation of an aesthetics liberated from the coherent coordinates of Self, World and God is the 'chaosmos.' This affirmation of divergence 'forms a "chaosmos" and no longer a world; the aleatory point which traverses them forms a counter-self, and no longer a self; the disjunction posed as a synthesis exchanges its theological principle for a diabolical principle' (Deleuze, 1969/2004b, p. 201). We might find these attributes present in what Jung refers to as the 'visionary artist,' the 'creative individual,' and the 'collective man' (1930/1950/1966, para. 157). We can productively compare this with Deleuze's equivalent of Nietzsche's overman, 'the thinker of the eternal return,' the 'universal individual,' and the 'man without a name' (1968/2004, p. 317). This individual designates a being who has relinquished the coherent identity of a subject with fixed boundaries and no longer assumes the 'psyche' to be a 'primary datum.' It affirms the 'system of a dissolved self' (Deleuze, 1968/2004, p. 100), which can only become possible when chaos is understood not as the negation of order but as a productive excess that has not been captured within the confines of consistency. In a deceptively simple passage Marlan articulates this excess-consistency dynamic in terms of 'unity.' Perhaps, he suggests:

> we can add the notion of chaosmos to the effort to express what Jung was after when speaking of the *complexio oppositorum*. Its further exploration can add a contemporary nuance to our mercurial understanding of just what we mean by the unity of opposites, which is never a simple unity or stable presence but rather a "dynamic hybridity", a unity that does not require that differences subordinate themselves to a unifying principle. Such a unity "affirms the very heterogeneity that would appear to dissolve it". As such, it is a unity in continuing self-deconstruction and so, an errant fugitive that maddeningly continues to escape our grasp while teasing us into conjunctions.
>
> (2013, p. 17, cited; Evans, 2009, p. 28)

Notes

1 Jung's speculations about the 'depth' of a 'psychoid' unconscious and archetype (1947/1954/1969, para. 420) could be included as another example of where the 'subjective viewpoint' is radically challenged. Recently Barentsen (2015) has proposed an 'onto-aesthetics' based upon his deduction that 'the archetype's psychoid co-implication of psyche and nature gives the collective unconscious a strange consubstantiality with the organic processes of Schelling's Nature' (2015, p. 74).

2 In this chapter I will draw from numerous works and ideas by Deleuze and his collaborator Félix Guattari (1930–1992). Not only was Deleuze profoundly influenced by Jung (see Kerslake, 2007), but of all the post-war continental philosophers, Deleuze wrote extensively about aesthesis and philosophy including individual works on Proust (1964), Kafka (1986), and Bacon (1981).

3 See Bishop, 2008a, p. 111, 132; Kerslake, 2007, pp. 111, 112, 115, 117, 120–123.

4 It is the 'Analytic of the Sublime' in the third *Critique* that suggests to Deleuze the *original* discord of the faculties. Smith relates that the 'lesson of the "Analytic of the Sublime" is that it discovers this discordant accord as the condition of possibility for the harmonious accords of the faculties that Kant evoked in the first two critiques, an accord that is not derived from pre-existent external "facts" (the "fact" of knowledge, the "fact" of morality), but is engendered internally in the subject' (2012, p. 93).

5 This is a lone reference to Kleist in Jung's corpus. Why? Perhaps Jung was influenced by Goethe's hatred for Kleist's work.

6 'A reflexive paradox has often been noted in the founding of psychoanalysis. Transference is supposed to be intrinsic to psychoanalysis, yet Freud somehow managed to analyze himself. Jung was the first to advocate that every analyst themselves be analyzed, but his own development of his theories only came through a period of withdrawal and a 'confrontation with the unconscious' (Kerslake, 2007, p. 186).

7 '[R]aises us above the human condition (*la philosophie nous aura élevés au-dessus de la condition humaine'*), making the effort to 'surpass' (*dépasser*) this condition' (Bergson, 1907/1983, p. 50, 193, translation modified).

References

Adkins, B. (2015). What is a Literature of War? Kleist, Kant and Nomadology. In Lundy, C. & Voss, D. (Eds.), *At the Edges of Thought: Deleuze and Post-Kantian Philosophy*. Edinburgh: Edinburgh University Press.

Barentsen, G. (2015). Silent Partnerships: Schelling, Jung and the Romantic Metasubject. *Symposium: Canadian Journal of Continental Philosophy*, 19(1), 67–79.

Bergson, H. (1983). *Creative Evolution* (A. Mitchell, Trans.). Lanham, MD: University Press of America. (Original work published 1907).

Berk, Van den, T. (2012). *Jung on Art: The Autonomy of the Creative Drive*. Hove and New York: Routledge.

Bishop, P. (2000). *Synchronicity and Intellectual Intuition in Kant, Swedenborg and Jung*. Lampeter, UK: Edwin Mellen Press.

——— (2008a). *Analytical Psychology and German Classical Aesthetics: Goethe, Schiller, and Jung: The Development of Personality* (Vol. 1). London and New York: Routledge.

——— (2008b). The Timeliness and the Timelessness OF The 'Archaic': Analytical Psychology, 'Primordial' Thought, Synchronicity. *Journal of Analytical Psychology*, 53(4), 501–523.

——— (2009). *Analytical Psychology and German Classical Aesthetics: Goethe, Schiller, and Jung: The Constellation of the Self* (Vol. 2). London and New York: Routledge.

——— (2017). *On the Blissful Islands with Nietzsche and Jung*. London and New York: Routledge.

Colman, W. (2017). Soul in the World: Symbolic Culture as the Medium for Psyche. *Journal of Analytical Psychology*, 62(1), 32–49.

Deleuze, G. (2000). *Proust and Signs* (R. Howard, Trans.). Minneapolis, MN: University of Minnesota Press. (Original work published 1964).

——— (1991). *Bergsonism* (H. Tomlinson & B. Habberjam, Trans.). London and New York: Zone Books. (Original work published 1966).

——— (2004a). *Difference and Repetition* (P. Patton, Trans.). London and New York: Continuum Press. (Original work published 1968).

——— (2004b). *The Logic of Sense*. In C.V. Boundas (ed.) (M. Lester & C. Stivale, Trans.). London and New York: Continuum Press. (Original work published 1969).

Deleuze, G. and Guattari, F. (1987). *A Thousand Plateaus: Capitalism and Schizophrenia*, (B. Massumi, Trans.). Minneapolis, MN: University of Minnesota Press. (Original work published 1980).

——— (1994). *What is Philosophy?* (H. Tomlinson & G. Burchell, Trans.). New York: Columbia University Press. (Original work published 1991).

Evans, F.J. (2009). *The Multivoiced Body: Society and Communication in the Age of Diversity*. New York: Columbia University Press.

Gaillard, C. (2006). The Arts. In R.K. Papadopoulos (Ed.), *The Handbook of Jungian Psychology*. London and New York: Routledge.

Harrington, A. (1999). *Reenchanted Science: Holism in German Culture from Wilhelm II to Hitler*. Princeton: Princeton University Press.

Hohl, R. (1983). Jung on Picasso (and Joyce). *Notes in the History of Art.* 3(1), 10–18.

Jung, C.G. (1970). After the Catastrophe. In Read, H., Fordham, M., Adler, G., & McGuire, W. (Eds.) (R.F.C. Hull, Trans.), *The Collected Works of C.G. Jung*, 20 vols. [hereafter *CW*]: *CW*, 10. *Civilisation in Transition* (2nd ed., pp. 194–217). London: Routledge and Kegan Paul. (Original work published 1945).

——— (1971). *Psychological Types. CW*, 6. London: Routledge and Kegan Paul. (Original work published 1921).

——— (1963). *Mysterium Coniunctionis, CW*, 14. London: Routledge and Kegan Paul. (Original work published 1955–1956).

——— (1969). *Archaic Man. CW*, 10 (2nd ed., pp. 50–73). London: Routledge and Kegan Paul. (Original work published 1931).

——— (1954). *The Development of Personality. CW*, 17 (2nd ed., pp. 165–186): London: Routledge and Kegan Paul. (Original work published 1932).

——— (1979). *Memories, Dreams, Reflections*, in Jaffé, A. (Rec. and Ed.) (R. Winston & C. Winston, Trans.), London: Collins, Routledge and Kegan Paul. Reprint, London: Collins Fount Paperbacks. (Original work published 1963).

——— (1969). *On the Nature of the Psyche. CW*, 8 (2nd ed., pp. 159–236). London: Routledge and Kegan Paul. (Original work published 1947/1954).

——— (1966a). *Psychology and Literature. CW*, 15 (pp. 84–105). London: Routledge and Kegan Paul. (Original work published 1930/1950).

——— (1966b). *"Ulysses": A Monologue. CW*, 15 (pp. 109–134). London: Routledge and Kegan Paul. (Original work published 1932).

——— (1966c). *Picasso. CW*, 15 (pp. 135–141). London: Routledge and Kegan Paul. (Original work published 1932).

——— (1983). Thoughts on the Nature and Value of Speculative Enquiry. In Read, H., Fordham, M., Adler, G. & McGuire, W. (Eds.) (J.V. Heurck, Trans.), *The Zofingia Lectures: CW: Supplementary Volume A* (pp. 59–88). London: Routledge and Kegan Paul. (Original work 1898).

Kerslake, C. (2004). Rebirth Through Incest: Deleuze's Early Jungianism. *Angelaki: Journal of the Theoretical Humanities*, 9 (1), 135–157.

——— (2007). *Deleuze and the Unconscious.* London and New York: Continuum Press.

Marlan, S. (2013). The Philosophers' Stone as Chaosmos: The Self and the Dilemma of Diversity. *Jung Journal: Culture and Psyche*, 7(2), 10–23.

Papadopoulos, R. (2006). Jung's Epistemology and Methodology. In R.K. Papadopoulos (Ed.), *The Handbook of Jungian Psychology*. London and New York: Routledge.

Rowland, S. (2005). *Jung as Writer*. London and New York: Routledge.

Smith, D.W. (2012). *Essays on Deleuze*. Edinburgh: Edinburgh University Press.

Wojtkowski, S. (2009). Jung's "Art Complex". *Aras/Art and Psyche Online Journal*, (3).

Chapter 13

Jung, Science, and Technology

Raya A. Jones

Carl Gustav Jung did not philosophize about science. He maintained that he was doing science. He was not averse to using technological apparatus, as evident in his word associations experiments (collated in Jung 1973). Nevertheless, his attitude toward science and technology was ambivalent: 'Science and technology have indeed conquered the world, but whether the psyche has gained anything is another matter' (Jung, 1942, para. 163). Jung's attitude should be considered in view of what he was trying to achieve against the backdrop of how science was generally understood, the history of psychology, and the view of technology as the practical application of science.

As Ihde (2016) summarizes, 'faith in progressive accumulation of knowledge, the approximation or attainment of universal natural laws, objectivity, and freedom from religion, culture, and values' were the underpinnings of early-modern philosophy of science, traceable to the seventeenth century (pp. 17–18). When Jung mentions science, he either fights shadows of this conception or endorses it, depending on the particular context. He was concerned with producing knowledge of practical use and cared little for intellectual purism. His disregard for the hypothetico-deductive method has cost analytical psychology dearly in terms of scientific credibility, for he developed his theory in the early twentieth century—a time when logical positivism and 'analytical styles' of philosophy established a certain relationship with science: 'Science produced knowledge; philosophy checked its logic and propositional form' (Ihde, 2016, p. 18). Fast forward past the mid-century classics of philosophy of science—works by Karl Popper, Thomas Kuhn, Imre Lakatos, and Paul Feyerabend, published when Jung was well set on his path or already dead—to a late twentieth-century shift towards historical, cultural, and material dimensions of science, as well as rising interest in technologies. The emergent consensus is that 'the understanding of science as acultural, ahistorical, unified, and triumphal ... is dead.' (Ihde, 2016. p. 22). It is from this standpoint that Jung's agenda for analytical psychology may be retrospectively appraised.

Jung's Timely Defense of Science

> Our aim is the best possible understanding of life as we find it in the human soul. What we learn through understanding will not, I sincerely hope, petrify into intellectual theory, but will become an instrument which, through practical application, will improve in quality until it can serve its purpose as perfectly as possible.
>
> (Jung, 1946, para. 172)

Jung made the above statement in the course of three lectures presented to the International Congress of Education in 1924 in London. The first published version (Jung, 1928a) was written in English. The version included in the *Collected Works* is a translation of a radically revised 1946 version in German. There are significant omissions and alterations in the later publication, which correspond to changes in the backdrop against which Jung was pitching analytical psychology and thus evince the historicity of his stance regarding its scientific status. The point to note here is how the early version constructs analytical psychology as embodying the voice of science and reason more strongly than the later version does.

In the early version, the counterpart of the above extract alludes to a systematic procedure or technique. It opens, 'Our method is the understanding ...' (Jung, 1928a, p. 348) and follows an acrimonious account of Freudianism. 'Immense damage is done ... through the Freudian doctrine', opined Jung, criticizing the reduction of all mental illnesses to a sex-problem ('we should not allow its sick phantasies to blindfold the eyes of science') and the assumption of universality ('To impute to the whole world our specifically western neurosis is more than ridiculous: it is insane') (p. 347). Freudianism had created a regrettable state of affairs ('people believe it is their duty to talk of sex incessantly ... in order to avoid repression') that required the scientific intervention offered by analytical psychology: 'I have to defend science against the intrusion of a mass-neurosis' (p. 347). The tirade has disappeared in the 1946 version. World War II barely over, the zeitgeist was different. Moreover, the substantive content of analytical psychology had increased in the interim two decades, and the exigency of defending his own school of thought against Freud's had abated. Freud was dead, and his contribution to knowledge is more appreciatively reviewed by Jung in 1946.

It was not enough, however, to claim that analytical psychology is more scientific than the Freudian doctrine. In the 1920s, Jung had to contend also with experimental psychologists, who anyway were inclined to dismiss Freud's theory as unscientific. The 1928 version of the lectures to educators characterizes 'academic' psychology as the science of normal consciousness and labors the contrast with analytical psychology and its study of the unconscious. This element is diffused, though still present, in the 1946 version. Both versions present Jung's approach to therapy as informed by scientific knowledge, and present analytical psychology as the science informing clinical practice. The lectures thus position analytical psychology as filling a gap in knowledge due to experimental psychology's focus on the 'normal' conscious mind; and further make moral claims for the necessity of filling this gap: 'We doctors are forced, for the sake of our patients, to treat obscure complaints which are hard or impossible to understand ... We have, for professional reasons, to tackle the darkest and most desperate problems of the soul'; and this 'higher necessity absolutely requires' a psychology of the unconscious (Jung, 1946, para. 170).

Jung's manifesto for analytical psychology involves downplaying the ideal of 'pure' science—an ideal to which Jung derogatorily alludes when expressing his hope that analytical psychology would not be petrified into intellectual theory of little practical use. He insists,

Our psychology is ... an eminently practical science. It does not investigate for investigation's sake, but for the immediate purpose of giving help. We could even say that learning is its by-product, but not its principal aim, which is again a great difference from what one understands by 'academic' science.

(Jung, 1946, para. 172; see also 1928a, p. 348)

Both versions identify two distinctive characteristics of analytical psychology: its subject matter and its methodology. The precise exposition, however, differs. Regarding the subject matter, the early version avers that unlike earlier psychologies, 'analytical psychology does not avoid dealing with admittedly complex mental phenomena' (Jung, 1928a, p. 348). Listing the four functions of consciousness (thinking, feeling, sensation, and intuition) as such phenomena, Jung confessed that 'we do not know what these functions really are,' but asserted that 'despite our ignorance of ultimate principles, we deal with these functions as if they were clearly definable organs of the mind' (p. 348). When the lectures were delivered in 1924, his most recent major work was the 1921 monograph *Psychological Types*, in which he expanded his theory of the four functions. The mention of the functions and admission of ignorance have vanished in the revision of the lectures, where the statement that analytical psychology 'does not hesitate to tackle even the most difficult and complicated processes' is immediately followed with, 'Another difference lies in our method of procedure' (1946, para. 171; 'method of investigation' in 1928a, p. 348).

Jung's Untimely Method of Investigation

> We have no laboratory equipped with elaborate apparatus. Our laboratory is the world. Our tests are concerned with the actual, day-to-day, happenings of human life, and the test-subjects are our patients, relatives, friends, and, last but not least, ourselves. ... There are no needle-pricks, artificial shocks, surprise lights, and all the paraphernalia of laboratory experiment; it is the hopes and fears, the pains and joys, the mistakes and achievements of real life that provide us with our material.
>
> (Jung, 1946, para. 171)

Rhetorically, this extract does more than inform about methodology. It implies that analytical psychology is attuned to what really matters—human life as lived by human beings—whereas other psychologies are bells and whistles, centering on artificially induced meaningless sensations by means of needle-pricks, artificial shocks, and so forth. The allusion is to the method of introspection developed by Wundt in the late nineteenth century, which involved exposing subjects to stimuli such as a light or a sound and asking them to report their thoughts and sensations, with the aim of identifying the constituent elements of the conscious process. Jung's dismissive stance might seem inconsistent with his own use of lab apparatus when conducting the word association experiments during the 1900s. Jung and his colleagues utilized not only a stop-watch to measure reaction times but also instruments of physiological psychology such as a galvanometer (the design of which Jung had improved) and a pneumograph to track physiological changes in subjects during the experiments. Nevertheless, by the 1920s, Jung no longer had practical uses for apparatus borrowed from physiological psychology.

Contrary to the statement in the above extract, however, Jung's primary sources of material were myths, legends, and fairytales, seemingly far removed from day-to-day life in his milieu. The claim that his tests concerned actual human life could be read as saying that real lives provided settings in which he could test hypotheses derived from analyzing fantasies, myths, and more. As a theorist, Jung wanted to get as close as possible to the 'raw' organizing process whereby the unconscious mind makes the bodily lived experience accessible to consciousness in the form of fantasies. In the 1912 monograph, *The Psychology of the Unconscious*, revised forty years later as *Symbols of Transformation*, he analyzed fantasies that he believed owed their existence exclusively to the activity of the unconscious (Jung 1912, 1952). The material, published by Théodore Flournoy in 1906, had been written by an American woman, Miss Frank Miller, who Jung assumed was Flournoy's patient. Unbeknown to him, she wrote the fantasies to help Flournoy with his publication (Bair, 2003). Nevertheless, the likelihood that Miss Miller's literary fantasies owed more to the conscious mind than Jung believed might be less detrimental to the credibility of his theory than the failure to validate it by a hypothetico-deductive procedure.

Jung was perceived by his contemporaries as betraying the dream of a scientific psychology. Piaget (1945/1962) commented on the 'anti-rationalist attitude' that Jung had adopted and suggested that 'a certain contempt for logic and rational activity, which he contracted through daily contact with mythical and symbolic thought, has made him inclined to be content with too little in the way of proof' (p. 196). Arguably, Jung took a thoroughly rationalist approach to myths, religion, beliefs in the supernatural, patients' delusions and so forth; but his transition from empirical observation to a full-blown theory was too rapid and sidestepped the hypothetico-deductive procedure. To some of his critics, Jung's fascination with myths and religions was itself the problem. Allen (1942), a British psychiatrist, seized the opportunity of reviewing an introduction to Jungian psychology by Jacobi to express disappointment with the direction Jung had taken. Allen applauded Jung's work between 1905 and 1907, 'Nothing could have been more promising than these observations based upon careful measurement. ... here at last clinical research was attaining definite scientific basis,' and disparaged the 1912 monograph, in which Jung 'abandoned his clinical work and most unfortunately started upon the study of religions and myths' (p. 622). Yet, it may be noted here, Jung never relinquished his professional commitment to medicine. On the contrary, he undertook the study of myths and religions as a necessary means towards understanding the workings of the unconscious mind so as to advance clinical practice.

Jung's Dilemma of Modern Psychology

This is the dilemma: psychology 'does not exclude the existence of faith, conviction, and experienced certainties of whatever description, nor does it contest their possible validity,' but it 'completely lacks the means to prove their validity in the scientific sense' (Jung 1948 para. 384). Strictly speaking, the doctrine of empiricism holds that theories ought to give a true account only of what is observable:

> One of the unbreakable rules in scientific research is to take an object as known only in so far as the inquirer is in a position to make scientifically valid statements about it. 'Valid' in this sense simply means what can be verified by facts.
>
> (Jung, 1948, para. 384)

Jung sums up, 'One may lament this incapacity on the part of science, but that does not enable [the psyche] to jump over its own shadow' (para. 384). The history of psychology in the twentieth century could be told as repeated confrontations with this dilemma. It was tackled from various different angles, often by redefining the subject matter of psychology, sometime denying that there is a 'psyche.'

Standard textbooks identify the birth of modern psychology as the moment that Wundt founded the Institute for Experimental Psychology in 1879 at the University of Leipzig, Germany, thus accomplishing the discipline's split from philosophy. It was a difficult birth, marked by schisms within nineteenth-century German universities and the vested interests of influential professors (Kusch, 1995, Scanlon, 1989). Dilthey (1870/1989) initially recommended designating psychology to the humanities (*Geisteswissenschaften*) since in his view it concerned relationships between human experience, expression, and understanding (*Verstehen*). He drew a contrast between the inner experience of psychic life, which is holistically presented to the subject as a living active reality, and the outer experience of nature, which is presented as phenomenal and in isolated data. For psychology to imitate a method that was successful in the natural sciences would involve treating an interconnected whole as if it were merely an assemblage of discrete entities; and, moreover, 'neglecting the lived sense of dynamic striving for intrinsically posited goals in favor of a non-teleological, hypothetico-deductive system' (p. 349).

Psychology as a natural science had no place in Dilthey's *Geisteswissenschaften* (literally, sciences of the spirit) and the nascent science of psychology, fashioning itself as a branch of physiology, had no place for spirit. Thirteen years after Wundt opened his laboratory, William James (1892) asserted that although psychology was still 'a mass of phenomenal description, gossip, and myth,' there was already enough 'real material' to justify optimism about psychology becoming 'worthy of the name of natural science at no very distant day' (p. 146). Two decades later, coinciding with Jung's parting of ways with Freud, the behaviorists would eschew even Wundt's method of introspection as too subjective, and redefine psychology as the study of behavior. 'Psychology as the behaviorist views it is a purely objective experimental branch of natural science,' declared Watson (1913, p. 158) in no uncertain terms. Although others at the time continued to uphold psychology as the study of mind, the classification of psychology as natural science was widely shared.

Against this backdrop, Jung could not regard psychology as anything but a natural science, and it behooved on him to persuade his peers that analytical psychology consisted of 'real material' and was worthy of a place in the *Naturwissenschaften*. At the same time, his description of analytical psychology echoes Dilthey's holism:

> Analytical psychology differs from experimental psychology in that it does not attempt to isolate individual functions (sense functions, emotional phenomena, thought-processes, etc.) and then subject them to experimental conditions for purposes of investigation. It is far more concerned with the total manifestation of the psyche as a natural phenomenon.
>
> (Jung, 1946, para. 170)

This statement casts analytical psychology as natural science (it is concerned with a natural phenomenon) and distances it from both the reductionist ethos of experimental psychology and, implicitly, the concerns of the humanities. For instance, a literary critic would analyze, evaluate, and interpret literary works, commenting on their aesthetic qualities; in contrast, when Jung analyzes literature he sees evidence that 'the human psyche is the womb of all the arts and sciences' (1950, para. 133). He is concerned—not with how particular works express human experiences—but with why such expressions occur at all, and what does their thematic content reveal about 'organs of the mind' (to borrow his phrase, e.g., 1928a, p. 348). Reiterating his epistemo-logical position in a prologue to 'The Phenomenology of the Spirit in Fairytales', Jung (1948) maintained that the natural phenomenon is the object of scientific inquiry, and in psychology such phenomena include verbal expressions such as fairytales. He thus positions himself as a naturalist who seeks to understand the human psyche, this natural phenomenon, through its outputs, not unlike a biologist who studies an organism by observing its behavior.

A more accurate analogy, however, would be someone purporting to describe an intangible entity whose existence is knowable only if we believe that certain phenomena are telltale signs of its existence. Jung excavated fairytales, myths, etymologies, alchemy and more, and investigated beliefs in the supernatural and UFOs, for what he believed was evidence for a collective unconscious. However, he embarked upon this line of inquiry when psychology was still trying to live down associations with its older namesake in philosophy. Comte (1830/2009) had relegated psychology to a prescientific stage, omitting it from the hierarchy of sciences, on grounds that 'those psychologists' (philosophers who studied the mind) mistook 'their own dreams for science' (p. 33). He defined the prescientific 'metaphysical' stage as characterized by postulations of 'abstract forces, veritable entities (that is, personified abstractions) inherent in all beings, and capable of producing all phenomena' (p. 26). This readily applies to the conception of Jungian archetypes as veritable personified abstractions inherent in all humans and producing all manner of mental phenomena. In Comte's scientific stage, the mind applies itself to the study of the laws of phenomena, describing their invariable relations of succession and resemblances. Entering the twentieth century, academic psychology became equated strictly with quantitative experimental methodology.

Jung (1954b) too noted that historically psychology consisted of numerous doctrines concerning the soul, and that philosophers' theories rested on a naïve belief in the universal validity of their subjective opinions—an attitude that is 'totally alien' to modern science (para. 343). He often characterized himself as an empiricist with the disclaimer that he was not a philosopher and with connotations caricaturing the philosopher. 'Not being a philosopher, but an empiricist, I am inclined in all difficult questions to let experience decide. Where it is impossible to find any tangible basis in experience, I prefer to leave the question unanswered,' he stated apropos intangible questions such as what is life and what is spirit (1926, para. 604). 'But I am an empiricist, not a philosopher; I cannot let myself presuppose that my peculiar temperament, my own attitude to intellectual problems, is universally valid,' a misconception in which 'only the philosopher may indulge,' Jung opined elsewhere (1954a, para. 149) as if echoing Comte's condemnation of philosophers who studied the mind. The objectivity of modern science is an improvement upon pre-Enlightenment thinking, Jung (1954b) affirmed; but unlike Comte—who had pointed out the absurdity of the mind trying to observe itself—Jung averred that we can never remove ourselves from the subjective situation: 'every science is a function of the psyche, and all knowledge is rooted in it' (para. 357). Consequently, psychology as a science finds itself in a conundrum. There is no Archimedean point from which to inquire into the meaning of empirical observations; 'only the psyche can observe the psyche' (Jung, 1948, para. 384).

Jung's Contemplation of Technology

The fact that only the psyche can observe the psyche does not rule out technological means for investigating it; but, as seen, Jung regarded laboratory apparatus as unnecessary for the purposes of analytical psychology. His attitude was pragmatic. Technology served him well towards discovering the autonomous complexes, but the kind of understanding he sought later on could not be furthered by instruments of measurement. Hence, by the 1920s, analytical psychology had 'no laboratory equipped with elaborate apparatus,' and, instead, its testbed was 'the actual, day-to-day, happenings of human life' (Jung, 1946, para. 171). Technology is always present in daily life, and yet did not enter Jung's sphere of interest. Nor did it enter the interests of philosophers until later in the twentieth century. Jung's indifference, however, could be understood as also epistemological. Jung (1912, 1952) drew a strict distinction between 'directed' thinking (speech-based, reality-oriented, and often intentional) and 'associative' thinking, which is image-based, fantasizing or dreaming. Jung was interested in fantasies because to him these reveal the structure and dynamics of the unconscious. In contrast, tools and machines are consciously crafted and applied to demands of reality.

Jung's only direct comment on technology seems to have been invited by the editors of *Zürcher Student* at the Federal Polytechnic Institute and takes the form of a letter to the editors. Technology's impact on human life became a poignant issue in the wake of World War II. The final paragraph of Jung's letter stipulates the danger of man 'discovering something that will destroy him if evilly used' and a reminder that humanity came 'very close to this with the atom bomb' (1949, para. 1407). Misgivings about technological innovations are hardly unique to Jung. Discussing the coming of age of atomic power, Heidegger (1959/1966) suggested that the greatest danger is that fascination with technological ingenuity might breed indifference towards meditative thinking, and then 'man would have denied and thrown away his own ... essential nature' (p. 56). Our nature was already compromised, according to Jung, though he conceptualized human nature as essentially instinctual (in contradistinction to Heidegger's emphasis of the meditative). For instance, he suggested elsewhere that 'disunity with oneself is the hall-mark of civilized man' due to the 'progressive subjugation of the animal in man' (1943, para. 17). This premise underpins also his letter to *Zürcher Student*.

The letter opens, 'The question you ask me, concerning the effect of technology on the human psyche, is not at all easy to answer' (Jung, 1949, para. 1403). His answer may disappoint contemporary readers expecting insights on how technologies mediate human experience and self-understanding. Instead, Jung superimposes 'technology' onto his understanding of the psyche as biologically pre-given. Since humans create technology, and even the most primitive cultures involve some technology, there must be innate 'modes of human adaptation' to enable people to 'meet the requirements of technology,' Jung speculated (para. 1404). The word 'requirements' in this context implies the imposition on embodied experience: 'Technological activities mostly consist in the identical repetition of rhythmical procedures,' and this 'corresponds to the basic pattern of primitive labor, which is never performed without rhythm or an accompanying chant' (para. 1404). In Jung's view, 'primitive man' is perfectly adapted, possessing the capacity to 'put up with an extraordinary amount of monotony'; and 'When the work is accompanied by drumming, he is able to heat himself up into ecstasy' (para. 1404). In modern civilization, people have lost touch with their instinctual nature and consequently lack the capacity to cope with the monotony of (factory) work: 'for modern man technology is an imbalance that begets dissatisfaction with work' (para. 1405).

In sum, while technology is 'a legitimate human activity ... neither good nor bad' (Jung, 1949, para. 1406), its negative effect on the psyche is a collateral damage of civilization. In other words, colloquially, technology puts a spanner in the works of individuation (self-realization through the achievement of inner balance). Jung proposed intervention to redress the psychic imbalance of technology-governed lifestyles. He warned his likely audience of polytechnic students that since technologists, like factory workers, deal 'mainly with mechanical factors,' they are in danger of having their 'other mental capacities atrophying,' and recommended that engineers cultivated philosophical interests (para. 1406).

Throughout the letter, technology remains a nebulous and undifferentiated concept, simply equated with 'mechanical factors' and monotony. There is no consideration of the fundamental difference between the embodied experience of the rhythmical activities of premodern life and the tedium of operating machines in a modern factory, for instance. As an undifferentiated concept, technology often carries connotations of unnatural contrivance and something that not only endangers life on Earth but also alienates us from our own nature.

Repositioning Analytical Psychology as a Technology of the Self

Modern technology is conventionally regarded as the practical application of science, but it could be truer to say that technology comes first. The telescope had to be invented before Galileo could make his discoveries. The stop-watch, galvanometer, and pneumograph had to exist before Jung could theorize the existence of autonomous complexes. For Galileo, however, the telescope amplified sight of natural objects, such as the moon and Jupiter that are visible with the naked eye even though not all their features can be seen from Earth. The instruments used by psychologists do not amplify sensory perception but enable an intellectual construction of abstract entities. In a way, the instruments deployed to study the mind facilitated the creation of the object of study.

Technology precedes science in a deeper sense, according to Heidegger (1953/1993). He contested definitions of technology in terms of instrumentality and human activity, for these construe technology as contrivance and thus place it in opposition to nature. The difference between craftsmanship (*techne*) and nature lies in the bringing-forth that is happening in the artisan's act; it brings forth a potential concealed in nature. In contrast, modern technology challenges nature. Whereas farmers used tools to cultivate the land, modern technology turns up the land to mine coal and ore (his example). Instead of bringing-forth, there is setting-upon. Energy is unlocked, transformed and stored up. Heidegger further articulated a concept of *enframing*, 'the way in which the actual reveals itself as standing-reserve' (p. 329). Even though chronologically modern physics began in the seventeenth century and machine-power technology emerged in the late eighteenth century, this technology (he argues) underpins the worldview upon which modern physics is founded. The rule of enframing 'demands that nature be orderable as standing-reserve' (p. 328). To go beyond Heidegger, the same rule demands also that the human soul be orderable as standing-reserve:

> Just as man has succeeded in inventing a turbine, and, by conducting a flow of water to it, in transforming the latter's kinetic energy into electricity capable of manifold applications, so he succeeded, with the help of psychic mechanism, in converting natural instincts, which would otherwise follow their gradient without performing work, into other dynamic forms that are productive of work.
>
> (Jung, 1928b, para. 82)

For Jung, the psyche reveals itself as standing-reserve for output such as 'dreams, fantasies, visions, and delusions of the insane' in which he recognized 'certain regularities' (1951, para. 309) upon which he staked the scientific status of the theory of archetypes.

The technology that directly enabled analytical psychology as a body of knowledge, however, is a technology of the self in the Foucauldian sense; namely, a set of culturally specific techniques that permit persons to perform certain operations on their bodies, souls, thoughts, and actions towards attaining desired states of perfection, happiness, purity, and so forth (Foucault, 1993). Jung could be viewed as offering to improve upon the Freudian technology of the self in terms of the precise operations to be performed on the so-called 'psychological man'—a term coined by Reiff (1959) in his study of Freud and rise of psychoanalysis in the early twentieth century. As Homans (1995) succinctly put it apropos Jung's historical context, psychological man is 'characterized by inner diffusioness' and therefore 'can organize or structure the inner, personal, and private dimension of his experience of the contemporary world only through psychology' (p. 5). The rise of psychological man could be tracked to historical conditions set in motion in the eighteenth century. Concepts such as psyche, personality, and consciousness, were created so as to carve out domains of analyzing the post-Enlightenment 'soul,' building upon it 'scientific techniques and discourses, and the moral claims of humanism' (Foucault, 1991, p. 30). Moral claims are indeed made in Jung's (1946) declaration that doctors must 'tackle the darkest and most desperate problems of the soul' and that this 'higher necessity absolutely requires' scientific knowledge (para. 170).

Artisans and engineers utilize materials at hand to make something. As a technologist of the self, Jung can be seen to utilize modern sciences as sources of raw materials for building and bolstering his model of the psyche. Biology and evolution theory enable him to argue for the logical necessity of archetypes: 'Just as the human body represents a whole museum of organs, with a long evolutionary history behind them, so we should expect the mind to be organized in a similar way' (1961, para. 522). The analogy perpetuates nineteenth-century psycho-physical parallelism, which many psychologists endorsed well into the twentieth century as a scientifically respectable doctrine that allowed psychology to coexist autonomously alongside physiology and other sciences (Heidelberger, 2003); and yet, Jung upheld the inseparability of psyche and body, contending that their unitary nature is evident in 'the undeniable fact that causal connections exist between the psyche and the body' (1955–1956, para. 767). Jung extrapolated the term *Unus Mundus* from medieval alchemy to convey the interrelatedness of all strata of existence. A contemporary trend within Jungian studies takes Jung's discussion of *Unus Mundus* as endorsing a metaphysics that attributes archetypes to the structure of the universe itself; but in an alternative reading, preferred here, Jung is simply reiterating his belief that 'every science is a function of the psyche' (1954b, para. 357). From quantum physics, Jung takes further support for the primacy of the psyche in any field of human understanding. Regarding the dis-covery that light behaves as both particles and waves, he reflects, 'This paradoxical conclusion obliged us to abandon, on the plane of atomic magnitudes, a causal description of nature ... and in its place to set up invisible fields of probability in multidimensional spaces' (para. 438). Indeed, 'a conception of reality that takes account of the uncontrol-lable effects the observer has upon the system observed' means that 'reality forfeits something of its objective character and that a subjective element attaches to the physicist's picture of the world' (para. 438).

Closing Reflections

Averring that psychology lacks an observation point outside the psyche, Jung (1948) reflected that this does not rule out 'the possi-bility that the atomic physics of the future may supply us with the said Archimedean point' (para. 384). Whether he said it wryly or in earnest, he consistently distanced himself from metaphysical speculations and positioned himself as a pragmatic psychologist. For instance, 'Whether energy is God or God is energy concerns me very little … But to give appropriate psychological explanations—this I must be able to do' (Jung, 1931, para. 678). Positioning himself as a medical psychologist—a physician of the soul, technologist of the self—carries responsibilities such as being able to provide empirical proof for particular explanations and thereby to demonstrate their appropriateness; but this is precisely where the scientific method has failed Jung.

Jung engaged with issues central to the formation of psychology as a modern science in the early twentieth century (see Shamdasani, 2003), but in the long run this science did not engage with Jung, mainly because he was perceived as violating the tenets of empirical inquiry. Jung's departure from the canons of the scientific method continues to be problematized within Jungian studies (e.g., Jones, 2013, 2014) while his legacy continues to inspire those engaged with it, conspicuously so at a personal level, and when cultivating a technology of the self is a matter of urgency.

References

Allen, C. (1942). A Mystical Psychology. *Nature*, 149, 622–623.

Bair, D. (2003). *Jung.* Boston, MA: Little, Brown & Company.

Comte, A. (1830/2009). *The Positive Philosophy of Auguste Comte*, Vol. I. New York: Cosimo.

Dilthey, W. (1870/1989). *Introduction to the Human Sciences* (Vol. 1). Princeton, NJ: Princeton University Press.

Foucault, M. (1991). *Discipline and Punish*. London: Penguin.

Foucault, M. (1993). About the Beginning of the Hermeneutics of the Self: Two Lectures at Dartmouth. *Political Theory* 21, 198–227.

Heidegger, M. (1953/1993). The Question Concerning Technology. In Krell, D.F. (ed.) *Martin Heidegger: Basic Writings* (pp. 311–341). San Francisco, CA: Harper.

Heidegger, M. (1959/1966). *Discourse on Thinking*. New York: Harper & Row.

Heidelberger, M. (2003). The Mind-Body Problem in the Origin of Logical Empiricism: Herbert Feigl and Psychophysical Parallelism. In Parrini, P. & Salmon, W. (Eds.) *Logical Empiricism: Historical and Contemporary Perspectives* (pp. 233–262). Pittsburgh, PA: Pittsburgh University Press.

Homans, P. (1995). *Jung in Context.* Chicago, IL: Chicago University Press.

Ihde, D. (2016). *Husserl's Missing Technologies.* New York: Fordham University Press.

James, W. (1892). A Plea for Psychology as a 'Natural Science'. *Philosophical Review,* 1, 146–153.

Jones, R.A. (2013). Jung's "Psychology with the Psyche" and the Behavioral Sciences. *Behavioral Science,* 3, 408–417.

Jones, R.A. (Ed.) (2014). *Jung and the Question of Science.* London: Routledge.

Unless otherwise stated, the following are from *The Collected Works of C. G. Jung* (CW) London: Routledge & Kegan Paul/Princeton, NJ: Princeton University Press:

Jung, C.G. (1912). *Psychology of the Unconscious.* London: Kegan Paul, Trench, Trubner & Co.

Jung, C.G. (1921). *Psychological Types. CW,* 6.

Jung, C.G. (1926). *Spirit and Life. CW,* 8.

Jung, C.G. (1928a). Analytical Psychology and Education. *Contributions to Analytical Psychology.* London: Kegan Paul, Trench, Trubner & Co.

Jung, C.G. (1928b). *On Psychic Energy. CW,* 8.

Jung, C.G. (1931). *Basic Postulates of Analytical Psychology. CW,* 8.

Jung, C.G. (1942). *Paraclesus as a Spiritual Phenomenon. CW,* 13.

Jung, C.G. (1943). *On the Psychology of the Unconscious. CW,* 7.

Jung, C.G. (1946). *Analytical Psychology and Education. CW,* 17.

Jung, C.G. (1949). *The Effects of Technology on the Human Psyche. CW,* 18.

Jung, C.G. (1948). *The Phenomenology of the Spirit in Fairytales. CW,* 9i.

Jung, C.G. (1950). *Psychology and Literature. CW,* 15.

Jung, C.G. (1951). *The Psychological Aspects of the Kore. CW,* 9i.

Jung, C.G. (1952). *Symbols of Transformation. CW,* 5.

Jung, C.G. (1954a). *Psychological Aspects of the Mother Archetype. CW,* 9i.

Jung, C.G. (1954b). *On the Nature of the Psyche. CW,* 8.

Jung, C.G. (1955–1956). *Mysterium Coniunctionis. CW,* 14.

Jung, C.G. (1961). *Symbols and the Interpretation of Dreams. CW,* 18.

Jung, C.G. (1973). *Experimental Researches. CW,* 2.

Kusch, M. (1995). *Psychologism.* London: Routledge.

Piaget, J. (1945/1962). *Play, Dreams and Imitation in Childhood.* London: Routledge & Kegan Paul.

Reiff, F. (1959). *Freud.* London: Victor Gollancz.

Scanlon, J. (1989). Dilthey on Psychology and Epistemology. *History of Philosophy Quarterly* 6, 347–355.

Shamdasani, S. (2003). *Jung and the Making of Modern Psychology.* Cambridge: Cambridge University Press.

Watson, J.B. (1913). Psychology as the Behaviorist Views it. *Psychological Review,* 20, 158–177.

Index